```
┌────────────────────────────────────────┐
│              WRITE MENU                 │
├────────────────────────────────────────┤
│                                         │
│        T - Type/Edit                    │
│        D - Define page                  │
│        P - Print                        │
│        C - Clear                        │
│        G - Get                          │
│        S - Save                         │
│        ─────────────────                │
│        U - Utilities                    │
│        M - Mailing labels               │
└────────────────────────────────────────┘
```

```
┌────────────────────────────────────────┐
│            UTILITIES MENU               │
├────────────────────────────────────────┤
│                                         │
│        P - Install printer              │
│        M - Modify font file             │
│        D - DOS file facilities          │
│        S - Set global options           │
│        A - Set alternate programs       │
└────────────────────────────────────────┘
```

```
┌────────────────────────────────────────┐
│               Assistant                 │
├────────────────────────────────────────┤
│                                         │
│     G - Get acquainted                  │
│     T - Teach me about your database    │
│     A - Ask me to do something          │
│     ─────────────────────────────       │
│     Q - Query Guide                     │
│     E - Teach Query Guide               │
└────────────────────────────────────────┘
```

Computer users are not all alike.
Neither are SYBEX books.

We know our customers have a variety of needs. They've told us so. And because we've listened, we've developed several distinct types of books to meet the needs of each of our customers. What are you looking for in computer help?

If you're looking for the basics, try the **ABC's** series. You'll find short, unintimidating tutorials and helpful illustrations. For a more visual approach, select **Teach Yourself**, featuring screen-by-screen illustrations of how to use your latest software purchase.

Mastering and **Understanding** titles offer you a step-by-step introduction, plus an in-depth examination of intermediate-level features, to use as you progress.

Our **Up & Running** series is designed for computer-literate consumers who want a no-nonsense overview of new programs. Just 20 basic lessons, and you're on your way.

We also publish two types of reference books. Our **Instant References** provide quick access to each of a program's commands and functions. SYBEX **Encyclopedias** provide a *comprehensive reference* and explanation of all of the commands, features and functions of the subject software.

Sometimes a subject requires a special treatment that our standard series doesn't provide. So you'll find we have titles like **Advanced Techniques, Handbooks, Tips & Tricks**, and others that are specifically tailored to satisfy a unique need.

We carefully select our authors for their in-depth understanding of the software they're writing about, as well as their ability to write clearly and communicate effectively. Each manuscript is thoroughly reviewed by our technical staff to ensure its complete accuracy. Our production department makes sure it's easy to use. All of this adds up to the highest quality books available, consistently appearing on best-seller charts worldwide.

You'll find SYBEX publishes a variety of books on every popular software package. Looking for computer help? Help Yourself to SYBEX.

For a complete catalog of our publications:

SYBEX Inc.
2021 Challenger Drive, Alameda, CA 94501
Tel: (415) 523-8233/(800) 227-2346 Telex: 336311
SYBEX Fax: (415) 523-2373

SYBEX is committed to using natural resources wisely to preserve and improve our environment. As a leader in the computer book publishing industry, we are aware that over 40% of America's solid waste is paper. This is why we have been printing the text of books like this one on recycled paper since 1982.

This year our use of recycled paper will result in the saving of more than 15,300 trees. We will lower air pollution effluents by 54,000 pounds, save 6,300,000 gallons of water, and reduce landfill by 2,700 cubic yards.

In choosing a SYBEX book you are not only making a choice for the best in skills and information, you are also choosing to enhance the quality of life for all of us.

Mastering Q&A 4

Mastering Q&A™ 4

Alan R. Neibauer

SYBEX ®

San Francisco • Paris • Düsseldorf • Soest

Acquisitions Editor: Dianne King
Developmental Editors: Christian T.S. Crumlish and Marilyn Smith
Copy Editor: Marilyn Smith
Project Editor: Janna Hecker
Technical Editor: Maryann Brown
Word Processors: Scott Campbell, Ann Dunn, and Susan Trybull
Series Designer: Eleanor Ramos
Chapter Art and Layout: Eleanor Ramos
Screen Graphics: Cuong Le
Desktop Publishing Specialist: Len Gilbert
Proofreader: Barbara Dahl
Indexer: Julie Kawabata
Cover Designer: Thomas Ingalls + Associates
Cover Photographer: Michael Lamotte
Screen reproductions produced by XenoFont.

XenoFont is a trademark of XenoSoft.

SYBEX is a registered trademark of SYBEX, Inc.

TRADEMARKS: SYBEX has attempted throughout this book to distinguish proprietary trademarks from descriptive terms by following the capitalization style used by the manufacturer.

SYBEX is not affiliated with any manufacturer.

Every effort has been made to supply complete and accurate information. However, SYBEX assumes no responsibility for its use, nor for any infringement of the intellectual property rights of third parties which would result from such use.

Library of Congress Card Number: 91-65090
ISBN: 0-89588-735-5

Manufactured in the United States of America

10 9 8 7 6 5 4 3 2 1

To Barbara

ACKNOWLEDGMENTS

I sincerely want to thank all of the talented people who helped make this book a reality. The professionalism of the SYBEX staff continues to make working with SYBEX a pleasure.

Special thanks go to Marilyn Smith, whose editing skills rank among the best, even when performed long distance from the mountainous wilds of the Northwest. My appreciation goes to Christian Crumlish and Janna Hecker, for their untiring coordination and organization; to proofreader Barbara Dahl; word processors Scott Campbell, Ann Dunn, and Susan Trybull; book designer Eleanor Ramos; typesetter Len Gilbert; and all of those at SYBEX whose efforts contributed to this project. Thanks also to Dianne King, for thinking of me, and to Dr. R. S. Langer, for keeping it all together.

I also want to thank Symantec Corporation for developing Q&A, an impressive program in many ways. The staff at Symantec has been helpful and supportive during the trials and tribulations of developing a program from beta versions to a final release.

My wife, Barbara, deserves more than a mention on these pages. Barbara, whose only lapse of common sense and good judgment was perhaps when she agreed to be my wife, has been the central force in my life for over 25 years now. She has played both my Watson and my Holmes and has been my tireless Mrs. Hudson during my probes into the mysteries of living.

CONTENTS AT A GLANCE

TABLE OF CONTENTS

Introduction

Q&A is a remarkably powerful program that can work in single-user and network environments. It features a new approach to database management.

At first glance, Q&A seems to lack the elements that make software salespeople stand up and cheer. Companies aren't fighting to produce the fastest Q&A compiler, or going to court over the rights to the Q&A interface. Q&A is a nonrelational, flat file manager, which does not have a dBASE-like programming language. You will never see a hundred-line Q&A program, but the advantage of Q&A is that you will never need to.

You can create complex business applications without writing even one line of program code. However, if you do want to program, you will find that a single line of Q&A program code can perform functions that would literally take more than a hundred lines in some other database language.

Q&A also has a unique feature called Intelligent Assistant, which allows you to access information in your database using plain English. After you "teach" Intelligent Assistant the words you will use to refer to your data, it will understand and process your requests.

This book covers Q&A version 4.0. If you are an experienced Q&A user just switching to version 4.0, you will be impressed with its enhanced capabilities. If this is your first use of a database manager, you will find Q&A easy to set up and use. If you are already familiar with other database programs, you may be dazzled by the ease that tasks can be performed without the yoke of lengthy programs and complex syntax.

WHAT THIS BOOK CONTAINS

Chapter 1 presents an overview of Q&A. You will learn how to start Q&A, interact with it, and set it up to work with your printer. The remaining chapters provide a comprehensive examination of each major Q&A function or application.

In Chapter 2, you will learn how to design and create a Q&A database; in Chapter 3, you will add and edit records; and in Chapter 4, you will learn how to manipulate information in your database. Chapter 5 shows you how to quickly print information in useful formats, and Chapter 6 describes how to produce sophisticated columnar and cross-tabulation reports.

The next three chapters provide details on Write, the word processing program built into Q&A. In Chapter 7, you will learn the fundamentals of working with Write. In Chapter 8, you will learn how to create form documents and labels using information from Q&A databases. Chapter 9 covers advanced word processing topics. You will learn how to import and export files and how to merge spreadsheets and graphics into Q&A documents.

Chapters 10 and 11 cover Query Guide and Intelligent Assistant, powerful features that allow you to interact with Q&A on a more natural level. In Chapter 10, you will learn how to use both Query Guide and Intelligent Assistant to generate reports and retrieve information. In Chapter 11, you will learn how to teach Intelligent Assistant so you can communicate with Q&A using English-language requests and commands.

Chapters 12 and 13 describe how to create macros and menus. You will learn how to record macros that automate database and word processing functions. You will also learn how to add options to Q&A menus, create menus, and even replace Q&A's menus with your own custom menus for complete applications.

In Chapter 14, you will learn how to customize your database. Customization options include restricting the values that can be entered into records, building templates for controlling input, indexing a database to speed up retrieval, and designing custom help messages.

Chapter 15 explains how to update any number of records at one time and use Q&A's powerful posting feature, which lets you update one database with information in another database. This chapter also describes how to use databases created with other programs, such as dBASE, Paradox, and Lotus 1-2-3.

For the power user, Chapter 16 covers Q&A programming. You will learn how to use several databases to build a complete application, and how to design and use built-in lookup tables for relational-like capabilities.

Several appendices supplement the chapters. Appendix A covers Q&A setup and installation. Appendix B summarizes the cursor-movement keys and the programming functions and commands. Appendix C details how to use printer fonts for professional Q&A output.

HOW TO USE THIS BOOK

To demonstrate the use of Q&A, the chapters in this book guide you through the development of a complete business application. You will design and build an invoicing and customer tracking application that includes several databases and macros.

If you are new to Q&A, follow the exercises in the book even if you do not need an invoicing system. By following the step-by-step instructions, you will quickly learn how to design and fine-tune your own applications.

If you are already experienced with an earlier version of Q&A, read all the chapters to become familiar with the new features in version 4.0. Concentrate on Chapters 13 through 16, which detail the more sophisticated and powerful extensions to Q&A's data-management capabilities.

If you are using Q&A primarily as a word processing program, pay special attention to Chapters 7 through 9. Do not ignore Q&A's database capabilities, however, because they can add greatly to the efficiency of your word processing tasks.

THE FAST TRACKS

Throughout this book, you will see special Fast Track synopses at the start of major topics or sections. Each Fast Track summarizes the major points, steps, or keystrokes explained in the section. In many cases, you will be able to perform the basic function just by following the Fast Track, although you should read the text for a more thorough and complete understanding of the material. After you have read the chapter, use the Fast Tracks when you need a review or want a quick reminder of the steps involved in performing a particular function.

CONVENTIONS USED IN THE TEXT

Throughout the book, several conventions are used to make the text clear and easy to read:

- Key combinations—keys to be pressed at the same time—are separated by a hyphen. For example, "press Shift-F8" means to press and hold down the Shift key while you press function key F8.

- Names of menu options and commands are in initial capital letters, even though they may not appear that way on the screen. For example, the Add data option on the File menu is shown as "Add Data."

- Characters to be typed in as part of the exercises are in boldface type. For example, you may read "Enter **<500** in the Amount field."

HARDWARE REQUIREMENTS

To run Q&A, you must have an IBM PC, PS/2, or compatible computer, with at least 512 kilobytes (K) of random access memory (RAM), or 640K RAM with DOS 4.0, and a hard disk drive. If you are using Q&A on a network, you will need at least 640K on the server and 484K on each local workstation after the network drivers have been loaded.

You must have DOS 2.0 or higher. DOS version 3.1 is required for network applications. DOS version 3.3 is required if you have a PS/2 or compatible computer. You can use either a color or monochrome monitor.

Q&A includes drivers for most dot-matrix, daisy-wheel, and laser printers, including PostScript. A mouse and expanded memory are optional.

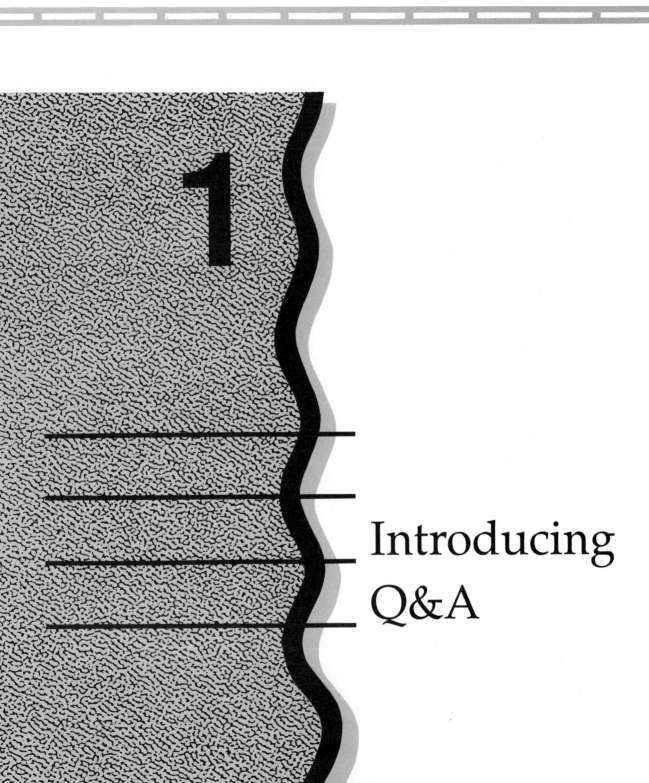

1

Introducing Q&A

Most software can be easily categorized as a word processing, database, spreadsheet, graphics, or another specific application (such as accounting) program. There are also integrated programs, such as Microsoft Works and Lotus Symphony, which combine elements of many applications. But for the most part, the individual applications in integrated programs are less powerful than their stand-alone competitors. For example, the word processing part of an integrated package generally has far fewer features than the popular word processors.

But then there is Q&A. On one hand, Q&A is a powerful and full-featured database manager, with sophisticated business features. But Q&A is also a robust word processing program, suitable for even the most complex documents. In addition, the two programs are fully integrated—you can share data between them to create all types of form documents and database reports.

Although Q&A does not include its own spreadsheet or graphics application, it can use spreadsheets and graphic files created with other applications. You can integrate Q&A with industry-standard applications, such as Lotus 1-2-3, to get the best of all worlds. And as you will learn in later chapters, you can even use Q&A with databases created by programs such as dBASE and Oracle, and with documents created by WordPerfect and other popular word processing programs.

In this chapter, you will learn about Q&A's functions and how to interact with the program. We will start with a brief summary of the major parts of Q&A.

INTRODUCING THE COMPONENTS

Q&A's main components are File, Report, Write, and Intelligent Assistant. Each of these components provides the tools you need to manage your database and produce reports and other documents.

USING Q&A FILE
FOR DATABASE MANAGEMENT

File is Q&A's database manager—an electronic version of your company's record room or filing cabinets. Like other database systems, Q&A allows you to collect, manipulate, and report on data.

Here are some examples of how you can use File:

- Maintain your company's inventory

- Keep track of customers, clients, or patients

- Maintain employee data

- Log contacts, phone calls, and appointments

- Keep records of your classes and student grades

- Catalog periodicals and collectables

- Maintain data for orders, invoices, and financial reports

Q&A is not a relational database, which is one that can combine data from more than one database or file. For example, with a relational database, you can create invoices by combining order information from one file with customer information and price data from other files. However, even though Q&A is not relational, you can perform these same functions by merging data from the various parts of Q&A.

Q&A also lacks a full-blown database language, which is a set of commands used to write custom applications for tasks that are not performed automatically by the program. But again, many of the tasks that you might program into other databases are already provided in Q&A. More advanced and custom functions can be performed by easy-to-use commands, functions, and macros from within your database file itself, not in a separate program—something Q&A calls *programming the form*. Once you become familiar with using Q&A, you will find that there is little that it cannot do.

DATABASE PUBLISHING WITH Q&A REPORT

Q&A Report lets you quickly and easily design and print sophisticated database reports, such as cross tabulations and standard deviation and variance calculations. With Report, you can gather information from multiple data files to perform relational-database-type functions.

In addition, you can take advantage of your printer's fonts and character formats to enhance your reports. You do not have to purchase special add-on database publishing software for professional-looking results.

WORD PROCESSING WITH Q&A WRITE

Q&A Write can be your primary word processing software. Although it lacks some of the features of more powerful programs, such as footnotes and index generation, it does include a spelling checker, thesaurus, and extensive formatting capabilities. You can create all types of documents with Write, as well as import documents and graphics created by other programs.

Q&A Write's main power lies in its integration with your data files. As part of the Q&A environment, it has direct access to your database. This means that you can merge data from multiple data files and produce a variety of useful materials:

- Catalogs, contracts, and proposals

- Agreements and leases

- Form letters, labels, and database reports

- Invoices and orders

Write's ability to use your database can replace thousands of lines of programming code necessary to produce the same results with other database products.

MAKING DECISIONS
WITH INTELLIGENT ASSISTANT

In order to be useful, a database must allow you to quickly and easily access the information you need to make timely and accurate decisions. With most database programs, you can only get specific information by learning complex syntax, such as

```
SELECT COMPANY FROM CLIENTS WHERE OWE > 500
LIST COMPANY FOR OWE > 500
```

With Q&A Intelligent Assistant, known as IA, however, you can "ask" Q&A questions and give it commands in plain English, such as

```
Who owes me more than 500?
Show me Smith's account.
Increase prices by 5 percent.
```

To communicate with IA this way, you "teach" it about your database and the words you want it to understand. Once you do this, you can access your information as if you were speaking to an administrative assistant. IA is a powerful and unique approach to database management, and it makes Q&A stand out among its competitors.

If you don't want to take the time to teach IA, you can still communicate with it. Since IA already understands about 600 words, you can give it requests as long as you know the structure of your database. For example, you can ask it to

```
Produce a report showing the names and addresses for records where
amount due is greater than $500
```

It is wordier than *Who owes over $500?*, but it accomplishes the same task.

You can also get answers using Query Guide, which is a menu-driven assistant that guides you through the process of generating reports, displaying records, and calculating statistics. You don't have to know how File and Report work, or even how your database is structured—just follow the prompts and menus.

Now that you're familiar with Q&A's main components, it's time to start the program, learn how to interact with it, and prepare it for printing.

STARTING Q&A

To start Q&A:

1. **Start your computer.**
2. **Type CD/QA and press ↵ to log onto the Q&A directory.**
3. **Type QA and press ↵.**

If you have not yet installed Q&A on your system, follow the instructions in Appendix A. (Version 4 requires a hard disk drive; you cannot run it from floppy disks.) When you're ready to start using the program, follow these steps:

1. Turn on your computer and respond to the date and time prompts if they appear.
2. When the DOS C:> prompt appears, log onto the directory containing the Q&A program. This is the drive and directory in which you installed the program. For example, if it is in the C drive and the QA directory, type **CD\QA** and press ↵.
3. Type **QA** and press ↵ to start the program. You will see the Q&A logo, a message indicating the program is loading, and then the Q&A Main menu.

If it seems as if there is something wrong with your screen, you may have to restart Q&A in a way that tells it the type of monitor you are using. Press X when the Main menu appears (or reboot your computer if necessary), and then start Q&A using one of the commands listed in Table 1.1. You only have to use a monitor command the first time you start the program. From then on, Q&A will automatically start correctly for your system when you load it with the QA command from the DOS prompt.

Table 1.1: Monitor Commands for Starting Q&A

MONITOR TYPE	STARTUP COMMAND
Color	QA -SCC
Monochrome	QA -SMC
Compaq monochrome	QA -SMM
Composite	QA -A
NEC multispeed	QA -ST
IBM PS/2 monochrome	QA -SMC -A
Toshiba 1100 or 3100	QA -SMC
Zenith laptop	QA -A
LCD display	QA -A or QA -ST

EXPLORING THE
Q&A MENU SYSTEM

▐▐▐➡ **To select options from Q&A menus, use one of the following methods:**
- **Highlight the option and press ↵.**
- **Type the initial letter and press ↵.**
- **Type the item's number.**
- **Click on the item with your mouse.**

Q&A's menu system helps you select options and perform tasks. The Main menu lists the major Q&A components and Utilities. You use the Utilities option to set up your printer, perform DOS commands, and import or export files to and from other applications, as you will learn in this and later chapters.

Notice that each menu option is preceded by a letter, such as F for File and R for Report. The first menu item is automatically highlighted (in white letters on black).

Use one of the following techniques to select a menu option:

- Press the ↓ or ↑ key to highlight the option and press ↵.
- Type the letter shown in front of the option to highlight it and press ↵.
- Type the number of the item on the menu, such as 1 for the first menu item or 2 for the second one. You do not have to press ↵ after typing the number.
- Click on the option with the mouse.

At the bottom of the screen is the Q&A copyright line, followed by the message line and the key-assignment line. On the message line, Q&A displays prompts and comments as you work. The key-assignment line shows functions you can perform, such as press X to exit from Q&A and return to the DOS prompt, press F1 to display a screen explaining the menu options, or press ↵ to continue with the highlighted option. The items listed in the key-assignment line depend on the function you're performing.

Selecting some menu options performs an action immediately, such as pressing X to leave Q&A. In other cases, Q&A displays another menu listing additional, related options. Continue selecting menu options until you perform the function desired.

As an example of navigating Q&A's menus, we'll step through the procedure for importing data from Lotus 1-2-3 into a Q&A file (we won't actually import the data now).

1. From the Main menu, press ↵ to select File, which is already highlighted. (You could also type 1 or click on File with your mouse.) The message

   Working...

   flashes briefly on the message line, and then the File menu appears, with the Main menu in the background.

2. Select Utilities from the File menu to display the File Utilities menu, shown in Figure 1.1.

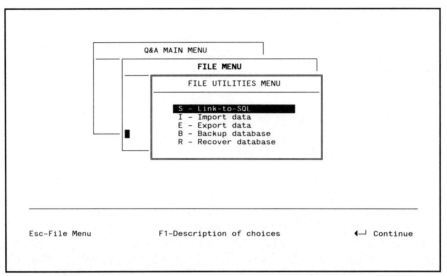

Figure 1.1: File Utilities menu

3. Select Import Data to display the Import menu, shown in
    Figure 1.2.

By leaving the previous-level menus in the background, Q&A reminds
you of the exact function you are performing. With the Import menu on
the screen, the background menus make it clear that you are importing
data into Q&A File.

The key-assignment line beneath each menu includes the F1-Description
of Choices and ↵ Continue options. It also shows how to return to the
previous-level menu. For example, with the File menu displayed, the key-
assignment line includes the Esc-Main Menu option.

When the File Utilities menu is in on the screen, the key-assignment
line shows Esc-File Menu. This means that you can press the Esc key to
remove the menu and return to the previous menu. We'll do this now to
return to the Main menu.

4. Press Esc, and the Import menu will disappear from the screen.

5. Press Esc twice more: once to clear the File Utilities menu and
    again to remove the File menu. Only the Main menu remains.

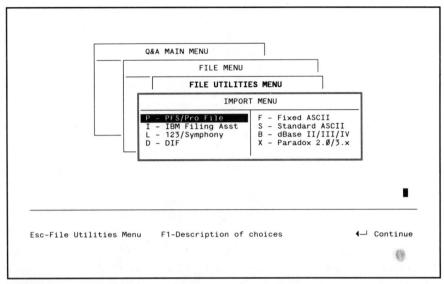

Figure 1.2: Import menu

You're now ready for a more practical example of using menus. In the next section, you will learn how to set up Q&A to print database reports and word processing documents.

PREPARING TO PRINT

To install your printer:

1. Select Utilities from the Main menu, then Install Printer.
2. Select Printer A through Printer E, a printer port, your printer's manufacturer, and the printer model.
3. Read the information screen, and then press ⌐.
4. Type N to continue, or Y to install another printer.

When you installed Q&A, you copied printer font files to your hard disk. These files contain the information Q&A needs to print reports and documents. But before printing with Q&A for the first time, you must install your specific printer into the Q&A environment to make it available to Q&A File, Write, and Report.

INSTALLING YOUR PRINTER

You can install up to five different printers in Q&A. This is especially useful if you have more than one printer with your system. For example, you can use your dot-matrix printer to produce quick database reports and your laser printer to print final documents that require graphics and different fonts.

When you install a printer, you tell Q&A its name and the port to which it is attached. Your printer may be either a serial or parallel type. You can't tell a serial printer from a parallel one by just looking at it, but you might be able to determine its type by how it's connected to the back of your computer.

You will see a plug, called a *port*, where the printer's cable is attached. If the port is labeled Printer, LPT 1, or Parallel, your printer is a parallel printer. If it's the only port on the back of the computer, it's probably a parallel port as well.

If the port is labeled COM 1 or Serial, you're using a serial printer, and you will have to read your printer's manual for special instructions. If you have more than one port of a type, they are called LPT2, LPT3, or COM 2. You can use these to attach more than one printer to your system.

When you are ready to install your printer, follow these steps:

1. Select Utilities from the Main menu to see the Utilities menu.

2. Press ↵ to choose the Install Printer option and display the Printer Selection menu.

As shown in Figure 1.3, this menu lists the current printers selected for use with Q&A and the port to which they are attached. Notice that the default port is LPT1, the parallel port. The default printer is listed as a Basic (Vanilla) Non-Laser Printer, which represents a dot-matrix or daisy-wheel printer. This setting allows you to print simple reports and documents with

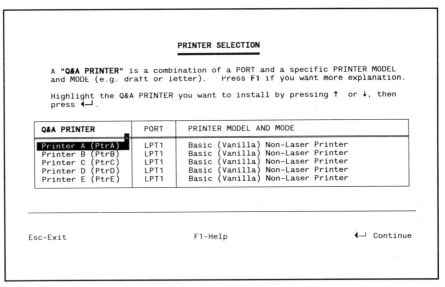

Figure 1.3: Printer Selection menu

almost any type of printer, but you will not be able to print graphics or take advantage of character formats (such as boldfaced and underlining) and fonts (such as italics).

3. Always assign your printer, or the one you plan to use most often, as Printer A (PtrA). Make sure Printer A is highlighted and press ↵. Q&A displays the Port Selection screen, shown in Figure 1.4.

4. Press ↓, ↑, or the spacebar to select the port, and then press ↵. (LPT 1 is the most common port.) Next, you will see the list of printer manufacturers shown in Figure 1.5.

5. Select the manufacturer of your printer from the list. If your manufacturer is not shown, press PgDn to display additional options. If you still don't see your printer, select Basic Vanilla (press PgUp to return to the first list if necessary).

6. Press ↵ to display the list of printer models. Figure 1.6 shows the list of Hewlett-Packard printers.

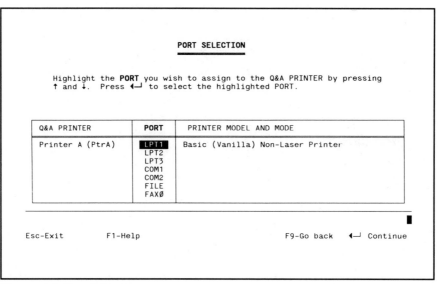

Figure 1.4: Port Selection screen

7. Select your specific model from the list. Press PgDn to see more if your model is not listed on the first screen. Then press ↵ to display information about your printer.

The information screen contains the options to press ↵ to continue with the setup, F8 for Special Options, or Esc to cancel the setup. If you have a serial printer, you must press F8 and specify the serial protocol. The protocol includes the settings your printer uses to accept characters from the computer. If you have a parallel printer, select Special Options only if you have difficulty printing with Q&A. The Special Options settings are summarized in Table 1.2.

8. Read the screen, and then press ↵. You'll see the prompt

   Your printer has been installed.
   Do you want to install another?
   　　Y - Yes   N - No

9. If you want to install a second printer, press Y then ↵, and

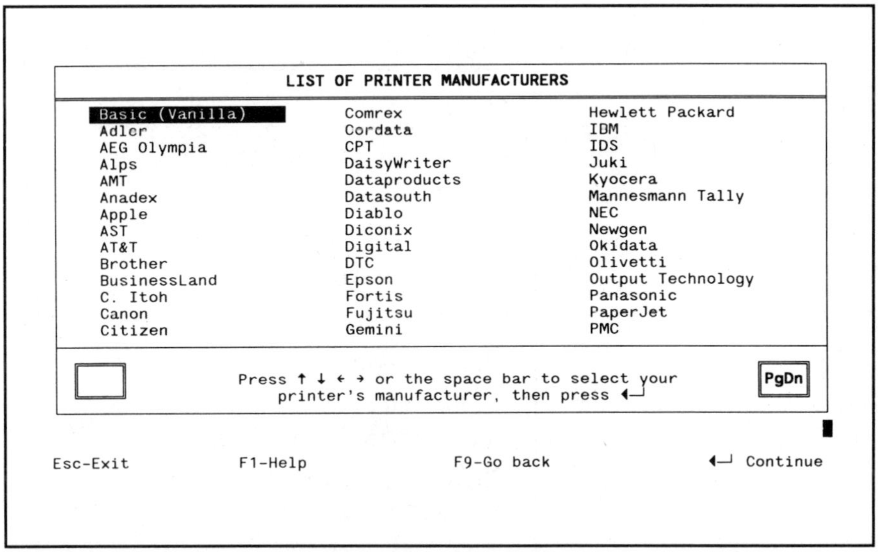

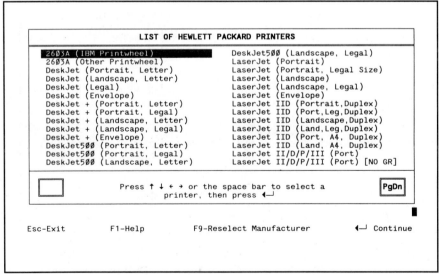

Figure 1.5: First Printer Manufacturers screen

Figure 1.6: List of Hewlett-Packard printer models

Table 1.2: Special Options for Installing Printers

SETTING	OPTIONS
Baud Rate	Choose 110, 150, 300, 600, 1200, 2400, 4800, or 9600.
Data Bits	Select 7 or 8 bits.
Stop Bits	Choose 1 or 2 bits.
Parity	Select Odd, Even, or None.
Check for printer timeout?	Choose Yes or No.
Length of timeout (in seconds)	Set the length of time for Q&A to wait until it responds to printer errors.
Check for printer ready signal?	Choose Yes or No.
Check for paper out?	Choose Yes or No.
Formfeed at end of document?	Choose Yes or No.
Font file name	Enter the name of the font file you installed when you set up Q&A.
Bin 1, 2, and 3 setup code	Enter the control codes your printer uses to select paper-feed bins.
Eject page code	Enter the control code to eject a sheet of paper.
Start of document code	Enter the control code you want Q&A to send to the printer at the start of each document.
End of document code	Enter the control code you want Q&A to send to the printer at the end of each document.
Envelope height	Enter the height of your envelope in lines.

repeat the steps above, selecting Printer B through E on the
Printer Selection menu. Press N at the prompt when you're
finished adding printers.

If you install more than one printer, you will be able to select the printer to use—PtrA, PtrB, and so on—before printing a document.

10.   Press Esc until you return to the Main menu.

Instructions for setting up Q&A to access your printer's fonts are in Appendix C.

PRINTING TO A DISK FILE

There may be occasions when you want the output of a report or document to be saved in a disk file instead of being sent to your printer to be printed. You might want to print the output at a later time or place, perhaps on a different printer than the one you have connected to your computer, or to transmit the file over a modem.

If you select File from the Port menu, Q&A will save the printed output to a disk file when you select to use the printer associated with it. All the special codes and commands used by the designated printer will be saved along with the text of the report or document. For example, suppose you installed Printer B as an Epson FX/80 on the File port. When you select PtrB, all printed output will be sent to a disk file, which will include codes that an Epson printer needs to format characters, control spacing, and print graphics.

Printing to a disk file is particularly useful if you have many documents that you would like to print at a later time. Since the codes are included in the file, you can print each document whenever it is convenient by using the DOS PRINT or COPY command. It will appear exactly as if you had printed it from Q&A.

You might also print to a disk file if you want to print the document on a printer at some other location, such as the laser printer at the office instead of your dot-matrix printer at home. You will have installed your main printer as Printer A. Set up the other printer (such as the office laser printer) as Printer B connected to the File port. You can then select PtrB and send the document to a disk file, carry the disk to the other printer, and print it from there.

When you are ready to print a document, you will be able to select from various printing options. Printing database records and reports is discussed in Chapter 5, and Chapters 7 and 8 describe the options for printing word processing documents.

GETTING HELP

▐▐▐▶ **To get on-line help from Q&A:**

1. **Press the F1 key to display context-sensitive information.**
2. **Press PgDn to see the next Help screen (if it exists).**
3. **Press PgUp to return to the previous Help screen.**

Whether you are printing a document, selecting a menu option, or performing any other function with Q&A, you can always display a screen with helpful information by pressing the F1 key.

Q&A's Help screens are context-sensitive; that is, they display information about the current function. For example, when a menu is on the screen, pressing F1 brings up a description of that menu's items. The Help screen will also show the number of the page in the Q&A manual that explains those particular options.

If the key-assignment line lists PgDn, there is more information. Press PgDn to see the next Help screen and PgUp to return to the previous one. When you're finished reading the Help information, press Esc to exit from the function.

CHANGING
THE WAY Q&A WORKS

▐▐▐▶ **To modify how Q&A operates:**

1. **Select Utilities from the Main menu, then Set Global Options.**

2. **Accept or change the default directories for documents, databases, and temporary files.**
3. **Select to execute menu items by pressing the initial letter.**
4. **If your computer is on a network, enter your name and telephone number.**
5. **Press F10 to continue.**

While you are setting up Q&A, you might want to adjust some ways in which it works. One adjustment you can make to speed up your work is to have Q&A execute menu items as soon as you press the item's first letter, so you do not have to press ↵.

You can also change the directory where Q&A stores your files. By default, Q&A stores all your files in the directory holding the Q&A program files. As you create databases and documents, this directory will become full, or at least contain more files than you can easily manage. Before this happens, you might want to specify separate directories for your own files.

Follow these steps now to switch to automatic execution:

1. Select Utilities from the Main menu.

2. Select Set Global Options to display the menu shown in Figure 1.7.

Use the first three options on the menu to specify default directories for your documents and databases, as well as the temporary files that Q&A creates during your work sessions. Press ↓ to select the option, and then enter a path and directory. Q&A will not check to be sure that the directory you enter exists, but if you specify a nonexistent directory, it will not be able to save your files. However, you can enter the directory name now, exit from Q&A, and create the directory before you begin working with the program.

3. Press ↓ to reach the Automatic Execution prompt.

4. Press Y to select Yes, so that you can choose a menu item by simply typing its first letter.

5. Press F10 to return to the Utilities menu.

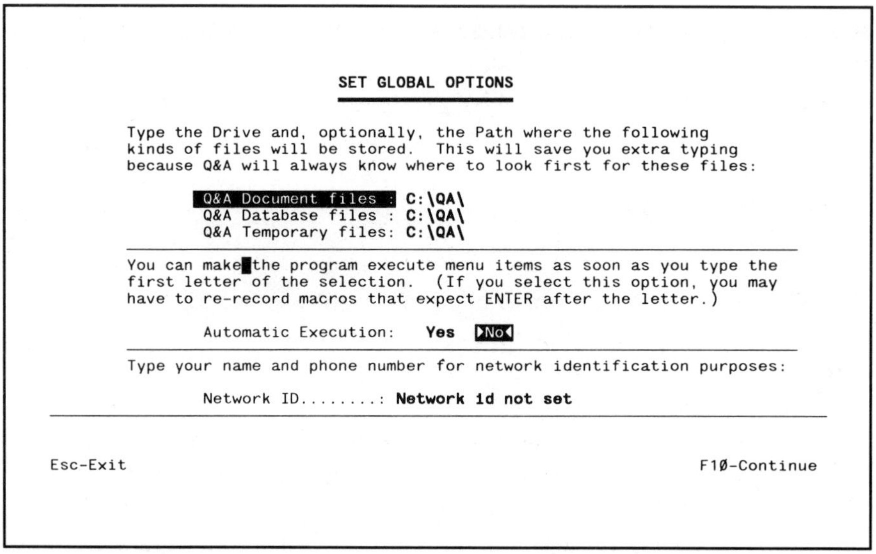

```
                        SET GLOBAL OPTIONS
                        ─────────────────

        Type the Drive and, optionally, the Path where the following
        kinds of files will be stored.  This will save you extra typing
        because Q&A will always know where to look first for these files:

                Q&A Document files : C:\QA\
                Q&A Database files : C:\QA\
                Q&A Temporary files: C:\QA\
        ─────────────────────────────────────────────────────────────
        You can make the program execute menu items as soon as you type the
        first letter of the selection.  (If you select this option, you may
        have to re-record macros that expect ENTER after the letter.)

                Automatic Execution:   Yes   ▶No◀
        ─────────────────────────────────────────────────────────────
        Type your name and phone number for network identification purposes:

                Network ID........: Network id not set
        ─────────────────────────────────────────────────────────────



   Esc-Exit                                              F10-Continue
```

Figure 1.7: Set Global Options menu

LEAVING Q&A

|||▶ **To exit from Q&A:**

1. Press Esc until the Main menu is displayed.

2. Choose Exit from the Main menu.

When you're finished working with Q&A, always leave the program before turning off your computer. If you don't, you might lose some of your work.

Follow these steps to exit from Q&A now:

1. Press Esc to retrun to the Main menu.

2. Type X to choose Exit.

If you were working on a database file, report, document, or other task, and you tried to leave the application without saving your work first, you would see a warning message. In this case, you would select No, save the file, and then press X from the Main menu.

Even though Q&A contains a word processing module, it is primarily a database-management system. Now that you're familiar with how Q&A works, you will learn how to create and work with databases.

2

Creating
Q&A
Databases

Chances are you already have a filing system of some sort. Perhaps you have a file cabinet full of client folders, inventory cards, or personnel data. You might keep index cards for recipes, a mailing list, or a record of your stamp collection.

A computer *database* is an electronic filing system. A database program provides speed, flexibility, and security that you can't achieve with a paper system.

In this chapter, you will create a sample database for client information. In later chapters, you will expand this example into an invoicing and billing system, which will give you an idea of just how powerful Q&A can truly be.

INTRODUCING
FORMS AND FIELDS

You create a database in three steps. First, you plan what information you want to maintain. Each category of information is called a *field*. For example, you might need fields for each client's name, address, and phone number. You can change the fields after you create the database, but it's best to plan them in advance, making sure you have all the required fields. In the planning process, you should decide on the names you will give the fields, their character width, and their type.

Second, you lay out or design the *form* as you want to see it on the screen. You position each field and draw the lines and boxes. Although you can have only one form for each client in the database, the form can include up to ten pages (screens of information), and you can link forms in other files to the database, as explained in Chapter 15. Each form can include up to 2045 fields, with a maximum of 248 fields per page. There are also limits on the number of characters and records in a Q&A database, as summarized in Table 2.1.

Table 2.1: Limitations on Q&A Databases

DATABASE ITEMS	MAXIMUM
Fields per form	2045
Fields per page	248
Characters per form	65,536
Characters per field	32,768
Records in a database	534,266
Characters in a database	1024 megabytes

In the third step, you specify the format of each field, or how its contents will appear on the screen.

After you create your database, you add your information to each form. Once you add information to a form, it becomes a *record*. A record contains all the information about one entity, such as a customer or inventory item. So if you have 100 customers, you will have 100 records.

Traditionally, the term *form* applies to the visual representation, or the layout of fields on the page. *Record* means the collection of information. However, Q&A often uses the terms interchangeably. For example, you will see one message saying

    50 Records are about to be removed PERMANENTLY

while another says

    Total Forms: 50

The second prompt refers to records, not 50 different layouts. In this book, we will use *form* to refer to layouts, and *record* to mean filled-in forms. Just remember that some of Q&A's prompts say forms but mean records.

You will learn how to add and work with records in your database in the next chapter. Now we will follow the steps to create a database.

PLANNING YOUR DATABASE

||||▶ **To prepare for creating your database:**

1. **Design the data input form on a piece of paper.**
2. **Assign each item, or field, a label. Field labels do not have to be unique.**
3. **Determine the appropriate width of each field.**
4. **Determine the type of each field: text, number, money, date, hours, yes/no, or keyword.**

The most important part of creating a database is done even before you turn on your computer. Design the form on a piece of paper, identifying the fields and adding descriptive titles or headings, just as you would if you were using a printed form.

On your form, each field is indicated by a field *label,* such as Name or Address. The label tells you the type of information that is to be entered at the place on the form. (You will learn in Chapter 15, however, that you can have fields without field labels.)

In many cases, the fields you will need are evident. For example, in an inventory database, you might include the item name, stock number, cost, quantity on hand, and the vendor that supplies the item.

When dealing with people, however, the division of the fields can be more complex. For example, you could refer to a name in one field:

Name: George M. Smith

or in three separate fields:

Last Name: Smith   First Name: George   MI: M

You could also use one large field for the entire address:

Address: 555 West Fifth Street
Madison, WI 15237

or four separate fields:

Address: 555 West Fifth Street
City: Madison   State: WI   Zip: 15237

Separating the information in several fields is usually the best approach, because it allows you to retrieve specific information more quickly and print more useful reports. For example, before making an out-of-town trip, you could print a list of customers in each city you plan to visit, as long as the city is in a separate field. If it were part of an address field, you would not be able to extract just the city, state, or zip code.

LABELING THE FIELDS

Your field labels can be more than one word long, and they should reflect the exact type of information desired. For example, the field label Profit could mean many things. A label such as Net Profit, Gross Profit, or After Tax Profit is more meaningful.

Although your field labels should be as descriptive as possible, you can use the same field label more than once if it makes your form easier to understand. Unlike most database systems, duplicate field labels do not confuse Q&A.

Field Labels Versus Field Names

In most database programs, each field label must be unique. That is, you cannot have two fields with the same label. For example, if you were designing a form that lists two persons, you would have to call one field something like Last-Name1 and call the other one Last-Name2. In a paper form, however, there may be labels that are not unique, as in the example shown in Figure 2.1.

Most database systems use the field label, which is the prompt that appears on the form or screen, as the field name that distinguishes one field from any others. So if you had two field names that were the same, such as Address, the database system wouldn't know which address to use when printing reports or form letters.

```
┌─────────────────────────────────────────────────────────────────┐
│  ┌───────────────────────────────────────────────────────────┐   │
│  │              Student Emergency Contact Form               │   │
│  │                        Father                             │   │
│  │  Name:_____ Home Phone:_____ Office Phone:_____│   │
│  │                        Mother                             │   │
│  │  Name:_____ Home Phone:_____ Office Phone:_____│   │
│  │                   Emergency Contact                       │   │
│  │  Name:_____ Home Phone:_____ Office Phone:_____│   │
│  └───────────────────────────────────────────────────────────┘   │
│                                                                   │
└─────────────────────────────────────────────────────────────────┘
```

Figure 2.1: Sample form with several identical field labels

However, Q&A distinguishes field labels from field names. If a field label is unique, Q&A assigns the field the same name as the label. For example, the only field with the label Client Code will be given the name Client Code. When two or more fields have the same label, Q&A assigns each field its own internal field name that is unique. For example, it would assign the first field labeled Phone the name Phone, the second Phone field Phone1, and the third Phone field Phone2. This means that your on-screen form can look just like a paper form.

Q&A uses the internal field names for its own purposes, but you do not have to consider them unless you are performing programming functions.

After you decide on your field labels, you must determine each field's width and its type.

DETERMINING FIELD WIDTHS

In some cases, the size of the field is obvious. For example, the State field in an address should be two characters wide, and the Zip Code field would have ten characters—a maximum nine-digit zip code, with a hyphen between the fifth and sixth numbers. Social security numbers are usually eleven characters. The width of fields for phone numbers depends on how you plan to enter the information: as eight characters without the area code (555-1234) or 12 with it (215 555-5555). Be sure to count each blank space and punctuation mark, such as a hyphen, as a character. (Actually, you will soon learn that you can enter any number of characters in a field, no matter what size you provide for it in the form.)

When you do not know the exact number of characters that will be in each field, such as for names or addresses, make sure to plan enough space for the longest possible entry.

PLANNING FIELD TYPES

More important than the size of the field, however, is its type. Q&A provides seven field types:

- Text
- Number
- Money
- Date
- Hours
- Yes/No
- Keyword

The following sections describe these field types in detail.

Text Fields

Any character you can type from the keyboard can be entered in a text field. This type is suitable for name and address fields, as well as fields that contain numbers and punctuation characters, such as phone numbers, social security numbers, and nine-digit zip codes. If you designate a phone number field as numeric, for example, you won't be able to enter hyphens or parentheses, as in (215) 651-9182.

In fact, even if you think a field will contain only numbers, designate it as text unless you plan to use it in arithmetic calculations. This will make it easier for you to format or add characters to the field later.

Number Fields

Assign a field a number type only if you plan to use it in calculations. For example, in our sample database, we will designate the field called Age as a number field so we can compute the average age of our customers, a common marketing practice.

Number fields can contain only the numbers 0 to 9, a comma, a period, a plus sign, and a minus sign. Q&A will not let you enter any other characters in a field with this type.

Q&A will automatically remove any leading zeros in numbers that you enter, since they do not affect the value of the field. Therefore, if you designated a zip code field as number, codes such as 01165 would appear with only four digits on the screen: 1165.

Money Fields

Q&A automatically formats entries in fields assigned as a money type as dollars and cents, with two decimal places. For instance, if you entered 123.45 into a money field, Q&A would display $123.45. When you enter whole numbers, such as 123, Q&A adds the decimal places for you, as in $123.00.

A money field is basically just a formatted number field, and you can use its contents in calculations. You can create formulas using any combination of money fields, number fields, and numbers. For example, in an inventory database, you might multiply a money field called Price by a number field called Quantity to calculate the total value of your stock on hand.

Date Fields

Keeping track of dates is important in any business. It is important to know when an item was ordered, a bill has to be paid, or an employee is planning a vacation. If you are maintaining data for personal use, you may have a list of your friends' birthdays.

You could type a date in a text field, but assigning the date type has two advantages: Q&A formats the field for you, and you can perform calculations with the dates. For example, you can enter a date in a variety of formats, such as 10/22/91, 22.10.1991, or even 91-10-22. Q&A will auto-matically convert the date and display it as Oct 22, 1991, or whichever of 20 styles you make the default.

You can also use date fields for date arithmetic, such as adding or sub-tracting days to arrive at a new date, or calculating the number of days or years between two dates. This would be useful, for example, if you plan to print aging reports of unpaid invoices or to calculate how long perish-able goods have remained in inventory.

Hours Fields

Keeping track of hours may also be part of your business. The hours field type records time in either standard or military format and can con-vert between them. This is convenient if you have to keep records in military time but have difficulty making the conversion yourself.

Assign the hours type to a field when you want to record the start and stop times of activities, such as to keep track of your time for billing pur-poses. You can subtract the fields, calculate the time spent on a project, and then multiply it by your hourly rate.

Yes/No Fields

There are times when you want a simple Yes or No answer from your database. Is the client tax-exempt? Is the inventory item perishable? Is your employee a member of the union?

The yes/no field type handles only two possible values: true or false. You can enter Yes, y, True, t, or 1 to represent a true condition; No, n, False, f, or 0 for a false condition.

By using yes/no fields with more advanced Q&A techniques, you can automate procedures in your database. For example, if the Taxable field were true, you could automatically add sales tax to an invoice. Automat-ing your Q&A tasks is covered in Chapter 15.

Keyword Fields

One problem with designing a database is the necessity for repeating fields, which contain the same type of information. For example, suppose you want to record the professional licenses that employees have obtained. You could create a number of similar fields—repeating fields—such as

    Name:
    License:
    License:
    License:
    License:

But since an employee could have any number of licenses, you do not know how many times to repeat the field—two License fields may not be enough, but ten of them might just waste space.

With most database software, you can avoid this problem only by creating multiple databases and linking them together with complex commands or programming statements. Q&A, however, provides the keyword field type just for this purpose.

A keyword field can contain a series of entries separated by semicolons. For example, in our sample database, we will have a keyword field called Products Purchased for item codes. This will allow us to enter data such as

    Products Purchased: 102; 201; 712; 762

listing as many items as necessary. We can then print reports showing which clients purchase particular products, because Q&A can separate the values in the field into individual items.

Q&A will match keywords regardless of capitalization, as long as they are spelled the same. If your keyword field contains the names of sports, for example, Q&A will consider *baseball*, *Baseball*, and *BASEBALL* as the same entry.

PUTTING THE PLAN ON PAPER

After you've planned your database's fields, put the initial design on paper. Make several copies of the paper form and fill them out with actual information—the same data you will be entering from the computer when your database is ready. If you make up information just to fill in the form, you might not notice some special requirements or problems that the actual entries would bring to your attention. For example, a common mistake is to create an address field with too few lines. Along comes an address with a suite or box number, and you have no place to enter it.

Try to pick a variety of records—some with long names, some with short ones, some with information for every field. Look for records that contain special entries or extra information.

It is also important to consider ways that you would like to use the database and make sure the form can accommodate them, even if you don't have the information to add at the current time. Including the fields now will save you a great deal of time later on.

Our sample database, for example, will not only store information about our customers, but will also be used to print reports and process invoices. In addition, we want it to provide the information we will need to promote our business.

LAYING OUT THE FIELDS

▐▐▐▶ **To lay out fields on the database form:**

1. **Select File from the Main menu, then Design File, then Design a New File.**
2. **Type the database name and press ⏎ to display the blank form.**
3. **Type the field labels where you want them to appear on the form. End each label with a colon (:) or less-than (<) symbol.**
4. **End the field at the end of the line, at the next field label on the line, or with a greater-than (>) symbol.**
5. **Align text and draw lines and boxes.**
6. **When you have completed the design, press F10.**

After you have planned your database, you can start Q&A and lay out the form.

COMPONENTS OF
THE FORM LAYOUT SCREEN

Figure 2.2 shows the screen that you use to design your database forms. The small horizontal line at the top of the screen is the *cursor,* which shows the position of characters that you type. The rectangle on the right side of the screen in Figure 2.2 is the *mouse pointer,* which appears when you have a mouse attached to your system. If you have a mouse, you can select items by placing the mouse pointer on the option and clicking the left mouse button.

Along the bottom of the screen is the *ruler,* which is marked in inches from 1 to 8. Each vertical line along the ruler represents a character position, and each T shows a tab stop. The box at the far left of the ruler is the *ghost cursor.* As you move the cursor horizontally on the form, the ghost cursor also moves, showing the exact position of the character. Use the ruler to judge spacing and align columns.

Below the ruler is the *status line.* It displays the name of the file, the percentage of your computer's memory being used by the form, the cursor position, the line number in which the cursor is placed, the current page number, and the total number of pages in the form. The location of the

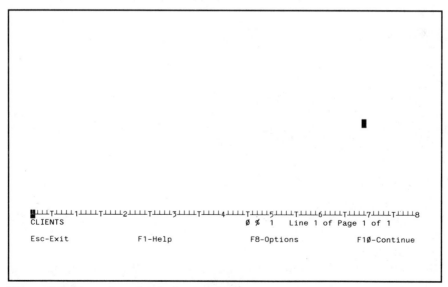

Figure 2.2: The screen for designing forms

cursor is shown in character positions, representing ten characters in each inch across the ruler. For example, when the cursor is on position 4 on the ruler, the indicator displays 40.

Below the status line is the *message line*. It displays messages, warnings, and prompts about the task you are performing or any problems that Q&A encounters. Follow any instructions that appear on the line to continue your work.

You can fit up to 21 lines on each page of the form. The line-number indicator increases as you move toward the bottom of the form; it decreases as you move to the top.

The final line is the key-assignment line. As you already know, this line lists the function keys that are available and the actions that they perform. The key-assignment line for this screen includes the following options:

- Esc, to return to the Main menu
- F1, to display Help information
- F8, to select options for arranging text on the screen and drawing lines
- F10, to continue with the database design process

ENTERING FORM ITEMS

You design your form by moving the cursor and entering characters. Table 2.2 lists the keystrokes for moving the cursor and editing and deleting characters. Most of these keystrokes are used within all parts of the Q&A system, including File and Write.

When the cursor is a small line, Q&A is in overtype mode, in which characters you type replace existing ones on the screen. If you want to insert new characters without deleting existing ones, press the Ins key. The characters Ins appear on the status line, indicating that you are in insert mode, and the cursor changes to a blinking box. When you type, characters to the right of the cursor will move over or down to make room. Press Ins again to return to overtype mode (Ins *toggles* between overtype and insert mode).

You must end each field label with a colon (:) or less-than (<) sign. You can use the greater-than sign (>) to indicate the end of the field. When you later add customer codes to the form, you will see only five characters in that field because there will be five spaces between the colon that ends the label and the > sign. If you do not enter the > symbol, you can see as many

Table 2.2: Cursor-Movement and Editing Keys

KEYPRESS	ACTION
↑	Moves up a line
↓	Moves down a line
→	Moves to the right one character
←	Moves to the left one character
Backspace	Deletes characters to the left of the cursor
Ctrl-→	Moves one word to the right
Ctrl-←	Moves one word to the left
Ctrl-End	Moves to the end of the last page of the form
Ctrl-F4	Deletes from the cursor position to the end of the line
Ctrl-Home	Moves to the beginning of the form
Del	Deletes the character above the cursor
End	
1st press	Moves to the end of the line
2nd press	Moves to the bottom of the screen
3rd press	Moves to the end of the last page of the form
F4	Deletes from the cursor position to the end of the word
Home	
1st press	Moves to the beginning of the line
2nd press	Moves to the top of the screen
3rd press	Moves to the beginning of the first page of the form
PgDn	Moves to the top of the next page
PgUp	Moves to the top of the previous page
Shift-F4	Deletes the line

characters as there are spaces remaining on the line, or up to the next field label on the same line.

You can design multiline fields for lengthier entries or for general information or comments about the subject of the form. Move the cursor down to where the field should end and place the > symbol there. If you end a multiline field label with a colon, Q&A starts the following lines in the field at the left edge of the screen. However, if you end the field label with the < symbol, your lines will align with the symbol.

SETTING UP
THE CLIENTS DATABASE

The database form we will design consists of two pages, as shown in Figures 2.3 and 2.4.

The first page contains the basic information we need to print invoices and other customer reports. The second page contains some personal information about the customer that will help in maintaining a friendly relationship, as well as data on a secondary, or alternate, contact in the same firm. You can picture the two pages as two sheets of paper you would store in a file folder.

The size of most fields is not critical, although date fields should be at

```
                        Customer Record
  Customer Code:
  Name:
  Address:
  City:               State:          Zip Code:

                        Primary Contact
  Last Name:          First Name:              MI:
  Title:              Phone:


                        Order Information
  Last Order Date:    Amount:         Total Orders:
  Taxable:            Credit Limit:
  Products Purchased:
  Shipping Zone:      Preferred Carrier:
```

Figure 2.3: First page of the sample client database form

```
┌─────────────────────────────────────────────────────────────────┐
│            Secondary Contact and Personal Client Data             │
│  ┌─────────────────────────────────────────────────────────────┐ │
│  │                       Primary Contact                        │ │
│  ├─────────────────────────────────────────────────────────────┤ │
│  │  Date of Birth:              Age:                            │ │
│  │  Hobbies:                                                     │ │
│  │  Secretary:                                                   │ │
│  └─────────────────────────────────────────────────────────────┘ │
│  ┌─────────────────────────────────────────────────────────────┐ │
│  │                      Secondary Contact                       │ │
│  ├─────────────────────────────────────────────────────────────┤ │
│  │  Last Name:               First Name:           MI:         │ │
│  │  Title:                   Phone:                             │ │
│  │  Date of Birth:           Age:                               │ │
│  │  Hobbies:                                                     │ │
│  │  Secretary:                                                   │ │
│  └─────────────────────────────────────────────────────────────┘ │
│     Notes                                                         │
└─────────────────────────────────────────────────────────────────┘
```

Figure 2.4: Second page of the sample database

least ten characters wide to store the default format. We will make the Customer Code field five characters long, the State field two characters, and the Zip Code field ten characters. The length of the other fields will be determined by their position on the form.

Most of the fields are assigned the text type, but the form will include all the field types except hours. Table 2.3 lists the field labels and types for the sample database.

Table 2.3: Field Types for the Sample Clients Database

FIELD NAME	TYPE
Customer Code	Text
Name	Text
Address	Text
City	Text
State	Text
Zip Code	Text
Last Name	Text
First Name	Text
MI	Text
Title	Text

Table 2.3: Field Types for the Sample Clients Database (continued)

FIELD NAME	TYPE
Phone	Text
Taxable	Yes/No
Credit Limit	Money
Products Purchased	Keyword
Shipping Zone	Text
Preferred Carrier	Text
Last Order Date	Date
Amount	Money
Total Orders	Money
Date of Birth	Date
Age	Number
Hobbies	Keyword
Secretary	Text
Last Name	Text
First Name	Text
MI	Text
Title	Text
Phone	Text
Date of Birth	Date
Age	Number
Hobbies	Keyword
Secretary	Text

We will call the database Clients. All Q&A file names must conform to the standard DOS file-naming conventions. Names can be from one to eight characters long, and they may contain letters, numbers, and the characters $, &, #, %, ', (,), @, ^, {, }, !, and -, but no spaces.

Follow these steps to begin setting up the database:

1. Start Q&A and then press ↵ to select the File option.

2. Press ↵ to select Design File. You will see the Design menu, shown in Figure 2.5.

3. Press ↵ to select Design a New File. Q&A displays the prompt

   Data file: C:\QA\

4. Type **CLIENTS** and press ↵. Q&A adds the extension DTF to the file name. Next, the form design screen appears (Figure 2.2).

Later in this chapter, we will draw borders around the form. You will place a blank line at the top of the form and press Tab in front of each of the fields to leave room for the lines and for the spaces between the lines and field labels.

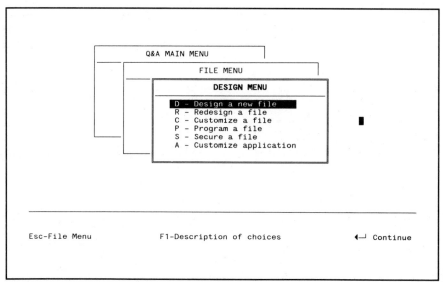

Figure 2.5: Design menu

5. Press ⏎ to insert a blank line at the top of the form.

6. Type **Customer Record** and press ⏎ twice. (You do not need to end this entry with a colon or < because it's an identifying heading, not a field.)

7. Press Tab, and then type **Customer Code:**.

8. Press → six times, and then type >. Figure 2.6 shows the screen at this point.

9. Press ⏎.

10. Press Tab, type **Name:**, and press ⏎.

11. Press Tab, type **Address:**, and press ⏎.

12. Press Tab and type **City:**.

13. Press Tab three times.

14. Type **State:**, press → three times, and then type >.

15. Press Tab.

16. Type **Zip Code:**, press → 11 times, and type >.

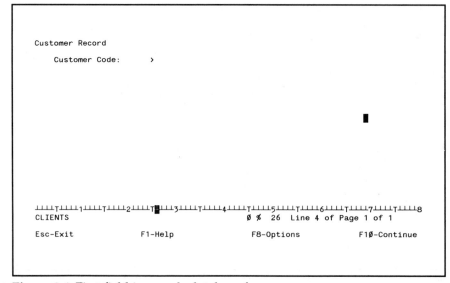

Figure 2.6: First field in sample database form

17. Press ↵ twice.

18. Type **Primary Contact**, and then press ↵ twice. Do not type a colon or > after the heading.

19. Press Tab, type **Last Name:**, press Tab twice, and then type **First Name:**.

20. Press Tab twice, type **MI:**, press → twice, type >, and press ↵.

21. Press Tab, type **Title:**, press Tab three times, type **Phone:**, and then press ↵ three times.

22. Type **Order Information** and press ↵ twice.

23. Press Tab, type **Last Order Date:**, press Tab twice, type **Amount:**, press Tab twice, type **Total Orders:**, and press ↵.

24. Press Tab, type **Taxable:**, press Tab three times, type **Credit Limit:**, and press ↵.

25. Press Tab, type **Products Purchased:**, and press ↵.

26. Press Tab, type **Shipping Zone:**, press Tab twice, and type **Preferred Carrier:**. Figure 2.7 shows the form at this point.

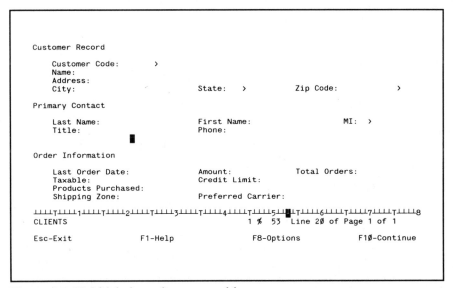

Figure 2.7: Field labels on first page of form

Text flows freely from one page of the form to the next. If you press ↵ twice after entering the last field label, the second page will automatically appear, much the way paginating works in a word processing program. Also as in a word processing program, inserting lines on one page might push other text onto the next page; deleting text on one page may cause text on following pages to scroll up.

Now let's complete the second page of our form before we format the text and add the lines and boxes.

27. Press PgDn. A blank screen appears, and the status line displays Page 2 of 2.

28. Type **Secondary Contact and Personal Client Data** and press ↵ twice. This is a heading to identify the purpose of this page of the form.

29. Type **Primary Contact** and press ↵ twice.

30. Press Tab, type **Date of Birth:**, press Tab twice, type **Age:**, and press ↵.

31. Press Tab, type **Hobbies:**, and press ↵.

32. Press Tab, type **Secretary:**, and press ↵ three times.

33. Type **Secondary Contact** and press ↵ twice.

34. Press Tab, type **Last Name:**, press Tab twice, type **First Name:**, press Tab twice, type **MI:**, press → twice, type >, and then press ↵.

35. Press Tab, type **Title:**, press Tab three times, type **Phone:**, and press ↵.

36. Press Tab, type **Date of Birth:**, press Tab twice, type **Age:**, and press ↵.

37. Press Tab, type **Hobbies:**, and press ↵.

38. Press Tab, type **Secretary:**, and press ↵ twice.

39. Press Tab and type **Notes<**.

40. Use the ↓ and → keys to place the cursor at position 80 on the last line of the screen.

41. Type >. Since that character is on the last space on the page, the next blank page appears on the screen.

42. Press PgUp to redisplay the second page of the form.

Notice that Notes is a multiline field; that is, it does not end at the end of the line, but at the > symbol several lines down. We used the < symbol after the Notes label so that the text will align with that symbol. You can also use the < symbol to indent the lines of the Notes field at some position to the right of the screen's edge. All the lines will align on the right at the position of the > symbol. A multiline field label must be the only field label on the line.

In this form layout, we used the Tab key to separate most of the fields, and placed a few fields on their own line. We only counted a specific number of spaces in a few cases. There are, however, some special factors to consider when you have an exact number of characters that you want displayed.

When you design your own forms, pay careful attention to the size or width of your fields. As mentioned previously, a field ends at the > symbol, the start of the next field label on the same line, or the end of the line if it is the only field on that line.

If you're ending a field with the > symbol, make sure it is one character past the desired maximum field size. For example, when you want to enter a two-character State field, press the → key three times after the field label, and then press >.

When you're using one field label to end the previous field, allow for two extra characters. For example, pressing Tab three times after the label Title leaves 24 character spaces before the next field. However, only 22 characters will be visible when you are actually entering data. Q&A leaves one space after the label's closing colon and one space before the next field label.

With yes/no fields, consider the type of entries you would like to allow. After entering the Taxable label, which we will designate as a yes/no field, you pressed Tab three times. Although this makes the field capable of storing 20 characters, you still can enter only the valid responses: yes, no, y, n, t, f, 1, or 0. If you wanted to restrict the field to only one-character responses, you would press → twice after the label, and then press > before entering the Credit Limit label.

ALIGNING TEXT

IIII▶ **To center text on the form:**

1. **Place the cursor on the line and press F8.**
2. **Select Align Text, then Center.**
3. **To return the text to left alignment, select Left from the Options menu.**

You can center text on the form by pressing F8 to display the Options menu, and then selecting the Align Text option. We will use this option now to format the headings on the form so they are centered on the screen.

1. Press PgUp to return to the first page of the form. The cursor will be on the first character of the first line.

2. Press ↓ to place the cursor on the heading *Customer Record*. The cursor can be anywhere on the line.

3. Press F8 to display the Options menu and submenu, as shown in Figure 2.8.

The menu on the left contains the categories of options that are available. The menu on the right shows the functions available for the selected category. Some of the items on both menus appear in gray, which means that they are not available (cannot be selected) when you are working on files. When you select an option from the menu on the left, the menu on the right changes to reflect available functions, and the cursor moves to the submenu. You can return the cursor to the Options menu on the left by pressing ←; pressing → moves the cursor to the submenu on the right.

4. Type **A** to select Align Text. The options Left and Center are now listed on the submenu, and the cursor is in that box. (If you did not turn on automatic execution, you must type A, and then press ↵.)

5. Type **C** to select Center. The heading will be centered on the screen. (If you did not turn on automatic execution, you must type C, and then press ↵.)

6. Place the cursor on the line containing the heading *Primary Contact*.

7. Repeat steps 3 through 5 to center the text.

8. Place the cursor on the line containing the heading *Order Information* and choose to center it as well.

9. Press PgDn to display the second page of the form.

10. Follow the same procedure to center the page title and the headings *Primary Contact* and *Secondary Contact*.

11. Press PgUp to display the first page of the form.

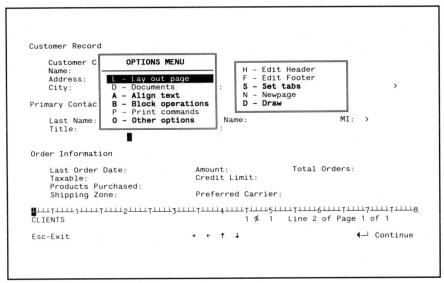

Figure 2.8: Options menu

DRAWING LINES AND BOXES

IIII➤ **To draw lines and boxes on a form:**

1. **Press F8, press →, and select Draw.**
2. **Draw single horizontal or vertical lines by moving the cursor with the arrow keys. Draw diagonal lines by using the 1, 3, 7, and 9 keys on the keypad.**
3. **Draw double lines by holding down the Shift key while moving the cursor.**
4. **Press F6 to move the cursor without drawing; press F6 again to resume drawing.**
5. **Press F10 to turn off draw mode.**

As you can see in Figures 2.3 and 2.4, the borders and lines surrounding the parts of the sample form divide it into distinct sections, each with items that relate to one another. By separating a form into sections, you make it easier to read and locate information.

Surrounding text in borders can be visually pleasing and useful for organizational reasons, but the lines do take up space, reducing the amount of characters that can be displayed on the screen.

You add borders by using the Draw option, which appears on the submenu when you select Lay Out Page from the Options menu. To draw lines, you move the cursor with the arrow keys (the mouse does not work in draw mode). You can also add diagonal lines by using the 1, 3, 5, 7, and 9 keys on the numeric keypad (with NumLock turned off). Use the position and line-number indicators on the status line to determine the cursor position. Hold down the Shift key while you move the cursor to draw double lines. If your printer cannot print double lines, only single lines will appear on the screen.

If you press F6, you can move the cursor without drawing lines. This lets you move the cursor from the end of one line to the start of the next without connecting them. Press F6 again to resume drawing. To erase lines, press F8, move the cursor back over the line you want to delete, and then press F8 to resume drawing.

Now we will add the borders to the Clients form. The cursor should already be at the top-left corner of the page.

1. Press F8 to display the Options menu.

2. Press → to move the cursor to the submenu, and then type **D** to select Draw.

The key-assignment line changes, as shown in Figure 2.9. Below the status line is a message that briefly explains how to draw lines. The message will disappear as soon you move the cursor.

```
                               Customer Record

       Customer Code:          >
       Name:
       Address:
       City:                     State:   >        Zip Code:              >

                               Primary Contact

       Last Name:                First Name:                 MI: ▉>
       Title:                    Phone:

                               Order Information

       Last Order Date:          Amount:             Total Orders:
       Taxable:                  Credit Limit:
       Products Purchased:
       Shipping Zone:            Preferred Carrier:
▉└┴┴┬┴┴┴┴1┴┴┴┴┬┴┴┴┴2┴┴┴┴┬┴┴┴┴3┴┴┴┴┬┴┴┴┴4┴┴┴┴┬┴┴┴┴5┴┴┴┴┬┴┴┴┴6┴┴┴┴┬┴┴┴┴7┴┴┴┴┬┴┴┴┴8
CLIENTS                                  2 % 1   Line 1 of Page 1 of 2
Use the cursor keypad to draw.  Press F8 to erase.  Press F1Ø when done.
Esc-Exit       →←↓↑   Shift →←↑↓    F6-Pen up    F8-Erase    F1Ø-Resume editing
```

Figure 2.9: Draw screen

3. Hold down the Shift key and press → to draw a double line to position 80, as shown in Figure 2.10.

4. Keep the Shift key depressed, and press ↓ to reach line 13.

5. Hold down the Shift key and press ← to draw to position 1, and then press ↑ to complete the box at line 1.

6. Press F6 to suspend drawing. The status line reads

   Pen is UP. Press F6 to put pen back down

7. Press ↓ to reach line 3.

8. Press F6 to resume drawing.

9. Press → (without using the Shift key) to draw to position 80.

10. Press F6 to suspend drawing, press ↓ to reach line 8, and press F6 to resume drawing.

11. Press ← to draw to position 1. Figure 2.11 shows the completed box and lines on the top of the form.

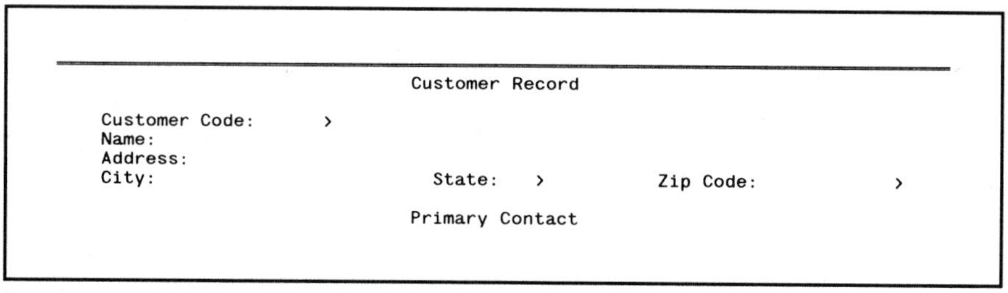

```
─────────────────────────────────────────────────────────
                        Customer Record
       Customer Code:       >
       Name:
       Address:
       City:                 State:   >      Zip Code:         >

                        Primary Contact
```

Figure 2.10: Double line drawn on top of the page

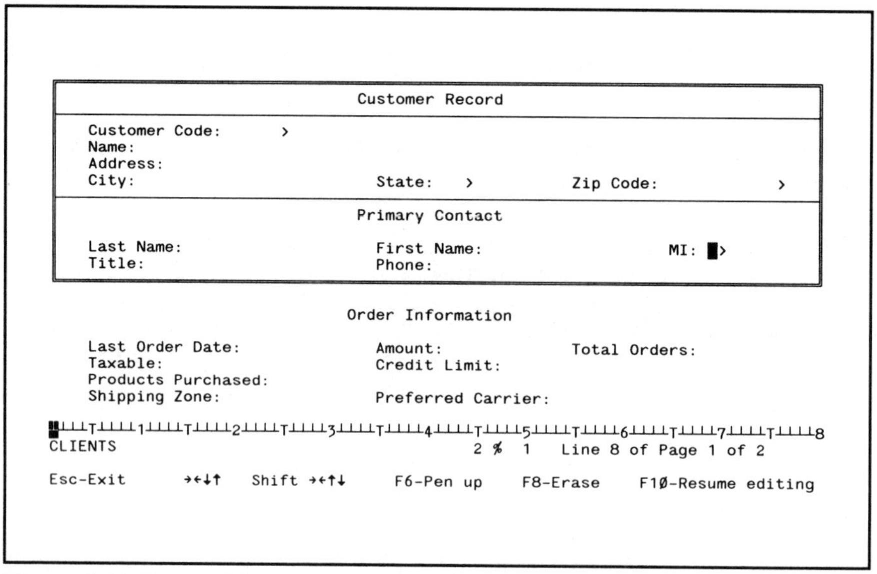

```
                        Customer Record
       Customer Code:       >
       Name:
       Address:
       City:                 State:   >      Zip Code:         >
                        Primary Contact
       Last Name:            First Name:            MI: ▮>
       Title:                Phone:

                        Order Information
       Last Order Date:      Amount:            Total Orders:
       Taxable:              Credit Limit:
       Products Purchased:
       Shipping Zone:        Preferred Carrier:
 ▮┴┴┴T┴┴┴┴1┴┴┴┴T┴┴┴2┴┴┴┴T┴┴┴3┴┴┴┴T┴┴┴4┴┴┴┴T┴┴┴5┴┴┴┴T┴┴┴6┴┴┴┴T┴┴┴7┴┴┴┴T┴┴┴8
 CLIENTS                              2 %   1    Line 8 of Page 1 of 2

 Esc-Exit       →←↓↑    Shift →←↑↓     F6-Pen up    F8-Erase     F1Ø-Resume editing
```

Figure 2.11: Box and lines on top of the form

Now we will draw the second box on the page. If you draw a line down past the bottom of the page, Q&A will automatically scroll to the next page and continue drawing. If this happens, press F8 to select Erase, retrace over the line to move back to the first page, and then press F8 to continue drawing.

12. Press F6 to suspend drawing; press ↓ to reach line 14, position 1; and then press F6 to continue drawing.

13. Hold down the Shift key and press → to draw to position 80.

14. Keep the Shift key down and press ↓ to draw to line 21, press ← to draw to position 1, and then press ↑ to complete the box at line 14.

15. Press F6 to suspend drawing, press ↓ to move the cursor to line 16, and press F6 again.

16. Press → to draw to position 80.

17. Press F10 to turn off draw mode.

Your form should look like Figure 2.3. Now we are ready to draw the boxes on the second page of the form.

18. Press PgDn to display the second page, and then move the cursor to line 2, position 1.

19. Press F8, and then select Draw from the Lay Out Page submenu.

20. Hold down the Shift key and press → to draw to position 80.

21. Keep the Shift key depressed and press ↓ to draw to line 8.

22. Hold down the Shift key, press → to draw to position 1, and then press ↑ to complete the box.

23. Press F6 to suspend drawing, press ↓ to reach line 4, and press F6.

24. Press → (without holding down Shift) to draw to position 80.

That completes the first box on this page. Now draw the second box on the page.

25. Press F6; press ↓ to move the cursor to line 9, position 80; and press F6.

26. Hold down Shift and press ← to draw to position 1.

27. Keep Shift down and press ↓ to draw to line 17, then → to draw to position 1, then ↑ to complete the box at line 8.

28. Press F6, press ↓ to move the cursor to line 11, and press F6.

29. Press ← to draw to position 1. Your form should appear as shown in Figure 2.4.

30. Press F10 to return to edit mode, and then press PgUp to view the first screen.

31. Press F10 to save the design.

Q&A flashes the message

Saving design...

as it records your form on the disk. You will then see the Format Spec (short for Specification) screen, with the Customer Code field highlighted, as shown in Figure 2.12.

This is just one of several Spec screens that you will use when working with Q&A. A Spec screen shows a representation of the database form, complete with the field labels. You add information to the screen to tell Q&A how you want it to process your data. On the Format Spec screen, you tell Q&A the type of each field and to how to format field information that you enter from the keyboard. Later you will use other Spec screens for sorting, printing, and retrieving data. All your specifications are saved as part of the database itself, so you won't see separate Spec files listed on your disk.

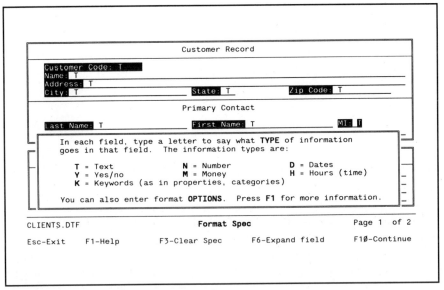

Figure 2.12: Format Spec screen

ASSIGNING FIELD TYPES

||||▶ **To assign field types:**

1. **Press F10 after designing the form to display the Format Spec screen.**
2. **Enter the field type identifier next to each field label: T for text, N for number, M for money, D for date, H for hours, Y for yes/no, or K for keyword.**
3. **Enter format entries next to the field types—press F1 to see the format codes.**
4. **Press F10 when you are finished assigning types.**

Q&A will assume that all your fields are the text type unless you tell it otherwise. Notice that each field on the Format Spec screen is followed by the letter T, for a text field. The Help window at the bottom of the screen reminds you which letters to use for the field types:

T   Text

N   Number

M   Money

D   Date

H   Hours

Y   Yes/No

K   Keyword

If you make a mistake when formatting the fields, use the cursor-movement keys, Ins, Del, and Backspace to correct it. You can press ↲, Tab, or the arrow keys to move from field to field.

The key-assignment line for this screen includes the Esc (Exit); F1 (Help); and F10 (Continue) options; as well as F3, to erase the field type letters; and F6, to expand the field so you can enter more information than fits on the form. You'll learn more about these options later in this chapter.

In addition to designating the field type, you can also tell Q&A how to format your entries. For example, you can control the number of decimal places in number fields and have Q&A insert commas in number and money fields, changing entries such as 1051500 to $1,051,500.00.

You can also convert the case of your characters. Controlling case is especially important when entering name and address information that you will use to create form letters. It would be rather obvious that a letter addressed to

Dear WILLIAM:

was not personally typed. When you designate a field type, however, you can tell Q&A to automatically convert your entries to uppercase, lowercase, or initial capitals.

Finally, you can control how the entry aligns in the blank space following the field label. By default, all entries are left-aligned; that is, they start one space after the colon or less-than symbol that ends the field label. But you can also have Q&A center your entries or right-align them, as in

Frame:	BN105	Cost:	$10.24
Shaft:	C34	Cost:	1.46
Cord:	OH123	Cost:	12.00

This example was created by centering the fields on the left and right-aligning the fields on the right. The first Cost field was designated as a money field so Q&A would automatically add the dollar sign at the start of the column. The other fields are number with two decimal places. This way, the last entry was typed in as 12 but formatted as 12.00.

To format an entry, add the formatting codes after the field type letter. For clarity, separate the characters with commas or a space, such as T, JR, or T I. However, Q&A will interpret the codes correctly if you type them together, as in TIJR.

Now, we will assign types to the fields in the Clients form:

1. From the Format Spec screen, press ↵ to accept the first field as a text field. The next field will be highlighted.

2. Press F1 to see the Help screen that explains how to format your fields, shown in Figure 2.13.

3. Press Esc to return to the form.

4. Type **T,I** to format the Name field as text with initial capital letters.

You could also press → to move the cursor past the format letter, and then type ,I. However, it is just as easy to type the entire field label over the existing one.

5. Press ↵ to reach the Address field.

6. Type **T,I** and press ↵ to reach the City field.

7. Type **T,I** and press ↵ to reach the State field.

You want Q&A to format the State field as all uppercase letters, the normal postal convention. However, the field is two characters wide, and the format T,U is three characters. You could enter the code as TU, but

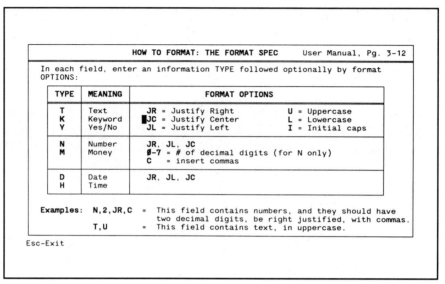

Figure 2.13: How to Format Help screen

instead let's see how to enter formatting instructions that are wider than the field.

8. Type **T,U**.

As soon as you type the comma, the cursor moves to the message line, which displays

  Expand field: T,U

When Q&A senses that the formatting information will not fit on the screen, it *expands* the field so you can enter up to 240 characters on the message line. On Spec screens, you can press F6 to expand a field when you want to add more data than will fit on the form.

9. Press ⏎ to return to the form.

The cursor moves to the next field in the form, and the State field appears as

  T→

The arrow indicates that the field is expanded, or that the formatting instructions are too large to fit on the screen but are still in effect.

10. Press ↵ to accept the Zip Code field as it is and move to the Last Name field.

11. Type **T,I** and press ↵ to reach the First Name field.

12. Type **T,I** and press ↵ to reach the MI field.

13. Press F6 to expand the field, type **T,I**, and press ↵ to reach the Title field. (You'll see why we formatted the middle initial as initial caps, not uppercase, in Chapter 8.)

Q&A automatically moved the Help window to the top of the screen to make the fields at the bottom of the screen visible.

14. Type **T,I** and press ↵ twice—once to accept the Phone field as it is and again to reach the Last Order Date field.

15. Type **D**, for a date field, and press ↵ to reach the Amount field.

16. Type **M,C** for a money field using commas, and then press ↵ to reach the Total Orders field.

17. Type **M,C** and press ↵ to reach the Taxable field.

18. Type **Y** for a yes/no field. Clients can be either taxable or nontaxable.

19. Press ↵ to reach the Credit Limit field.

20. Type **M,C** and press ↵ to reach the Products Purchased field.

21. Type **K** for a keyword field, and then press ↵ twice to reach the Preferred Carrier field.

22. Type **T,U** and press ↵ to reach the Date of Birth field on the next page.

23. Type **D** and press ↵ to reach the Age field.

24. Type **N**, for a number field, and press ↵ to reach the Hobbies field.

25. Type **K** and press ↵ to reach the Secretary field.

26. Type **T,I** and press ↵ to reach the Last Name field.

27. Type **T,I** and press ↵ to reach the First Name field.

28. Type **T,I** and press ↵ to reach the MI field.

29. Press F6 to expand the field, type **T,I**, and press ↵ to reach the Title field.

30. Type **T,I** and press ↵ twice to reach the Date of Birth field.

31. Type **D** and press ↵ to reach the Age field.

32. Type **N** and press ↵ to reach the Hobbies field.

33. Type **K** and press ↵ to reach the Secretary field.

34. Type **T,I** and press F10 to accept the field assignments. Q&A displays the Global Format Options screen, as shown in Figure 2.14. (You will learn more about this screen shortly.)

35. Press F10 to save the form design and return to the File menu.

Your disk now has two files: CLIENTS.DTF and CLIENTS.IDX. Both of these files are required. The DTF file contains the form design and your

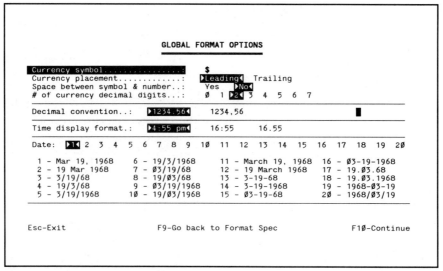

Figure 2.14: Global Format Options

data. The IDX file stores an index that Q&A uses to locate information in your database.

CLEARING SPEC FORMS

In the Clients form, most of the fields were text, so it was easy to skip over a field without changing its designation. If you're creating a database whose fields are mostly another type, you might find it easier to clear the Spec screen before entering the field type letters.

To clear any Spec screen of its data, press the F3 function key. All the data after the field labels will be erased. On the Format Spec screen, if you fail to enter a field type, Q&A will automatically designate it as text when you press F10 to save the form.

GLOBAL FORMATTING OPTIONS

IIII➡ **To set global formats for fields:**
1. **Press F10 after you have completed the Format Spec screen.**
2. **Complete the Global Options menu.**
3. **Press F10 to save the database design.**

The Global Format Options screen appears only if your form includes number, money, date, or hours fields. On this screen, you can change the default formats that Q&A uses to display your field information.

The specific format information that you enter after a field type letter affects only that field. Changes you make on the Global Format Options screen, however, affect all number, money, date, and hours fields on the form.

To select a new format, press ↵ or Tab to reach the option you want to change, and then press the arrow keys to highlight your choice.

The first four options control money field formats. You can enter another character to substitute for the $ sign, and have Q&A place it before or after the dollar amount. You can also select to have a blank space between the currency symbol and the number, such as $ 125.00, and change the number of decimal places. If you're dealing with large whole numbers, for example, you might not want to show any decimal places, so you would enter 0 for the # of Currency Decimal Digits.

The Decimal Convention option affects both money and number fields. The default selection separates decimal points with a period. You can choose the European method of using a comma.

The Time Display Format option selects between standard and two versions of military (24-hour) time.

Finally, the Date option offers formats for date fields, numbered from 1 to 20. Press → or ← to select the corresponding number next to the Date option.

After making your selections, press F10 to save the formats and display the File menu.

The form you create provides the structure of your database. Your next step is to fill the fields in with information to add each record. Once your database includes data, you can manipulate it in many ways. The next chapter describes how to add and work with data.

3

Adding,
Retrieving,
and
Editing
Database
Records

You handle the data in your database in the same way that you would in a paper filing system. For example, when you get a new customer, you enter the information at the appropriate blanks on the form, then file the form with your other customer records. You might file forms alphabetically by the customer's name, or assign each a customer number.

If one of your customers moves, you retrieve the form from the file and change the information on it. And if the customer goes out of business, you probably remove the form from the file entirely, or delete it from your records.

You might have a complete folder on each client, containing several different forms. One form could contain name and address information, another form a history of customer transactions, and a third form with credit data. While each form contains different information, all the forms in the folder relate to the same client.

In this chapter, you will learn how to perform these types of tasks with your Q&A database.

ADDING DATA TO YOUR FORMS

To add information to a database form:
1. **Select Add Data from the File menu.**
2. **Type the database name and press ↵.**
3. **Add the appropriate information following the field labels.**
4. **Press F10 to save the record and add another or press Shift-F10 to save the record and return to the File menu.**

One of the nicest features of Q&A is that your database form appears on the screen as it would on a sheet of paper in a manual system. There are no abbreviated field labels. Also, if necessary, you can enter up to 32,768 characters in a field, about 16 pages, no matter how wide the field is on the screen.

Unlike a manual system, Q&A will warn you if you try to enter improper characters in a field. This can greatly reduce data-entry errors.

To add a record to a database, select the Add Data option from the File menu, and enter the name of the database.

The first page of the form appears. Figure 3.1 shows the first page of the Clients form. Each of the field labels appear in reverse, and the cursor is on the first field. The status line shows that you are entering the first new record for that editing session and that there are currently no records in the database. The key-assignment line includes a few new options: F3, to delete a record; F7, to search for specific records; and F8, to calculate mathematical formulas. You will learn about these functions in this and later chapters.

Type the data on the form, and then press F10 to add another record, or press Shift-F10 to save the record and return to the File menu. (Press Esc to return to the File menu without saving the record.)

Now you will add the information for the first record of the Clients database. Follow these steps:

1. Select Add Data from the File menu. Q&A prompts you to enter

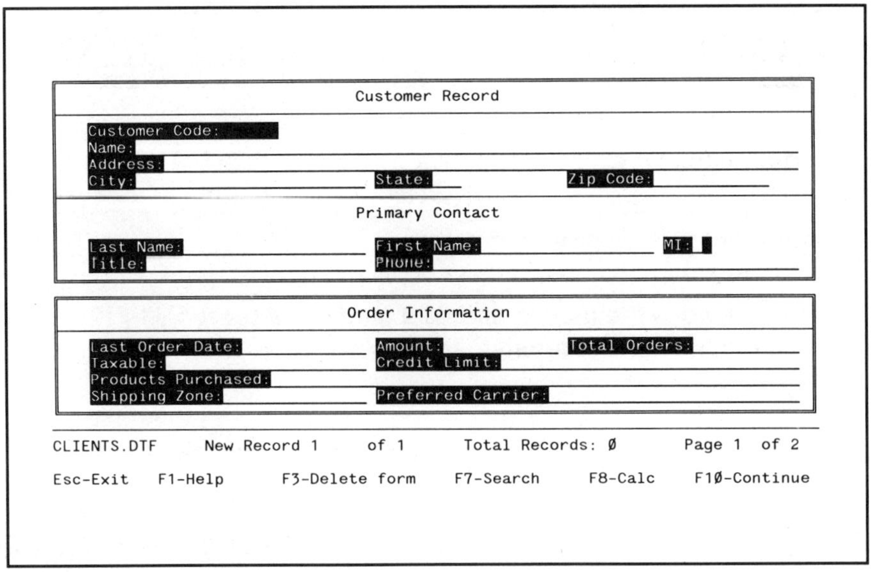

Figure 3.1: Data entry form

the database name, but CLIENTS, the name of the database you last used, already appears at the prompt.

2. Press ↵ to accept the name of the database.

When you want to use another database, just enter its name and press ↵. Q&A will add the DTF extension for you.

3. Type **101** and press ↵.

When you press ↵ or Tab, the cursor moves to the next field, from left to right across a line that contains several fields. If you press ↓ or ↑, the cursor will move to the closest field in the line below or above.

4. Type **Chesin Pharmacy, Inc.** and press ↵.

5. Type **182 Walnut Street** and press ↵.

6. Type **Newark** and press ↵.

7. Type **NJ** and press ↵. (Remember that we set up the State field so that it will accept only two characters.)

8. Type **08192** and press ↵.

9. Type **CHESIN** (all uppercase) and press ↵. Because of the formatting instructions for this field, Q&A displays the name with an initial capital letter (Chesin).

10. Type **Adam** and press ↵.

Now before entering the client's middle initial, assume for the moment that the client is very proud of his middle name, Mycroft. In fact, he gets downright angry when he receives letters using only the first initial. Even though this field is set for only one character, you can still accommodate this customer. Q&A allows you to enter more characters than can be displayed in the field by using the expand function (function key F6).

11. Press F6. An editing window appears near the center of the screen, as shown in Figure 3.2.

In this window, you can enter up to 16 pages of data in the field. The cursor-movement and editing commands that are available when you lay

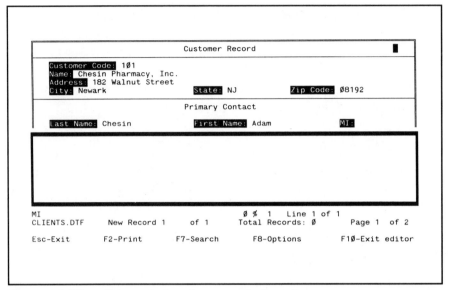

```
                              Customer Record                         ▮

      Customer Code: 101
      Name: Chesin Pharmacy, Inc.
      Address: 182 Walnut Street
      City: Newark                    State: NJ            Zip Code: 08192

                              Primary Contact

      Last Name: Chesin           First Name: Adam              MI:




   MI                                    0 %   1   Line 1 of 1
   CLIENTS.DTF     New Record 1     of 1    Total Records: 0       Page 1  of 2

   Esc-Exit       F2-Print       F7-Search       F8-Options      F10-Exit editor
```

Figure 3.2: The editing window for expanded entries

out the form also work here.

When you are expanding text, keyword, and yes/no fields, the editing window appears as in Figure 3.2. However, when you expand date, hours, number, and money fields, you will see the prompt

     Expand field:

below the status line, instead of an editing window. This is because you can enter only one line of data in these fields. In these cases, press ↵ when you're finished to return to the form (if you press F10, Q&A will assume you're finished entering data for the entire record).

    12.   Type **Mycroft**, and then press F10 to exit from the editing window.

The field contains only →, but the status line displays

     Expand field: Mycroft

When you expand a field, Q&A displays as many characters as it can fit in the form followed by →. In this case, the arrow fills the entire area. When you place the cursor on a field that has an →, the first 66 characters of the field will appear on the status line.

13. Press ↵ to move to the next field.

14. Type **President** and press ↵.

15. Type **555-7654** and press ↵.

16. Type **10/52/91** and press ↵.

Q&A knows this date has something wrong with it and displays the message

    This date can't be reformatted -- is it a valid date?

You either entered an incorrect date or set aside too few spaces on the form to display the date in the selected format.

17. Press ← to place the cursor on the *5* in *52*, type **2**, and press ↵.

Q&A automatically formats and displays the date in the default format: Oct 22, 1991.

18. Type **1250** and press ↵.

Q&A displays $1,250.00. If you entered any characters that are not valid in a money field, Q&A would have displayed the message

    This doesn't look like a money value. Please verify

You would correct the error as you did the date, and then press ↵ to move onto the next field.

19. Type **2500** and press ↵. Q&A formats the Total Orders entry for you.

In Chapter 4, you will program the Total Orders field to calculate the total for you.

20. Type **Y** and press ↵. As with the other nontext fields, Q&A will display a message if you make an invalid entry in a yes/no field.

21. Type **1500** and press ↵. Q&A formats the field for you.

22. Type **102; 103; 105**, and then press ↵.

Because Products Purchased is a keyword field, you can enter a series of items, each separated by a semicolon. In this case, the entries are inventory stock numbers representing the items this client purchases. In Chapter 16, we will create an inventory database and enter corresponding items.

23. Type **1** and press ↵.

24. Type **UPS** and press ↵. The second page of the form automatically appears.

25. Type **11-16-45** and press ↵ twice.

Q&A converts the date to the default format and moves to the Hobbies field. In Chapter 4, we will have Q&A compute the age.

26. Type **Martial arts; skiing; basketball** and press ↵.

27. Type **Nancy Harriet**.

To save time, we will not enter information for the secondary contact or notes. Instead, we will skip that section and move to the next record.

28. Press F10 to display the start of the next record.

29. Enter the records shown in Figure 3.3.

30. After you finish entering the last record, press Shift-F10 to save it and return to the File menu.

If you press F10 instead, Q&A displays the next blank record. You can press Esc to return to the File menu. If you press Esc while the record you're adding is still on the screen, you'll see the warning shown in Figure 3.4. Select Yes if you do not want to save the record, or press ↵ to return to the form.

While you are entering records, you can review those you've already added during the session. Press F9 to display the previous record, or F10

```
Customer Code: 102
Name: Williams Engine Company
Address: 347 West Fifth Street
City: Margate               State: NJ          Zip Code: 08126
Last Name: Peterson         First Name: John   MI: J
Title: President            Phone: 431-9871
Last Order Date: Dec 1, 1991  Amount: $238.00    Total Orders: $2,510.00
Taxable: Y                   Credit Limit: $750.00
Products Purchased: 102; 103; 106
Shipping Zone: 1            Preferred Carrier: UPS
Date of Birth: Jan 12, 1938  Age:
Hobbies: Bowling; stamps
Secretary: Paul Hamilton


Customer Code: 103
Name: Dershaw, Inc.
Address: 17th And Locust Streets
City: Philadelphia          State: PA          Zip Code: 19101
Last Name: Dershaw          First Name: Terry  MI:
Title: President            Phone: 565-1267
Last Order Date: Mar 8, 1990  Amount: $125.00    Total Orders: $1,025.00
Taxable: Y                   Credit Limit: $750.00
Products Purchased: 101; 104; 107; 110
Shipping Zone: 1            Preferred Carrier: FED EX
Date of Birth: May 8, 1949   Age:
Hobbies: Hockey; sailing; baseball
Secretary: Marge Simpson


Customer Code: 104
Name: Samual Engineering
Address: 809 Walden Road
City: Margate               State: NJ          Zip Code: 08456
Last Name: Samual           First Name: Bernice MI: K
Title: President            Phone: 823-1911
Last Order Date: Dec 1, 1991  Amount: $1,050.00   Total Orders: $3,560.00
Taxable: Y                   Credit Limit: $1,000.00
Products Purchased: 104; 106; 108; 109; 110
Shipping Zone: 1            Preferred Carrier: FED EX
Date of Birth: Mar 5, 1940   Age:
Hobbies: Sailing; racing
Secretary: Joan Tippler


Customer Code: 105
Name: City Of Newark
Address: 129 State Road
City: Newark                State: NJ          Zip Code: 08163
Last Name: Ronish           First Name: Sally  MI: M
Title: Buyer                Phone: 512-8716
Last Order Date: May 9, 1990  Amount: $2,500.00   Total Orders: $6,800.00
Taxable: N                   Credit Limit: $1,500.00
Products Purchased: 102; 103; 104; 105
Shipping Zone: 2            Preferred Carrier: UPS
Date of Birth: Dec 1, 1953   Age:
Hobbies: Baseball; skiiing
Secretary: Raymond Kohl
```

Figure 3.3: Information for remaining records

to display the next one. You'll learn other ways to add records later in this chapter.

```
Customer Code: 106
Name: Ajaz Refining, Inc.
Address: 23 Delaware Avenue
City: Wilmington              State: DE          Zip Code: 20192
Last Name: Paulson            First Name: Patrick MI: G
Title: Vice President         Phone: 876-1200
Last Order Date: Apr 4, 1991  Amount: $127.00    Total Orders: $1,250.00
Taxable: Y                    Credit Limit: $1,000.00
Products Purchased: 102; 108
Shipping Zone: 3              Preferred Carrier: UPS
Date of Birth: Jun 1, 1958    Age:
Hobbies: Basketball
Secretary: Georgette Rolands


Customer Code: 107
Name: Williams College
Address: 45 Market Walk
City: Philadelphia            State: PA          Zip Code: 10871
Last Name: Bryan              First Name: Stuart  MI: J
Title: Director Of Finance    Phone: 827-9812
Last Order Date: Dec 1, 1991  Amount: $756.00    Total Orders: $2,150.00
Taxable: N                    Credit Limit: $750.00
Products Purchased: 104; 108; 109
Shipping Zone: 2              Preferred Carrier: UPS
Date of Birth: Jun 21, 1961   Age:
Hobbies: Bowling; skiing
Secretary: Mary Province


Customer Code: 108
Name: Stack And Gallagher
Address: 98b Benett Avenue
City: Margate                 State: NJ          Zip Code: 08761
Last Name: Stack              First Name: Faye    MI:
Title: Vice President         Phone: 921-5600
Last Order Date: May 9, 1990  Amount: $115.00    Total Orders: $1,876.00
Taxable: Y                    Credit Limit: $1,000.00
Products Purchased: 102; 103; 104
Shipping Zone: 1              Preferred Carrier: UPS
Date of Birth: Jun 1, 1945    Age:
Hobbies: Sailing
Secretary: Mike Stack


Customer Code: 109
Name: Harding Junior High School
Address: 45 Frankford Avenue
City: Philadelphia            State: PA          Zip Code: 19101
Last Name: Richards           First Name: Mary    MI: M
Title: Principal              Phone: 765-1200
Last Order Date: Dec 21, 1991 Amount: $745.00    Total Orders: $1,850.00
Taxable: N                    Credit Limit: $1,500.00
Products Purchased: 105; 107
Shipping Zone: 1              Preferred Carrier: UPS
Date of Birth: Jun 16, 1946   Age:
Hobbies: Swimming; sailing
Secretary: Peter Harvey


Customer Code: 110
Name: Sparkling Water, Inc.
Address: 56 West Marytown Pike
City: Margate                 State: NJ          Zip Code: 08156
Last Name: Kaufman            First Name: Herb    MI:
Title: President              Phone: 876-0500
Last Order Date: Dec 4, 1991  Amount: $256.00    Total Orders: $5,050.00
Taxable: Y                    Credit Limit: $1,000.00
Products Purchased: 101; 103; 105
Shipping Zone: 3              Preferred Carrier: UPS
Date of Birth: May 1, 1938    Age:
Hobbies: Civil War; model planes
Secretary: Sandy Kaufman
```

Figure 3.3: Information for remaining records (continued)

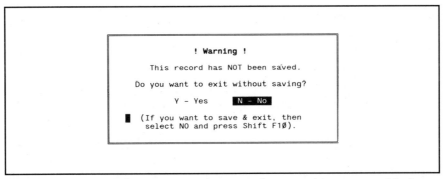

Figure 3.4: Warning that appears when you choose to leave a record before saving it

Q&A provides a number of features to streamline data entry. You can automatically number your records, insert a default or initial value into a field, or design a template for entering phone numbers and other information that has a standard format. We will discuss these features in Chapters 4 and 14.

Now that you've created the database and added records, let's see how you can use its information.

RETRIEVING DATABASE RECORDS

To display a database record:

1. **Select Search/Update from the File menu.**
2. **Type the name of the database and press ⏎ to display the Retrieve Spec screen.**
3. **Press F10 to recall all the records, or enter information in fields to identify the records you want to recall and press F10.**

Having data in a database would be useless if you could not get information out of it. When you retrieve a record from the database, it appears on the screen so you can read it or make changes. You might want to retrieve a client record to check on an order date or phone number, or you might want to change a credit limit or information in another field.

You can retrieve all your records from a Q&A database or selected records based on the contents of their fields. To begin, select the Search/Update option from the File menu. Press ↵ to accept the current database or enter the name of another database. Q&A displays the Retrieve Spec screen, shown in Figure 3.5.

In the fields, enter as much information as necessary for Q&A to identify the specific records you want to edit or view. For example, if you want to edit the record for client 101, type 101 in the Customer Code field. Since only one client has that code, Q&A will retrieve just one record. If you enter PA in the State field, Q&A will locate all the records for clients in Pennsylvania.

You can customize your retrieval by entering data in more than one field. To see the records for all taxable clients in Pennsylvania, for instance, enter PA in the State field and Yes, y, t, or 1 in the Taxable field (to indicate a true value).

When you're finished filling in the screen, press F10 to display the first record that matches the specifications. If you want to display all your records, press F10 without filling in any of the fields.

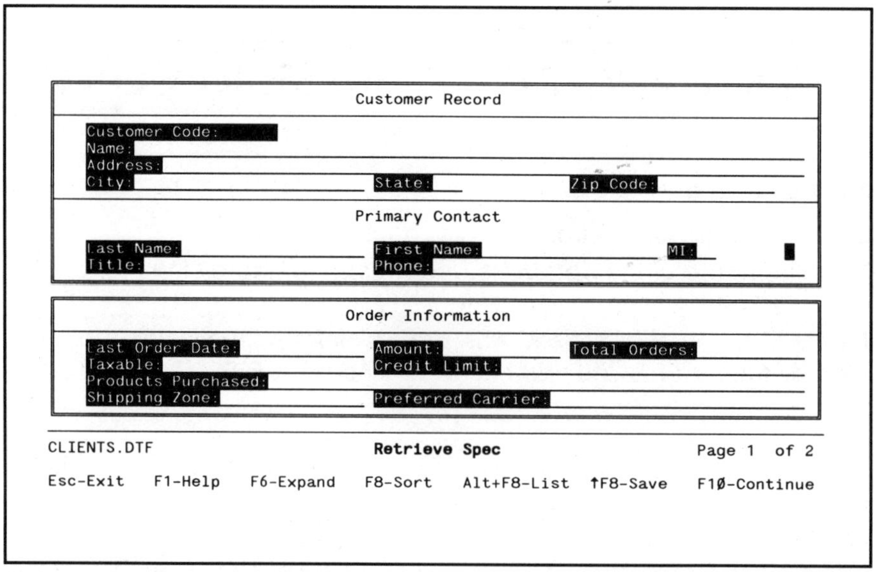

```
                            Customer Record
Customer Code:
Name:
Address:
City:                      State:              Zip Code:

                            Primary Contact
Last Name:                 First Name:                MI:
Title:                     Phone:

                           Order Information
Last Order Date:           Amount:             Total Orders:
Taxable:                   Credit Limit:
Products Purchased:
Shipping Zone:             Preferred Carrier:


CLIENTS.DTF            Retrieve Spec              Page 1  of 2

Esc-Exit   F1-Help   F6-Expand   F8-Sort   Alt+F8-List   ↑F8-Save   F10-Continue
```

Figure 3.5: Retrieve Spec screen

New key assignments available on the Retrieve Spec screen are F8, to sort records; Alt-F8, to list available retrieval specifications; and Shift-F8 (Shift is indicated by the ↑), to save your retrieval specifications. Saving and reusing retrieval specifications will be discussed shortly. Sorting records is covered in Chapter 4.

The status line reports information about the records in your database using the term *form*. This includes the total number of records in the file and the relative number of the record displayed on the screen. For example, Form 1 of -- means that you are looking at the first record that meets your retrieval criteria, not necessarily the first record in the database. When you begin the retrieval process, Q&A doesn't know how many records will match your criteria. But if you press Ctrl-End, Q&A scans the file and displays the last matching record, then shows the number of matching records, such as Form 25 of 25. Press Ctrl-Home to return to the first record, Form 1 of 25.

When Q&A cannot find another record that matches the specifications, it displays

Form 1 of 1

on the status line. Below this is the message

No more records. Press Esc to exit or F9 for previous form

If you want to search for other records, press F7 to display the Retrieve Spec screen, press F3 to clear the fields, enter the new retrieval criteria, and press F10.

SAVING RETRIEVAL CRITERIA

||||➡ **To save and recall retrieval criteria:**

- **Save the criteria on the Retrieve Spec screen by pressing Shift-F8, typing a name of up to 31 characters, and pressing ↵.**
- **Recall stored retrieval criteria by pressing Alt-F8, typing the name or selecting its name from the List Manager screen, and then pressing ↵.**

Since some of your retrieval criteria can be quite complex, you might want to save the retrieval specification so that you can use it again to quickly locate records at some other time. To save the criteria, after completing a specification, press Shift-F8. Q&A displays the prompt

Save retrieve spec as

Type a name for the specification, and then press ↵. Use a descriptive name, such as Commissions over $5000, or Clients in PA with No Credit. Specification names can be up to 31 characters, including spaces.

The retrieval criteria are saved with the database itself, and the specification will only be available for that database.

RETRIEVING RECORDS
WITH LIST MANAGER

When you want to use the retrieval criteria you've saved, press Alt-F8 from the Retrieve Spec screen. As shown in Figure 3.6, Q&A displays a list of saved specifications for that database, along with the prompt

Enter name:

This screen is called the List Manager. You will see the List Manager screen when you recall databases and specifications of all types.

Type the name of the specification that you want to use, or select it with the arrow keys or mouse, and then press ↵. The form will appear on the screen. Press F10 to retrieve the records that match the saved criteria.

The List Manager screen key-assignment line includes the options F3, to delete; F5, to copy; F7, to search for; and F8, to rename items listed. To delete, copy, or rename an item, highlight its name in the list, press the appropriate function key, and follow the instructions on the screen.

If your list contains more items than can fit on a single screen, press PgDn to display the additional items. Press PgUp to return to the previous list.

Instead of scanning the entire list to find a specific item, you can use the search function (function key F7). Type the first few characters of the item you're looking for, followed by two periods, such as *Comm..*, and then

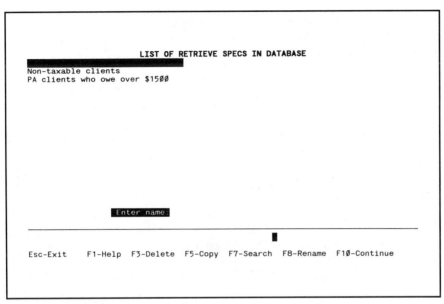

Figure 3.6: List Manager screen

press F7. The first item starting with those characters will be highlighted, and the status line will display

Comm.. found. Hit F7 to search for next match

If the highlighted item is not the one you want, press F7 until it is selected.

DISPLAYING RECORDS IN A TABLE

To display retrieved records in table view:

1. Select Search/Update from the File menu.
2. Type the name of the database and press ⏎ to display the Retrieve Spec screen.

3. **Press F10 to see all the records, or enter information to limit the retrieval and press F10.**
4. **When a record appears on the screen, press Alt-F6.**

Using the Retrieve Spec screen to find records has disadvantages:

- You have to enter specific information in a field. If you type the entry incorrectly, such as *PE* instead of *PA*, Q&A will not find the correctly spelled word. If you don't notice that you entered the retrieval criteria incorrectly, you might assume that there were no customers in Pennsylvania.

- You can display data from just one record at a time. This forces you to scroll through the database record by record to find the one you are looking for (if more than one meets all the retrieval specifications).

You can overcome these problems by using table view. To display records in table view, press Alt-F6 from a record. In table view, your data is listed in rows and columns, 17 partial records at one time. The record that you pressed Alt-F6 from will be highlighted. You can quickly scan the list looking for a specific record, or press PgDn to display the next 17 partial records.

Table view displays all the records located using your retrieval specifications. If you press F10 from the Retrive Spec screen without entering any field information, all your forms will be listed in the table. However, if you limit the retrieval to specific records by entering data in one or more fields, only those records will appear in table view.

To display fields that do not appear on the screen, press the → or ← key to scroll them into view. Press Ctrl-→ and Ctrl-← to scroll left and right five fields at a time.

To display a record on the screen in its full form, highlight any of its fields in the table using ↓ or ↑, and then press F10. Press Home to reach the first record on the list; press End to reach the last one.

Let's see how our Clients database looks in table view:

1. Select Search/Update from the File menu.

2. Press ↵ to accept the Clients database.

3. Press F10 to display the first of your records.

4. Press Alt-F6 to display the records in table view. Your screen should look like Figure 3.7.

The first record is highlighted, and the status line shows its record number and the total records in the file.

5. Press → five times. The Customer Code field scrolls off the left side of the screen, and the Zip Code field comes into view on the right.

6. Press ← until the Customer Code field comes back into view.

```
┌──────────────────────────────────────────────────────────────────────┐
│                                                                        │
│   ┌──────────────┬──────────────┬──────────────┬──────────────┬───────┐│
│   │Customer Code │    Name      │   Address    │    City      │State ▋││
│   ├──────────────┼──────────────┼──────────────┼──────────────┼───────┤│
│   │101           │Chesin Pharmac→│182 Walnut Str→│Newark        │NJ     ││
│   │102           │Williams Engin→│347 West Fifth→│Newark        │NJ     ││
│   │103           │Dershaw, Inc. │17th And Locus→│Philadelphia  │PA     ││
│   │105           │City Of Newark│129 State Road│Newark        │NJ     ││
│   │106           │Ajaz Refining,→│23 Delaware Av→│Wilmington    │DE     ││
│   │107           │Williams Colle→│45 Market Walk│Philadelphia  │PA     ││
│   │108           │Stack And Gall→│98b Benett Ave→│Margate       │NJ     ││
│   │109           │Harding Junior→│45 Frankford A→│Philadelphia  │PA     ││
│   │110    )      │Sparkling Wate→│56 West Maryto→│Margate       │NJ     ││
│   │104           │Samual Enginee→│809 Walden Road│Margate       │NJ     ││
│   │              │              │              │              │       ││
│   └──────────────┴──────────────┴──────────────┴──────────────┴───────┘│
│   CLIENTS.DTF      Retrieved record 1     of 10      Total records: 10  │
│   Esc-Exit  F1-Help  ( ↓ ↑ → ← Home End PgUp PgDn )-Navigate  F10-Show form│
│                                                                        │
└──────────────────────────────────────────────────────────────────────┘
```

Figure 3.7: Clients database in table view

7. Press ↓ to highlight the next record, then F10 to display it in full on the screen.

8. Press Alt-F6 to return to table view.

CUSTOMIZING TABLE VIEW

||||➡ **To rearrange the fields in table view:**

1. **Press Shift-F6 to display the Table View Spec screen.**
2. **Number the fields in the order you want them to appear.**
3. **Press F10 to return to table view.**

You can change the order in which the fields are displayed in table view so that you will be able to see particular information at a glance. In table view or while a record is displayed, press Shift-F6 to display the Table View Spec screen, shown in Figure 3.8.

Notice that each of the fields are numbered in increments of 10, starting at 10. The numbers indicate the order that fields are displayed in the table: field 10, then field 20, and so on. To change the order of fields in table

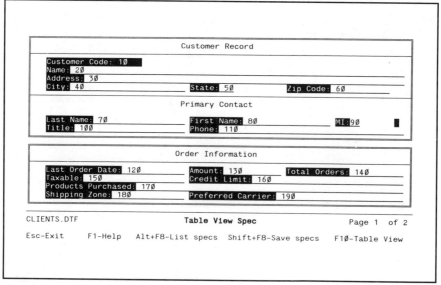

Figure 3.8: Table View Spec screen

view, you change the numbers following the field. The numbers are in increments of 10, so you can change the order without renumbering the entire form. You will see how this works shortly.

The changes you make to the table view will be saved with the database and serve as the default when you use it. So before making the changes, you should save the original specification that displays all the fields. Like retrieval specifications, saved table view specifications can be recalled later by displaying the Table View Spec screen and pressing Alt-F8. The List Manager screen will show the saved table specifications for that database.

Now, we will change the table view of the Clients database so we can see the name and phone number of the primary contact next to the customer's code and name:

1. In table view, press Shift-F6.

2. Press Shift-F8 to display the prompt

    Save table view spec as

3. Type **Full Form** and press ↵.

Since you saved the original table view specification under the name Full Form, you can easily retrieve it to display the fields in that order.

4. Press ↓ four times to move to the Last Name field, and then type **21**.

5. Press Tab to move to the First Name field and type **22**.

6. Press ↓ to move to the Phone field, type **23**, and press Del to erase the extra character.

7. Press F10 to return to table view. The fields are now listed according to the order you specified, as shown in Figure 3.9.

8. Press Esc to return to the File menu.

```
┌─────────────────────────────────────────────────────────────────────┐
│                                                                       │
│  ┌─────────────┬────────────────┬─────────────┬─────────────┬───────────┐ │
│  │Customer Code│      Name      │  Last Name  │ First Name  │  Phone ▋  │ │
│  ├─────────────┼────────────────┼─────────────┼─────────────┼───────────┤ │
│  │ 101         │Chesin Pharmac→ │Chesin       │Adam         │555-1200   │ │
│  │ 102         │Williams Engin→ │Peterson     │John         │431-9871   │ │
│  │ 103         │Dershaw, Inc.   │Dershaw      │Terry        │565-1267   │ │
│  │ 105         │City Of Newark  │Ronish       │Sally        │512-8716   │ │
│  │ 106         │Ajaz Refining,→ │Paulson      │Patrick      │876-1200   │ │
│  │ 107         │Williams Colle→ │Bryan        │Stuart       │827-9812   │ │
│  │ 108         │Stack And Gall→ │Stack        │Faye         │921-5600   │ │
│  │ 109         │Harding Junior→ │Richards     │Mary         │765-1200   │ │
│  │ 110         │Sparkling Wate→ │Kaufman      │Herb         │876-0500   │ │
│  │ 104         │Samual Enginee→ │Samual       │Bernice      │823-1911   │ │
│  │             │                │             │             │           │ │
│  │             │                │             │             │           │ │
│  │             │                │             │             │           │ │
│  │             │                │             │             │           │ │
│  │             │                │             │             │           │ │
│  │             │                │             │             │           │ │
│  └─────────────┴────────────────┴─────────────┴─────────────┴───────────┘ │
│                                                                       │
│  CLIENTS.DTF      Retrieved record 1       of 10      Total records: 10│
│                                                                       │
│  Esc-Exit  F1-Help   ( ↓ ↑ → ← Home End PgUp PgDn )-Navigate    F10-Show form│
│                                                                       │
└─────────────────────────────────────────────────────────────────────┘
```

Figure 3.9: Table view in new order

REFINING YOUR SEARCH

You have learned how to enter information in fields on the Retrieve Spec screen to limit the retrieval search to records that exactly match the criteria, such as all records in which the customer code is 101 or the state is Pennsylvania.

By using retrieval codes, you can refine your search even further to locate selected groups of records.

USING SEARCH CRITERIA TO LOCATE RECORDS

▐▐▐▶ **To customize retrieval of records:**

- **Enter the less-than symbol to find field entries less than a value.**

- **Enter the greater-than symbol to find field entries more than a value.**
- **Enter a slash followed by characters you want to exclude from the search.**
- **Enter two dots to indicate a range.**
- **Enter a semicolon to represent a logical OR.**
- **Use MAX or MIN to find the maximum or minimum field values, respectively.**

Suppose that you would like to see a list of all your customers whose purchases total $5,000 or more. If you entered 5000 in the Total Orders field of the Retrieve Spec screen, Q&A would list only those customers whose orders equaled exactly $5,000. Instead, you would use the greater-than symbol to find the specific records:

> = 5000

Q&A will locate just the records in which the Total Order field entry is greater than or equal to $5,000.

The less-than (<), greater-than (>), and equal (=) symbols also work in text fields. Entering <M in the Name field, for example, will locate clients whose name starts with the letters A through L, regardless of case.

Use the slash (/) symbol in all types of fields to exclude the characters following the symbol from the search. In all fields except yes/no types, you can also use two dots (..) to indicate a range, and a semicolon (;) to represent a logical OR. Here are some examples of how these criteria work:

Smith or =Smith	Exact match. Retrieves records in which the entry is Smith, ignoring capitalization
/SMITH	Retrieves records in which the field entry is not Smith
=	Retrieves records in which the field entry is empty (contains no data)
/=	Retrieves records in which the field entry is not empty (contains some data)

>5..<10	Retrieves records in which the field entry contains a value greater than 5 but less than 10 (or from 6 to 9)
>5..<=10	Retrieves records in which the field entry contains a value greater than 5 but less than or equal to 10 (or from 6 to 10)
<5;>=10	Retrieves records in which the field entry contains a value less than 5 or equal to or greater than 10 (or all numbers except 5 through 9)
5..<10	Retrieves records in which the field entry contains a value greater than or equal to 5 but less than 10 (or from 5 to 9)
>5..10	Retrieves records in which the field entry contains a value greater than 5 but less than or equal to 10 (or from 6 to 10)
Ball; Bat	Logical OR match; retrieves records in which the field entry contains the value ball or bat

Two other criteria you can use for all fields except keyword and yes/no fields are MAXn and MINn. Entering MAXn, where n is a number, retrieves records in which the field entry contains a value equal to the nth highest in the database. For example, entering MAX1 in the Total Orders field locates the client who has purchased the most; entering MAX2 would find the two customers with the most purchases. By using MINn, you can retrieve records in which the field entry contains a value equal to the nth smallest in the database, such as the customers who have ordered the least merchandise.

Criteria for Date, Hours, and Money Fields

By using criteria in date fields, you can locate clients who haven't purchased anything recently. For example, enter <10/22/91 in the Last Order Date field to locate clients who haven't made a purchase since October 21, 1991.

Here are some examples of how you can use the range symbol (..) in date, hours, and money fields:

5..   Retrieves records in which the field entry contains a value equal to or greater than 5

..5   Retrieves records in which the field entry contains a value equal to or less than 5

5..10   Retrieves records in which the field entry contains a value between 5 and 10 (or from 5 to 10)

Criteria for Keyword and Text Fields

Suppose that UPS, or some other shipper, decides to increase its rates for items over 100 pounds when shipped to all zones except zone 1. You have only two items that large in your inventory—items 105 and 111—so you're not sure what effect the rate change will have on your business. To find out, you could locate all clients who purchase item 105 or 111 *and* who are not in zone 1 by entering 105;111 in the Products Purchased field and /1 in the Shipping Zone field. The code 105;111 means "a keyword field that contains either 105 or 111," and /1 means "a field that contains a zone other than 1."

In keyword fields only, you can use an ampersand to represent a logical AND. For example, the entry &Stamps;Coins retrieves records in which the field entry contains the keywords stamps and coins.

Two other criteria that can be used in only text or keyword fields are the question mark (?) to represent any single character, called a *wildcard*; and the tilde (~), which finds words that sound like the characters following it.

Here are some examples of criteria for text and keyword fields:

C..   Retrieves records in which the field entry contains an entry starting with the letter *c*

..C   Retrieves records in which the field entry contains an entry ending with the letter *c*

h..e	Retrieves records in which the field entry contains an entry starting with the letter *h* and ending with the letter *e*
..C..	Retrieves records in which the field entry contains the letter *c*
..C..A..T..	Retrieves records in which the field entry contains the letters *CAT*, in that order
C..A..T	Retrieves records in which the field entry starts with *C*, ends with *T*, and includes an *A* anywhere in between
?????	Retrieves records in which the field entry contains any five-character entry. A wildcard ? is substituted for any one character. To use a wildcard with date fields, precede the criteria with], such as]1990/??/?? to locate all dates in 1990 (dates must be in *YYYY/MM/DD* order)
~Newarc	Retrieves records in which the field entry contains a word that sounds like *Newarc*, such as Newark

USING LOGICAL
OPERATORS BETWEEN FIELDS

To locate records based on an OR condition across fields:

1. **From the Retrieve Spec screen, press Ctrl-F7.**
2. **Press ↓ and select ANY.**
3. **Press F10 to locate records.**

You can use the semicolon symbol to perform a logical OR search on the contents of a keyword field, but these are logical AND operations across multiple fields. This means that only records matching all the criteria are located, such as clients who are in Pennsylvania *and* whose purchases total more than $5,000.

Locating clients who are either in Pennsylvania *or* who purchased more than $5,000 (no matter what state they are in) is a different type of search. In this case, you want to list, for example, a California client who has purchased $6,000, as well as a Pennsylvania client who has purchased nothing. This is called an OR search because it locates records matching either one criteria or the other. Actually, OR searches can include as many criteria as you want.

To conduct a logical OR search involving multiple fields, you go through the search options window (Ctrl-F7). As an example, we will locate clients in our sample database who have either purchased an item since November 16, 1991, or whose last purchase was more than $500. Follow these steps:

1. Select Search/Update from the File menu, and then press ↵ to accept the Clients database and display the Retrieve Spec screen.

2. Enter **>11/16/91** in the Last Order Date field.

3. Enter **>500** in the Amount field.

4. Press Ctrl-F7 to display the search options window, shown in Figure 3.10.

As you can see, the default search will locate *all* records who *do* meet the search criteria.

5. Press ↓, then → to select ANY.

6. Press F10 to locate records meeting any of the criteria, rather than all of them.

7. Press Esc twice to return to the Main menu.

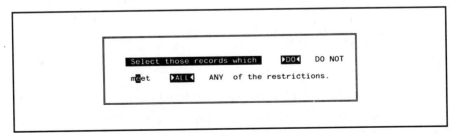

Figure 3.10: Search options window

REVISING AND DELETING RECORDS

IIII➡ **To change a record:**

- **Edit the record by displaying it, making your changes, and pressing F10 or Shift-F10.**
- **Delete the record by displaying it and pressing F3, then Y.**

When you need to update a record with new or revised information or delete one that you no longer need, you must first retrieve it, using any of the methods described in this chapter. Then you can proceed to make the changes.

EDITING RECORDS

You can edit the record using the cursor-movement and editing keys (see Table 2.2). Move the cursor to the field you want to change, and then enter the new information, in either insert or overtype mode.

You might find it easier to first delete the existing entry in the field. If the entry is one word, press F4. When the entry is several words, press Ctrl-F4 or Shift-F4 to delete all the words at one time.

In search/update mode, editing affects only the field contents, not the form design. This means that you can insert and delete characters without changing the appearance of the form or the border lines. If you try to edit an expanded field, Q&A displays the message

Press F6 to edit long input on a line that can scroll

Press F6 to edit the field in the expand window.

As an example, we will change some information in two of our sample records.

1. Select Search/Update from the File menu.

2. Press ↵, then F10 to display the first record in the Clients database.

3. Press ↓ five times, press Tab to reach the Phone field, and enter **555-1200**.

4. Press F10 to save the change and display the next record.

The status line now includes the F9 option, which displays the previous record in the file. Also, when you move to another record, the cursor remains in the field it was in before, so the cursor is still in the Phone field.

5. Press ↑ twice to reach the City field, press F4 to delete the name already there, and then type **Newark**.

6. Press F9 to save the changes and go back to the previous record.

If you edit a record, but then change your mind about the changes, press Esc while the record is still on the screen. You will see a warning that your changes will not be saved. Select Yes to return to the File menu.

DELETING INDIVIDUAL RECORDS

When you must delete a record from your database—perhaps a customer went out of business or you traded an item in your collection—display it on the screen using the Search/Update option, and then press F3. Q&A will warn you that the record will be permanently deleted.

Press Y to delete the record, or N to cancel the operation. If other records met the retrieval criteria, the next one will be displayed. Otherwise, the File menu will reappear.

DELETING MULTIPLE RECORDS

▐▐▐➡ **To delete multiple records:**

1. **Select Remove from the File menu.**

2. **Enter the database name and press ↵.**

3. **Choose selected records.**

4. **Complete the Retrieve Spec screen and press F10.**

If you want to delete a group of records at one time, or all of the records in your database, use the Remove option on the File menu.

When you're ready to delete records, select Remove from the File menu, and then enter the name of the database. Q&A will display the menu shown in Figure 3.11.

Choose the Selected Records option to display the Retrieve Spec screen, complete the fields and press F10. Press F10 alone to delete every record in the database. Before deleting all your records, you might want to make a backup copy of the database in case you later change your mind. Copying a database is explained in Chapter 4.

Q&A scans your database for records meeting the retrieval criteria, and then displays a message warning you that your records will be permanently erased. Select Yes and press ↵ to delete the records. Press Esc to return to the File menu.

The other options on the Remove menu delete duplicate records. Both erase records from the database, but the Duplicate Records to ASCII option saves the deleted records in a separate file. This way, you can retrieve the records if you find that you've erased them by mistake.

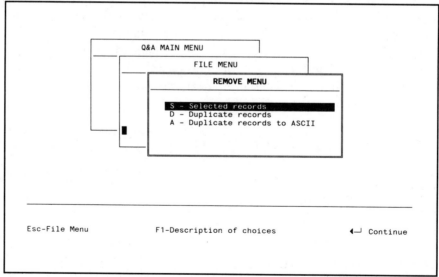

Figure 3.11: Remove menu

When you select either of the Duplicate Records options, Q&A will display the Duplicate Spec screen, which looks like the Retrieve Spec screen. Type D in the fields you want Q&A to check for duplicate information. For instance, if you enter a D in only one field, Q&A will assume that all records having the same information in that field are duplicates. So if you enter D in just the City field, for example, Q&A will assume that all records with the same city are duplicates, even though the records might only have that one field in common.

It is best to enter D in a number of fields to ensure that you delete the correct records. In some instances, you might have several records that have a number of fields in common. Enter D in enough fields so that these common elements are not assumed to represent a duplicate record.

Press F10 after filling in the Duplicate Spec screen. Q&A searches the database for duplicates of the marked fields, and then displays a message similar to

```
2 Records will be deleted
Do you want to confirm each deletion individually?
(Press Esc to cancel this process)
Y - Yes     N - No
```

If you select No, Q&A saves the first of each duplicate and deletes the others. If you select Yes, the first duplicated record will appear on the screen. Press Shift-F10 to delete it, Ctrl-F10 to save the displayed record and delete its duplicates, or F10 to save all of the duplicates. The process will be repeated for each of the duplicate sets.

REVISING RECORDS IN TABLE VIEW

▐▐▐▐➤ **To revise a record in table view:**

1. **Highlight the field you want to change.**
2. **Make the changes.**
3. **Press F10 or Shift-F10.**

To edit a record in table view, highlight the field, press F5 to turn on edit mode, and then make your corrections or additions. Remember to press F6 to expand a field, if necessary. When you're finished making your changes, press Shift-F10 to return to the File menu.

To delete a record in table view, highlight it in the list, press F3, then Y, then ↵ to confirm the deletion.

To insert a record, press Ctrl-F6 to enter the Add function. If you want to return to table view after inserting a record, press F7 to display the Retrieve Spec screen, enter any criteria for the search, and then press F10 to display the first record. Finally, press Alt-F6 to enter table view.

NAVIGATING BETWEEN ADD AND SEARCH/UPDATE

||||▶ To switch between the search/update and add modes:

- **Press Ctrl-F6 to add records after choosing Search/Update from the File menu.**
- **Press F7 to retrieve records after choosing Add Data from the File menu.**

So far, you've used the Add option to enter new records, and the Search/Update option to view and edit existing ones. You do not, however, have to return to the File menu to move from one function to the other.

If you want to add a new record while viewing one you found by using Search/Update, press Ctrl-F6. The Add form will appear.

If you want to search for existing records while adding new ones, press F7 to display the Retrieve Spec screen. Fill in the retrieval criteria and press F1.

Using the techniques you have learned so far, you could create a database for almost any purpose. In Chapter 4, you will learn how to sort the records and redesign your database form, and also get a preview of some more advanced database techniques.

4

Managing Your Database

After you have created one or several databases, you will need to open the data file you want to work with and arrange the records in some meaningful order. While working with a database, you may find that your form is not designed properly.

This chapter describes how to access your data files, sort your records, and redesign your database forms. You will also learn some techniques for streamlining data entry.

OPENING DATA FILES

▶ **To open a data file, use one of these methods:**

- **Enter the command to start Q&A followed by the name of the file.**
- **Enter the name of the file at any file name prompt.**

You can start Q&A and open the data file you want to use at the same time by entering **QA** followed by the file name at the DOS prompt. For example, you would enter **QA CLIENTS** to open the Clients database you created in Chapter 2. The file name you enter will automatically appear at the file name prompt when you select options from the File menu.

When you do not start Q&A with a file name, you must enter a database name when you first select a function from the File menu. During the remainder of the session, that name will automatically appear at file name prompts.

If you cannot remember the name of the file you want to use, you can have Q&A list the available files for you by pressing ↵ at a file name prompt. We will use this method now to open our database:

1. Start Q&A and press ↵ to accept File.

2. Select the Search/Update option. Since you have not named a file, a file name does not appear at the file name prompt.

3. Press ↵ without typing a name at the prompt. The List Manager
    screen will display the names of the data files on your disk.

If you want to list files later in the session, press Ctrl-F4 to delete the
name that appears at the file name prompt, and then press ↵.

4. Press ↓ to highlight CLIENTS. Under the status line, you will
    see the message

    No description available. Press F6 to add one.

Each database can have a description of up to 72 characters. If you
want to add a description to the database, press F6, type the text, and then
press F10. The description will appear under the status line when you
highlight a file name on the List Manager screen.

5. Press ↵ to display the Retrieve Spec screen for the database. If
    you have a mouse, you can open the file by clicking on its name
    with the left button.

Now we will continue working with the Clients database to demonstrate how to display your records in any order.

SORTING YOUR RECORDS

You added the records to the Clients database in the order of their customer number. Therefore, when you retrieve the records or display them
in table view, they appear in customer number order.

However, you will not always have the luxury of entering records in
a specific order. More typically, you will enter data haphazardly. For example, you might create a mailing list by typing in names and addresses
as you receive them, not in alphabetical order. Even if you can initially
enter records in some order, they will not remain that way as you update
your database by deleting and adding new records.

In order to display your records in some order, such as by customer
code or alphabetically, you arrange the records by *sorting* them. As you

work with your data, you may discover many useful arrangements. You might want to display customers by the amount of their total orders, for example, so you can identify your best clients. Or, you might want to display them by their last order date.

KEYS FOR SORTING

To sort records, you tell Q&A which field is the *key*, or the field you want to base the sort on, and if you want them in ascending or descending order. If you designate the customer name field as the key, for example, your records will appear in alphabetic order according to their names.

Sometimes, the key that you use to sort your data will be unique; that is, no two records will have the same exact data in the key field. Key fields such as customer numbers and social security numbers are unique because the same number is never assigned to more than one record.

Other times, the key you will use will not be unique. For example, if you sort your data by city, there may be several records with the same entry in the City field. Your records will appear in city order, but they will not be in a particular order within that group.

You can arrange groups of records in a particular order by using more than one key: a *primary* key and one or more (up to 9998) *secondary* keys.

The primary key is the first field that the records will be sorted by, and the secondary key is the field that will be used to order the records that have the same primary key data. If you were creating a mailing list for bulk mail, you might use the zip code as the primary key (for delivering the mail presorted to the post office), and the last name as a secondary key (so you could check for duplicates).

Sorting your records affects only the order in which records are displayed on the screen or printed. Q&A does not physically arrange the records in that order on your disk; they always remain in the order in which they were entered.

ENTERING SORT SPECIFICATIONS

▰▶ **To sort records to be displayed:**

1. **Select Search/Update from the File menu.**

2. Press F8 to display the Sort Spec screen.

3. Number the fields in the order you want them sorted, followed by AS for an ascending sort or DS for a descending sort.

4. Press F10 to sort and display the records.

To sort records, press F8 from the Retrieve Spec screen to display the Sort Spec screen. Except for some of the options on the key-assignment line, this screen looks just like the Retrieve Spec screen.

On this screen, you designate the primary key by entering 1 after the field label, a comma, and then either AS for an ascending sort or DS for a descending sort. You must type in AS or DS. There is no default value, and Q&A will display a warning if you forget to supply one. Designate second-ary keys with numbers from 2 to 9999, again followed by a comma and AS or DS. You do not have to use the same order for all keys—some can be descending while others are ascending.

You can sort just selected records by entering the retrieval criteria on the Retrieve Spec screen before pressing F8.

Now suppose that we want to display the records in our Client database grouped by city, and also in order of the amount each customer has purchased. For example, the list of all Philadelphia customers will have the customer who purchased the most first, and the one who bought the least last. For this sort, the City field is the primary key, and the Total Orders field is the secondary key. Follow these steps:

1. From the Retrieve Spec screen, press F8 to display the Sort Spec screen.

2. Press ↓ three times to reach the City field.

3. Type **1,AS** to designate the field as the primary key to be sorted in ascending order.

4. Press ↓ three times, press Tab twice to reach the Total Orders field, and type **2,DS**.

You can return to the Retrieve Spec screen to add or change search criteria by pressing F9. Instead, let's sort the records and display them on the screen.

5. Press F10 to sort the records. You will see the message

Please wait...

Now scanning record   of   selected records

Then Q&A will display the first of the sorted records.

6. Press Alt-F6 to enter table view.

The records are sorted by city, then by total orders, but these fields do not appear on the screen. Let's rearrange the view so that these fields are visible.

7. Press Shift-F6 to display the Table View Spec screen.

8. Press F3 to clear the fields.

9. Enter **30** after the Name field, **10** after the City field, and **20** after the Total Orders field.

10. Press F10 to return to table view.

As shown in Figure 4.1, the records are sorted as you specified.

```
┌─────────────────────────────────────────────────────────────────────┐
│                                                                       │
│   ┌──────────────┬──────────────┬──────────────┬─────────┬─────────┐ │
│   │     City     │ Total Orders │     Name     │         │    █    │ │
│   ├──────────────┼──────────────┼──────────────┼─────────┼─────────┤ │
│   │ Margate      │   $5,050.00  │Sparkling Wate→│         │         │ │
│   │ Margate      │   $3,560.00  │Samual Enginee→│         │         │ │
│   │ Margate      │   $1,876.00  │Stack And Gall→│         │         │ │
│   │ Newark       │   $6,800.00  │City Of Newark │         │         │ │
│   │ Newark       │   $2,510.00  │Williams Engin→│         │         │ │
│   │ Newark       │   $2,500.00  │Chesin Pharmac→│         │         │ │
│   │ Philadelphia │   $2,150.00  │Williams Colle→│         │         │ │
│   │ Philadelphia │   $1,850.00  │Harding Junior→│         │         │ │
│   │ Philadelphia │   $1,025.00  │Dershaw, Inc.  │         │         │ │
│   │ Wilmington   │   $1,250.00  │Ajaz Refining,→│         │         │ │
│   └──────────────┴──────────────┴──────────────┴─────────┴─────────┘ │
│                                                                       │
│   CLIENTS.DTF      Retrieved record 1      of 10       Total records: 10 │
│   Esc-Exit  F1-Help   ( ↓ ↑ → ← Home End PgUp PgDn )-Navigate    F10-Show form │
│                                                                       │
└─────────────────────────────────────────────────────────────────────┘
```

Figure 4.1: Records sorted by city and total orders

11. Press Esc twice to return to the Main menu, and then type **X** to exit from Q&A.

As your database grows larger, it will take Q&A longer to sort records, especially if you are using secondary keys. To save time, use secondary keys only when necessary (and only when the contents of the primary key field are not unique).

SAVING AND RECALLING SORT SPECIFICATIONS

||||➡ **To save and reuse sort specifications:**

- **Save the specification by pressing Shift-F8 from the Sort Spec screen, typing a name, and pressing ↵.**
- **Recall the specification by pressing Alt-F8 from the Sort Spec screen and selecting its name from the list displayed.**

When you want to save your sort specifications, press Shift-F8 from the Sort Spec screen. Q&A displays the message

Save sort spec as...

Enter a specification name up to 31 characters, and then press ↵.

To reuse a saved sort specification, display the Sort Spec screen and press Alt-F8 to display the List Manager screen. Select the specification from the list and press ↵.

CHANGING YOUR DATABASE DESIGN

Once you start using your database, no matter how well you planned it, you may find that it could be improved. This may become apparent when you add new records or when you find that printed reports are missing important information.

Fortunately, Q&A allows you to change your form by adding and deleting fields, as well as by changing field types and formats. It is easier to change a form before entering data, but you can redesign a database that already contains records. You just have to make sure your changes will not cause you to lose information. For example, if you shorten the width of a field, any existing data that exceeds the new size will be lost.

Q&A also allows you to copy a database form. When you need to create a new database form that is similar to one that you already have, you can save time by copying the existing one, and then redesigning the copy as necessary.

In the following sections, we will build another database for our sample business-management system. This will be a database of vendors, which will include fields for the name, address, primary contact information, and order information. Because the form will not be much different from the Clients form, we will make a copy of that form and redesign it instead of designing an entire new form.

COPYING DATABASE DESIGNS

IIII➡ **To copy a database form:**

1. **Select Copy from the File menu.**
2. **Enter the name of the file you want to copy.**
3. **Select to copy the design only.**
4. **Enter the name of the new file.**

You could copy the CLIENTS.DTF and CLIENTS.IDX files with the DOS COPY command, but then the new database would contain the old records. Since we want to copy only the form, not the information, we will use the Copy option on Q&A's File menu. Follow these steps to copy the Clients database form under the name Vendors:

1. Select File from the Main menu, and then choose Copy. Q&A displays the prompt

   Copy from: C:\QA\CLIENTS.DTF

2. Press ⏎. You will see the options

   D - Copy design only
   I - Copy design with IA/QG
   S - Copy selected records

3. Select to copy the design only. The next prompt is

   Copy to: C:\QA\

4. Type **Vendors** and press ⏎. The final message is

   Please wait...
   Your form is being copied.
   This may take several minutes

Although Q&A does not copy any records with the form, it does copy all the stored specifications, such as those for record retrieval and sorting, which are part of the Clients database. The List Manager screen will list these specifications when you use the new database.

5. Press Esc to return to the File menu.

After making a copy of the database, you can copy selected records to it by using the Copy Selected Records option on the Copy submenu. Q&A will display a Retrieve Spec screen in which you enter the criteria for locating the records you want to copy.

The Copy Design with IA/QG option copies specifications for Intelligent Assistant and Query Guide along with the design. You will learn how to use these features in Chapters 10 and 11.

Copying Entire Databases

If you want to copy a database and all its records, select Utilities from the Main menu, and then select DOS File Facilities. You will see the submenu shown in Figure 4.2. Choose the Copy a File option, and you will be prompted

   Copy from: C:\QA\

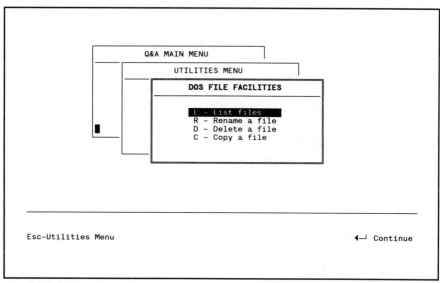

Figure 4.2: Dos File Facilities menu

Type the name of the file you want to copy, including the DTF extension, and press ↵. The next prompt is

    Copy to: C:\QA\

Type the name of the new database (you can leave out the extension) and press ↵. Because you are copying a DTF file, Q&A makes a copy of the associated IDX file as well. You do not have to copy the IDX file yourself. If you decide you do not want the records in the new database, use the Remove option to delete them.

Listing, Renaming, and Deleting Files

The other option on the DOS File Facilities menu allow you to perform file manipulation functions without returning to the DOS prompt, as follows:

- List Files displays a directory of your disk, allowing you to use the * and ? wildcards as you do with the DOS DIR command.

- Rename a File changes the name of files. Changing the name of a DTF file renames the IDX file at the same time.

- Delete a File erases files from your disk. When you delete a DTF file, Q&A also deletes the associated IDX file.

CHANGING YOUR FORM

||||▶ **To change a database form:**

1. **Select Design File from the File menu.**
2. **Select Redesign a File.**
3. **Edit the form, and then press F10 to display the format design screen.**
4. **Press F10 to display the Global Options screen.**
5. **Press F10 to save the design.**

To display an existing form in order to change it, choose the Design File option from the File menu, and then select Redesign.

The form design screen that appears shows your form with two letter codes after each field, as shown in Figure 4.3. Q&A uses these codes to keep track of your fields. Do not change the codes or delete them, unless you intend to delete the field itself. If you move a field from one location on the form to another, move the two-letter code along with it.

You can edit the form in either insert or overtype mode. In overtype mode, be careful not to replace characters that you do not want to change. For example, do not enter a new field name that runs into a field you want to keep.

Inserting and deleting characters will change the position of other fields and borders. After making your changes, you might need to redraw some of your borders. The best way to avoid this is to remain in overtype mode as much as possible and delete characters by entering a space in their place. Use the arrow keys to reach any line you want to change. Just make sure that fields you do not want to change are not affected by your editing.

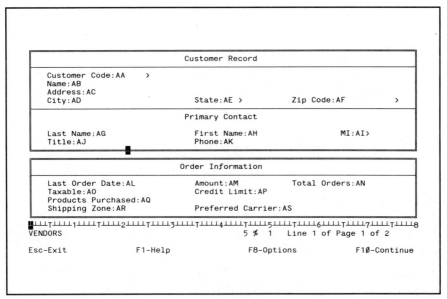

Figure 4.3: Form redesign screen with Q&A's internal codes

Now we will use the Redesign option to set up the Vendors form:

1. Select Design File from the File menu.

2. Select Redesign a File, enter **Vendors** at the prompt, and press ↵.

3. Make sure the characters INS do not appear on the status line. If they do, press Ins to turn off insert mode.

4. Place the cursor on the *C* in *Customer Record*.

5. Press the spacebar to delete the *C*, type **Vendor Record**, and then press the spacebar to delete the letter *d* that remains from the old title.

6. Place the cursor on the first letter *C* in *Customer Code*, and then type **Vendor**.

7. Press Del twice to delete the extra characters. Notice that the double line at the end of the form shifted two spaces to the left, as shown in Figure 4.4.

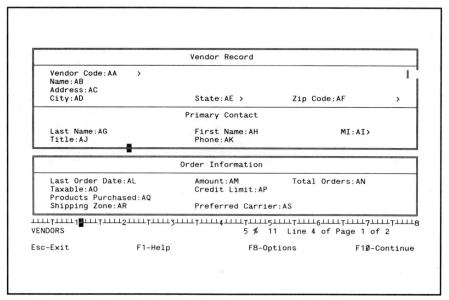

Figure 4.4: Effect of form editing on the border

8. Press End to move the cursor to the end of the line, and then press ← twice.

9. Press Ins, then the spacebar twice to move the line back into the border.

10. Press Ins to turn off insert mode.

11. Press Home to move the cursor to the left side of the screen, and then move the cursor to line 18, which contains the Taxable field.

12. Press Shift-F4 to delete the line, moving the field below it up into its place.

Because you deleted the entire line, text on the second page of the form scrolled onto the first page. We will take care of that shortly.

13. Place the cursor on the *P* in *Purchased.*

14. Type **Sold**, and then press Del five times.

Now you must readjust the border to the right of that line.

15.   Press End, then ← twice.

16.   Press Ins, the spacebar five times, then Ins.

17.   Press ↓ to move the cursor to the Shipping Zone field, and then press Shift-F4 to delete it.

18.   Press ↓ to reach the line that scrolled from the second page, press Ins, and then press ↵ twice.

Inserting two lines moves the text back to, and displays, the second page.

19.   Press Ins to turn off insert mode.

20.   Press PgUp to return to the first page.

Figure 4.5 shows the changes you have made so far. In the next section, we will use a different technique to complete the redesign of the form.

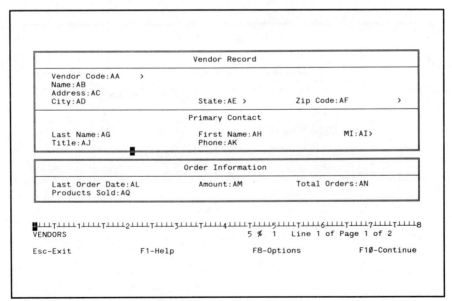

Figure 4.5: Partially redesigned first page

PERFORMING BLOCK OPERATIONS

||||➡ **To perform block operations:**

1. **Press F8, type B, and choose the operation desired; or press F3 to delete a block, F5 to copy a block, or Shift-F5 to move a block.**

2. **Use the cursor-movement keys to highlight the text you want to manipulate, and then press F10.**

3. **Position the cursor at the new location for moved or copied text, and then press F10.**

Block operations allow you to manipulate larger amounts of text on the form. You can quickly delete any amount of text, or move or copy text from one location to another.

Block Operations is a choice on the Options menu (F8). Figure 4.6 shows the options available on this menu while you are using Q&A File. Notice that most of the options have a function key or key combination

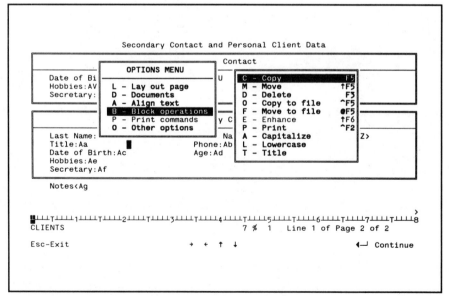

Figure 4.6: Block Operations menu

assigned to them. You can activate functions by selecting them from the menu or by pressing the keys from within the form.

All the block operations work the same way. Place the cursor at one end of the text you want to manipulate, select the option, move the cursor to the other end of the block, and then press F10.

For our final changes to our form, we will delete all the fields for the secondary contact on the second page of the form and move the order information before the primary contact fields on the first page. You will use block operations to make these revisions.

1. Press PgDn to return to the second page.

2. Place the cursor on the *S* in the title *Secondary Contact.*

3. Press F8 to display the Options menu, and then type **B** to select Block Operations.

4. Type **D** to select Delete. The status line will display the message

    Use the arrow keys to select the text you want to delete, then press F10

5. Press → to place the cursor in the space before the word *Personal*, and then press F10.

The selected characters are deleted, and the remaining part of the heading is automatically centered.

6. Place the cursor on line 9, position 1.

7. Press F3, the function key for the Delete option.

8. Move the cursor to line 18, position 1, and press F10. The secondary contact fields will be deleted.

9. Press PgUp to return to the first page of the form.

10. Place the cursor on line 14, position 1, and then press Shift-F5, the key combination for the Move option. The message that appears on the status line is the same as the one displayed when you choose the Delete operation.

11. Move the cursor to line 20, position 1, to highlight the block you want to move, and then press F10. The status line will now display

> Move the cursor to the place you want the text moved, then press F10

12. Place the cursor at line 9, position 1, and press F10.

The order information fields are now before the ones for personal contact information.

13. Press F8 and type **L**, then **D** to turn on draw mode.

14. Adjust the lines of the boxes on the form. Your completed page should look like Figure 4.7.

15. Press F10 to save the form and display the format design screen.

16. Press F10 to display the Global Format screen.

17. Press F10 to save the completed form and return to the File menu.

You can use block operations while creating a new form as well as when you are redesigning one. The same techniques are also available for working with documents in Q&A Write.

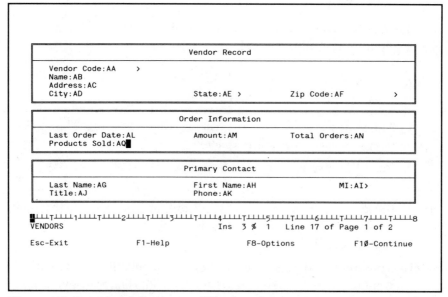

Figure 4.7: Completed first page of Vendors form

STREAMLINING DATA INPUT

Q&A provides a number of ways to automate your data-management functions. The following sections introduce some useful features that you can apply immediately to your own work. You will learn how to set initial values, copy data from one record to the next, and create field values that are the calculated results of other field values.

SETTING INITIAL VALUES

▐▐▐▊➤ **To set initial (default) field values:**

1. **Select Design File from the File menu and enter the database name.**
2. **Select Customize a File.**
3. **Select Set Initial Values.**
4. **Enter the field data that you want to appear automatically in new records.**
5. **Press F10 to save the form.**

In many databases, there are certain field entries, or *values*, that a number of records have in common. For example, most of your friends may live in the same city, or you might want to assign the same initial credit rating to all new customers. Rather than typing the same information with each new record, you can tell Q&A to insert it automatically as the default initial value. Then, while you are filling in the form, you can accept the default value or edit the field to make a different entry.

You set initial values through the Customize submenu, shown in Figure 4.8. You access this menu by selecting the Design File option from the File menu, and then choosing Customize a File.

Now let's suppose that because of state regulations in the industry, we must purchase all products from companies within the state. To simplify data entry, we will customize the Vendors database so that there is a default initial value for the State field.

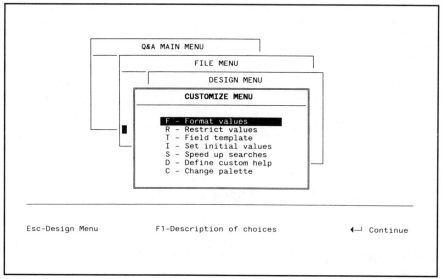

Figure 4.8: Customize menu

1. From the File menu, select Design File, and then choose Customize a File.

2. Press ↵ to accept the Vendors database and display the Customize menu.

3. Select Set Initial Values to display the Initial Values Spec screen.

Any information you enter in the fields on this screen will automatically appear on your Vendors form.

4. Press ↵ four times to reach the State field.

5. Type **PA**, and then press F10 to save the form and return to the Customize menu.

6. Press Esc twice to return to the File menu.

You can have Q&A automatically insert sequential numbers in a field by entering @NUMBER in the field on the Initial Values Spec screen. The first record you add will have the number 1 in the field, the second will have number 2, and so on. This is handy for customer numbers or other numeric codes you assign.

COPYING DATA
WITH THE DITTO FEATURE

IIII➤ **To copy data when adding records:**
- **Press F5 to copy the field contents from the previous record.**
- **Press Shift-F5 to copy all the data in the previous record.**

Setting initial values is useful if most of your records contain the same information in a particular field. If only a few records have data in common, it isn't a good idea to set an initial value because you might forget to change it, and then the field would contain the wrong information.

Instead of setting initial values, you can simply repeat certain information from one record to the next record by using the Ditto feature. For example, use this feature when you are entering records for two customers who are located in the same city, or two persons with the same last name. When you want to copy data, place the cursor in the field you want to fill in on the new form and press F5. If most of the data in one record is duplicated in the next, you can press Shift-F5 to copy the entire previous form. Then edit the record to change the field values that are different.

Now you will add records to the Vendor database and see the result of adding an initial value. You will also use the Ditto feature to repeat field information.

1. Select Add Data from the File menu and press ↵ to accept Vendors as the file name.

2. Enter the information for vendor 101 shown in Figure 4.9.

3. Press F10 to display the next blank record.

4. Enter **102** for the Vendor Code, **Siravo, Inc.**, as the Name, and **35 West Kingsessing Avenue** as the address.

5. Move the cursor to the City field and press F5. The entry in the City field of the previous record is automatically copied to the new record.

6. Complete the rest of this record as shown in Figure 4.9, and then press F10 to display the next blank form.

7. Complete the database with the information shown in Figure 4.9, and then press Esc to return to the File menu.

CALCULATING FIELD VALUES

▌▌▌➡ **To calculate field values:**

1. **Select Design File from the File menu.**
2. **Select Program a File, and then enter the database name.**
3. **Select Program Form.**
4. **Enter field numbers and formulas, and then press F10 to save them.**
5. **When adding or updating records, press F8 to calculate the formulas.**

```
Vendor Code: 101
Name: Marvin Supply, Inc.
Address: 35 West Fifth Street
City: Philadelphia            State: PA           Zip Code: 19101
Last Order Date: May 5, 1991  Amount: $365.00     Total Orders: $2,500.00
Products Sold: 101; 103
Last Name: Marvin             First Name: James   MI: J
Title: President              Phone: 555-8730
Date of Birth: May 1, 1939    Age:
Hobbies: Bowling
Secretary: Mary Martinelli


Vendor Code: 102
Name: Siravo, Inc.
Address: 35 West Kingsessing Avenue
City: Philadelphia            State: PA           Zip Code: 19101
Last Order Date: Dec 1, 1990  Amount: $320.00     Total Orders: $1,620.00
Products Sold: 102; 108
Last Name: Siravo             First Name: Don     MI:
Title: President              Phone: 555-8467
Date of Birth: Jul 1, 1949    Age:
Hobbies: Scuba
Secretary: Kathy Siravo


Vendor Code: 103
Name: Capital Manufacturing
Address: 493 Route 309
City: Flemington              State: PA           Zip Code: 19023
Last Order Date: May 12, 1991 Amount: $1,025.00   Total Orders: $5,672.00
Products Sold: 107; 109; 110
Last Name: Salledi            First Name: Dalores MI: L
Title: President              Phone: 653-9328
Date of Birth: Sep 1, 1952    Age:
Hobbies: Fencing
Secretary: William Nichol
```

Figure 4.9: Vendor records

```
Vendor Code: 104
Name: Dershaw, Inc.
Address: Fifth And Wyoming Avanues
City: Hatboro              State: PA          Zip Code: 19056
Last Order Date: Oct 7, 1991   Amount: $765.65     Total Orders: $8,701.54
Products Sold: 104; 105
Last Name: Armitage        First Name: Gertrude MI:
Title: Vice President      Phone:   651-1987
Date of Birth: Apr 23, 1938   Age:
Hobbies: Swimming; bowling
Secretary: Hazel Jackson

Vendor Code: 105
Name: Wellington, Inc.
Address: 976 Old Lincoln Highway
City: Feasterville         State: PA          Zip Code: 19023
Last Order Date: Feb 6, 1990   Amount: $1,025.00   Total Orders: $3,421.90
Products Sold: 106
Last Name: Paulson         First Name: Peter    MI: P
Title: Vice President      Phone:   765-0091
Date of Birth: Feb 6, 1930    Age:
Hobbies: Baseball; football
Secretary: Teresa Ferguson
```

Figure 4.9: Vendor records (continued)

You can use field values in calculations by assigning each field a *logical field number:* the # symbol followed by a number, such as #1. You can then use the field number as a variable in a formula. Whenever Q&A sees the field number in a calculation, it uses the numeric value in that field. You can also use the field name in the formula instead of a field number. However, all formulas must begin with a field number.

For example, suppose you have an inventory database with the fields Number on Hand, Price per Unit, and Total Value. You could calculate your total inventory value this way:

```
Number on Hand: #1
Price per Unit: #2
Total Value: #3 = #1 * #2
```

This calculation multiplies the value in field #1, Number on Hand, times the value in field #2, Price per Unit, and places the results in field #3, Total Value. You could also use this combination of field numbers and names (notice that the formula still starts with a field number):

```
Total Value: #3 = Number on Hand * Price per Unit
```

If your database has some field labels that are the same, remember that Q&A assigns them unique field names, such as Amount and Amount1. Be sure to use the correct field name in the formula.

Our Clients database has a field called Total Orders. This field is designed to store the running totals of entries in the Amount field, which contains the amount of the most recent order. Each time we update a record with a new order date and amount, we want to add the amount to the Total Orders field, using the basic formula

Total Orders = Total Orders + Amount

Computer programmers will recognize this as an accumulator algorithm in the general form:

$$X = X + Y$$

This formula says "The new value of X is now equal to the old value of X plus Y."

Adding Field Numbers and Formulas

You add field numbers and formulas to forms by using the Program Form function. This is a sophisticated feature that lets you automate the data-entry process. You will learn more about it later in the book. For now, we will use it to maintain the Total Orders field.

1. Select Design File from the File menu, and then choose Program a File.

2. Type **Clients** and press ↵ to display the Programming menu, shown in Figure 4.10.

3. Select Program Form to display the Program Form Spec screen.

4. Press ↓ six times, then Tab to reach the Amount field.

5. Type **#7**. (You will assign field numbers to other fields later on.)

6. Press Tab to reach the Total Orders field.

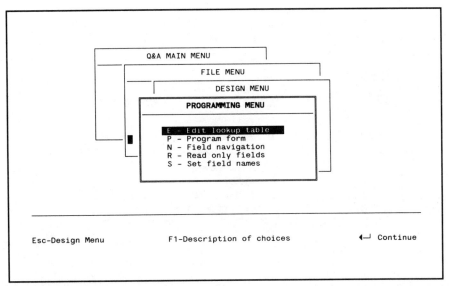

Figure 4.10: Programming menu

7. Press F6 to expand the field.

8. Type **#8 = #8 + #7**, and then press F10. Your screen should look like Figure 4.11.

This formula assigns the Total Orders field the number #8, and allows it to accumulate, or total, the contents of the Amount field. The formula could also be written as #8 = Total Orders + Amount.

9. Press F10 to save the specification and return to the Programming menu.

10. Press Esc twice to return to the File menu.

Using Formulas

To use a formula for a field value, press F8 from the form. Let's see how this works:

1. Select Search/Update from the File menu and press ↵ to accept Clients.

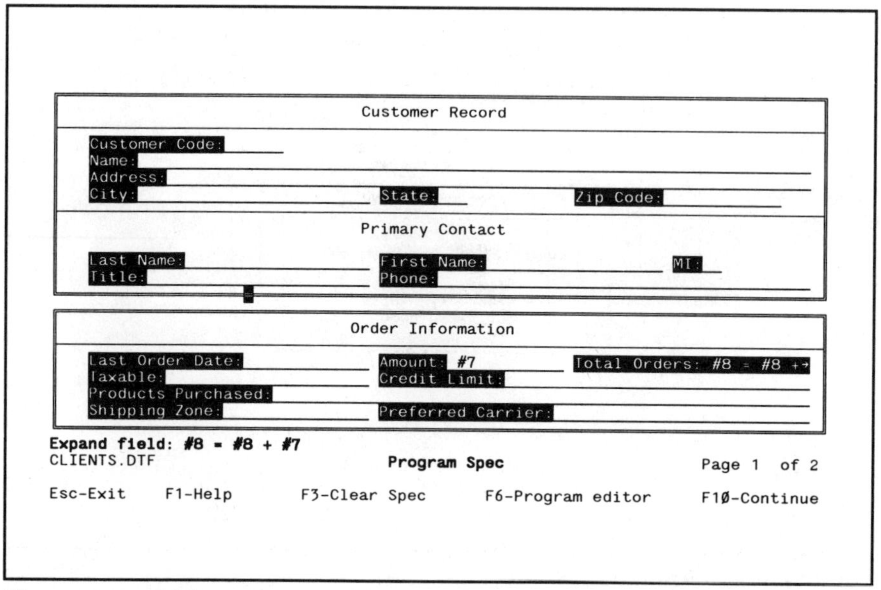

Figure 4.11: Field numbers and formula in Program Form Spec screen

2. Press F10 from the Retrieve Spec screen to display the first record.

3. Place the cursor in the Date of Last Order field, press Ctrl-F4 to delete the entry, and then type **11/16/91**.

4. Press Tab to move to the Amount field, press Ctrl-F4 to delete the entry there, and type **500.90**.

5. Press F8. The figure in the Total Orders field increases by 500.90, from 2500 to 3000.90.

6. Press Esc, and **Y** to return to the File menu without saving the changes to the record.

Pressing F8 calculates all the formulas in the form and displays the results. In Chapter 15, you will learn how to have Q&A calculate the results automatically for you.

There are two important warnings when using accumulators in your records:

- Press F8 *only* when you add new data to the field being accumulated. For example, every time you press F8 in a Clients database form, the figure in the Amount field will be added to the figure in the Total Orders field. After entering a new amount, press F8 to add it to the total orders. But do not press F8 a second time, or the amount will be added again, even though only one order for the amount had been placed.

- Use only one accumulator in a record. When you press F8, every formula in the record is recalculated. If you have two accumulators, but only make a change that affects one of them, both will be recalculated when you press F8—one correctly, the other adding the accumulated amount a second time.

In Chapter 15, you will learn how to use accumulators without these unwanted side effects.

There is a similar algorithm, called a *counter*, that works like an accumulator. You can use it to keep a running count, such as the number of a client's orders. You would create a field called Number of Orders and insert a formula like this:

    #9 = #9 + 1

Every time you enter another order and press F8, the Number of Orders field value would increase by one.

WORKING WITH DATES AND TIMES

To handle the date and time in records:

- **Use the @DATE and @TIME functions as initial values.**
- **When adding or updating records, press Ctrl-F5 to insert the date or Alt-F5 to insert the time.**
- **Use date and hours fields with calculations.**

Some of your database records may contain fields for the current date or time. For example, suppose you create a database to help with your client billing. Each record contains information about a block of time that you spent on a specific activity, such as a phone call giving the client advice or research for the project.

You would record the client's name, the project you are working on, the specific activity, and the starting and stopping time of that block of time. You can then use the information to bill the client for your time spent. Your basic form might look something like this:

```
Client: Project:
Activity:
Date:
Start Time:       End Time:
Minutes Spent:
```

Date would be defined as a date field, Start Time and End Time as hours fields, and Minutes Spent as a number field.

You could enter the date and the starting and ending times manually. But if you create the record on the date and at the time you begin the activity, you can have Q&A insert the date and time for you.

You can use one of two methods to add the date and time:

- Place the @DATE function in the Date field and the @TIME function in the Start Time field as initial values. Q&A will use the format you designated in the Global Options menu—you cannot override it.

- Press Ctrl-F5 to insert the date, or Alt-F5 to insert the time. When you create the record, move to the Date field and press Ctrl-F5. Q&A will insert the current system date in the field. Then move to the Start Time field and press Alt-F5 to insert the current time. When you complete the activity, move to the End Time field and type the time yourself or press Alt-F5 to insert the current system time.

Calculating with Dates

Q&A can perform arithmetic with date and hours fields, such as subtracting two fields to calculate time spent on an activity or adding days to arrive at a new date.

If you subtract two date fields, as in

```
Start Date: #1
End Date #2
Days Spent: #3 = #2 – #1
```

Q&A will calculate the number of days between fields #1 and #2.

You can use arithmetic on date and time field values very effectively. For example, you could program a billing form like this:

```
Client: #1
Project: #2
Activity: #3
Date: #4
Start Time: #5       End Time: #6
Minutes Spent: #7 = #6 – #5
```

This calculates the number of minutes between the start and end times and places the result in the Minutes Spent field. You could modify the billing method in many ways. For example, if you bill in 15-minute intervals, modify the last field to be

```
Periods: #7 = (#6 – #5)/15
```

The Clients form has fields for the date of birth and age of both the primary and secondary contacts. By using the contents of the Date of Birth field and the @DATE function for obtaining the current date, we can calculate each contact's current age. Follow these steps to enter the formula:

1. Select Design File from the File menu, choose Program a File, and press ↵ to accept Clients.

2. Select Program Form and press PgDn to display the second page of the form.

CHAPTER FOUR

3. Type **#14** in the Date of Birth field.

4. Press Tab to reach the Age field and type **#15 = @INT((@DATE – #14)/365.25)**.

This formula finds the number of days between the current date and the contact's date of birth using @DATE – #14. It then divides that number by 365.25 (the decimal accounts for leap years), and takes the integer value, or the closest whole number.

5. Press ↓ five times to reach the Date of Birth field for the secondary contact and type **#22**.

6. Press Tab to reach the Age field and type **#23 = @INT((@DATE – #22)/365.25)**. Figure 4.12 shows the formulas.

7. Press F10 to save the specification and return to the Programming menu.

8. Press Esc twice to return to the File menu.

```
                    Secondary Contact and Personal Client Data
   ┌──────────────────────────────────────────────────────────────────┐
   │                           Primary Contact                         │
   │  Date of Birth: #14              Age: #15 = @INT((@DATE - #14)/365.25) │
   │  Hobbies:                                                          │
   │  Secretary:                                                        │
   └──────────────────────────────────────────────────────────────────┘

   ┌──────────────────────────────────────────────────────────────────┐
   │                          Secondary Contact                        │
   │  Last Name:              First Name:              MI:             │
   │  Title:                  Phone:                                   │
   │  Date of Birth: #22      Age: #23 = @INT((@DATE - #22)/365.25)    │
   │  Hobbies:                                                          │
   │  Secretary:                                                        │
   └──────────────────────────────────────────────────────────────────┘

   Notes

   CLIENTS.DTF              Program Spec                Page 2  of 2

   Esc-Exit    F1-Help      F3-Clear Spec     F6-Program editor   F1Ø-Continue
```

Figure 4.12: Formulas to compute age from date of birth

9. To use the formula, select Search/Update from the File menu and press ↵.

10. Press F10 from the Retrieve Spec screen. Notice that $2500.00 appears in the Total Orders field.

11. Press PgDn to display the second page of the form.

12. Press ↓ five times and type **11-16-50** in the secondary contact's Date of Birth field.

13. Press F8. The ages are calculated and appear in the Age fields.

14. Press PgUp to display the first page of the form.

The Total Orders field now contains $3750.00, showing that the figure in the Amount field was incorrectly added to the accumulator.

15. Press Esc, and type **Y** to return to the File menu without saving the changes to the record.

16. Press Esc, and then type **X** to exit from Q&A.

So far, you have learned how to maintain your records as well as the database forms. Another very important aspect of database management is printing paper copies of your records. Printing records is the topic of the next chapter.

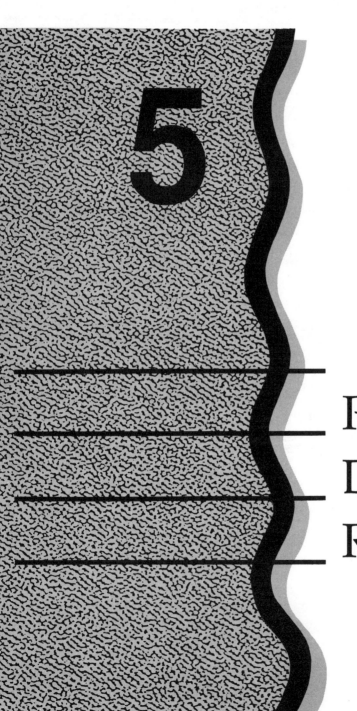

5

Printing
Database
Records

You can print data in your database through Q&A File, Report, or Write. This chapter describes how to print records from Q&A File. Use File when you want to print records as they appear on the screen, complete with lines, boxes, and field labels.

Even though it doesn't provide the same capabilities as Report, you can still produce useful and informative reports quickly and easily with File. You can print records as you add or retrieve them, or by using the Print command on the File menu.

CHOOSING PRINTING OPTIONS

IIII▶ To select print option for records:

1. **Choose to print (press F2 or Ctrl-F2 from the record or select Print from the File menu), and the Print Options menu will appear.**
2. **Select the printer, port, and other options from the menu.**
3. **Press F10 to print the report.**

Before printing any records, you can select printing options from the File Print Options menu, shown in Figure 5.1. You can display this menu in a variety of ways: when you add or update records, complete a printing specification, or change the default global values. You will learn about these printing techniques later in the chapter.

To make selections from the Print Options menu, press ↵, Tab, or ↓ to move down the list; press ↑ or Shift-Tab to move up. Some options have choices to select from on the right. Press ←, →, or the spacebar to highlight your choice. For the other options, enter the desired setting.

Since you will go through this menu for each printing, you should become familiar with its options. The following sections describe how to use the File printing options.

```
                    FILE PRINT OPTIONS

    Print to.....:    ▶PtrA◀  PtrB   PtrC   PtrD   PtrE   DISK   SCREEN

    Page preview..................:    Yes  ▶No◀

    Type of paper feed............:    Manual  ▶Continuous◀  Bin1   Bin2   Bin3

    Print offset..................:    Ø

    Printer control codes.........:    _____

    Print field labels............:    ▶Yes◀   No

    Number of copies..............:    1
                                                                    ▮
    Number of records per page....:    1

    Number of labels across.......:    ▶1◀  2   3   4   5   6   7   8

    Print expanded fields.........:    Yes  ▶No◀
    _____
    CLIENTS.DTF          Print Options for current form
    Hewlett Packard LaserJet (Portrait) »» LPT1
    Esc-Exit             F1-Help           F8-Define Page          F1Ø-Continue
```

Figure 5.1: File Print Options menu

SELECTING THE PRINTER AND PORT

The first option, Print To, allows you to select one of the printers you installed in Q&A (using the Install Printer option on the Utilities menu). The name of the printer will appear under the status line.

Select Disk to save the output as an ASCII disk file rather than sending it to your printer. You can then print the file later by using the DOS PRINT command.

If you want to see the record before printing it, select Screen for the first option. When you choose to print the document, it will appear on the screen.

DISPLAYING GRAPHIC IMAGES

Select Yes for the Page Preview option to display a graphic representation of the printed page. Previewing the printout gives you the opportunity to confirm that it will appear as you want. You can display up to two pages at a time, and zoom in (enlarge) the display to see specific details.

SELECTING THE PAPER SOURCE

For the Type of Paper Feed option, select the type of feed your printer uses:

- Manual for individual sheets
- Continuous for continuous, perforated pages
- Bin1 for the top drawer of a multidrawer printer
- Bin2 for the second drawer of a multidrawer printer
- Bin3 for the third drawer of a multidrawer printer

Choose Continuous if you are using a paper cassette in a laser printer, or a sheet feeder in a daisy-wheel printer.

INDENTING TEXT ON THE LEFT

The Print Offset option lets you specify the number of spaces you want to indent the printed output from the left edge of the paper. If you plan to bind the report in a folder or three-ring binder, you can use the Print Offset option to create a wide margin. Enter a number large enough to ensure that the text will not be obscured by the binding.

SELECTING PRINTER FEATURES

Q&A File uses your printer's default settings for the font and the orientation. For example, you can install a LaserJet printer in either portrait or landscape mode. When you print, Q&A will use the orientation you selected and the default 10-point Courier font.

If fonts and other printing features of your printer are not supported by Q&A, you may still be able to use them by entering the proper codes for the Printer Control Codes option.

Control codes are special sequences of numbers that turn on or off printer functions. Your printer manual lists your printer's control codes. They might be shown in hexadecimal (a 16-base numbering system), decimal, or ASCII. For example, for some dot-matrix printers, the codes for turning on italics might be shown in one of these ways:

1B 34	Hexadecimal
27 52	Decimal
ESC 4	ASCII

Each of these codes represents the same two numbers, the Escape code (1B, 27, or ESC) followed by the representation of the character 4.

A control code may also include several numbers, as in ESC I1, which turns on italics for IBM Graphics and compatible printers. This code has three characters: ESC followed by the characters *I* and *1*. In ASCII, 4 and 1 represent characters, not the numeric values 4 and 1.

Your printer manual should include a conversion chart showing the decimal equivalents of ASCII characters and hexadecimal numbers. With Q&A, you must enter the codes in decimal, not hexadecimal or ASCII. For example, suppose that you want to print the entire report in boldface type, and your printer lists the bold control code as ESC G. If you look up the character G in an ASCII chart, you will see that it is equivalent to the decimal number 71. So to print in boldface, you would enter 27 71 for the Printer Control Codes option.

Keep in mind, however, that if you enter codes that change the page orientation or the pitch of characters (the number of characters printed per inch), you will have to adjust the page size and margins using the Define Page menu options, which are discussed later in the chapter.

IDENTIFYING FIELDS

Select Yes for the Print Field Labels option when you want to print the field labels along with the values in the fields. Any boxes and lines you have drawn on your forms will print only when you choose to print field labels.

Print the labels if the field values do not clearly indicate what they represent. For example, without field labels, the record

```
Inventory Item: Ham
Shippable: Yes
Taxable: No
```

would be printed as

Ham

Yes

No

If you are printing an address list or mailing labels, however, field labels are not necessary.

PRINTING DUPLICATE RECORDS

If you want to print multiple copies of each record, enter the number you want for the Number of Copies option. File will print all copies of the first record, then all copies of the second, and so on.

PRINTING RECORDS ON THE SAME PAGE

By default, Q&A will print one record on a page. For example, if you print 100 records, your report will be 100 pages long. To print more than one record on each page, enter the number for the Number of Records per Page option.

A sheet of $8\frac{1}{2}$-by-11-inch paper can hold 66 lines using your printer's default font, and Q&A will add a blank line between records. Compute the maximum number of records per page by dividing 66 by the number of lines you are printing for each record plus 1. For example, if you are printing six lines for each record, you can print nine records per page. Note that the actual number of lines you can print on each page is controlled by the Define Page menu settings, which are discussed shortly.

If you specify more records than can fit on a page, Q&A will print as many as possible on the page and add the rest to the next page. Q&A will not divide records across pages. To print a continuous report without having to count lines, just enter a large number for this option.

When you are printing one copy of each record, print the most you can on each page to produce a listing of your database. However, if you want more than one copy of the listing, do not use the Number of Copies option because Q&A will print the copies of each record in a row. For multiple copies of reports, set the Number of Copies option to 1 and print the report several times.

PRINTING IN COLUMNS

Use the Number of Labels Across option to print records in columns across the page, such as for mailing lists. The records print next to each other in sequence from left to right. If you are printing two labels across, record 1 will be on the left, record 2 on the right, then record 3 on the left again.

The Q&A Write module has an automatic function for printing labels from your database, so you probably will not print labels with File. However, this option is useful when you are producing narrow lists that would normally print in one column, leaving the right half of every page blank.

PRINTING THE FULL TEXT

Select Yes for the Print Expanded Fields option to print the full content of expanded fields. The default setting of No prints only as many characters of each field as will fit on the form.

Keep in mind that printing expanded fields may cause a record to take up more lines than you planned, which will affect the number of records that can fit on a page.

DEFINING THE PAGE

To define the page:

1. Press F8 from the Print Options menu.
2. Enter settings for the paper size, margin, and characters per inch options.
3. Type header and footer text in the lines at the bottom of the menu.

You can customize your File printouts by using the Define Page menu options, shown in Figure 5.2. Defining the page gives you control over the final output and also allows you to adjust for fonts and orientation you specified by entering printer control codes on the File Print Options menu. To display the Define Page menu, press F8 from the Print Options menu.

SETTING THE PAPER WIDTH AND LENGTH

By default, the page width is set in character spaces, and the page length is the number of lines. You can also enter measurements in inches by ending them with the " symbol. If you enter 14 as the page length, for example, Q&A assumes your page is only 14 lines long. So to use legal-size paper, enter either 14" or 84 for the number of lines.

If you select to print to a laser printer in landscape mode, change the width to 110 or 11", and the length to 51 or 8.5". Q&A does not automatically adjust the settings for you.

```
                              DEFINE PAGE
                              ───────────

            Page width : 24Ø          Page length..: 66_____

            Left margin: Ø_____        Right margin : 24Ø____

            Top margin : 3_____        Bottom margin: Ø_____

            Characters per inch:  ▶1Ø◀   12    15    17
                                  █
        ──────────────────────── HEADER ────────────────────────
        1:
        2:
        3:
        ──────────────────────── FOOTER ────────────────────────
        1:
        2:
        3:
        ─────────────────────────────────────────────────────────
        CLIENTS.DTF          Define page for current form

        Esc-Exit      F1-Help      F9-Go Back to Print Options    F1Ø-Continue
```

Figure 5.2: Define Page menu

SETTING MARGINS

You can set the left and right margins in character positions, or in inches by following the number with ". When you enter the right margin in character positions, it is relative to the left edge of the page. A right margin of 75, for example, ends each line 75 character positions from the left edge of the paper, giving you a 1-inch right margin using the default font. If you set the right margin in inches, however, Q&A assumes you mean inches from the right edge of the page. So for a 1-inch right margin, enter either 1" or 75. Q&A will warn you if your right margin is set wider than the page.

Set the top and bottom margins in lines (six lines per inch) or inches. Most laser printers cannot print within $\frac{1}{2}$-inch of the top and bottom edges of the page, so make sure to set the margins accordingly.

SETTING CHARACTERS PER INCH

The Characters per Inch (cpi) setting determines the printer font being used. If your printer has a number of built-in fonts, you can select the setting for the one you want to use. Q&A will turn on that font when it prints the report. If you select a setting that is not available, the report will still print, but you will see the message

The selected printer cannot print at the chosen CPI

Q&A will then select the closest size that your printer has available. For example, using a LaserJet Plus with only Courier and Line Printer installed, any character per inch setting other than 10 will turn on the Line Printer font.

Note that character-based settings for width and margins are affected by the Characters per Inch setting. For example, consider a page set at 85 characters wide, with right and left margins set at 10 and 75. At 10 cpi, these settings result in a page that's $8\frac{1}{2}$ inches wide with 1-inch left and right margins. Each line will be 65 characters long.

However, if you change the setting to 15 cpi, Q&A thinks the page is only 5.66 inches wide. This is because the 85 character positions take up less space at 15 cpi than they do at 10. Even though you are using a smaller font, your lines will still be 65 characters long—the difference between 10 and 75. In addition, the left and right margins will be about .66 inch each. Since you are really printing the report on 8½-inch paper, you will have a .66-inch left margin and a more than 3-inch right margin.

If you want to print on an 8½-inch page with 1-inch margins at 15 cpi, set the page width to 127, and the left and right margins to 15 and 112, respectively. The lines will be 97 characters wide.

If you do not want to recalculate width and margin settings when you change the Characters per Inch setting, enter your measurements in inches so that Q&A will automatically maintain the same page width and margins. A page set at 8.5" with 1" margins will always be that size. Only the number of characters that print on each line will change when you enter a different number of characters per inch.

PRINTING HEADERS, FOOTERS, AND PAGE NUMBERS

Through the Define Page menu, you can add headers and footers to your printouts. These are standard lines of text that print at the top or bottom of every page.

You can enter up to three lines of text for a header or footer and include codes for the date, time, and page number, as well as alignment. If you want two header (or footer) lines with a blank line between them, enter text in only the first and third lines.

To print the current date in a header or footer, enter @DATE on the appropriate line of the Define Page menu. Use @TIME to print the current system time. Q&A adds the date and time in the formats set on the Global Options menu for that database. For example, if you selected the second time format and sixth date format when you created your database, and it is now November 16, 4:30 p.m., the date will appear in the format 16/11/1991 and the time as 16:30. If you didn't change the formats in Global Options, the date will appear as Nov 16, 1991, and the time will be in 12-hour (nonmilitary) style.

You can override the default date and time formats by following the @DATE or @TIME function with the number of the format in parentheses. Entering @DATE(11), for example, will display dates with the month spelled out.

Include a page number in your header or footer by entering the # sign, as in Page #. If you want to print the # symbol itself in the text, precede it with a backslash; Page \## will create Page #1.

To center text on the page, precede it with an exclamation point (!). For example, add a centered title, date, and page number to a printout like this:

```
!Client Phone List
!as of @DATE
!Page #
```

Right-align text using a second exclamation point. The footer

```
@DATE!Page #!@TIME
```

will print the date on the left, the page number centered, and the time aligned on the right.

If you want to right-align text without any in the center, you still need two exclamation points. Entering

```
@DATE!!@TIME
```

inserts the date on the left and time on the right.

PRINTING WHILE
RETRIEVING OR ADDING RECORDS

To print records while adding or updating:

- **Print a single record by pressing F2 when the record is displayed. Choose settings on the Print Options and Define Page menus, and then press F10.**
- **Print multiple records by pressing Ctrl-F2 when a record is displayed.**

After you choose the Search/Update or Add Data option from the File menu, you can print a single record or multiple records.

PRINTING A SINGLE RECORD

To print a single record, display it on the screen using the Search/Update option, and then press F2 to access the File Print Options menu. Select your options from the menu, and then press F10 if you do not want to change the page settings or add a header or footer.

If you want to change the page settings, press F8 to display the Define Page menu, and then make your selections. Press F9 to return to the File Print Options menu, or press F10 to print the record.

If you are adding new records, you can print a single record using the same technique. To print more than one record, however, you will need to use a slightly different method, as explained in the next section.

PRINTING MULTIPLE RECORDS

To print multiple records, after selecting Search/Update, complete the Retrieve Spec screen, and then press F10, or just press F10 to print all your records. Press Ctrl-F2 when a form is displayed and complete the File Print Options and Define Page menus. Press F10 to begin printing.

Now we will explore the Page Preview and Print to Screen printing options, and then print the records in the Clients database. Follow these steps:

1. Start Q&A and select Search/Update from the File menu.

2. Type **Clients** and press ⏎.

3. Press F10 to select all the records.

4. Press Ctrl-F2 to display the File Print Options menu.

5. Press ↓ to reach the Page Preview option, then ← to select Yes.

6. Press ↓ six times to reach the Number of Records per Page option and type **3**.

7. Press F8 to display the Define Page menu.

8. Type **85** for the Page Width option.

9. Press ↓, then Tab to reach the Right Margin option and type **80**.
    If the margins were any larger, the form would not fit on the
    page.

10. Press F10 to display the form on the screen.

Because you selected Page Preview, the screen changes to a full-page
graphic display, as shown in Figure 5.3.

The line at the bottom of the screen shows some of the commands that
you can use in preview mode, and the length of the page in lines. These
and the other commands that you can use in preview mode are summarized in Table 5.1.

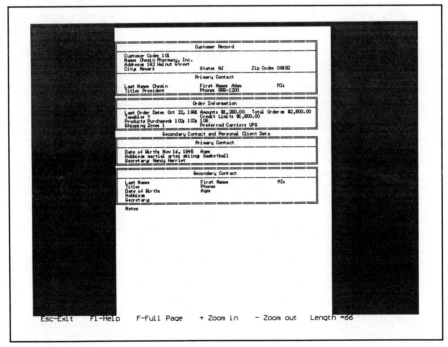

Figure 5.3: Full page in preview mode

Table 5.1: Preview Mode Commands

COMMAND	FUNCTION
+	Zooms in (enlarge) the display
–	Zooms out the display
2	Displays two facing pages
Ctrl-PgDn	Displays the next page
Ctrl-PgUp	Displays the previous page
Esc	Exits and returns to File menu
F	Displays full page
F1	Displays help information
F2	Returns to Print Options menu
H	Half view (same as pressing + from full-page view)
N	Normal view (same as pressing + twice from full-page view)
PgDn	Scrolls down on the current page
PgUp	Scrolls up on the current page

11. Press + to zoom in. This enlarges a portion of the screen, as shown in Figure 5.4.

12. Press + a second time to enlarge the display even further.

13. Press PgDn to scroll down the page.

14. Type **F** for a full-page display (or press – twice).

15. Press F2 to return to the File Print Options menu.

16. Type **S** to select Screen for the Print To option.

17. Press ↓, then → to turn off preview mode.

18. Press F10. Because you selected to print to the screen, the first record appears, as shown in Figure 5.5.

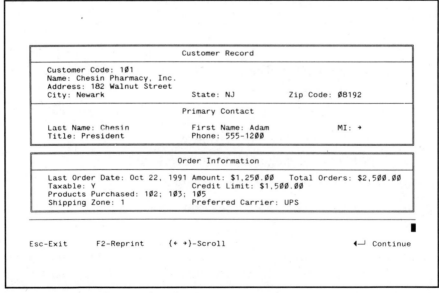

```
 ======================================================================
 ‖                          Customer Record
 ‖----------------------------------------------------------------------
 ‖ Customer Code: 101
 ‖ Name: Chesin Pharmacy, Inc.
 ‖ Address: 182 Walnut Street
 ‖ City: Newark                  State: NJ            Zip Code: 08192
 ‖----------------------------------------------------------------------
 ‖                          Primary Contact
 ‖----------------------------------------------------------------------
 ‖ Last Name: Chesin            First Name: Adam              MI:
 ‖ Title: President             Phone: 555-1200
 ‖======================================================================
 ‖                          Order Information
 ‖----------------------------------------------------------------------
 ‖ Last Order Date: Oct 22, 1991 Amount: $1,250.00  Total Orders: $2,500.0(
 ‖ Taxable: Y                   Credit Limit: $1,500.00
 ‖ Products Purchased: 102; 103: 105
 ‖ Shipping Zone: 1             Preferred Carrier: UPS
 ‖======================================================================
 ‖              Secondary Contact and Personal Client Data
 ‖======================================================================
 ‖                          Primary Contact
 ‖----------------------------------------------------------------------
 ‖ Date of Birth: Nov 16, 1945   Age:
 ‖ Hobbies: martial arts: skiing; basketball
 ‖ Secretary: Nancy Harriet
 ‖======================================================================

 Esc-Exit    F1-Help    F-Full Page    + Zoom in   - Zoom out   Length =66
```

Figure 5.4: Zoomed in preview

```
   +------------------------------------------------------------+
   |                      Customer Record                       |
   |------------------------------------------------------------|
   | Customer Code: 101                                         |
   | Name: Chesin Pharmacy, Inc.                                |
   | Address: 182 Walnut Street                                 |
   | City: Newark             State: NJ        Zip Code: 08192  |
   |------------------------------------------------------------|
   |                      Primary Contact                       |
   |------------------------------------------------------------|
   | Last Name: Chesin        First Name: Adam          MI: →   |
   | Title: President         Phone: 555-1200                   |
   +------------------------------------------------------------+

   +------------------------------------------------------------+
   |                     Order Information                      |
   |------------------------------------------------------------|
   | Last Order Date: Oct 22, 1991 Amount: $1,250.00  Total Orders: $2,500.00
   | Taxable: Y               Credit Limit: $1,500.00          |
   | Products Purchased: 102; 103; 105                         |
   | Shipping Zone: 1         Preferred Carrier: UPS           |
   +------------------------------------------------------------+


Esc-Exit      F2-Reprint     (← →)-Scroll               ←┘ Continue
```

Figure 5.5: Record printed to the screen

19. Press ↵ to display the next part of the record.

20. Press ↵ again to display the next record.

21. Press F2 to return to the File Print Options menu.

22. Select PtrA, and then press F10 to print the forms.

Q&A will report the page and line number being sent to the printer. The key-assignment line shows the options Esc, to cancel printing and return to the Print menu; and F2, to cancel printing and return to the File Print Options menu (so you can modify and reprint the report).

23. When the report is printed, press Esc to return to the File menu.

You can print single or multiple records from the Add Data or Search/Update function, but you cannot select specific fields, change their order, or print in neatly aligned columns. If you want to control these aspects of your printout, create printing specifications, as described in the next section.

USING PRINTING SPECIFICATIONS

When you use the F2 or Ctrl-F2 keystrokes to print records, all the fields print for each page of the record, even if the fields are blank. However, by using the Print option on the File menu, you can select which fields to print, their order, and the spacing on the page, as well as enhance the text with boldface, underlining, italic, and other fonts available on your printer. You can also align fields on columns. However, you cannot perform arithmetic on columns, such as calculating subtotals and totals.

Using the Print command, you create a printing specification, which is a description of the report you want to print. By saving the specification, you can quickly reprint the same report, or modify it to print different records.

You create a printing specification in five basic steps:

1. Complete the Retrieve Spec screen to select records.

2. Complete the Sort Spec screen, if desired.

3. Complete the Fields Spec screen to select and arrange fields.

4. Select options from the File Print Options menu.

5. Set the options on the Define Page menu.

The only new element in this process is the Fields Spec screen. This looks like the Retrieve Spec screen, except you use it to designate which fields should be printed, in what order, how they should be spaced, and if they should be enhanced. You control spacing using either of two methods: free-form or coordinate.

FREE-FORM PRINTING

In *free-form* printing, you determine the spacing between fields relative to each other. So, for example, you can tell Q&A to print the first name, skip one space, then print the last name. You can also set how many characters of a field prints.

If you want to print all the fields on your form, each on its own line, just press F10 when the Fields Spec screen appears.

Printing Specific Fields

When you want to print specific fields, you must designate the spacing between fields and, optionally, the order in which the fields will print. To print the contents of a field and then perform a carriage return, place an X after its label. To print the field on the same line as the next field you mark, enter a + next to the label. For example, the specification

```
Last:+      First:+      MI:X
Phone: X
```

will print the last name, first name, and middle initial on one line (in that order), then the phone number on the next line. Each of the fields will be separated with a space.

Add a number after + or X to increase the spaces. For example, +5 prints the field, then skips five spaces, X2 prints the field then performs two carriage returns before printing the next field.

Printing Fields in Custom Order

To print the fields in a special order, type a number from 1 to 9999 to indicate the order of the fields. Fields with numbers will be printed in that order, followed by fields with just an X or +.

When you number fields, however, you must follow the number with an indicator of how you want to space the following fields—you cannot have just a number by itself. Enter an X after the number to place the following field on the next line, or a + to leave one space between fields. For example, the specification

Last Name:3x2   First Name:1+   MI:2+

will print the person's full name on a line: the first name, followed by a space, the middle initial, followed by a space, then the last name. After the last name, Q&A will double space, then print the next field, if any. Add extra spaces between fields by including a number after the + sign, such as 1+2.

Limiting Field Width

If your field specification calls for more characters on a line than will fit, Q&A will automatically move extra text to the next line. You can, however, control how many characters of a field print using the syntax

$N + A, B$

where N is the field number, A is the number of spaces to leave between fields, and B is the number of characters to print.

For example, the specification to print the first three characters of a phone number, then skip three lines is

Telephone: 1x3,3

Use this syntax if you want to print several long fields on the same line. While you might lose some characters in some fields, your printout will be spaced as you planned.

COORDINATE PRINTING

With the coordinate printing method, you specify the exact line and character position where each field prints on the page. Use this method for aligning fields in columns or for printing on preprinted forms.

Follow each field with the line and column number where you want the field to print, such as

```
Last Name: 1,15      First Name:1,5      MI:
Telephone: 2,5
```

This specification will print the first name on the first line, starting at position 5, the last name on the first line at position 15, and then the phone number on the second line, position 5.

If you print more than one form per page, the line numbers become relative. The first record will print exactly as indicated. Subsequent records print in relation to the end of the last. For example, if the first field is marked to print on the fifth line, as in 5,5, the first record prints five lines down from the top of the page. Other records start five lines after the previous record.

You can use this method to create columnar reports quickly. Enter 1 as the row for all fields, then use the length of the field to determine where each column starts. Set the File Print Options menu to print multiple records on the page, and each record will appear as another row in the report, with the columns neatly aligned. If a field is longer than the column, add a third number indicating the number of characters to print; otherwise, text could be intermixed and unsightly. The specification 1,5,20, for instance, prints up to 20 characters of the field, starting on line 1, position 5. Since the longest entry in the column would end at position 25, you could start the next field at any position after that.

PRINTING FIELD LABELS

To print field labels, add L after the specification, as in 1,25,L. If a field label is too long or doesn't clearly indicate the field's meaning, you can specify another label to use instead. For example, the specification

```
Customer Code: 1,5,L(Code:)
Name: 2,5,L(Customer:)
Address: 3,15
```

will print as

Code: 101

Customer: Chesin Drugs

128 West Fifth Street

Notice that you do not have to label each field. Also, although the label was not printed with the address, the starting position aligns it under the start of the name. Using a colon with field labels that are added this way is optional.

PRINTING EXPANDED FIELDS

To print the full text of an expanded field, add E after the specification, as in 5XE. Use this technique to expand selected fields.

If you want to print all the expanded fields, use the Print Expanded Fields option on the Print Options menu.

CREATING A PRINTING SPECIFICATION

▮▮▮➤ **To define a print specification:**

1. **Select Print from the File menu and enter the database name.**

2. **Select Design/Redesign a Spec and enter a name.**
3. **Complete the Retrieve Spec and Sort Spec screens.**
4. **Designate the fields, their order, and specifications on the Fields Spec screen.**
5. **Use the Print Options and Define Page menu options if necessary, and then press F10.**

In this section, you will create a printing specification for a simple report that lists order information for each of the clients. This is the type of report you would print to review important information from your database.

Follow these steps to set up the report:

1. Select Print from the File menu and press ↵ to accept the Clients database. The Print menu will appear, as shown in Figure 5.6.

2. Press ↵ to select Design/Redesign a Spec, and the List Manager screen will display the available printing specifications for that database.

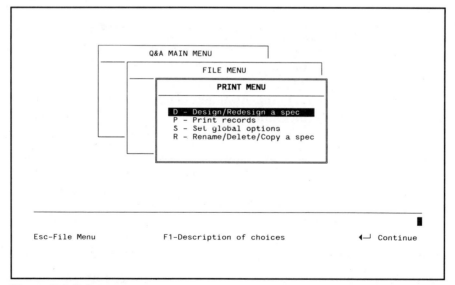

Figure 5.6: Print menu

3. Type **Order Information** and press ↵.

4. From the Retrieve Spec screen, press F8 to display the Sort Spec screen.

5. Press ↓ six times, then Tab twice to reach the Total Orders field.

6. Type **1, AS** to sort the records by this field in ascending order.

7. Press F10 to display the Fields Spec screen.

8. Press ↵ to reach the Name field and type **1X**, so that the name will print on its own line.

9. Press ↓ five times, press Tab twice to reach the Total Orders field, and type **2+,10,L**. This prints the Total Order field second, preceded by the field label, then skips 10 spaces.

10. Press Shift-Tab twice to reach the Last Order Date field, and press F6 to expand the field.

11. Type **3X,L(Most Recent Order:)** and press ↵.

12. Press Shift-Tab five times to reach the First Name field and type **4+,L(Contact:)**.

13. Press Tab to reach the MI field, press F6, type **5+**, and press ↵.

14. Press ↑ to reach the Last Name field and type **6+,10**.

15. Press ↓, then Tab to reach the Phone field and type **7X**. Figure 5.7 shows the completed Fields Spec screen.

In designing this specification, we went back and forth between fields to enter the numbers in sequential order. If you plan your specification in advance, you can enter the numbers in any sequence, moving from the first field to the last in the order they appear in the form.

Now, let's complete the printing specification and print the report.

16. Press F10 to display the File Print Options menu.

17. Press ↓ and select Yes for the Page Preview option.

18. Press ↓ six times to reach the Number of Records per Page option and type **10**.

19. Press F8 to display the Define Page menu.

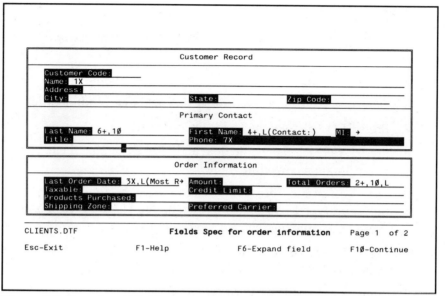

Figure 5.7: Completed Fields Spec screen

20. Type **85** for the Page Width option.

21. Press ↓ to reach the Left Margin option and type **10**.

22. Press Tab to reach the Right Margin option and type **75**.

23. Press ↓ three times to reach the Header option.

24. Type **!Order Information Report** on the first header line.

25. Press ↵ to reach the next header line and type **!@DATE**.

26. Press ↵ twice to reach the first footer line and type **!PAGE #**.

27. Press F10. Q&A saves your entries and displays the message

     Your print spec has been saved.
     Do you want to print the forms now?
     Y - Yes   N - No

28. Press ↵ to accept Yes.

Q&A looks for records meeting the listed criteria, and then displays the preview on the screen, as shown in Figure 5.8.

29. Press F2 to return to the File Print Options menu.

30. Press ↓, then ← to turn off preview mode.

31. Make sure your printer is turned on, and then press F10, then ↵ to print the records.

32. Press Esc to display the File menu.

Once Q&A starts to print the document, you can press Esc to cancel the printing and return to the Print menu, or press F2 to cancel and return to the File Print Options menu.

In the steps above, you reviewed the report in preview mode before printing it. After you saw that the fields were set up correctly, you pressed F2 to return to the Print Options menu, turned off the Page Preview option, then saved the specification again and printed the forms. If you had pressed Esc from the preview, the Print menu would have reappeared.

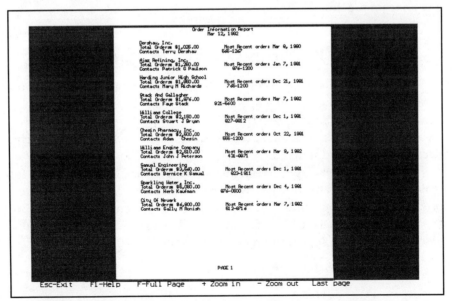

Figure 5.8: Results of the printing specification in preview mode

Previewing is a good way to make sure your printout will appear as you had envisioned, without wasting paper and waiting for an improperly designed report to print. If a report does not appear correct in preview mode, press F2 to return to the File Print Options menu. Change the options on this menu and the Define Page menu if necessary, or press F9 to go back to the Fields Spec screen; press F9 again to return to the Retrieve Spec screen. Redesign any aspect of the form, and then preview it again before printing it.

If you press Shift-F9 while a record is printing, Q&A displays the message

Which Spec? R-Retrieve S-Sort F-Fields P-Print A-Page

at the bottom of the screen. Press the indicated letter to return directly to one of the screens listed. For example, if you want to cancel a printout and change the Sort Spec screen, press Shift-F9 S. When you change the specification and press F10, printing will begin automatically—you do not have the opportunity to return to the File Print Options menu first. Shift-F9 works when you select any Print To option, but it does not have any effect in preview mode.

USING PRINTING SPECIFICATIONS

After adding or editing records, you might want a printout of the updated data. Since the printing specification is saved with your database, you can print reports using that specification at any time. Select Print from the File menu, enter the name of the database, and then choose Print Records from the Print menu.

When the List Manager screen displays the printing specifications for that database, select the one you want to use and press F10. You will see a prompt asking if you want to make any temporary changes to the printing specification. If you select No, the report will be printed. If you select Yes, you can change the specification before printing the report.

MODIFYING A PRINTING SPECIFICATION

To make permanent changes to a printing specification, select the Design/Redesign a Spec option from the Print menu, and then choose its name from the list that appears. Q&A will take you through each of the steps you followed to create the form, giving you the opportunity to change the Retrieve Spec, Sort Spec, and Fields Spec screens, as well as the File Print Options and Define Page menus.

OTHER PRINT MENU OPTIONS

To use other Print menu options:

- **Select Set Global Options to change the default settings for all File printing operations.**
- **Use the Rename/Delete/Copy option to manipulate printing specifications.**

The Print menu has two other options: Set Global Options and Rename/Delete/Copy.

Select Set Global Options to change the default values on the File Print Options and Define Page menus. You can change two separate sets of default values: one to use when printing records from the Add and Search/Update functions, and another set for printing records with the Print option.

The Rename/Delete/Copy option lets you organize and manipulate your printing specifications. Use it to change a specification's name, remove unwanted specifications from the database, or make duplicate copies that you can modify for other purposes. You can also perform these functions from the List Manager screen.

If you always use 8½-by-11-inch paper, set the default values in the

Define Page menu so that you do not have to adjust them each time you create a specification or print a record. We will do this now.

1. Select Print from the File menu and press ↵ to accept the Clients database.

2. Select Set Global Options to display the menu shown in Figure 5.9.

The first two options change the defaults used when printing with the Print option on the File menu. Your selections will affect any new printing specifications that you create, regardless of the database. However, existing printing specifications will not be affected.

Select the last two options to change default settings used when printing records with the Add and Search/Update options (F2 or Ctrl-F2).

3. Select Change Define Page Defaults.

4. Type **85** for the Page Width option.

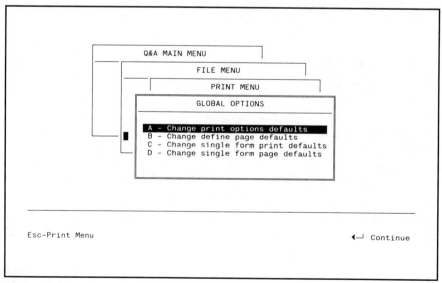

Figure 5.9: Global Options menu

5. Press ↓ to reach the Left Margin option and type **10**.

6. Press Tab to reach the Right Margin option and type **75**.

7. Press F10.

8. Select Change Single Form Page Defaults.

9. Type **85** for the Page Width option.

10. Press ↓ to reach the Left Margin option and type **10**.

11. Press Tab to reach the Right Margin option and type **75**.

12. Press F10.

13. Press Esc twice to return to the File menu.

ENHANCING YOUR PRINTOUTS WITH CHARACTER FORMATS AND FONTS

To enhance printouts with character formats and fonts:
1. **Place the cursor on the field specification.**
2. **Press Shift-F6 to display the enhancement menu.**
3. **Select the enhancement.**
4. **Use the arrow keys to highlight the text, and then press F10.**

On the Fields Spec screen, you can format your printout on a field-by-field basis using any of the character formats or fonts that Q&A supports for your printer.

FORMATTING FIELD DATA AND LABELS

You can format just the field data, the field label added with the L option, or both. Place the cursor on the first character of the specification you want to format, and press Shift-F6 to display the menu shown in Figure 5.10.

Select the format or font you want and press ⏎. You will see a message on the status line similar to

> Use the arrow keys to select the text you want to underline, then press F10

Move the cursor over the part of the specification you want to format and press F10. The formatted section will appear highlighted on the screen.

The position of the cursor before you press Shift-F6 is important. For example, suppose a field has the format 3X,L(Most Recent Order:). To format the entire specification, the cursor must be on the 3 or following the custom label so that you can press → or ← to select the entire specification.

To format just the data in the field, not the label, start with the cursor on the 3 or X to highlight just *3X*. To format just the label, start with the cursor on the L or) to highlight *L(Most Recent Order:)*.

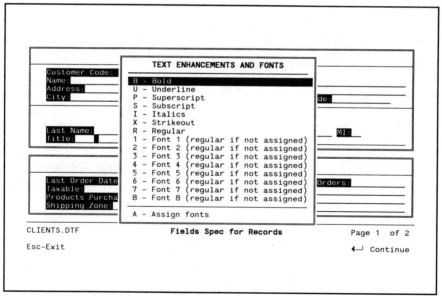

Figure 5.10: Enhancement options

ENHANCING HEADERS AND FOOTERS

You can use the same techniques to enhance the text of your headers or footers. Display the Define Page menu, and then place the cursor at the start of the text you want to enhance. Press Shift-F6, select the format or font, and then move the cursor to highlight the text.

PRINTING COLUMNAR REPORTS

If you want to print only a few fields for each record, it's best to align them in columns using the coordinate method. This makes the report easier to read and allows you to scan the page looking for specific information.

As an example, we will create the table of shipping information shown in Figure 5.11. Follow these steps:

1. Select Print from the File menu and press ↵.

3. Press ↵ to select Design/Redesign a Spec.

3. Type **Shipping Table** and press ↵ to display the Retrieve Spec screen.

4. Press ↓ nine times, then Tab to reach the Preferred Shipper field,

```
                    Shipping Information

   Zone                Name            City          State     Zip
    1         Chesin Pharmacy, Inc     Newark          NJ     08192

    1         Stack And Gallagher      Margate         NJ     08761

    1         Harding Junior High      Philadelphia    PA     19101

    1         Williams Engine Comp     Newark          NJ     08126

    2         City Of Newark           Newark          NJ     08163

    2         Williams College         Philadelphia    PA     10871

    3         Ajaz Refining, Inc.      Wilmington      DE     20192

    3         Sparkling Water, Inc     Margate         NJ     08156
```

Figure 5.11: Columnar report

type **UPS**, and then press F8 to display the Sort Spec screen.

5. Press ↓ nine times to reach the Shipping Zone field, type **1, AS**, and press F10 to display the Fields Spec screen.

6. Press ↓ nine times to reach the Shipping Zone field, and then type **1,2,1**.

7. Press ↑ eight times to reach the Name field and type **1,15,20**.

8. Press ↓ twice to reach the City field and type **1,40,15**.

9. Press Tab to reach the State field, press F6 to expand the field, and type **1,59,2**.

10. Press ↵ to reach the Zip Code field and type **1,66,5**.

11. Press F10 to display the Print Options menu. Figure 5.12 shows the completed Fields Spec screen.

12. Press ↓ seven times to display the Number of Records per page option and type **50**.

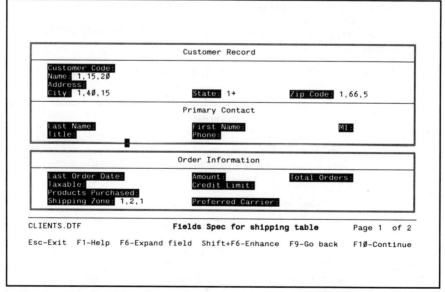

Figure 5.12: Columnar reportCompleted field specification for column printout

13. Press F8 to display the Define Page menu.

The new default values are already in place. Since this report is wide, however, let's change the left margin to five spaces.

14. Press ↓ to reach the Left Margin option, press F4 to delete its contents, and then type **5**.

15. Press ↓ three times to reach the Header option and type **!Shipping Information**.

16. Press ↵ twice to reach the last header line.

Now you can enter the column headings for the report.

17. Type **Zone**, press the spacebar 17 times, type **Name**, press the spacebar 15 times, type **City**, press the spacebar 13 times, type **State**, press the spacebar 4 times, and then type **Zip**.

18. Press ↵ twice to reach the second footer line and type **!PAGE #**.

19. Press F10, then ↵ to print the records.

20. Press Esc to return to the Main menu.

If your columns are not aligned properly, you did not leave adequate spacing between fields. You will have to either limit the number of characters that print or adjust the spacing.

In this chapter, you learned about the options and methods for printing your database records. The next chapter takes record printing one step further—you will learn how to create and print sophisticated columnar and statistical reports using the information in your database.

6

Building
Q&A
Reports

Q&A File's printing function allows you to print records and produce quick reports. For more control over the format and content of your database reports, you can use the Report option on the Main menu.

Report lets you construct two types of reports: columnar and crosstab. After you design a report, you can quickly reprint it at any time to reflect the current data in your file. You can have up to 200 reports per database, although you can create any number of temporary reports by modifying others.

PRODUCING COLUMNAR REPORTS

As when you print reports with File, you select from Print Options and Define Page menus to set page size, margins, headers, footers, and specify printing options. Also, your reports are stored with individual databases. For example, a report you design for and save with the Clients database will not be available for the Vendors database, even though the forms are similar.

You start creating a report by filling in the Retrieve Spec screen to designate which records you want to include. However, instead of completing the Sort Spec and Fields Spec screens, you use the Column/Sort Spec screen, shown in Figure 6.1. Here you designate which fields print and in what order, as well as create column breaks for calculating subtotals and other results.

DEFINING COLUMN BREAKS

A *column break* (also known as a *control break*) occurs when the contents of a field change, and it signals Q&A to perform some special processing.

The report shown in Figure 6.2 illustrates how column breaks are used. It lists the prices of properties sold by real estate agents. Each of the

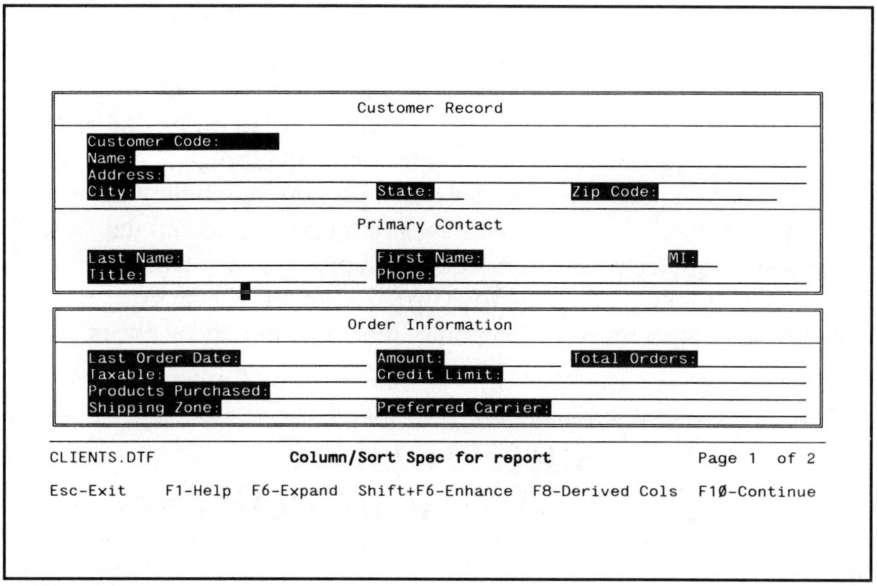

```
                          Customer Record

 Customer Code:
 Name:
 Address:
 City:                          State:        Zip Code:

                          Primary Contact

 Last Name:                     First Name:              MI:
 Title:                         Phone:

                          Order Information

 Last Order Date:               Amount:        Total Orders:
 Taxable:                       Credit Limit:
 Products Purchased:
 Shipping Zone:                 Preferred Carrier:

 CLIENTS.DTF          Column/Sort Spec for report          Page 1  of 2

 Esc-Exit    F1-Help  F6-Expand  Shift+F6-Enhance  F8-Derived Cols  F1Ø-Continue
```

Figure 6.1: Column/Sort Spec screen

prices is taken from a different record. Notice that the agent's name in the first column appears only once; it is not repeated on each line of the report. Sorting the file by agent grouped the records together so it isn't necessary to repeat the agent name next to each sale.

The column break occurs when the contents of the Agent field change from one value to another. In this case, when the field changes from Chesin to Hall, Q&A calculates and prints the subtotal of Chesin's sales, then prints the next agent's name. The next column break occurs when the agent's name changes from Hall to Walker. Again, Q&A calculates and prints the subtotal, then prints the next agent's name, Walker. The final column break occurs after the last record. Q&A calculates and prints both Walker's subtotal and the grand total.

The column break is useful because it groups information based on the value of the field. In this case, you can quickly see the total of each agent's sales.

```
Agent          Price
------         ---------------
Chesin          $147,650.00
                $143,250.00
                 $79,050.00
                $158,150.00
                $374,100.00
                $165,650.00
               ---------------
Total:        $1,067,850.00

Hall            $99,250.00
                $37,000.00
                $427,400.00
                $157,375.00
                 $18,275.00
                $100,025.00
                $142,250.00
                $129,275.00
               ---------------
Total:        $1,110,850.00

Walker          $141,500.00
                $283,800.00
                $727,250.00
                $147,500.00
                 $98,075.00
                $138,700.00
                 $76,030.00
                 $62,475.00
                $184,425.00
               ---------------
Total:        $1,859,755.00

======        ===============
Total:        $4,038,455.00
```

Figure 6.2: Report with one column break

Figure 6.3 illustrates two levels of column breaks: one on the first column, with subtotals being calculated for each agent; and another on the second column for the Style field. The break in that column occurs when the style changes from Condo to Single. Subtotals are calculated on both column breaks—for each style and for each agent.

If the field is a date field, you can also specify the column break to occur when the day, month, or year changes. For example, you could get a printout of your daily invoices or monthly bills.

You specify the order in which the fields appear by numbering the field labels on the Column/Sort Spec screen, as you do in a File printing specification. After the number, you indicate the sort order, the type of break, and any calculation and formatting codes.

```
Agent      Style      Price           Commissions
------     ------     --------------- -----------
Chesin     Condo          $79,050.00    $3,952.50
                      --------------- -----------
           Total:         $79,050.00    $3,952.50

           Single        $147,650.00    $7,382.50
                         $165,650.00    $8,282.50
                         $158,150.00    $7,907.50
                         $374,100.00   $18,705.00
                         $143,250.00    $7,162.50
                      --------------- -----------
           Total:        $988,800.00   $49,440.00

                      --------------- -----------
Total:               $1,067,850.00    $53,392.50

Hall       Condo         $142,250.00    $7,112.50
                         $100,025.00    $5,001.25
                      --------------- -----------
           Total:        $242,275.00   $12,113.75

           Single         $99,250.00    $4,962.50
                          $37,000.00    $1,850.00
                         $157,375.00    $7,868.75
                         $129,275.00    $6,463.75
                         $427,400.00   $21,370.00
                          $18,275.00      $913.75
                      --------------- -----------
           Total:        $868,575.00   $43,428.75

                      --------------- -----------
Total:               $1,110,850.00    $55,542.50

Walker     Condo          $62,475.00    $3,123.75
                         $184,425.00    $9,221.25
                          $98,075.00    $4,903.75
                      --------------- -----------
           Total:        $344,975.00   $17,248.75

           Single        $727,250.00   $36,362.50
                         $147,500.00    $7,375.00
                         $283,800.00   $14,190.00
                          $76,030.00    $3,801.50
                         $141,500.00    $7,075.00
                         $138,700.00    $6,935.00
                      --------------- -----------
           Total:      $1,514,780.00   $75,739.00

                      --------------- -----------
Total:               $1,859,755.00    $92,987.75

======     ======   =============== ===========
Total:               $4,038,455.00   $201,922.75
```

Figure 6.3: Report with two column breaks

Indicating the Sort Order

Your first column break must be in the first column. Second and third column breaks occur in the second and third columns.

You create a column break by sorting the column break field or fields using one of these codes:

AS Ascending sort

DS Descending sort

MS Ascending sort by the month and year (must be the only sort/break code)

YS Ascending sort by the year (must be the only sort/break code)

The records will be listed in the sorted order, with the column break occurring when the data in a field changes. Entering 1,AS in the State field, for example, would place the state in the first column, in ascending order, and process a column break when the state changes.

To print a list of clients by their last order date, for example, you would enter 1,MS in the Last Order Date field. Your records will be grouped according to the month and year, with the column break occurring when the month and year change—all clients who last ordered in November 1991 will be grouped together; clients who last ordered in December 1991 will be in the next group.

You can further refine the column break by following AS or DS with any of the following codes:

AB Column break on the first letter

CS Cancel subcalculations and skipped lines

DB Column break when the day changes

MB Column break when the month changes

P Start a new page on the column break

R Repeat the sorted values

YB Column break when the year changes

Entering 1,AS,AB in a name field, for example, will sort records in ascending order by the last name but process a column break when the first letter of the name changes. All your clients whose names start with A will be in one group, B in another, and so on.

Use DB, MB, and YB to refine a column break on a date field when you use AS or DS for the sort. Use the R code to repeat the contents of the field for each line of the report, rather than print it only once in each group.

Calculating in Column Breaks

You define the processing that takes place at a column break by entering the following codes:

A	Column averages
C	Column counts
MAX	Maximum value
MIN	Minimum value
SA	Subaverages
SC	Subcounts
SMAX	Submaximum value
SMIN	Subminimum value
SSTD	Substandard deviation
ST	Subtotals
STD	Standard deviation
SVAR	Subvariance
T	Column total
VAR	Variance

If you want to calculate and print a subtotal at each column break, for example, add ST after the specification of the field you want to subtotal. Use T to print a grand total at the end of the column. Q&A will automatically insert the word *Total:*, *Average:*, or other appropriate label at the column breaks.

Place the code in the field you want to calculate, not the one used for the column break. For example, suppose you want to print a report on total orders by state. Your specification would include these entries:

State: 1,AS
Total Orders: 2,ST,T

The State field will be used for the first column, in ascending order. The values in the Total Orders field will appear in the second column. At each column break—when the state changes—Q&A will calculate and print the subtotal of total orders for that state. At the end of the report, Q&A will calculate and print the grand total for all states.

Formatting Columns

To adjust the format of the contents of the column, use the following codes:

F(C)	With commas (money and numbers)
F(Dn)	Use date format n
F(Hn)	Use time format n
F(JC)	Justify center
F(JL)	Justify left
F(JR)	Justify right
F(M)	Format as money
F(Nn)	Use n decimal digits
F(T)	Format as text
F(TR)	Truncate to fit
F(U)	Format in uppercase
F(WC)	Format without commas

H(*A:B:text*)   Set column width at *A*, indent the second and following lines *B* characters, replace the column heading with *text* (use the options by themselves or in any combination)

You can use more than one format code in a column, but only one of each type. For example, use only one of the codes JR, JL, or JC; one of the codes C or WC; one of the codes D*n*, H, N*n*, M, or T. Combine codes within one set of parentheses, as in F(JR, T).

Q&A separates the column heads and subcalculations with a single dashed line (------) and final calculations with a double line (=======). You can print other characters for the column head separator lines by using the code HS followed by the characters you want to appear. Entering HS(+), for example, will separate the column heads with a lines of + symbols. To change the subcalculation separator lines, use the code SL followed by the characters. For example, SL(*-*) will separate subcalculations with lines that look like *-**-**-**-*.

The field's name is used as the column heading, and each column is as wide as the heading or the largest entry in the column, whichever is greater. If a field name is three characters long, and the longest entry is ten characters, the column will be ten characters wide.

Calculated subtotals or totals, however, may be wider than the largest number in the column. Adding two five-digit numbers, for instance, might result in a six-digit total. If the subtotal or total is wider than the column, Q&A prints a series of asterisks in its place:

```
Sales      989.11

Rentals    246.44

           ======

Total:     ******
```

If this occurs in your report, widen the column by designating a new column width with the H command, such as 30,T,H(12). To include a new column heading as well, separate it with a colon, as in 30,T, H(12:Totals). Q&A assumes the number indicates width in characters. To set columns in inches or centimeters, use " or CM, as in H(1") or H(25CM).

If you want each section of the report to print on its own page, add the code P at the appropriate column break field. For example, you could print the information for each state or city on a separate page.

If your report has more columns than will fit across a page, Q&A displays the message shown in Figure 6.4 when you try to print or preview the report.

To stop the process, choose Cancel Printing. If you select Split Report Across Pages, Q&A prints as many columns as will fit on a page and continues with additional pages until all the columns have been printed. If you want to print the report on a single page, select Edit Option & Reprint. Then you can group the columns, as explained later in the chapter, or try a smaller font or different margins. To print only what will fit on a page, choose Truncate Report and Continue.

SETTING UP A COLUMNAR REPORT

Now let's suppose that you would like to visit your clients to stimulate business. In planning your visits, you need to know which states and cities generate more business. We will start by creating a report with two column breaks that calculates subtotals and totals.

1. Select Report from the Main menu to display the Report menu.

This menu includes the same options as the Print menu, but they relate to reports rather than printing specifications for records.

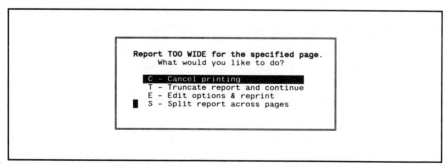

Figure 6.4: Warning message for wide reports

2. Press ↵ to accept Design/Redesign a Report.

3. Type **Clients** at the file name prompt and press ↵ . The List Manager screen will display the names of any existing reports for that database.

4. Type **Sales by State** and press ↵ . You will see a prompt with the options

   C - Columnar Report   X - Crosstab Report

5. Press ↵ to accept Columnar Report and display the Retrieve Spec screen.

When you want to limit the report to specific records, enter the criteria on this Retrieve Spec screen.

6. Press F10 to display the Column/Sort Spec screen.

7. Press ↓ three times to reach the City field and type **20,AS**.

This will create a column break, with city names in ascending order, in what will be the second column. The processing that you define for the Total Orders column will occur when the city name changes.

8. Press Tab to reach the State field, and then press F6 to expand the field.

9. Type **10,AS** and press ↵ .

The first column will contain a column break on the state name in ascending order. Processing will occur when the state name changes.

10. Press ↓ three times, press Tab to reach the Total Orders field, press F6, type **30,ST,T,H(12:Total!Orders)**, and then press ↵ . Your screen should look like the one shown in Figure 6.5.

This will create a third column containing the Total Orders field, with

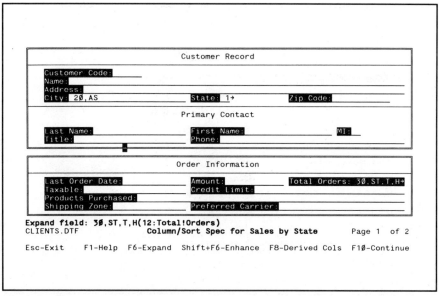

Figure 6.5: Completed Column/Sort Spec screen

subtotals on the two column breaks—one subtotal for each city and one for each state—and a grand total at the end of the column. The H option changes the default heading. Although we used the same field name, we included an exclamation point between the words to divide the heading into two lines.

11. Press F10 to display the Report Print Options menu.

As shown in Figure 6.6, the menu is similar to the File Print Options menu you used in Chapter 5. We will describe the options that are specific to Report after we complete this sales report.

12. Press ↓, press ← to select Preview Page, and then press F10. You will see the prompt

Your design has been saved.

Do you want to print the report now?

 Y - Yes   N - No

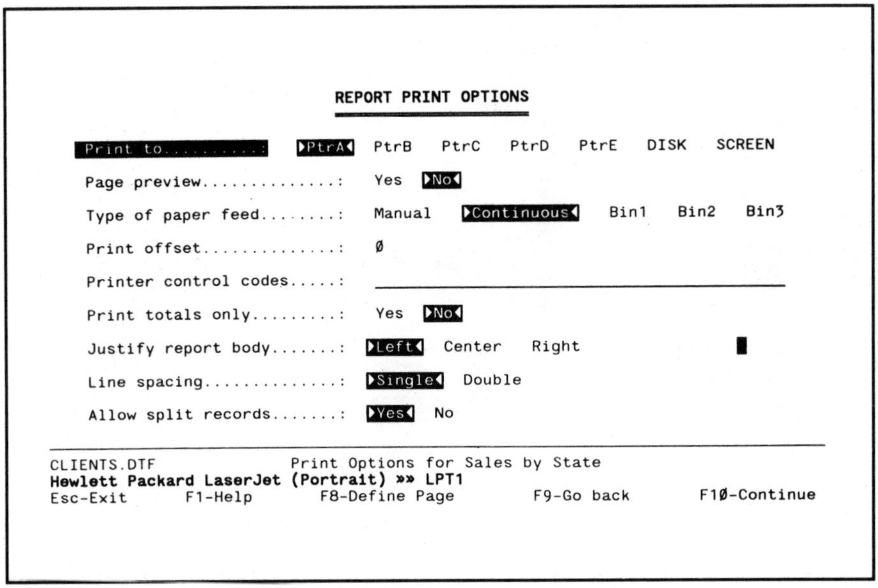

```
                        REPORT PRINT OPTIONS


          Print to..........:     ▶PtrA◀   PtrB   PtrC   PtrD   PtrE   DISK   SCREEN

          Page preview..............:    Yes   ▶No◀

          Type of paper feed........:    Manual   ▶Continuous◀   Bin1   Bin2   Bin3

          Print offset..............:    Ø

          Printer control codes.....:    _____

          Print totals only.........:    Yes   ▶No◀

          Justify report body.......:    ▶Left◀   Center   Right              ▮

          Line spacing..............:    ▶Single◀   Double

          Allow split records.......:    ▶Yes◀   No

         _____
         CLIENTS.DTF            Print Options for Sales by State
         Hewlett Packard LaserJet (Portrait) »» LPT1
         Esc-Exit      F1-Help       F8-Define Page      F9-Go back      F1Ø-Continue
```

Figure 6.6: Report Print Options menu

13. Press ↵ to accept Yes. Your preview should look like Figure 6.7.

14. Press Esc to return to the Report menu.

The other options on the Report Print Options menu allow you to control the contents and format of your reports:

- Print Totals Only: By default, this is set to No, and Q&A prints the data from individual records. To print just the subcalculations and totals, select Yes.

- Justify Report Body: This option controls the alignment of the report in relation to the left and right margins. Your choices are Left, Center, and Right.

- Line Spacing: Choose between single- or double-line spacing.

- Allow Split Records: By default, this option is set to Yes, and a record may be split at a page break. If you select No, Q&A will move the entire record to the next page.

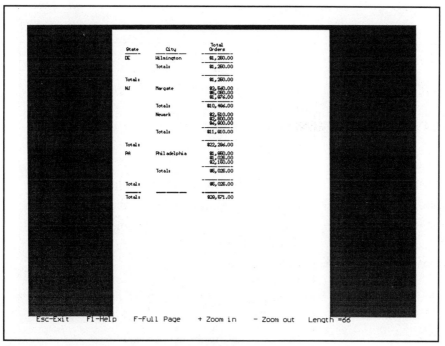

Figure 6.7: Preview of Sales by State report

ADDING INFORMATION WITH DERIVED COLUMNS

To create a derived column:

1. **From the Column/Sort Spec screen, press F8.**
2. **On the Derived Columns screen, enter the column heading, formula, and column specification.**

A derived column is one calculated from information in other fields. For example, the database used to create the report shown in Figure 6.3 does not include a Commissions field. The information in that column—a derived column—was calculated by taking five percent of the Sales Price field.

You can use addition, subtraction, multiplication, and division in the calculations, as well as the functions listed in Table 6.1. For example, you

Table 6.1: Q&A Functions Useful for Database Reports

FUNCTION	RESULT
@TOTALS(n)	Calculates the grand total of the values in column n.
@AVERAGE(n)	Calculates the grand average of the values in column n.
@COUNT(n)	Counts the values in column n.
@MINIMUM(n)	Finds the minimum value in column n.
@MAXIMUM(n)	Finds the maximum value in column n.
@TOTAL(n, m)	Calculates the total values in column n at the break in column m.
@AVERAGE(n, m)	Calculates the average values in column n at the break in column m.
@COUNT(n, m)	Counts the values in column n at the break in column m.
@DATE	Inserts the current date.
@MINIMUM(n, m)	Finds the minimum value in column n at the break in column m.
@MAXIMUM(n, m)	Finds the maximum value in column n at the break in column m.
@TIME	Inserts the current time.

could subtract a date field, such as one called Date Started, from @DATE (the current date) to derive a column called Time Spent on Project. You will learn how Q&A functions work in this and later chapters (also refer to Appendix B for a summary of the functions).

Now we will improve the Sales by State report by adding a derived column.

1. Press ↵ twice to accept Design/Redesign a Report and the Clients database.

2. Select Sales by State, and then press ↵ to display the Retrieve Spec screen.

3. Press F10 to display the Column/Sort Spec screen.

4. Press F8 to display the Derived Columns screen, shown in Figure 6.8.

You can create up to 16 derived columns in a report. The cursor is at the Heading prompt for the first derived column.

5. Type **Percent of !State Total**.

6. Press ↵ to reach the Formula prompt.

7. Type **#30 / @TOTAL(#30, #10) * 100**.

This formula tells Q&A to calculate the record's total orders percent of the overall total for the state. In essence, it says "divide the figure in column 3 (the total order amount for a single record) by the total figure in column 3 (caused by the column break in column 1), then multiply the result by 100." Since column 1 represents the state, the state total will be

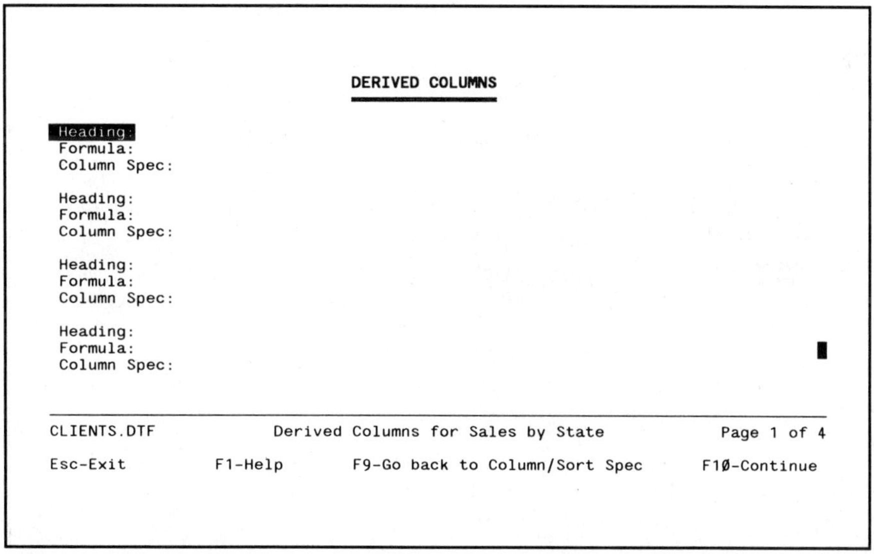

```
                          DERIVED COLUMNS
                          ━━━━━━━━━━━━━━━━

        Heading:
        Formula:
        Column Spec:

        Heading:
        Formula:
        Column Spec:

        Heading:
        Formula:
        Column Spec:

        Heading:
        Formula:
        Column Spec:                                        ▮
        ────────────────────────────────────────────────────────────
        CLIENTS.DTF          Derived Columns for Sales by State      Page 1 of 4

        Esc-Exit        F1-Help      F9-Go back to Column/Sort Spec    F10-Continue
```

Figure 6.8: Derived Columns screen

used in the calculation. The spaces in the formula make it easier to read, but they are not required.

8. Press ↵ to reach the Column Spec prompt and type **40,F(N2)**.

This designates the fourth column, formatted with two decimal places.

9. Press ↵ to reach the Heading prompt of the next column and type **Percent of !Grand Total**.

10. Press ↵ to reach the Formula prompt.

11. Type **#30 / @TOTAL(#30) * 100**.

This calculates the percent each record is of the grand total in column 3, because a column break was not specified.

12. Press ↵ to reach the Column Spec prompt and type **50,F(N2)**. Figure 6.9 shows the derived column specifications.

13. Press F10 to display the Report Print Options menu.

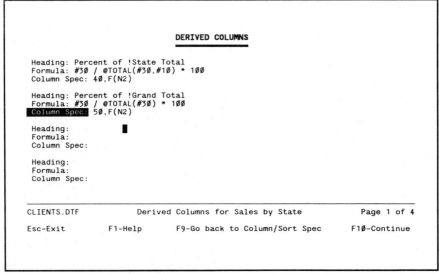

```
                         DERIVED COLUMNS
                         ───────────────

      Heading: Percent of !State Total
      Formula: #30 / @TOTAL(#30,#10) * 100
      Column Spec: 40,F(N2)

      Heading: Percent of !Grand Total
      Formula: #30 / @TOTAL(#30) * 100
      Column Spec: 50,F(N2)

      Heading:                  █
      Formula:
      Column Spec:

      Heading:
      Formula:
      Column Spec:

      ──────────────────────────────────────────────────────
      CLIENTS.DTF      Derived Columns for Sales by State      Page 1 of 4

      Esc-Exit      F1-Help     F9-Go back to Column/Sort Spec      F10-Continue
```

Figure 6.9: Derived column specification

14. Press ↓, then ← to select Preview Page.

15. Press F10, then ↵ to save the design.

Q&A scans the database for matching records, and then displays a message notifying you that it has to make several passes through the database to process the report. Each line of the report cannot be generated until the subtotals and grand totals are calculated. Q&A has to make one entire pass through the database to calculate the subtotals and grand totals, then make a second pass to print the individual lines.

After the calculations are completed, the report will appear on your screen, as shown in Figure 6.10. Now let's add headers and footers to this report.

16. Press F2 to return to the Report Print Options menu.

17. Press F8 to display the Define Page menu.

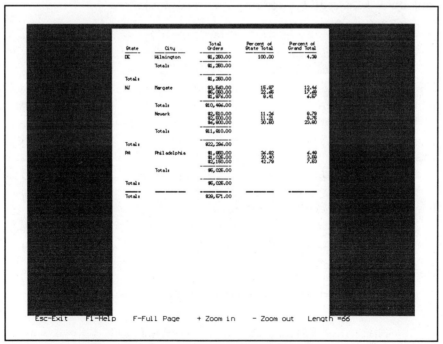

Figure 6.10: Report with two derived columns

18. In the first header line, type **!Total Orders by State and City**.

19. In the third header line, type **Prepared on: @DATE!!@TIME**.

20. In the first footer line, type **!Page /##**.

21. Press F10, then ↵ to save the design and preview the report.

22. Press Esc to return to the Report menu.

CALCULATING WITH INVISIBLE COLUMNS

To create an invisible column:

1. **Choose to design or print a columnar report.**
2. **If you select to print, press Y to make temporary changes.**
3. **On the Column/Sort Spec screen, enter an I at the end of the column specification for the field. The data in that field will not print, but will be used for derived column calculations.**

An *invisible column* is one that does not appear in the report but is generated internally as the report is printed. The figures in the column, as well as any subtotals, totals, and other calculations, are then available for use by derived columns.

For example, suppose that you are only interested in the two percentage columns of our Sales by State report, not the actual amount of total orders for each state. You couldn't leave out the third column of the report because the total order amounts and the subtotals and totals are needed to derive the percentages. Instead, you can make the column invisible by adding the I code to its column specification.

Follow these steps to make a temporary change to the Sales by State report so it displays only the state, city, and two derived percentage columns:

1. From the Report menu, select Print a Report and press ↵ to accept Clients.

2. Select Sales by State and press ↵. You will be asked if you want to make any temporary changes to the report.

3. Press Y, then ↵ to display the Retrieve Spec screen.

4. Press F10 to display the Column/Sort Spec screen.

5. Press ↓ six times, then Tab twice to reach the Total Orders field.

6. Press F6 to expand the field.

7. Press End to reach the end of the specification, type **I**, and press ↵.

8. Press F8 to display the Derived Columns screen.

9. Edit the Column Spec entry for the first derived column to read **40,ST,F(N2)**.

If the ST command were after the F(N2), only the detail lines would be formatted as two decimal places, not the subtotals.

10. Edit the Column Spec entry for the second derived column to read **50,ST,F(N2)**.

11. Press F10 twice to display the report.

The finished report appears as shown in Figure 6.11. The Total Orders column does not appear, but its contents are used to calculate the derived columns. The percentages are shown for each individual record; however, without any additional information about the record, these figures are meaningless. So, let's change the report just to list the state subtotals.

12. Press F2 to return to the Report Print Options menu.

13. Press ↓ five times to reach the Print Totals Only option.

14. Press ← to select Yes, then F10 to print the report. It should look like Figure 6.12.

15. Press Esc to return to the Report menu.

Because of the way Q&A rounds figures to display two decimal places, some totals might appear as 99.99 instead of 100.

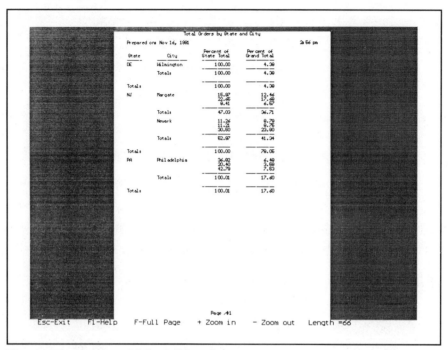

Figure 6.11: Report with invisible column

GENERATING KEYWORD REPORTS

In Chapter 2, you learned that a keyword field can store repeated values. The usefulness of keyword fields becomes apparent when you have Q&A separate the values in a field to generate reports.

The Clients database contains several keyword fields: the Products Purchased and Hobbies fields for the primary and secondary contacts. As an example, we will use the Products Purchased field to print a report analyzing sales. In planning a marketing campaign, we would like to see which clients purchase each of our products. We'll also count the number of clients who purchase each product. Follow these steps:

1. Press ↵ twice to accept Design/Redesign a Report and the Clients database.

2. Type **Products** and press ↵.

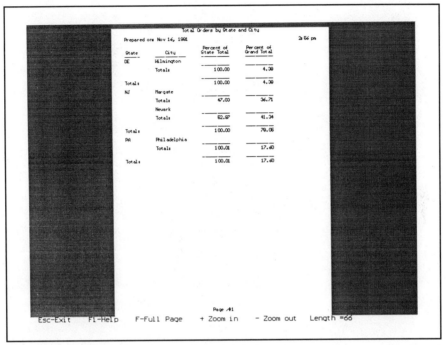

Figure 6.12: Report showing totals only

3. Type **C** to create a columnar report and to display the Retrieve Spec screen.

4. Press F10 to display the Column/Sort Spec screen.

5. Press ↵ to reach the Name field and type **2,SC.**

6. Press ↓ seven times to reach the Products Purchased field and type **1,K,AS**.

7. Press F10 to display the Report Print Options menu.

8. Press ↓, then ← to select Preview Page.

9. Press F10, then ↵ to save the report. Your preview should look like Figure 6.13.

10. Press Esc to return to the Report menu.

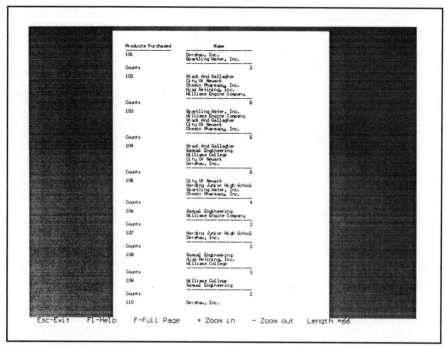

Figure 6.13: Keyword report

If you were only interested in the number of clients who purchased each product, not their names, you would select Yes for the Print Totals Only option.

The only problem with keyword reports is that they will include all the keywords in the field. For example, suppose you want a list of the primary contacts interested in baseball. On the Retrieve Spec screen, you would enter Baseball in the Hobbies field. In the Column/Sort Spec screen, you would enter 1,K in the Hobbies field, then number the name and phone fields as desired. Your report would be similar to the one shown in Figure 6.14. As you can see, Q&A located only the records that contain baseball in the Hobbies field, but it also printed the other hobbies listed in those records.

```
        Hobbi es       Last Name      First Name     MI
        --------       ---------      ----------     --
        Baseball       Roni sh        Sally          M
                       Dershaw        Terry

        Hockey         Dershaw        Terry

        sailing        Dershaw        Terry

        skiiing        Roni sh        Sally          M
```

Figure 6.14: Keyword report showing extra data

COMBINING COLUMN SPECIFICATIONS FOR USEFUL REPORTS

By specifying both derived and invisible columns in a report, you can produce informative reports. As an example, Figure 6.15 shows a report from a student database. This report includes student names, their grades, and a running grade average. Although the report doesn't appear to be in order of any of the columns, it is sorted in descending order by the Attendance field to show how attendance affects overall grade average.

The report was created from a database that contains, among other fields, each student's name, grade for the course, number of days attendance, and class (freshman, sophomore, junior, or senior). The Column/Sort Spec screen for the report looks like this:

    Name: 2, F(JR,U), H(15)
    Grade: 3
    Attendance: 1, DS, I
    Class:

Because the first column is invisible, Q&A doesn't process a column break when the values change, but it still sorts the records in that order.

Three derived columns were used to calculate the running averages:

    Heading:
    Formula: #4 + 1
    Column Spec: 4,I

```
figure
                                       Running
                     Name        Grade Averages
                ---------------   -----  --------
                     COLRIDGE      95     95.00
                      WALLACH      98     96.50
                      ROBERTS      91     94.67
                     CORTLAND      95     94.75
                       RIVERA      97     95.20
                    ENGLEHART      95     95.17
                        JONES      95     95.14
                    GOLDSMITH      95     95.13
                        EWING      93     94.89
                         YANG      85     93.90
                       SIRAVO      93     93.82
                    JEFFERSON      84     93.00
                         RYAN      94     93.08
                       KOPLAN      85     92.50
                      ROSSINI      94     92.60
                        ADAMS      86     92.19
                        WELSH      86     91.82
                     AUERBACH      86     91.50
                     BUCHANAN      89     91.37
                       SAVAGE      74     90.50
                       CHESIN      75     89.76
                     NEIBAUER      73     89.00
                          KIM      73     88.30
                       MARTIN      76     87.79
                      FLEMING      75     87.28
                        KELLY      75     86.81
                         KANE      74     86.33
                      FORMANN      65     85.57
                  HILDENBRAND      46     84.21
                   MONTGOMERY      55     83.23
                      GERBINO      56     82.35
```

Figure 6.15: Report using invisible and derived columns

Heading:
Formula: #5 + #3
Column Spec: 5,I

Heading:Running!Average
Formula: #5 / #4
Column Spec: 6,F(N2)

Column 4 keeps a running, invisible count of students using a counter algorithm. Column 5, another invisible column, accumulates the grades. Finally, column 6, the third printed column in the report, calculates the running average by dividing the running total by the count. The average is displayed with two decimal places.

PRODUCING CROSSTAB REPORTS

A *crosstab* report is a statistical analysis that shows the relationship between two or three fields. Figure 6.16 shows an example of a crosstab report for a database containing student grades, days of attendance, and year (1 for freshman, 2 for sophomore, and so on). The report shows the relationship between the days of attendance and the average grade by class. You can see that as attendance decreases, so does the average grade. Students that attend 170 days or more, for example, have an average grade of 93.90, while those attending between 160 and 169 days have an average grade of only 88.56.

The report also breaks down the analysis by class. The bottom row of the report indicates that the average grade increases somewhat with class; the average freshman grade is 76.60, and the average senior grade is 85.73. The other rows of the report reflect the general relationship between attendance and grades, although well-attending freshman seem to have a slightly higher average grade (95) than well-attending seniors (93).

When you create a crosstab report, you tell Q&A which fields to use for the analysis. You must designate the field to use for the rows of the report, the field to use for the columns, and the field to summarize. The row field determines the values listed down the left side of the report. The column field determines the values, or headers, on top of each column. The summary field determines all the other calculated and displayed values.

For the report in Figure 6.16, the Grade field was selected to be summarized, or analyzed in relation to the other two fields. All the figures in the report, except the row and column labels, represent grades.

```
                              Year
                  --------------------------   Average
                                                Grade
Attendance          1      2      3      4
----------------  -----  -----  -----  -----   =======
>=170             95.00  91.00  96.00  93.00    93.90
>=160..<=169      85.00  89.00  89.75  88.00    88.56
>=150..<=159      74.00  74.50  75.00  74.50    74.43
<=149             55.00  56.00  60.00  65.00    59.20
================  =====  =====  =====  =====    =======
Average Grade     76.60  77.00  84.20  85.73    82.35
```

Figure 6.16: Crosstab report using three fields

The Attendance field was used for the rows, and attendances were grouped together in four ranges. The first row represents the average grades (the summarized field) of students who attended 170 or more days. The second row represents the average grades of students who attended between 160 and 169 days. If attendances were not grouped, the report would have a separate row for each different number in the Attendance field.

The Year field was used for the columns. Therefore, the figures under column 1 are the average grades of freshmen students broken down by the four attendance ranges.

Figure 6.17 shows another crosstab report generated from the same database but using only the Grade and Year fields, not Attendance. Although this report is useful for summarizing average grades by year, it does not provide the same insights as the previous report. In this case, the same field, Grade, was used for both the row and summary fields.

```
                           Year
                 --------------------------------  Average
       Grade        1      2      3      4         Grade
       --------- ------ ------ ------ ------     =======
       >=90       95.00  91.00  95.00  94.80       94.58
       >=80..<=89 85.00  89.00  86.00  85.00       85.86
       >=75..<=79 75.00  75.00  75.00  76.00       75.25
       >=70..<=74 73.00  74.00  74.00  73.00       73.50
       <=69       55.00  56.00  46.00  65.00       55.50
       ========== ====== ====== ====== ======    =======
       Average Grade 76.60  77.00  84.20  85.73    82.35
```

Figure 6.17: Crosstab report using two fields

Q&A can total, average, and count the summarized field; find the maximum and minimum values; and compute the standard deviation and variance. You can include as many of these analyses as you want to appear in the report.

You can format crosstab reports with the same techniques and codes you use for columnar reports, except that you add the formatting codes in the row field.

SETTING UP A CROSSTAB REPORT

Using our Clients database, we will now create the crosstab report shown in Figure 6.18 to analyze the relationship between client location (the City field), credit limit, and amount of orders.

This type of report is useful for determining if higher credit limits encourage clients to order. If you find that there is an increase in orders as credit limits increase, you might want to consider raising the credit limits for certain clients. If there appears to be no relationship, you must consider reducing the credit limit to avoid possible collection problems.

```
                                 Credit Limit
                          ------------------------------------   Total
    City                  $750.00    $1,000.00   $1,500.00   Total Orders
    -------------------   ---------   ---------   ---------   ============
    Margate                  $0.00   $10,486.00       $0.00   $10,486.00
    Newark               $2,510.00        $0.00   $9,300.00   $11,810.00
    Philadelphia         $3,175.00        $0.00   $1,850.00    $5,025.00
    Wilmington               $0.00    $1,250.00       $0.00    $1,250.00
    ==================   =========   =========   =========   ============
    Total Total Orders   $5,685.00  $11,736.00  $11,150.00   $28,571.00
```

Figure 6.18: Crosstab report for Clients database

Adding the City field to the analysis makes the report even more useful. You can tell which cities generate the most business, or if there is any relationship between the city, credit limit, and orders.

Follow these steps to create the report:

1. Select Report from the Main menu to display the Report menu.

2. Press ↵ twice to accept Design/Redesign a Report and the Clients database.

Q&A displays a list of all existing reports for the database, both columnar and crosstab. If you want to be able to identify crosstab reports on the list, include a special indicator in their names, such as the letter *X* or the word *Cross*.

3. Type **City, Limit, Orders Crosstabs** and press ↵.

4. Type **X** to select a crosstab report. Q&A displays the Retrieve Spec screen.

5. Press F10 to display the Crosstab Spec screen.

6. Press ↓ three times to reach the City field and type **ROW**.

Unless you designate otherwise, Q&A sorts rows and columns in ascending order. If you want to use a descending sort, add DS after Row or Col, as in Row,DS.

7. Press ↓ three times, press Tab twice to reach the Total Orders field, and type **SUM**.

8. Press ↓ to reach the Credit Limit field and type **COL**.

9. Press F10 to display the Report Print Options menu.

10. Press ↓, then ←, then F10, then ↵ to preview the report and save the design.

Q&A automatically adds the word *Total* to the last row and column.

11. Press F2 to return to the Report Print Options menu.

The only option unique to the Crosstab Print Options menu is Show Results As. By default, Q&A displays all summary figures as numbers, but you can select to display figures as a percentage of the total, percentage of the total or count of each row or column, or normalized. *Normalized* assigns the average of the summary figures an index number of 100. It then displays the results as a percentage above or below the index. Numbers less than 100 are below the average; numbers above 100 are above the average.

DEFINING CROSSTAB CALCULATIONS

If you do not specify the type of summary, Q&A totals money and number fields and counts nonnumeric fields. To use a different type of summary, or specify several types in one report, use the following codes:

T   Total the summaries

A	Average the summaries
C	Count the summaries
MIN	Minimum of the summaries
MAX	Maximum of the summaries
STD	Standard deviation of the summaries
V	Variance of the summaries

As an example, let's change our crosstab report to include both totals and averages.

1. Press F9 to return to the Crosstab Spec screen.

2. Press ↓ six times, then Tab twice to reach the Total Orders field. Q&A will display the word *SUMMARY* in place of *SUM*.

3. Press F6 to expand the field, then End to move the cursor after *SUMMARY*.

4. Type **,T,A** and press F10 twice to display the report on the screen.

Figure 6.19 shows the report preview. When you have both a total and average in the same report, Q&A places the average first.

5. Press Esc to return to the Report menu.

SETTING A SCALE FACTOR

If your report includes very large or very small numbers, you can scale how they appear. For example, it is common to represent large dollar amounts in thousands, such as displaying 50 in place of 50,000 and 12 in place of 12,000.

To add a scale factor, place the code SCALE(n), where n is a number, after the other format instructions. For example, to display totaled summary results in thousands, enter SUM,T,SCALE(1000).

Scale factors smaller than 1 will scale numbers up. For example, suppose you have a chemical database with fields in decimals of grams. You want to print a report but do not want to show the numbers in decimal

```
                              Credit Limit
                         -----------------------------------
       City               $750.00   $1,000.00   $1,500.00  Total Orders
       ------------       --------  ----------  ----------  ============
       Margate      Avg             $3,495.33               $3,495.33
                    Tot    $0.00    $10,486.00    $0.00     $10,486.00

       Newark       Avg    $2,510.00            $4,650.00   $3,936.67
                    Tot    $2,510.00    $0.00   $9,300.00    $11,810.00

       Philadelphia Avg    $1,587.50            $1,850.00   $1,675.00
                    Tot    $3,175.00    $0.00   $1,850.00    $5,025.00

       Wilmington   Avg             $1,250.00               $1,250.00
                    Tot    $0.00    $1,250.00     $0.00      $1,250.00
       ============ ===  ========== ========== ==========  ============
       Total Orders Avg   $1,895.00  $2,934.00  $3,716.67    $2,857.10
                    Tot   $5,685.00 $11,736.00 $11,150.00   $28,571.00
```

```
Esc-Exit   F1-Help   F-Full Page   + Zoom In   - Zoom out   Length =66
```

Figure 6.19: Both totals and averages in a summary report

places. By setting a scale factor of .001, your summary figures would appear as milligrams.

GROUPING FIELD VALUES

▶ **To group rows or columns:**

1. **From the Crosstab Spec screen, press F7.**
2. **On the Group Spec screen, specify the criteria to designate the range for rows, columns, or both.**

In the crosstab report you created, the fields used for rows and columns included a definite number of values. For example, the credit limit was $750, $1000, or $1500. But now suppose that you want to use the Total Orders field for the rows. If you had 100 clients, each with a different number in the field, you would have 100 rows.

Take a second look at Figures 6.16 and 6.17. Even though a student's attendance might range anywhere from 0 to 180 days, there are only four rows. For this report, ranges of possible attendances were placed in *groups*.

To explore the use of groups, we will create a crosstab report to analyze the relationship between total orders and credit limit. First, we will set up the report without groups to see why groups are necessary. Follow these steps:

1. Select Design/Redesign a Report from the Report menu and press ⏎ to accept the Clients database.

2. Type **Credit and Orders Crosstabs** and press ⏎.

3. Type **X** for a crosstab report.

4. From the Retrieve Spec screen, press F10 to display the Crosstab Spec screen.

5. Press ↓ six times, then Tab twice to reach the Total Orders field.

6. Press F6, type **ROW, SUM, A** and press ⏎. This specifies the Total Orders values to serve as rows in descending order and to be summarized as averages.

7. Press Tab to reach the Credit Limit field and type **COL**.

8. Press F10 to display the Report Print Options menu.

9. Press ↓, then ←, then F10, then ⏎ to save and preview the report.

As Figure 6.20 shows, the rows are in ascending order, and there are some rows that are very close in value, such as $1850 and $1876. The difference between these values is not statistically important. In addition, since no two clients have the same amount of total orders, the figures in the Average column are the same as the ones in the Total Orders column.

Instead of listing each total orders figure in its own row, let's group them together into four ranges. We will use orders under $2,000 to represent the lowest range, followed by orders between $2,000 and $4,000, between $4,000 and $6,000, and over $6,000 as the other ranges.

10. Press F2 to return to the Report Print Options menu, then F9 to return to the Crosstab Spec screen.

```
                              Credit Limit
                    --------------------------------    Average
Total Orders          $750.00  $1,000.00  $1,500.00   Total Orders
--------------------  --------  ---------  ---------   ============
$1,025.00             $1,025.00                        $1,025.00
$1,250.00                       $1,250.00              $1,250.00
$1,850.00                                  $1,850.00   $1,850.00
$1,876.00                       $1,876.00              $1,876.00
$2,150.00             $2,150.00                        $2,150.00
$2,500.00                                  $2,500.00   $2,500.00
$2,510.00             $2,510.00                        $2,510.00
$3,560.00                       $3,560.00              $3,560.00
$5,050.00                       $5,050.00              $5,050.00
$6,800.00                                  $6,800.00   $6,800.00
==================    ========  =========  =========   ============
Average Total Orders  $1,895.00 $2,934.00  $3,716.67   $2,857.10
```

```
Esc-Exit    F1-Help    F-Full Page    + Zoom in    - Zoom out    Length =66
```

Figure 6.20: Credit and Order crosstab report without grouping

11. Press F7 to display the Group Spec screen.

On this screen, you enter the groups you want for the rows, columns, or both, using the same criteria you use for designating ranges in retrieval specifications. The default value @ALL tells Q&A to use every value.

12. Type **<2000** and press ↓.

13. Type **>=2000..<4000** and press ↓.

14. Type **>=4000..<6000** and press ↓.

15. Type **>=6000**.

16. Press F10 three times to display the report on the screen. It should look like Figure 6.21.

17. Press Esc to return to the Report menu.

```
                                  Credit Limit
                        ------------------------------    Average
                         $750.00  $1,000.00 $1,500.00  Total Orders
         Total Orders   ---------  --------- ---------  ============
         ---------------------
         <2000           $1,025.00  $1,563.00 $1,850.00   $1,500.25
         >=2000..<4000   $2,330.00  $3,560.00 $2,500.00   $2,680.00
         >=4000..<6000              $5,050.00             $5,050.00
         >=6000                                $6,800.00   $6,800.00
         ===================  =========  =========  =========  ============
         Average Total Orders $1,895.00  $2,934.00 $3,716.67   $2,857.10
```

Figure 6.21: Credit and Order crosstab report grouped in ranges

If your groups overlap, Q&A will count some records twice. For example, suppose you group total orders into the ranges <1000, <3500, and <80000. The second range will include all records under $3,500, including those already counted in the first range. The third range will include every record.

In addition to your own groupings, you can use the built-in group functions listed in Table 6.2. For example, if you want rows of clients in four equal-sized groups between the smallest and largest amount in total orders, enter @I(4) as the row group. Then use the @MONTH, @DAY, and @YEAR functions to quickly organize rows or columns using a date field.

REPORTING WITH DERIVED FIELDS

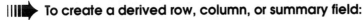 **To create a derived row, column, or summary field:**

1. **From the Crosstab Spec screen, press F8.**
2. **On the Derived Field Spec screen, enter the column heading, formula, and crosstab specification.**

A *derived field* is one created using a formula based on actual database fields. They are similar to the derived columns you can use in columnar reports. Derived fields can be used for crosstab report rows, columns, or summaries.

For example, suppose you have a database with the fields Salary, Overtime, and Total Deductions, and you want to average your employees' net pay for the summary. Net pay is total salary, including

Table 6.2: Q&A Report Grouping Functions

FUNCTION	RESULT
@ALL	Places each unique value in its own group.
@ALPHA	Groups data by the first letter in the field.
@DAY	Groups values by date.
@DOM	Groups values by the day of the month, regardless of the month. You will have a maximum of 31 groups.
@DOW	Groups values by the day of the week, for a maximum of seven groups. Days are abbreviated Mon, Tue, etc.
@I(n) or @INTERVAL(n)	Groups values into n equal-sized ranges between the smallest and largest value in the field. If n is missing, Q&A calculates the "ideal" grouping.
@MONTH	Groups values by month and year. Abbreviates the month name as Jan, Feb, etc.
@MOY	Groups values by month only, regardless of year. You will have a maximum of 12 groups, Jan to Dec. Useful for determining seasonal or monthly trends.
@R(x,y,z) or @RANGE(x,y,z)	Groups values in z specified ranges starting at x, in intervals of y. @R(0,10,1000) would create 10 ranges between 100 and 1000 in intervals of 100 (100, 200, 300, etc.).
@YEAR	Groups values by year.

overtime, less deductions. To create this report, from the Crosstab Spec screen, press F8 to display the Derived Field Spec screen, with the options

    Heading:
    Formula:
    Crosstab Spec:

Fill in the information, and then press F9 to return to the Crosstab Spec screen. The specification for using net pay as the summary might appear as

Heading: Net Pay
Formula: Salary + Overtime – Total Deductions
Crosstab Spec: SUM, A

REPRINTING REPORTS

||||▶ To reprint a report:

1. Select Print a Report from the Report menu.
2. Select the report name from the List Manager screen.
3. To make a temporary change to the report, select Yes when prompted.

To print a report using an existing report specification, select Print a Report from the Report menu, enter the name of the database, and then press ↵. Select the report specification name from the list that appears on the screen. You will see a prompt asking if you want to make any temporary changes to the specification. If you select No, the report will be printed. If you select Yes, you will be able to revise the specification before printing the report.

MODIFYING A REPORT SPECIFICATION

||||▶ To modify a report:

1. Select Design/Redesign a Report from the Report menu.
2. Select the report name from List Manager screen.
3. Change the retrieval, column sort, or crosstab specifications as necessary.

To make permanent changes to a report specification, select Design/Redesign a Report from the Report menu, enter the name of the database, and press ↵. Select the specification name from the list that appears. Q&A will take you through the steps you followed to create the report, giving you the opportunity to change the Retrieve Spec, Column/Sort Spec, or Crosstab Spec screen entries, as well as the Report Print Options and Define Page menu settings.

To make sure your report appears as you planned, select Preview Page from the Report Print Options menu. If it is correct, press F2 to return to the menu and turn off preview mode. If the report is incorrect, you can press F8 to display the Define Page menu, or press F9 to work your way back through the specifications used to design the report.

If you want to modify a report while it is displayed on the screen or being printed, press Shift-F9. For a columnar report, Q&A displays the message

    Which Spec? R-Retrieve C-Column/Sort D-Derived Cols P-Print A-Page

For a crosstab report, you will see

    Which Spec? R-Retrieve C-Crosstab D-Drvd Flds G-Group P-Print A-Page

Press the indicated letter to return directly to the Spec screen you want to revise, make your changes, and then press F10 to print the report.

When you edit the Crosstab Spec screen, Q&A will not change the groupings automatically. For example, if you switch the fields for rows and columns, Q&A will maintain the same groupings; you must change the ranges yourself.

Create complex reports in stages. Preview each stage on the screen to make sure it is correct, and then return to the Column/Sort, Crosstab, Derived Field, or Derived Column Spec screen to refine the report further. Any error that you see on the display will have been caused by your last change to the report. Return to that stage, make your correction, and preview the report again. When you're sure the report is correct, turn off preview mode and print the final output.

OTHER REPORT PRINTING OPTIONS

IIII➤ **To use other report options:**

- **Select Set Global Options from the Report menu to change default settings.**
- **Select Rename/Delete/Copy from the Report menu to manage report specifications.**

The Set Global Options and Rename/Delete/Copy options on the Report menu are similar to those options on the Print menu.

Select Set Global Options to change report default values. You can change two separate sets of defaults: one to use when printing columnar reports and another for crosstab reports. You can change the defaults on the Print Options and Define Page menus, set column widths, and define column and row headings.

You can also change format options. For both columnar and crosstab reports, you can set the spacing between columns and choose whether missing values are left blank or appear as 0. With crosstab reports, you can establish how Q&A is to handle rows and columns when the field values are blank. You can also set columnar reports to print repeated values in sorted columns, and whether or not to skip a blank line on column breaks.

The Rename/Delete/Copy option lets you organize and manipulate your report specifications. Use it to change a specification's name, remove unwanted specifications from the database, or copy a specification that you want to modify.

ENHANCING REPORTS

IIII➤ **To enhance reports with character styles and fonts:**

1. **On the Column/Sort or Crosstab Spec screen, position the cursor on the column specification.**

2. Press Shift-F6 and select the enhancement.

3. Highlight the appropriate section of the specification and press F10.

You can enhance sections of your reports with boldfacing, underlining, italics, and other formats and fonts. From the Column/Sort or Crosstab Spec screen, place the cursor in the field you want to enhance, and then press Shift-F6 to display the enhancement menu. Select the feature you want and highlight the section of the report code. For example, in columnar reports, you might highlight T to format grand totals or ST to format subtotals.

To format just the labels, such as *Total:* or *Average:,* add and enhance one of the codes listed in Table 6.3. You can change the default label by adding your own in parentheses after the label code. Enter AL(Norm), for example, to display the word *Norm* in place of the default *Average.* In columnar reports, add the code in the field that causes the column break.

Table 6.3: Codes to Enhance Report Labels

CODE	ENHANCES
Columnar and Crosstab Reports	
TL	Total
AL	Average
CL	Count
MINL	Minimum
MAXL	Maximum
STDL	Standard
VARL	Variance
HS	Heading separator lines
SL	Subcalculation and break separator lines
DL	Double separator lines for grand totals

Table 6.3: Codes to Enhance Report Labels (continued)

CODE	ENHANCES
Crosstab Reports	
H	Heading of the column, row, or summary field
SH	Subheading of the column, row, or summary field
Columnar Reports	
MCL	Month count
MMAXL	Month maximum
MMINL	Month minimum
MSTDL	Month standard
MTL	Month total
SAL	Subaverage
SCL	Subcount
SMAXL	Submaximum
SMINL	Subminimum
SSTDL	Substandard
STL	Subtotal
YAL	Year average
YCL	Year count
YMAXL	Year maximum
YMINL	Year minimum
YSTDL	Year standard
YTL	Year total

To enhance crosstab reports, highlight COL to enhance all the columns, ROW to enhances all the rows, or SUM to enhance all the summary information. To format just the final row and column (which contains the total or average information, for example), highlight A, T, or the other code that specifies the type of summary.

If you want to format a specific row or column, you must create groupings (using the Group Spec screen). Highlight the group of the row or column you want to enhance in the report.

In this chapter, you learned how to create reports using derived columns. The columns used formulas to calculate values based on other fields in the database. In Chapter 16, you will learn how to create derived columns that obtain values from other databases and from lookup tables, a special source of information you can build right into your database. Using these techniques, you can build sophisticated applications for automating your work.

7

Introducing
Q&A
Write

This chapter introduces Write, Q&A's word processing component. By itself, Write is a worthwhile program that can be used to create documents of all types. But as part of the Q&A system, it can access information in your databases to provide you with a powerful business tool. Although most of the major word processing programs can be used to create form letters, it is Write's integration with File that gives it some unique and impressive abilities.

WORKING WITH WRITE

Selecting Write from the Q&A Main menu displays the Write menu, which provides the following options:

- Type/Edit: Use this option to enter and edit text in the current document.

- Define Page: This option lets you set the margins, page size, characters per inch, header and footer position, and page number position.

- Print: Select this option to print the current document.

- Clear: This option erases the current document from memory.

- Get: Choose this option to recall a document from the disk and make it the current document.

- Save: Use this option to save the current document.

- Utilities: This option lets you change default values, import and export documents, perform DOS file functions, and recover damaged document files.

- Mailing Labels: Use this option to format and print mailing labels from Write database files.

Each time you start a document or recall one from the disk, it becomes the *current document*. The Type/Edit, Define Page, Print, and Save commands on the Write menu relate to the current document—selecting Save will save the current document; choosing Print prints it. When you select Clear, the current document is erased from memory, but not from the disk if you saved it. If you select to Get another document, it replaces the one in memory and becomes the new current document.

WRITE'S DEFAULT SETTINGS

Q&A automatically sets the standard page size, line spacing, and other formats, so you can begin producing documents immediately.

The following are Q&A Write's default settings:

- Line length of 10 characters per inch
- Page width of 78 characters
- Page length of 66 lines
- Top and bottom margins of 6 lines each (1 inch)
- Left margin set at 10 characters
- Right margin set at 68 characters from left
- Single spacing
- Tab stops set at 5, 15, 25, and 35

These settings result in a page with 54 lines of text, aligned at the left margin. Each line is 58 characters (or just less than 6 inches) wide.

Standard business stationery is actually 85 characters wide, not 78. Add the extra 7 characters to get a right margin of 17 characters, or about than 1¾ inches.

You can specify different settings for individual documents. When you do, the new settings are stored as part of the document, and they do not affect other documents on your disk or new documents that you will create. You can also change the default settings if you want to use other specifications for *every* new document.

EXPLORING THE WRITE SCREEN

||||➡ **To display the Write screen:**

1. **Select Write from the Main menu.**
2. **Select Type/Edit from the Write menu.**

When you select Write from the Main menu and accept Type/Edit, you will see the Write screen, shown in Figure 7.1. This screen is similar to the Q&A File form design screen. It has a ruler, status line, and key-assignment line. The rectangular mouse pointer will appear if you have a mouse attached to your system.

The small horizontal lines on the left and right near the top of the screen represent the top margin of the page. The position of these lines will change if you change the top margin setting.

On the ruler, the left and right margins are indicated by the [and] symbols. Each vertical line on the ruler represents a character position, and each *T* is a tab stop. The numbers on the ruler represent distances in

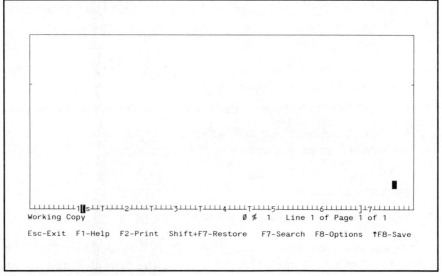

Figure 7.1: The Write screen

inches from the left edge of the page. For example, when the ghost cursor is on the 2, the cursor is 2 inches from the left page border.

The letter *s* next to the left margin indicates that your document is single spaced. The letter will change to *d* when you select double spacing, or *t* when you select triple spacing (from the Options menu).

The status line contains the same elements as the status line in File: the name of the document, percent of memory being used, horizontal character position, and line and page indicators. The character-position indicator, however, represents the position relative to the left *margin,* not the left edge of the page. For example, using the default margins and font, the indicator will show 40 when the cursor is on position 5 in the ruler. The ruler shows that the cursor is 5 inches, or 50 positions, from the left edge of the paper. The status line indicates that it is 40 characters from the left margin.

The words *Working Copy* on the status line indicate that you are creating a new document that has not yet been named and saved on the disk.

The key-assignment line includes the following options:

- Esc: Exits from the current function and returns to the Write menu, without affecting the current document.

- F1-Help: Displays context-sensitive help information. When you are typing or editing, you will see the template of function-key commands shown in Figure 7.2.

- F2-Print: Displays the Print Options menu. From this menu you can also select to change the Define Page menu settings.

- Shift-F7-Restore: Restores the block of text most recently deleted.

- F7-Search: Allows you to search for, and optionally replace, text anywhere in your document.

- F8-Options: Displays the Options menu listing the options summarized in Table 7.1.

- Shift-F8: Saves the current document.

The space in front of the memory indicator will be used to indicate the status of certain keys: *Num* for Num Lock, *Caps* for caps lock, and *Ins* for

```
        Alt F1  Thesaurus                     Ctrl F2  Print text block
  F1    Ctrl F1  Check spelling (word)   F2   Shift F2  Use macros
        Shift F1  Check spelling (doc)              F2  Print document
              F1  Info
                                           Ctrl F4  Delete to end of line
  F3    Ctrl F3  Document statistics   F4  Shift F4  Delete line (Ctrl Y)
              F3  Delete block                   F4  Delete word (Ctrl T)

        Alt F5  Move block to file         Alt F6  Hyphenate
        Ctrl F5  Copy block to file       Ctrl F6  Define Page
  F5    Shift F5  Move block           F6  Shift F6  Enhance text
              F5  Copy block                     F6  Set temporary margins

        Alt F7  List fields
        Ctrl F7  Go to page/line            Ctrl F8  Export document
  F7    Shift F7  Restore text         F8   Shift F8  Save document
              F7  Search & Replace                F8  Options Menu        ▮

        Alt F9  Calculate
        Ctrl F9  Make font assignments
  F9    Shift F9  Scroll screen down  F10
              F9  Scroll screen up              F10  Continue

Esc-Exit                        → PgDn-More ←
```

Figure 7.2: Main Write Help screen

Table 7.1: Write Options Menu Commands

OPTION	DESCRIPTION
Layout Page	
Edit Header	Type or edit a header for the top of each page.
Edit Footers	Type or edit a footer for the bottom of each page.
Set Tabs	Set and delete tab stops.
Newpage	Enter a hard page break.
Draw	Draw a line and boxes.
Documents	
Get a document	Retrieve a new current document.
Insert a document	Insert a document into the current document.
Align Text	
Left	Align text on the left.

Table 7.1: Write Options Menu Commands (continued)

OPTION	DESCRIPTION
Center	Center text between the margins.
Right	Align text on the right.
Temp Margins	F6—set or clear temporary left and right margins. Use for indenting paragraphs.
Single Space	Single space text below the cursor.
Double Space	Double space text below the cursor.
Triple Space	Triple space text below the cursor.
Block Operations	
Copy	F5—copy text to another location.
Move	Shift-F5—move text to another location.
Delete	F3—delete a block of text.
Copy to file	Ctrl-F5—copy text to a new disk file.
Move to file	Alt-F5—move text to a new disk file.
Enhance	Shift-F6—enhance text with character format and fonts.
Print	Ctrl-F2—print a block of text.
Capitalize	Convert selected text to uppercase.
Lowercase	Convert selected text to lowercase.
Title	Convert selected text to initial capitals.
Print Commands	
Date	Insert the @DATE code.
Filename	Insert the name of the document.
Graph	Insert a Lotus .PIC or PFS:Graph file into the document.
Join	Insert another Write file when printing.
Justify	Turn on and off microjustification.
Linespacing	Change line spacing from 1 to 9. This spacing does not appear on the screen, only in the printed document.

Table 7.1: Write Options Menu Commands (continued)

OPTION	DESCRIPTION
Postfile	Insert a PostScript program file.
Postscript	Insert a PostScript command.
Printer	Insert printer control codes.
Program	Insert a Q&A programming statement.
Queue	Create a print queue of named documents. This prints each document separately.
QueueP	Prints queued documents as one document.
Spreadsheet	Insert a Lotus 1-2-3 spreadsheet into the document.
Stop	Pauses printing. Press ↵ to resume printing.
Time	Inserts the @TIME code.
Other Options	
Spellcheck	Shift-F1—spell check the entire document.
Spellcheck word	Ctrl-F1—spell check the word at the cursor.
Thesaurus	Alt-F1—Look up synonyms for the word at the cursor.
Statistics	Ctrl-F3—display the number of words, lines, and paragraphs in the current document.
Hyphenate	Alt-F6—insert a soft hyphen at the cursor position.
Search & Replace	F7—Search for and replace text.
Restore	Shift-F7—restore the text last deleted using F3.
Go to page/line	Ctrl-F7—move the cursor to a specific line or page.
List fields	Alt-F7—display database fields for creating form documents.
Save	Shift-F8—save the current document in Write format.

Table 7.1: Write Options Menu Commands (continued)

OPTION	DESCRIPTION
Save as ASCII	Ctrl-F8—save the current document as ASCII text.
Assign fonts	Ctrl-F9—specify available printed fonts for enhancement.
Calculate	Alt-F9—Add, average, count, multiply, or divide numbers on rows and columns.

insert. The status line will also indicate any enhancement that has been applied to the character above the cursor. You will see *Bold, Undl, Ital, Supr, Subs, Sout,* or *Font1* through *Font8,* corresponding to the enhancement.

ENTERING TEXT

▐▐▐▶ To create and save a document:

1. On the Write screen, enter the text. Press ↵ only to end paragraphs, short lines, or to insert blank lines.
2. Press Shift-F8 when the document is displayed or select Save from the Write menu.
3. Enter the name of the file and press ↵.

If you know how to use a typewriter, you will be able to create documents in Write. The most obvious difference between the Q&A screen and the printed page, however, is the number of lines they hold. The Q&A screen can display only 21 lines of text at one time.

As you type, when one line becomes full, Q&A will automatically move the cursor to the next line—a feature called *word wrap.* The cursor will continue to move down the page and the line indicator on the status line will change. When you pass the last line on the screen, the lines at the top will scroll up out of view into the computer's memory. You can scroll the lines back into view using the cursor-movement keys.

As your text grows even longer, you don't have to worry about ending one page and beginning another—just continue typing. When you type enough text to fill one page, a double line will appear across the screen to mark the end of the page, and the page indicator on the status line will increase by one. This is *autopagination*. If you later add or delete lines from a page, the page breaks will change so that each page holds as many lines as it can. You can manually begin a new page using the Newpage command on the Options menu.

All the cursor-movement and editing keystrokes that work in File can be used in Write as well (see Table 2.2). Write also has the same typing modes. In overtype mode, new characters will replace existing ones. When you turn on insert mode, new characters are inserted between existing ones. The words to the right of the cursor will move over, and down if necessary, to make room for the new ones. To enter insert mode, press the Ins key. The characters *Ins* will appear on the status line. Press Ins again to return to overtype mode.

CREATING A DOCUMENT

Now that you have some background information on Write, let's begin creating a brief document.

1. Start Q&A and select Write from the Main menu.

When you start Q&A with a file name, even the name of a Write document, that name will only appear at file name prompts in File, Report, and Intelligent Assistant.

2. Press ↵ to accept Type/Edit. The Write screen will appear.

3. Type the text below. Do not press ↵ when the cursor reaches the right edge of the screen; just continue typing. If you make a mistake, press the Backspace key to move the cursor back through your text and erase the existing characters.

> **Q&A is a powerful database manager as well as a word processing program.**

As you typed the word *processing,* Q&A sensed it would not fit on the line, so it moved the whole word down to the next line, as shown in Figure 7.3. The carriage return at the end of the first line is called a *soft return.* If you insert or delete text on the line, the rest of the line will adjust automatically, moving characters down or up as necessary.

4. Press ↵ twice after typing the sentence.

Pressing ↵ inserts a *hard carriage return.* You press ↵ as you type to end a paragraph or to insert blank lines in the document.

5. Type the next sentence.

> **Q&A can merge information from a database into a document to create form letters, envelopes, and labels.**

6. Press ↵.

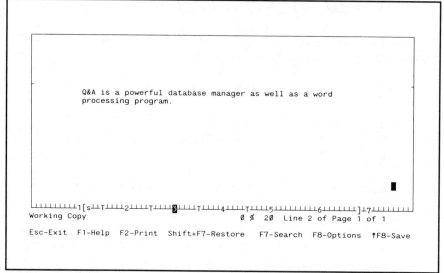

Figure 7.3: Word wrap moves text to the next line

SAVING YOUR DOCUMENT

You can save your document either by pressing Shift-F8 when it is displayed on the screen or by selecting Save from the Write menu. Follow these steps to save the text you just entered:

1. Press Shift-F8. Q&A will display

   Save as: C:\QA\

2. Type **MYFIRST** and press ↵.

Q&A saves your document without an extension. If you want to add an extension, such as .TXT or .DOC, type it after the file name.

EDITING YOUR DOCUMENTS

One of the main advantages of a word processor is the flexibility it provides for revising your documents. You can easily insert and delete text. Additionally, all the block operations described in Chapter 4 can be used to make major changes to your Write documents.

INSERTING AND DELETING CHARACTERS

If you make a mistake while typing, you can always press Backspace to erase characters. But what if you notice a mistake in the middle of the paragraph? If you press Backspace to erase all the characters up to the mistake, you will have to retype the rest of the paragraph.

Instead, use the cursor-movement and editing keys to delete and insert characters anywhere in the document. As an example, we will make some changes to the current document.

1. Place the cursor on the letter *p* in *powerful* in the first sentence.

2. Press Del nine times—eight times to erase the word *powerful,* a ninth time to delete the space following the word.

Pressing the Del key erases characters under the cursor. Since remaining characters move over to take its place, use Del when you want to erase characters to the right of the cursor.

3. Place the cursor on the *b* in *database,* and then press F4.

F4 deletes all characters up to the next blank space. To delete an entire word, place the cursor on the word's first character and then press F4.

4. Place the cursor on the letter *r* in *manager* and type **ment**.

The characters you typed replaced the existing ones, erasing the word *as*. This is because you are in overtype mode.

5. Press the Ins key, and the characters *Ins* will appear on the status line to indicate that Write is in insert mode.

6. Press the spacebar and type **program as**. The sentence now reads

   Q&A is a database management program as well as a word processing program.

7. Move the cursor to the start of the first paragraph and press Tab.

The first sentence moved over five characters. Because there was enough room at the end of the line, none of the characters at the end of the line wrapped to the next.

8. Press Shift-F6 to display the text enhancement options.

9. Press ↵ to accept Bold.

10. Press → twice, then F10. The word *Bold* will appear on the status line.

11. Place the cursor at the start of the next paragraph and press Tab.

This time, the word *to* wrapped to the next line automatically.

12. Press Shift-F6, then ↵ to accept Bold.

13. Press → twice, then F10.

SPLITTING AND COMBINING PARAGRAPHS

The key to splitting a paragraph into two, or joining two into one, is the ↵ key. When you press ↵, you are really inserting a return code in the text. By deleting the code that separates two paragraphs, you can join them together. By inserting a return code in a paragraph, you divide it into two.

To split one paragraph into two, first make sure you are in insert mode. If the characters *Ins* do not appear on the status line, press the Ins key. When you are not at the end of the document, you must be in insert mode to add a return code. If you are in overtype mode, the cursor will simply move to the next line without affecting the text.

Next, position the cursor at the beginning of the sentence that you want to start the new paragraph and press ↵. The text of that paragraph, from the cursor position down, will move to the next line. Insert a tab stop, press ↵ again to doublespace between paragraphs, or otherwise adjust the spacing as necessary.

To combine two paragraphs, position the cursor immediately after the first paragraph that you want to combine, and then press Del. The paragraph below will move up one line. If you double spaced between paragraphs by pressing ↵ twice, you must press Del twice. If the paragraph was indented with a tab space, press Del five more times to delete the spaces.

DELETING A BLOCK OF TEXT

To delete a block of text using the keyboard, place the cursor at one end of the block and press F3. Then move the cursor to the other end of the block and press F10.

Using a mouse, you can delete a block of text by dragging the mouse pointer over the block and then pressing Del. Alternatively, you can place the cursor at one end of the block, press F3, place the mouse pointer at the other end of the block, and then click the left mouse button.

If you change your mind about deleting the text, press Shift-F7. The last block you deleted will appear at the position of the cursor.

COPYING AND MOVING A BLOCK OF TEXT

To copy or move a block of text using the keyboard, follow these general steps:

1. Place the cursor at one end of the block.

2. Press F5 to copy the block or Shift-F5 to move it.

3. Move the cursor to the other end of the block and press F10.

4. Move the cursor to the new location and press F10.

With a mouse, you can copy or move a block of text by dragging the mouse pointer over the block and pressing F5 to copy the block or Shift-F5 to move it. Next, place the pointer at the new location and click the left button.

Another method is to place the cursor at one end of the block, press F5 (to copy) or Shift-F5 (to move), position the mouse pointer at the other end of the block, and click the left button. Finally, move the pointer to the new location and click the left button again.

CLEARING AND RECALLING DOCUMENTS FROM MEMORY

To clear and recall documents from memory:

- Select Clear from the Write menu to erase a document from the computer's memory.

- **Select Get from the Write menu or from the Options (F8) Document menu to recall a saved document.**

When you are done working on a document and want to start another new one, you must first erase, or *clear*, it from the computer's memory. Then you can recall it when you want to work on it again.

CLEARING A DOCUMENT

Follow these steps to clear our MYFIRST document:

1. Press Esc to return to the Write menu.
2. Select Clear. Q&A will display the warning message shown in Figure 7.4.

This warning appears when you try to return to the Main menu, clear a document, or get a new one, and you made changes to the current document since you last saved it. You can select Yes if you do not want to save the changes.

3. Select No.
4. Select Save and press ↵ to save the document.
5. Select Clear from the Write menu.

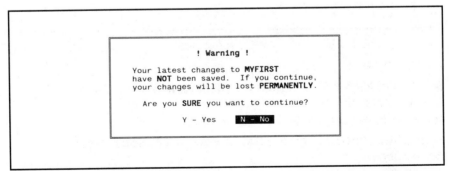

Figure 7.4: A warning message appears when you did not save your edited document

RECALLING A DOCUMENT

You can recall a document that you saved on the disk in two ways. One method is to select Get from the Write menu. This displays the prompt

Document: C:\QA\

Type the name of the document you want to recall and press ↵, or just press ↵ to display the List Manager screen with a list of your files.

You can also recall a document by using the Options menu from within the Write screen. We will use this method to recall our MYFIRST document.

1. Press F8 and then type **D** to display the Options menu and list the document options.

MYFIRST, the name of the document you just saved, is listed along with the options Get a Document and Insert a Document. This menu shows the names of the last 12 documents you worked on. You can recall any of these documents, making it the current document, by selecting its name from the list.

2. Select MYFIRST.

The document is retrieved from the disk and displayed on the Write screen.

PRINTING YOUR DOCUMENTS

IIII➤ **To print a document:**

1. **Select Print from the Write menu or press F2 when the document is on the screen.**
2. **Select options from the Print Options menu.**
3. **Press Ctrl-F6 and change the Define Page menu settings if necessary.**
4. **Press F10 to start printing.**

You can print a document in two ways: by selecting Print from the Write menu or by pressing F2 when the document is displayed on the screen. Before printing your document, you can select printing options.

SPECIFYING PRINTING OPTIONS

The Write Print Options menu is shown in Figure 7.5. Some of the selections are the same as those you used when printing records and reports. Table 7.2 summarizes the settings.

DEFINING THE PAGE

You can customize your printouts even further by using the options on the Define Page menu, shown in Figure 7.6. Display the menu by selecting Define Page from the Write menu or by pressing Ctrl-F6 from the Print Options menu.

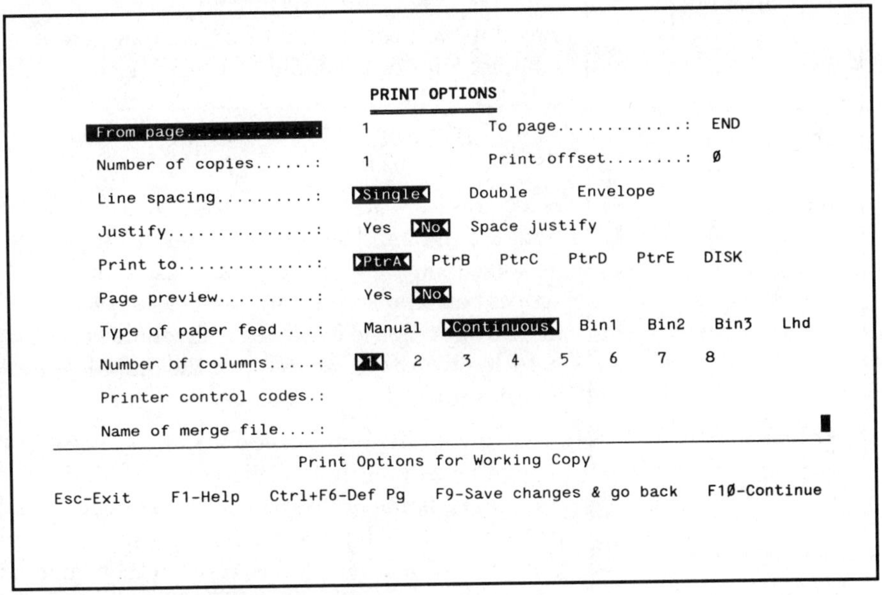

```
                              PRINT OPTIONS

      From page.............:   1              To page............:   END

      Number of copies......:   1              Print offset........:   Ø

      Line spacing..........:  ▶Single◀    Double      Envelope

      Justify...............:   Yes  ▶No◀  Space justify

      Print to..............:  ▶PtrA◀   PtrB    PtrC    PtrD    PtrE    DISK

      Page preview..........:   Yes  ▶No◀

      Type of paper feed....:   Manual  ▶Continuous◀  Bin1    Bin2    Bin3    Lhd

      Number of columns.....:  ▶1◀    2      3      4      5      6      7      8

      Printer control codes.:

      Name of merge file....:                                              ▮
      ─────────────────────────────────────────────────────────────────────
                     Print Options for Working Copy

      Esc-Exit    F1-Help    Ctrl+F6-Def Pg    F9-Save changes & go back    F1Ø-Continue
```

Figure 7.5: Print Options menu

Table 7.2: Write Printing Options

OPTION	DESCRIPTION
From Page	Enter the first page you want to print. Leave the default 1 to print from the beginning of the document.
To Page	Enter the number of the last page you want to print. Set at End to print to the last page in the document.
Number of Copies	Enter the number of copies of the document you want to print.
Print Offset	Enter the number of spaces you want to indent the printout from the left edge of the paper. If you plan to bind the report in a folder or three-ring binder, enter a number large enough to ensure that all the text will be clearly visible.
Line Spacing	Select Single, Double, or Envelope. Use Envelope to print addresses on envelopes (see Chapter 8 for details). This setting does not affect how the document appears on the screen. To change the spacing on the screen, use the Options menu.
Justify	Select Yes or Space Justify to align lines on both the right and left margins. Yes applies *microjustification,* which is small increments of spaces between letters and words to align text on the right. Space Justify inserts whole spaces between words. Choose No for the default left justification only.
Print To	Select one of the printers you installed in Q&A using the Install Printer option on the Utilities menu. The name of the printer will appear under the status line. Select Disk to save the printer output as a disk file. You can then later print the file using the DOS PRINT command. (Print to Screen is not available in Write; use Page Preview instead.)

Table 7.2: Write Printing Options (continued)

OPTION	DESCRIPTION
Page Preview	Select Yes to display a graphic representation of the printed page and confirm that the printout will appear as you want. You can display up to two pages at a time, and zoom in (enlarge) the display to see specific details.
Type of Paper Feed	Select the type of paper feed your printer uses. Use Manual for individual sheets; Continuous for continuous, perforated pages; Bin1 for the top drawer of a multidrawer printer; Bin2 for the second drawer of a multidrawer printer; Bin3 for the third drawer of a multidrawer printer; or Lhd to print the first page from Bin1, subsequent pages from Bin2. When you select Manual and start to print, Q&A will display a message telling you to put a new page in the printer and press ↵ to begin printing.
Number of Columns	Select a number greater than 1 to print your document in newspaper-like columns. Printing in more than two columns on 8$1/2$-inch wide paper is not recommended for normal text. Columns are not shown on the screen as you type, but they appear in preview mode and in the printout.
Printer Control Codes	Insert codes that turn on and off features of your printer that are not directly supported by Q&A (see Chapter 5 for details).
Name of Merge File	When creating form documents, enter the name of the database file containing the variable merge information.

```
                           DEFINE PAGE


          Left margin: 1Ø            Right margin : 68

          Top margin : 6             Bottom margin: 6

          Page width : 78            Page length  : 66
                          ■
          Characters per inch............:  ▶1Ø◀   12    15    17

          Begin header/footer on page #...:   1

          Begin page numbering with page #:   1

       _____

                  Page Options for Working Copy

    Esc-Exit          F1-Help          F2-Print Options       F1Ø-Continue
```

Figure 7.6: Write Define Page menu

The page size and margin settings are the same as those for printouts of database records and reports. Remember that right margin settings in characters are relative to the left edge of the paper; in inches they are from the right side of the page. If you select a proportionally spaced font or another characters per inch setting, set the measurements in inches to maintain the proper spacing.

The Begin Header/Footer on Page # setting determines the first page on which headers or footers will print. The Begin Page Numbering with Page # option determines the number to print on the first page. Headers, footers, and page numbers are discussed in Chapter 9.

PRODUCING A PRINTOUT

If you select Print from the Write menu before typing or calling a document, Q&A displays the message

You must get a document before you can print it

We will now print the MYFIRST document twice—once as single spaced and then as double spaced—to show the effects of printing options. Make sure your printer is turned on and ready to print, and then follow these steps:

1. Press F2 to display the Print menu.

2. Press F10 to print the document using the default page settings.

The document reappears on the screen after it is printed.

3. Press F2 to display the Print menu.

4. Press ↓ twice, then → to select double spacing.

5. Press F10 to print the document.

The printed document is double spaced, but it is still single spaced on the screen.

6. Press Home three times to place the cursor at the start of the document.

7. Press F8 to pull down the Options menu.

8. Type **A**, then **D** to select Double Space.

The document appears double spaced on the screen, and the letter *d* is next to the left margin on the ruler.

9. Press F2 to display the Print menu.

10. Press ↓ twice, then ← to select single spacing.

If you choose double spacing for the document on the screen and on the Print Options menu, the printout will have three blank spaces between each line of text.

11. Press F10 to print the document.

12. Press Esc to return to the Write menu.

13. Press Esc to return to the Main menu.

Q&A will display a warning message because you changed the spacing of the document but did not resave it.

14. Type **Y** to display the Main menu, then **X** to exit from Q&A.

In the next chapter, you will learn how to use Q&A Write to produce form documents, labels, and envelopes from your databases.

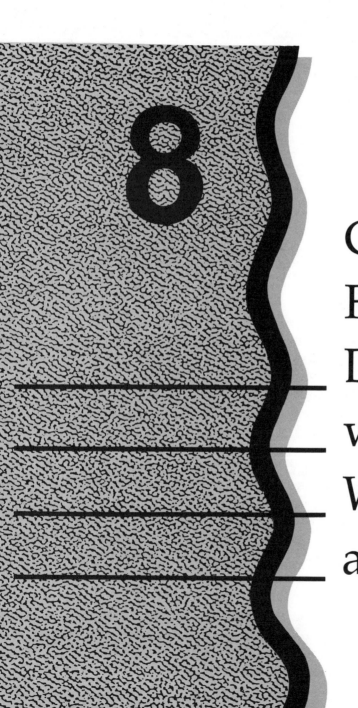

8

Creating
Form
Documents
with Q&A
Write
and File

Many people think of form letters as junk mail. This is because some form letters are obviously mass produced and are as "personal" as the phone directory.

But professional-looking form letters can be invaluable tools. They can be used to advertise promotions, place orders, and process invoices. For your personal affairs, you can use form letters as requests for information, invitations to a party, or letters of complaint.

In this chapter, you will learn how to produce personalized form letters by merging your Q&A File data with a Write document.

PREPARING FORM LETTERS

Preparing a form letter requires the following basic steps:

- Write a document that contains the text common to all copies of the form letter. You write this letter once, no matter how many copies will be printed. In each location where you want to insert the contents of a database field, you insert a merge code that includes the field name.

- Create, or have available, a database that contains the variable information to be inserted into each letter. You can use the same database for any number of different form documents, as well as for envelopes and mailing labels. You can even merge data from several databases into a form letter.

- Merge the document and database together. Q&A inserts the field information from the database wherever the field name is used in the form letter.

Since we already created the Clients database, we can prepare a form letter to our customers using Write. Follow these steps:

1. Start Q&A and select Write from the Main menu.

2. Press ↵ to accept Type/Edit and display the Write screen.

3. Type the following inside address.

   Aardvark International

   35 West Appleton Drive

   Alaway, AL 08765

If you will be printing your letters on preprinted letterhead, press ↵ enough times to move past the letterhead area before entering the address (using the default font, every six lines is 1 inch).

4. Press ↵ twice to end the address and insert a blank line.

5. Press F8 to display the Options menu.

6. Type **P** to select Print Commands, then **D** to select Date. At the position of the cursor, Q&A will insert

   @DATE(n)

7. Press Ins to turn on insert mode, type **11**, and then press Del to erase the *n.*

The code *@DATE(11)* inserts the current date into the document using format 11 (for example, November 16, 1991). This code is the same as the one you use to enter dates into the headers and footers of reports, except that it is surrounded by asterisks. You can also enter the code by typing it manually into the document instead of selecting it from the Options menu.

8. To center the lines between the margins, place the cursor in the first line of the address, press F8, type **A**, and then type **C**.

9. Use the same technique to center the remaining lines of the inside address and the date.

10. Press End three times to reach the end of the document, and then press ↵ to insert a blank line after the date.

INSERTING VARIABLE INFORMATION

||||▶ **To insert variable information in form documents:**

- **Enter the first field by pressing Alt-F7, entering the database name, and then selecting the field name from the list that appears.**
- **Add other fields by typing the field name surrounded by asterisks or by pressing Alt-F7 and selecting from the list of field names.**

You want to address your form letters to the clients in your database. To do this, you insert codes into the document using the field names from the Clients form. This is called *variable information* because the actual names and addresses will change with each copy of the form letter.

You add the field names by typing them surrounded by asterisks, or by selecting them from a list of fields. When you select them from the list, Q&A will automatically insert the name of the database on the Print Options menu.

With the standard heading in the letter, you can now enter the variable information:

1. Press Alt-F7. You will see the prompt

    Date file name: C:\QA\

2. Type **Clients** and press ↵ to display the list of field names shown in Figure 8.1.

The names, not the field labels, are listed in alphabetical order. For example, the database contains two fields with the label Age: one for the primary contact and one for the secondary contact. Q&A has assigned the names Age for the primary contact and Age1 for the secondary contact.

The ↓ at the bottom of the box means that there are additional field names. Scroll these into view by using the arrow keys or PgDn. To select a field, highlight its name and press ↵.

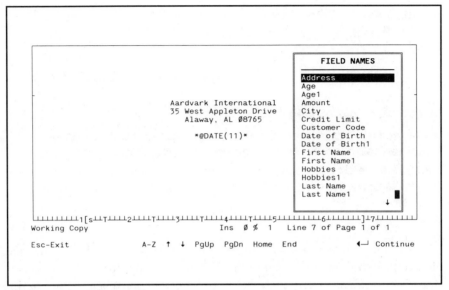

Figure 8.1: Field names list

3. Press ↓ nine times to highlight First Name and press ↵ to select it.

The field name appears in the document as

   First Name

The asterisks indicate that this is a variable value.

4. Press the spacebar.

5. Press Alt-F7 and select Last Name. (You will learn how to handle the middle initial later.)

6. Press ↵, then Alt-F7, then PgDn, and select Name.

7. Press ↵, then Alt-F7, and select Address.

8. Press ↵, then Alt-F7, and select City.

9. Press the spacebar, then Alt-F7, then PgDn, and select State.

10. Press the spacebar, then Alt-F7, then PgDn twice, and select Zip Code.

11. Press ↵ twice, type **Dear**, and press the spacebar.

12. Press Alt-F7 and select First Name.

You can use the same fields as many times as you want in a single document.

13 Type **:** (a colon). Your screen should look like the one shown in Figure 8.2.

14. Press ↵ twice.

15. Type the start of the first paragraph:

    In preparation for the busy summer season, we want to confirm the shipping information we have on file for

16. Press the spacebar, then Alt-F7, then PgDn, and select Name.

17. Type **.** (a period) to end the sentence.

18. Press the spacebar and continue typing the letter:

    If any of the information below is incorrect, please call your

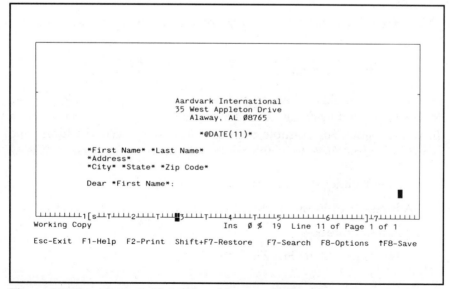

```
                    Aardvark International
                    35 West Appleton Drive
                    Alaway, AL Ø8765

                       *@DATE(11)*

        *First Name* *Last Name*
        *Address*
        *City* *State* *Zip Code*

        Dear *First Name*:                              ▮


Working Copy                    Ins   Ø %  19  Line 11 of Page 1 of 1

Esc-Exit  F1-Help  F2-Print  Shift+F7-Restore  F7-Search  F8-Options  ↑F8-Save
```

Figure 8.2: Form letter with inside address and salutation

Aardvark representative as soon as possible.

19. Press ↵ twice.

20. Type **Preferred Carrier:** and press Tab.

21. Press Alt-F7, then PgDn, and select Preferred Carrier.

22. Press ↵, type **Shipping Zone:**, and press Tab.

23. Press Alt-F7, then PgDn, and select Shipping Zone.

24. Press ↵, type **Taxable?:**, and press Tab twice.

25. Press Alt-F7, then PgDn, and select Taxable.

26. Press ↵ twice.

27. Type the letter closing:

    Sincerely,

    Alvin Aardvark

Your screen should look like the completed letter shown in Figure 8.3.

28. Press Shift-F8, type **Confirm**, and press ↵ to save the document.

MANAGING BLANK FIELDS

If one of the fields to be merged is empty, and it is the only text on the line, Q&A will not insert an extra carriage return and leave a blank line in the printed letter. For example, suppose we stored a second address line in our Clients database to handle room, suite, or box numbers, such as

Name: Wonder Welding, Inc.

Address: 9601 West Street

Address: Suite 304

City: Tampa   State: FL   Zip Code: 16192

```
          *First Name* *Last Name*
          *Address*
          *City* *State* *Zip Code*

          Dear *First Name*:

              In preparation for the busy summer season, we want to
          confirm the shipping information we have on file for
          *Name*. If any of the information below is incorrect,
          please call your Aardvark representative as soon as
          possible.

          Preferred Carrier:      *Preferred Carrier*
          Shipping Zone:          *Shipping Zone*
          Taxable?:               *Taxable*

          Sincerely,


          Alvin Aardvark                                   ▋
  └┴┴┴┴┴┴┴┴1[s┴┴T┴┴┴┴2┴┴┴▌┴┴┴3┴┴┴┴T┴┴┴┴4┴┴┴┴T┴┴┴5┴┴┴┴┴┴┴6┴┴┴┴┴┴]┴7┴┴┴┴┴┴
  Working Copy                          Ø %  15  Line 26 of Page 1 of 1

  Esc-Exit  F1-Help  F2-Print  Shift+F7-Restore   F7-Search  F8-Options  ↑F8-Save
```

Figure 8.3: Completed form letter

The inside address in form letters would include a line for the second part of the address:

```
*Name*
*Address*
*Address1*
*City* *State* *Zip Code*
```

When there isn't a second address for a client in the Address1 field, Q&A will skip it entirely and will not print a blank line between the first address line and the city, state, and zip code.

However, if there are other fields or text on the same line as the empty field, blank spaces will appear on that line. For example, it would be better etiquette if we included the middle initial with the name in the inside address. We could add the initial field like this

```
*First Name* *MI* *Last Name*
```

But then the inside addresses for clients without middle initials would include an extra blank space between the first and last names, as in

    Faye   Stack

Instead, you must include the MI field by using the *Program command:

    Program {First Name +" "+MI} *Last Name*

*Program is a special command that allows you to include programming expressions in form letters. It tells Q&A to process the instructions that follow.

In this case, the expression

    Program {First Name +" "+MI}

constructs a string by combining the value in the First Name field, a space, then the value in the MI field. If the second field is blank, however, Q&A ignores the spaces and uses only the first name. The string is followed by a space, then the value in the Last Name field.

You can add a *Program command by typing *Program, or by selecting it from the Print Command submenu displayed from the Options menu (F8). We will use the *Program command later in the chapter to perform calculations on the values being merged into the document.

Before we leave the subject of middle initials, remember Adam Mycroft Chesin, the client who insists that we use his full middle name? When we created the Clients database, we formatted the middle initial fields as TI, meaning initial capitals. If we had formatted it as TU, assuming that all our clients used only an initial, Mr. Chesin's form letter would be addressed to

    Adam MYCROFT Chesin

Because we used the TI code, his middle name is stored as Mycroft, but all single-character middle initial fields are uppercase.

PRINTING FORM DOCUMENTS

||||➡ **To print form documents:**

1. **Display the Print Options menu.**
2. **If necessary, enter the file name at the name of merge file prompt.**
3. **Press F10, complete the Retrieve Spec screen, and press F10 twice.**

Now we are ready to merge the form letter with the database. In the following steps, you will merge the information for all clients in New Jersey and sort the letters by zip code. Instead of printing copies of the letters, you will preview them on the screen.

1. Press F2 to display the Write Print Options menu. The name of the database appears at the name of merge file prompt.

2. Press ↓ five times, and then type **Y** to select Page Preview.

3. Press F10, and the Retrieve Spec screen for this database will appear.

When you want to merge data from every record, press F10. But in this case, we want only the records of clients in New Jersey.

4. Press ↓ three times, press Tab to reach the State field, and type **NJ**.

5. To sort the letters by zip code, press F8 to display the Sort Spec screen.

6. Press ↓ three times, press Tab twice to reach the Zip Code field, and type **1,AS**.

7. Press F10. Q&A will scan the database looking for clients who meet the retrieval criteria, and then displays a message indicating the number of records to be merged, as shown in Figure 8.4.

8. Press ↵. Each of the matching records will appear briefly on the screen. Under the status line, Q&A flashes the message

   preparing to merge print

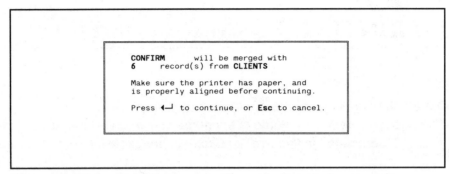

Figure 8.4: Q&A reports the number of records about to be merged

After all the records have been located, the first one appears on the screen in preview mode, as shown in Figure 8.5.

9. Press Esc to return to the document.

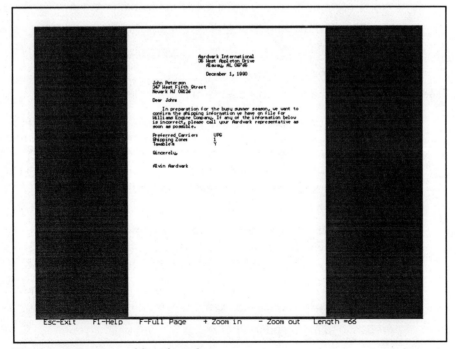

Figure 8.5: Preview of first form letter

As Q&A merged the database with the form document, it inserted the field values at the position of the field names surrounded by asterisks.

PERFORMING CALCULATIONS IN FORM DOCUMENTS

▐▐▐▐▶ **To perform calculations in form documents:**

1. **Where you want the results to appear, use the *Program command to include programming expressions—type *Program or press F8 and select it from the Print Command submenu.**
2. **Follow the *Program command with the formula in brackets, then an asterisk.**
3. **Use either the field name or logical field number (assigned on the Program Spec screen) to represent field values.**

When you merge number and money fields into a document, you can also perform calculations whose results will appear in the printed form letter.

ENTERING FORMULAS WITH THE *PROGRAM COMMAND

You use the *Program command to perform math on number and money fields as they are being merged into a document. Where you want the results of a calculation to appear, type or choose *Program, then enter the formula in brackets, followed by an asterisk.

Represent field values using either the field name (*not* field label) or the logical field number if you assigned one to the field. For example, the Clients database includes the money fields Amount and Total Orders. Amount represents the last order, and it is accumulated in the Total Orders field. To calculate and print the total order figure before the last order was added to it, you would include the line

Program {Total Orders – Amount}

where you want the number to appear in the document.

Because we assigned logical field numbers to these fields (in Chapter 4), you could also enter the line as

Program {#8 – #7}

or with any combination of field names and numbers. The word *program* can be abbreviated *pg*, as in this formula, which calculates 10 percent of the Total Orders field:

*pg {Total Orders * .1}*

Do not surround the field names with asterisks as you do when merging the field values directly into the document. If you forgot the field names, you can press Alt-F7 to display the list. However, if you select the field name from the list, you must delete the asterisks surrounding the name.

If you leave the asterisks, use an invalid field name, or make some other error in the formula, Q&A will display the message

Invalid programming expression found in the *pg{}* command

under the status line when you try to merge print. Correct the formula, and then try merging the file again.

CREATING A DOCUMENT WITH CALCULATION COMMANDS

Now let's suppose that because business has been slow, we want to offer our clients a special incentive. We will discount the next order by 10 percent of the last order. For example, if a client's last order was $500, we will subtract $50 from the next order. We will perform the calculations while merging the letters by using the *Program command.

This second form letter will also include the client's name and address and Mr. Aardvark's standard closing. Instead of retyping this information, you will save the beginning and the closing of the letter that you already typed and use it again.

Follow these steps to create the second letter:

1. Press Home three times to place the cursor at the start of the letter.

2. Press Ctrl-F5 to copy a block to a file.

3. Move the cursor to the blank space in front of the first paragraph and press F10. You will see the prompt

   Copy to: C:\QA\

4. Type **Discount** and press ↵.

5. To save the closing, place the cursor in the blank line above *Sincerely*, and press Ctrl-F5.

6. Move the cursor to the blank line under *Alvin Aardvark* and press F10.

7. Type **Closing** and press ↵.

Now that the text we will reuse is saved on disk, you can clear the screen and begin the new document. In this case, we want to start the document with the contents of DISCOUNT, the address information that we saved from the previous form letter.

8. Press F8 to display the Options menu.

9. Type **D** to list the document options.

Confirm has been added to the list of available documents, however, DISCOUNT and CLOSING, the names of the saved blocks, are not on the list.

10. Type **G** to select Get a Document. This displays the prompt

    Document to get: C:\QA\

Before pressing G or I to select options from this menu, check the documents listed. If a document starts with *G* or *I*, typing the letter will recall that document instead of executing the Get or Insert command.

11. Type **Discount** and press ↵ to make it the current document.

12. Press End three times to reach the end of the document, and then press ↵ twice to insert a blank line.

13. Type the following paragraph exactly as it appears—do *not* use Alt-F7 to insert the field names or the Program command:

   Because we value your business, Aardvark International is pleased to offer you a special discount of $*program { #7 * .10 }* on your next order. That's 10% of the last order you placed with us, *Amount* on *Last Order Date*.

The *Program command multiplies the value in the Amount field, which we assigned the number 7 in Chapter 4 (on the Program Form Spec screen), by 10 percent. A dollar sign will print in front of the results.

14. Press ↵ and continue typing the rest of the letter:

   However, if you place an order over $*program { #7 * 2 }*, we will double the discount. That's a full $*program { #7 * .20 }*!

   This discount, which we plan to offer periodically, is our way of saying Thank You.

Figure 8.6 shows the letter at this point. Now, instead of typing the closing, we will insert the CLOSING document.

15. Press ↵ twice, then F8 to display the Options menu.

16. Type **D**, then **I** to select Insert a Document.

17. Type **Closing** and press ↵.

The Insert a Document option adds the document to the current one, without replacing it.

18. Press Shift-F8, then ↵ to save the document.

19. Press F2 to display the Print Options menu.

Notice that the name of the database is not at the name of merge file prompt. This is because you typed the merge commands instead of using Alt-F7.

```
                          35 West Appleton Drive
                          Alaway, AL 08765

                              *@DATE(11)*

              *First Name* *Last Name*
              *Address*
              *City* *State* *Zip Code*

              Dear *First Name*:

                  Because we value your business, Aardvark International
              is pleased to offer you a special discount of $*program (
              #7 * .10 )* on your next order. That's 10% of the last
              order you placed with us, *Amount* on *Last Order Date*.
                  However, if you place an order over $*program ( #7 * 2
              )*, we will double the discount. That's a full $*program (
              #7 * .20 )*!
                  This discount, which we plan to offer periodically, is
              our way of saying Thank You.

  └┴┴┴┴┴┴┴┴1[s┴┴T┴┴┴┴2┴┴┴┴T┴┴┴┴3┴┴┴T┴┴4┴┴┴┴T┴┴┴5┴┴┴┴┴┴┴┴┴6┴┴┴┴┴┴┴]┴7┴┴┴┴┴
  DISCOUNT                                    0 %   29  Line 21 of Page 1 of 1

  Esc-Exit  F1-Help  F2-Print  Shift+F7-Restore   F7-Search  F8-Options  ↑F8-Save
```

Figure 8.6: Form document with calculations

20. Press ↓ five times, and then type **Y** to preview the letters.

21. Press ↓ four times and type **Clients**.

22. Press F10 to display the Retrieve Spec screen.

23. Press F10 to generate form letters for all clients.

24. Press ↵ to merge the files. The first letter will appear on the screen, as shown in Figure 8.7.

25. Press Ctrl-PgDn to disply the next letter, and then press Esc to return to the document.

We added a dollar sign in front of the *Program command so it would appear on the merged letters, but some of the calculated numbers do not have the two decimal places that should appear with dollar amounts. Let's experiment a little to see how Q&A would format the numbers themselves if we made a small change to the letter.

26. Delete each of the three dollar signs by placing the cursor under each one and pressing Del.

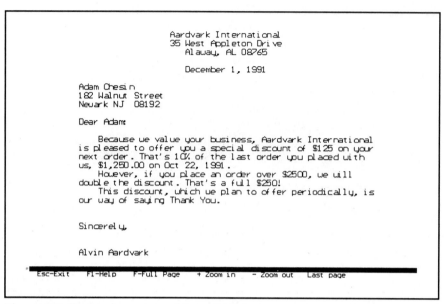

```
                    Aardvark International
                    35 West Appleton Drive
                    Alaway, AL 08765

                    December 1, 1991

        Adam Chesin
        182 Walnut Street
        Newark NJ  08192

        Dear Adam:

            Because we value your business, Aardvark International
        is pleased to offer you a special discount of $125 on your
        next order. That's 10% of the last order you placed with
        us, $1,250.00 on Oct 22, 1991.
            However, if you place an order over $2500, we will
        double the discount. That's a full $250!
            This discount, which we plan to offer periodically, is
        our way of saying Thank You.


        Sincerely,


        Alvin Aardvark

  Esc-Exit   F1-Help    F-Full Page   + Zoom in   - Zoom out   Last page
```

Figure 8.7: Zoomed preview of form letter

27. Edit the second sentence in the first paragraph to read:

    That's 10% of the last order you placed with us, *Amount*.

28. Press F2 to display the Print Options menu.

29. Press F10 twice to display the Retrieve Spec screen and generate form letters for all clients.

30. Press ↵ to merge the files.

In the first letter, the calculated number in the first paragraph is not formatted as money, but the two numbers in the second paragraph are. Q&A formats calculated numbers according to the merged field that precedes them. Since a merged money field, not the Last Order Date field, is now just before the second paragraph, the two calculated figures in that paragraph are formatted as money fields, with two decimal places.

31. Press Ctrl-PgDn to display the next letter.

The first calculated figure in this letter, as in all subsequent letters, is formatted as money. Q&A is still using the format of the Amount field from the previous letter. The only way to format the initial calculated field in the first letter as money is to include a money field, such as Amount or Total Orders, before the *Program command.

32.   Press Esc to return to the document.

33.   Press Esc and type **Y** to return to the Main menu.

34.   Type **X** to exit from Q&A.

FORMATTING VARIABLE INFORMATION

To format variable information:

- **Enhance the field name in the merge document to format the inserted variable information.**
- **Follow the field name with (R) to right-align variable information with the ending asterisk.**
- **Restrict the length of printed fields with the (R) and (L) codes.**
- **Delete trailing spaces and combine multiline fields with the (T) code.**

You can enhance the merged information by applying the format to the merge code. If you underline *Amount*, for example, Q&A will underline the amount value in the form letter.

You can also control the position of merged information, aligning it on the left or right, or trimming extra spaces. This is particularly useful when trying to align field values in columns, since Q&A normally places merged values at the starting asterisk in the code.

For example, suppose that you want to print a document with this text:

Total Orders: $2500.00

Last Order: $500.00

Previous Total: $2000.00

You enter these codes into the document:

```
Total Orders:      *Total Orders*
Last Order:        *Amount*
Previous Total:    *Program { #8 – #7 }*
```

Q&A will merge the data and align it like this:

Total Orders: $2500.00

Last Order: $500.00

Previous Total: $2000.00

Aligning the codes on the closing asterisk, like this:

```
              *Total Orders*
                 *Amount*
       *Program { #8 – #7 }*
```

would result in

        $2500.00

          $500.00

    $2000.00

Each number still starts at the position of the code's first asterisk. To align merged data on the right, line up the closing asterisks and insert (R) before each one:

```
            *Total Orders(R)*
               *Amount(R)*
     *Program { #8 – #7 }(R)*
```

However, the (R) code has another function: it limits the length of the printed field to the number of characters in the merge code. For example, if you tried to right-align the Name and Address fields like this:

```
*Name(R)*
*Address(R)*
```

Q&A will print this:

Chesin Ph

182 Walnut S

When you use the (R) code, make sure that the line is long enough to handle the longest entry in the database. If you have to, insert blank spaces before the closing asterisk, such as

```
*Name(R)      *
```

There may be times when you want to intentionally limit the number of characters, such as when you want to print a sample of a multiline notes field, or when you're trying to fit text into labels or narrow columns. In this case, add the (R) code if you want the field right-aligned, or add (L) if you want it left-aligned. Then make the code the proper length by adding spaces before the asterisk. For example, entering

```
*Notes(L)                *
```

will print the first 14 characters of the Notes field, left-aligned.

If you leave out the (R) or (L), Q&A will print the entire contents of the field, no matter how many spaces you add.

One final code that you can add to merge codes is (T), for truncate. This code deletes any extra spaces and is used for combining multiline fields on one printed line. As an example, suppose your database includes two multiline fields

```
Address<
```

```
Notes<
```

and a record that looks like this:

```
Address   182 Fifth Avenue
          Suite 405
Notes     1 - Call every Friday
          2 - Bill on December 3
```

Including the two lines

```
*Address*
*Notes*
```

in the form letter would result in four lines being printed since each field is two lines long. Adding the (T) code in each

```
*Address(T)*
*Notes(T)*
```

combines the two lines of each field, resulting in

182 Fifth Avenue Suite 405

1 - Call every Friday 2 - Bill on December 3

MISMATCHED FIELD NAMES

||||▶ **To match field names:**
1. **When Q&A warns you that it cannot find a field name, press F8.**
2. **On the Identifier Spec screen, enter the name you used in the document next to the field label.**
3. **Press F10 to continue to the Retrieve Spec screen.**

If you type the names of fields surrounded by asterisks instead of selecting them from the list, there is always the possibility of entering the field name incorrectly, such as Zip instead of Zip Code, or Telephone instead of Phone.

If this happens, Q&A will not be able to locate the field information in the database. Fortunately, instead of leaving spaces in the letters or canceling the operation, Q&A will give you a chance to match the field names you entered with the actual fields in the database.

After you press F10 from the Print Options menu, Q&A checks each of the field codes in your document against the actual field names in the database. When it encounters a field that is not in the file, Q&A displays a warning similar to the one shown in Figure 8.8. You can press Esc to return and edit the document, F10 to skip the unknown fields, or F8 to match the field names.

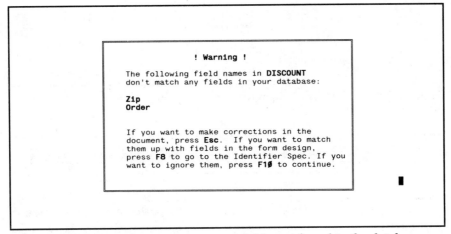

Figure 8.8: Warning that you've entered fields not found in the database

When you press F8, Q&A displays the Identifier Spec screen, shown in Figure 8.9. Enter the name that you typed in the document next to the field label. If you forgot how you entered the names in the document, press F10 to redisplay the warning message with the unknown field names.

After you have matched all the fields, press F10 to display the Retrieve Spec screen and continue the printing process.

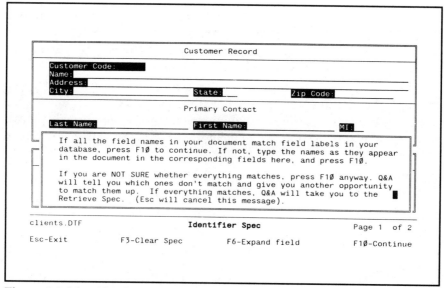

Figure 8.9: Identifier Spec screen for matching your fields with those in the database

'OTHER PROGRAM FUNCTIONS

You can use the *Program command to perform a wide range of sophisticated tasks during the merge process. You will learn how to use Q&A's programming functions throughout this book, and all the functions are listed in Appendix B. As a preview of the type of advanced programming possible in Q&A, the following sections describe how to use functions to perform calculations and manipulate text for form letters.

USING MATHEMATICAL FUNCTIONS FOR FORM LETTERS

To use the *Program command for form document math:

- **Use the @INT function to calculate an integer.**
- **Use the @ROUND function to round off decimal places.**

- **Use the @AVG, @MAX, @MIN, and @SUM functions for averages, maximums, minimums, and totals, respectively.**

In addition to performing simple arithmetic, the *Program command can be used with number and money fields to round off numbers, calculate the total and average of a list of fields, and find the largest and smallest values in a list.

In Chapter 4, you used the @INT function to calculate a person's age from the date of birth. This function returns the integer of a number (the number without decimal places). To use the @INT function in a form document, include it in the *Program command, such as

          Program { @INT((@DATE – #14)/365.25)}

The @ROUND function rounds off decimal places. This is especially useful when you do not want to deal with cents in money fields. The syntax for the command is

          *Program { @ROUND(*value, number-of-places*)}*

When the field is merged, Q&A rounds off the value to the number of places specified in the command. For example, if a value in an amount field is $125.46, the command

          Program { @ROUND(Amount, 1)}

would result in $125.50. The value can be a number, a field, or an expression, as in

          *Program { @ROUND(Total Orders * .13, 0)}*

In this case, a calculated result of $1,562.36 would be rounded to $1,562.00.

Other Q&A functions deal with lists, or *ranges*, of values. You designate a range by using logical field numbers or the field names. List the first item in the range and the last item in the range separated by two periods.

As an example, suppose you have a database with the following field labels and logical field numbers:

Salary: #3
Salary: #4
Salary: #5
Salary: #6

Q&A assigns the fields the internal names Salary, Salary1, Salary2, and Salary3.

You could calculate the average salary with the command

Program { @AVG(#3..#6)}

To find the highest and lowest salaries, use

Program { @MAX(#3..#6)}
Program { @MIN(#3..#6)}

Quickly total the salaries with the command

Program (@SUM(#3..#6)}

MANINULATING TEXT

IIII▶ To use the *Program command to manipulate form letter text:

- Use the @LEFT, @RIGHT, and @MID functions to extract characters on the left side of the field, right side of the field, or at the specified position, respectively.
- Use the @LEN and @WIDTH functions to find the number of characters in a field and the number of spaces between fields, respectively.

Some program functions manipulate text instead of numbers. The @LEFT function, for example, returns a specific number of characters that start the field, using the syntax

Program {@LEFT(field, number-of-characters)}*

Suppose that we wanted to print a list with just Adam Mycroft Chesin's middle initial, but his full middle name is in the MI field. We could extract the initial with the command

Program {@LEFT(MI, 1)}

The @RIGHT function's result is just the opposite: it returns characters on the right of the field, using the syntax

Program {@RIGHT(field, number-of-characters)*}*

@MID, on the other hand, locates characters at any starting position, using the syntax

Program {@MID(field, starting-position, number-of-characters)*}*

For example, if the City field contains the value Alameda, the command

@Program {@MID(City,2,4)}*

returns *lame*—the four characters starting at the second position.

If you stored phone numbers in the format (215) 555-1111, you could separate the area code, exchange, and extension by using these commands:

```
Area Code:   *Program { *MID(Phone, 2,3)}*
Exchange:    *Program { *MID(Phone, 7,3)}*
Extension:   *Program { *RIGHT(Phone, 4)}*
```

Two other useful commands are @LEN and @WIDTH. @LEN prints the number of actual characters in a field. @WIDTH reports the number of spaces between fields on the form. For example, you could determine how much space an address field required by using these functions:

The value in the Address field takes up *Program { @LEN (Address)}* characters of a total of *Program { @WIDTH (Address)}* characters.

The number of spaces between fields is not the same as the number of characters that can appear. For instance, the @WIDTH function will show that the State field is three characters wide, even though it displays two, and the MI field is two characters, although it displays one.

PRINTING ENVELOPES AND LABELS

Printing the form letters is only part of the mailing process. You need to print envelopes or address labels to complete the task. The following sections describe how to merge your database information to produce addressed envelopes or labels.

MERGING TO ADDRESS ENVELOPES

To print envelopes for form documents:

1. **From the Write screen, press F2.**
2. **Select Print Options.**
3. **Choose Envelope and press F10.**
4. **Complete the Retrieve Spec screen and press F10.**

You can print a single envelope or merge variables from a database to print any number of envelopes.

Now we will print envelopes for our sample form letters.

1. Press F2 to display the Print menu.

2. Press ↓ twice, then → twice to select Envelope.

3. Press F10 twice to display the Retrieve Spec screen and generate envelopes for all clients.

4. Press ↵ to merge the files. The first envelope appears in preview mode.

5. Press Esc to return to the document.

Q&A assumes that you've created the form document using a standard format. Your own address, if you're not using preprinted letterhead, is centered at the top of the page, followed by the date either centered or left-aligned. Following the date is the recipient's name and address aligned at the left margin.

When you select Envelope for the Line Spacing option on the Write Print Options menu, Q&A scans the document looking for the first block of text at the left margin. A *block* is defined as lines of text with a blank line above and below. If the block is a date—either a @DATE code or an actual date—the program ignores it and looks for the next block followed by a blank line. Q&A assumes the block is the address.

When you are merging data from a database, Q&A uses the variables in the block to format and print each envelope. If you are typing a single letter, it uses the text in the block for the address. It formats the address to print on standard business-sized envelopes, ten lines down and 3½ inches from the left edge.

Q&A has no way of knowing if you really entered the address in the expected format. If you include some other text at the left margin before the address, such as a reference number, Q&A will assume it is the address block and print it on the envelope.

If you want to print a set of envelopes without typing a form letter, just create a document with the appropriate codes:

```
*Program {First Name +" "+MI}* *Last Name*
*Name*
*Address*
*City* *State* *Zip Code*
```

Enter the name of the database at the name of merge file prompt. In fact, it would be a good idea to have a separate document with just those codes on your disk. When you are creating a form letter, insert it into the document after the date.

If you are using a LaserJet printer, make sure you installed the LaserJet (Envelope) or LaserJet II/D/P/III (Envelope) model. If not, return to the

Main menu, choose Utilities, and install the proper envelope model as one of your printers.

When you print envelopes, Q&A will turn on the printer's manual feed mode, and you will see a message on your printer's control panel requesting that you insert an envelope. Insert the envelope with the printing side face up and the top of the envelope towards the right side of the printer. With a LaserJet Plus, place the bottom of the envelope flush against the paper feed. With other models, center the envelope in the feed tray.

PRINTING MAILING ADDRESS LABELS

IIII➡ **To print mailing labels:**

1. **Select Mailing Labels from the Write menu.**
2. **Select the predefined label, or create your own from an existing template.**
3. **Make sure that the field names correspond to your database fields.**
4. **Complete the Mailing Label Print Options menu, and then press F10 twice.**

Formatting and printing labels with most word processing programs can be a time-consuming process. Q&A Write, however, has a built-in function that prints labels from your database. Labels can include field information as well as standard text to be printed on each one. You can select from 50 predefined label formats or create your own format for nonstandard labels.

We will use this function to print labels for a mailing to our clients. The labels will be sorted by zip code and formatted as two-up, or two labels across the page.

1. Select Mailing Labels from the Write menu. The List Manager screen will display the first page of predefined label formats, which are those designed for Avery labels and a LaserJet printer, as shown in Figure 8.10.

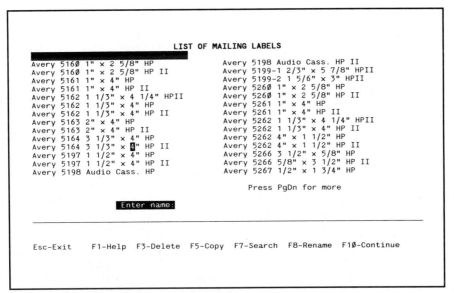

Figure 8.10: First screen of defined labels

2. Press PgDn to display a second page of label formats. The ones marked Pin Fed can be used with most printers that accept continuous label stock.

3. Press PgUp to return to the first page.

4. Choose the third label format on the right, Avery 5161 1" x 4" HP, and press ↵. Q&A will display the form document screen for this label, as shown in Figure 8.11.

The document is formatted as a single label, and it includes the most common field codes used for address information. In our Clients database, however, we have a field called Zip Code instead of just Zip. We could use the Identifier Spec screen to match Zip with Zip Code, but instead, we will edit this document to match our field name.

5. If necessary, turn on insert mode (Ins should appear on the status line).

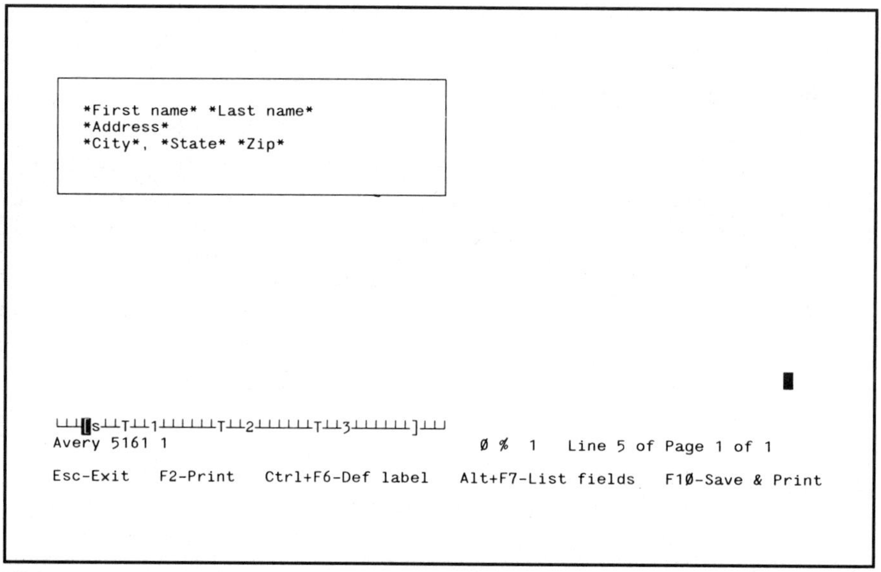

```
*First name* *Last name*
*Address*
*City*, *State* *Zip*
```

```
LLLLsLLTLL1LLLLLLLTLL2LLLLLLLTLL3LLLLLLL]LL
Avery 5161 1                          Ø % 1   Line 5 of Page 1 of 1

Esc-Exit   F2-Print   Ctrl+F6-Def label   Alt+F7-List fields   F1Ø-Save & Print
```

Figure 8.11: Form document screen for selected label

6. Place the cursor on the asterisk after Zip, press the spacebar, and type **Code**.

The key-assignment line on this screen includes the options Esc, to return to the Write menu; F2, to display the printing options without saving your changes to the label (so that the changes will only be used during this session); Ctrl-F6, to adjust the size, margins, and font of the label; Alt-F7, to list the field names in the database; and F10, to save any changes you made to the label and display the printing options.

7. Press F2 to display the Mailing Label Print Options menu, shown in Figure 8.12, without saving your changes.

All the options are set for the selected label format. You can change the Number of Labels Across, Space Between Labels, and Lines per Label Sheet options to create custom labels, as explained in the next section.

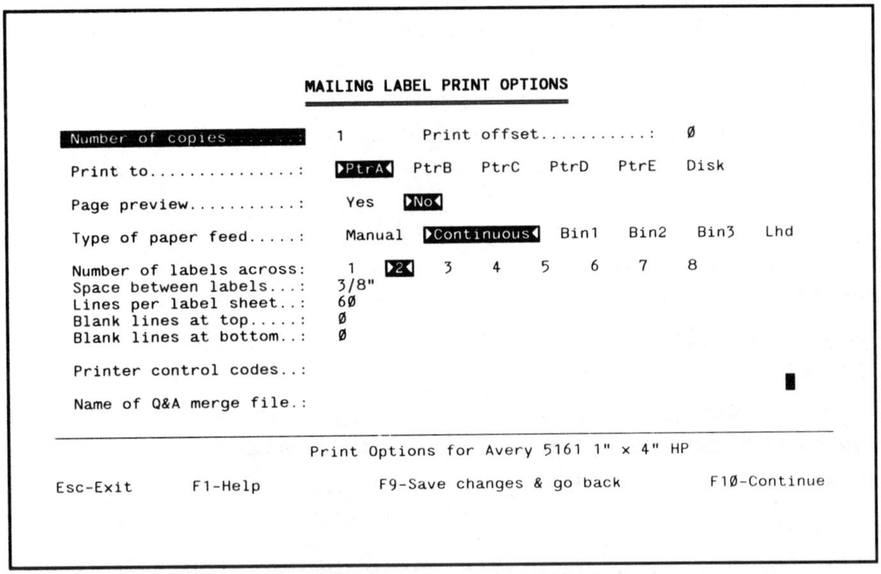

```
                        MAILING LABEL PRINT OPTIONS

      Number of copies.........:    1         Print offset..........:    Ø

      Print to..............:    ▶PtrA◀   PtrB    PtrC    PtrD    PtrE    Disk

      Page preview..........:    Yes    ▶No◀

      Type of paper feed.....:    Manual   ▶Continuous◀   Bin1   Bin2   Bin3   Lhd

      Number of labels across:    1    ▶2◀    3    4    5    6    7    8
      Space between labels...:    3/8"
      Lines per label sheet..:    6Ø
      Blank lines at top.....:    Ø
      Blank lines at bottom..:    Ø

      Printer control codes..:                                              ▮

      Name of Q&A merge file.:
      _____
                        Print Options for Avery 5161 1" x 4" HP

      Esc-Exit       F1-Help           F9-Save changes & go back        F1Ø-Continue
```

Figure 8.12: Mailing Label Print Options menu

Adjust the Print Offset setting by entering a positive number if your text prints too far to the left, or a negative number if it is too far to the right. If text is printing above the first label, increase the Blank Lines at Top setting. Entering 1, for example, will start the first label one line down from the default position. If text prints below the last label, increase the Blank Lines at Bottom setting; decrease it if the last label is not being printed.

8. Press ↓ twice to reach the Page Preview option, and then type **Y**.

9. Press ↓ eight times to reach the name of merge file prompt and type **Clients**.

The name of the merge file will automatically appear when you press Alt-F7 to select field names from the list.

10. Press F10 twice, then ↵ to preview the label sheet.

11. Press Esc to display the document.

12. Press Esc and type **Y** to return to the Write menu.

If you are printing on narrow labels, it is possible that a field will be too long to fit on a line. In this case, consider truncating the field by adding the (L) or (R) command to the field code. If you do not like the results, try changing the label's margins, as explained in the following section.

CREATING CUSTOM LABELS

||||➡ **To customize a label format:**

1. **Select Mailing Labels from the Write menu and choose the label that is the most similar to the format you want.**
2. **Press F5 to copy the label and edit the copy as necessary.**
3. **Press Ctrl-F6 and adjust the size settings as necessary.**
4. **Press F2 to display the Mailing Label Print Options menu.**

Although Q&A provides a wide selection of labels, you might want to print on a type that is not supported. By adjusting the page definition and printing options of one of the built-in labels, however, you can create your own custom format.

Instead of making permanent changes directly to one of the existing labels, make a copy of it first under a new name. This way, the original label will be available if you need it.

As an example, suppose that you are preparing materials for a convention. Your company purchased 4-inch by 4-inch continuous adhesive name tags, with the company's name printed on the top inch. You want to print the name of the primary contact and company name for each of your clients on the tags.

Follow these steps to format labels for name tags:

1. Select Mailing Labels from the Write menu.

2. Press PgDn to display the second page of labels.

3. Highlight the label closest in size, Pin fed 4" x 2 15/16" - 1 up.

4. Press F5 to display the prompt

   Copy to:

5. Type **Pin fed tag 4" x 4" - 1 up** and press ↵.

The label will be copied, and the new name will appear at the bottom of the list.

6. Highlight the new name and press ↵ to display the form with field names.

7. Press ↑ to reach the Address line, and then press Shift-F4 twice.

8. Type ***NAME***.

9. Press F8 and type **A**, then **C** to center the second line.

10. Press ↑, press F8, type **A**, and then type **C** to center the first line. Figure 8.13 shows the edited label.

11. Press Ctrl-F6 to display the Define Label screen, shown in Figure 8.14.

This screen allows you to change the width, height, margins, and characters per inch settings for the label. The width is correct, but we need to adjust the height, which is set as 3 inches. We also need to change the top margin to leave room for the preprinted company name. Finally, we must alter the left margin, because if it remains set at 2, the text on the label will be two characters to the right off center.

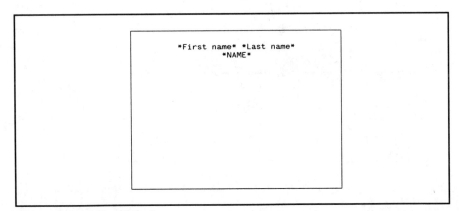

Figure 8.13: Edited label

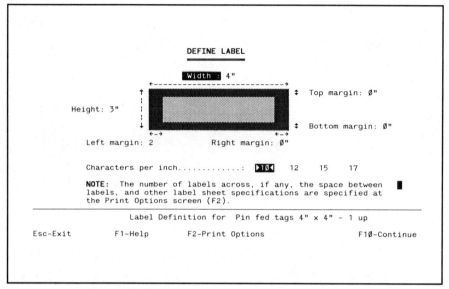

Figure 8.14: Define Label screen

12. Press ↵ to move to the Top Margin option and type **1.5"**.

13. Press ↵ to move to the Height option and type **4"**.

14. Press ↵ twice to reach the Left Margin option (the cursor moves from Height to Bottom Margin, and then to Left Margin), and type **0**.

If you entered 0 for both the left and right margins, Q&A would display the warning

    Left/right margins are too close together. Please respecify

Enter 0" for both options if you do not want any left or right margin.

15. Press F2 to display the Mailing Label Print Options menu.

16. Press ↓ twice and type **Y** to select Page Preview.

17. Press ↓ four times to reach the Lines per Label Sheet option and type **24**.

18. Press ↓ four times to reach the name of merge file prompt and type **Clients**.

19. Press F10 twice, then ↵ to display the first label on the screen. It should appear as shown in Figure 8.15.

If the label is set up correctly, you can press F2, turn off preview mode, and then print the labels.

20. Press Esc to return to the document.

21. Press Shift-F8 to save the completed template.

22. Press Esc twice, and type **X** to exit from Q&A.

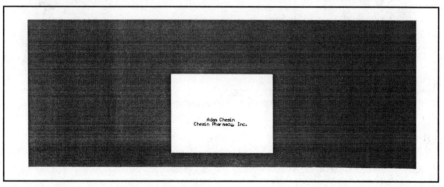

Figure 8.15: Preview of custom label

Since Q&A labels can include text as well as field names, you can produce all sorts of short form documents by customizing a label format. Figure 8.16 shows an example of invitations with client names merged from a database. The invitations were formatted as 3½-by-4-inch labels, printed six-up on 8½-by-11-inch paper. The label form included the client's First Name and Last Name fields, as well as the text of the invitation. Two lines of text were set in different fonts (fonts are discussed in Appendix C).

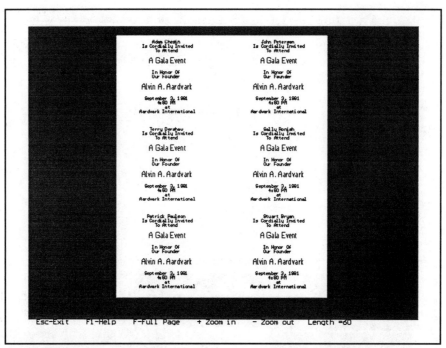

Figure 8.16: Custom labels used to print personalized invitations

This and the previous chapter have introduced some of the features of Q&A Write. In the next chapter, you will learn how to use the word processor's other capabilities, including finding and replacing text and checking the spelling in your documents.

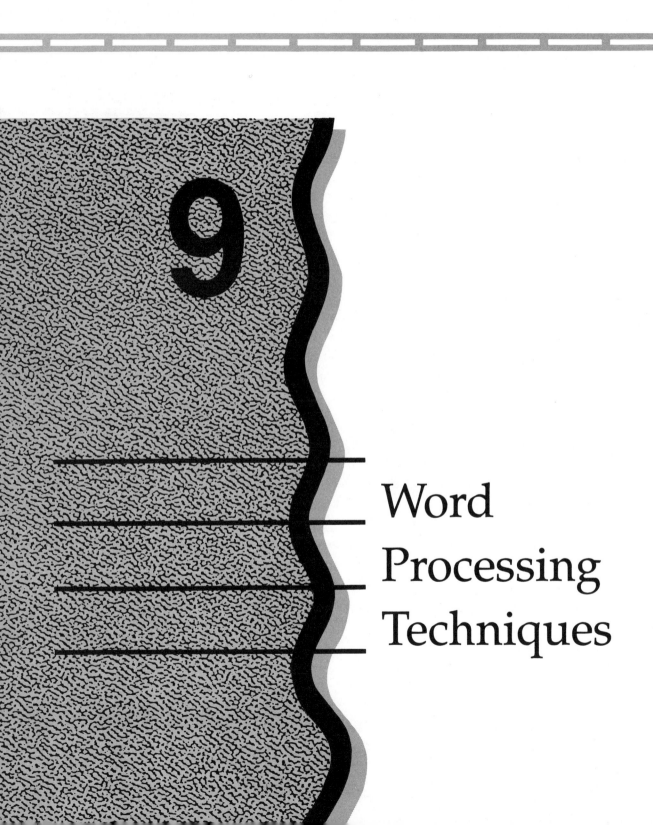

9

Word Processing Techniques

In the previous chapters, you learned the fundamentals of word processing using Q&A Write, including how to merge information from a Q&A database file. This chapter covers Write's word processing features for preparing documents of all types.

You will start by learning how to customize various Write options from the Write Utilities menu. Then you will learn about formatting techniques, special printing methods, and ways to import and export files.

CHANGING Q&A WRITE'S DEFAULT SETTINGS

||||▶ **To change Write's default settings:**

1. **Select Utilities from the Write menu, then Set Global Options.**
2. **Select Set Editing Options to reset editing defaults on the Editing Options menu.**
3. **Choose one of the other selections on the Global Options menu to reset printing, page, or import defaults.**

To customize how Q&A Write works, select Utilities from the Write menu, and then choose Set Global Options. The Global Options menu, shown in Figure 9.1, allows you to change the settings on the Print Options and Define Page menus, as well as settings for imported documents.

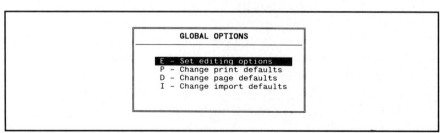

Figure 9.1: Write Global Options menu

You can also change default settings for editing options. Choose Set Editing Options from the Global Options menu to display the menu shown in Figure 9.2. On the menu, the default values for the editing options are surrounded by small triangles or listed after the option. You can select the other settings or enter new tab stop positions and column spacing. Table 9.1 summarizes the editing options.

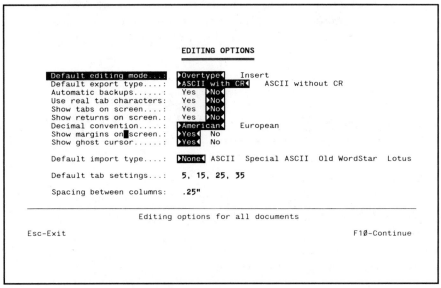

Figure 9.2: Editing options menu

Table 9.1: Settings on the Editing Options Menu

OPTION	SETTING
Default Editing Mode	Determines if Q&A Write is in overtype or insert mode when you start the program. If you frequently find yourself accidentally overtyping existing text, you might want to change the default mode from overtype to insert. Then the characters Ins will appear on the status line automatically, and you must press the Ins key to change to overtype mode.

Table 9.1: Settings on the Editing Options Menu (continued)

OPTION	SETTING
Default Export Type	Lets you select how ASCII files are saved when you press Ctrl-F8. The default setting, ASCII with CR, changes each soft return inserted by word wrap into a hard carriage return. The ASCII without CR setting saves only the hard returns created by pressing ↵.
Automatic Backups	Saves the original document with the extension .BAK when you save an edited version. If you have enough room on your disk to store both versions and want to be able to retrieve the original, change the default from No to Yes.
Use Real Tab Characters	Inserts a tab code instead of blank spaces when the Tab key is pressed.
Show Tabs on Screen	When you choose to use tab codes, allows you to display a ➤ symbol when the Tab key is pressed.
Show Returns on Screen	Allows you to display paragraph symbols (¶) where ↵ is pressed.
Decimal Convention	Determines whether American style (a period) or European style (a comma) decimal indicators are used in automatic calculations and decimal tab values.
Show Margins on Screen	Establishes whether or not left, right, top, and bottom margins are indicated by blank spaces on the screen. Change the default setting from Yes to No to remove the spaces and display the maximum number of lines and characters on the screen. This is particularly useful with wide documents that would otherwise scroll off the right edge of the screen.
Show Ghost Cursor	Allows you to remove the cursor indicator on the ruler.

Table 9.1: Settings on the Editing Options Menu (continued)

OPTION	SETTING
Default Import Type	Allows you to bypass the Import menu by selecting a file type (ASCII, Special ASCII, Old WordStar, or Lotus 1-2-3). With the default None setting, Q&A automatically displays the Import menu when you are importing a file. However, if you change the default setting and try to get a document that is not in Q&A's format or the selected type, the import operation will fail.
Default Tab Settings	Allows you to change the default tab stops, set at 5, 15, 25, and 35. Any new tab settings you enter will be used with every new document, but will not affect existing ones—they maintain the tab settings that were set when they were created.
Spacing Between Columns	Allows you to change from the default spacing of ¼ inch between columns in multicolumn documents. Enter the new value in inches, centimeters, or character spaces.

Two of the Editing Options menu settings can affect exported files. The Default Export Type option is set to change soft returns—those created by word wrap—into hard carriage returns—those inserted when you press ↵. Use the default setting if you want to print the document as an ASCII text file, but not if you plan to use it with another word processor. If you do, each line will be treated as an individual paragraph, and it will be difficult to change margins and other formats.

When you change the default setting so that the file is saved without ↵, the return codes are inserted only at the end of each paragraph, where you pressed ↵. When you import the document, the word processor will add its own soft returns, keeping the text in paragraphs.

The other setting that can be useful for exported files is Use Real Tab Characters. When you press the Tab key, Q&A moves the cursor to the next tab stop, inserting blank spaces up to that position. You can delete any or all of the spaces to adjust the alignment. If you choose real tab characters, a tab code will be inserted instead of spaces. The code tells Q&A to move the cursor to the specific position on the line indicated by the next tab stop. With real tab characters, you cannot delete the spaces in the tab area until you remove the code.

You should select to use real tab characters if you plan to export the document for use with another word processor. Using the default setting, the exported document will have the same spacing as in Q&A; if a tab setting indented a paragraph five spaces, it will be indented five spaces when it is brought into the other program. When you insert a real tab character, the spacing will conform to the other word processor's tab settings.

You should also select real tab characters when you are using proportionally spaced fonts and creating tables.

FORMATTING LINES AND PARAGRAPHS

To format lines and paragraphs:

- **Indent paragraphs from the left or right by positioning the cursor and pressing F6, then L or R.**
- **Return to the default margin by pressing F6, then C.**
- **Insert a soft hyphen by pressing Alt-F6.**

Formatting means to arrange the placement of text on the page. In Chapter 7, you learned how to center and right-align text by using the Align text settings on the Options menu (F8). However, Q&A Write provides other ways to format text.

For example, the default paragraph format is the block style. Every line, including the first one in a paragraph, starts at the left margin. To indent the first line of a paragraph, you press the Tab key.

But you might want to indent a whole paragraph, like this one, from the left margin. This helps to make a specific point stand out.

You might also want to indent a paragraph from both the right and left margins. This is frequently required for long quotations.

The following sections describe how to create these and other types of indentations.

INDENTING FROM
THE LEFT OR RIGHT MARGIN

When you want to change the left or right margin of the entire document, use the Define Page menu. To change the margin of a single paragraph or line, press F6, the Indent key, to create a temporary margin. This command allows you to format individual paragraphs quickly without affecting other text.

Move the cursor to the position where you want the left margin to appear and press F6. You will see the prompt

Set temporary margin: L-Left R-Right C-Clear

Press L to set the left margin or R to set the right one. The > (for a left margin) or < symbol (for a right margin) will appear in the ruler to indicate the temporary margin position. As you type, word wrap will return the cursor to the indented position, not the original margin, until you change or clear the margin position.

To return to the original margin, press F6 and then type C to select Clear.

To change the margin of existing text, move to the beginning of the paragraph, and then insert the spaces or tab positions necessary to indent the start of the first line to the desired position. When that line is in the correct position, press F6 and type L or R. All the text in the paragraph will realign along the temporary margin.

If you want both margins indented for a long quotation or another special section, you must set both left and right temporary margins.

CREATING HANGING INDENTATIONS

Standard paragraphs have only the first line indented with remaining text starting at the left margin. Hanging indentations are just the opposite; the first line starts to the left of the rest of the paragraph. Use hanging indentations when you want paragraphs to stand out from each other, as in numbered paragraphs and outlines.

1. These lines are an example of a numbered paragraph with a hanging indentation. The main text is indented to the right of the level number. In this case, the level number is at the far left margin. Because the level number stands out from the text, it is easy to see and can be differentiated from other paragraphs and levels.

To create numbered paragraphs using hanging indentations, type the number, move the cursor to the indented position, and press F6, then choose Left. To create the next lower level, type the number at the indented position, and then reset the indentation further to the right. To move back to a higher outline position, reset the margins again.

As an example, we'll create the sample entries for the topical outline shown in Figure 9.3. Follow these steps:

1. Type **1.** to begin the outline.

2. Press Tab to reach position 5 on the ruler, press F6, and choose Left.

3. Type the following indented text.

   The choice of media used for data communications depends upon the speed of the transmission and the distance it must travel. There are three general classifications of media.

The text is indented to the first tab position, while the level number "hangs" at the left margin.

4. Press ↵. The indentation remains in effect for the next paragraph.

5. Type **a.**, and then press the spacebar three times to move the cursor to position 10.

```
1.   The choice of media used for data communications depends
     upon the speed of the transmission and the distance it must
     travel. There are three general classifications of media.
     a.   Wire media include open copper wire, twisted pair, and
          coaxial cable.
     b.   Airborne media include broadcast and microwave
          transmission.
     c.   New technology includes fiber optics and laser beam
          transmission.
2.   The communications protocol depends on the hardware being
     used, and the protocol selected by the recipient.
```

Figure 9.3: An outline using hanging indentations

6. Press F6, choose Left, and then type the first entry at this level.

   Wire media include open copper wire, twisted pair, and coaxial cable.

7. Press ↵.

8. Press Shift-Tab to move the cursor to position 5, type **b.**, and press Tab. Q&A treats the temporary margin as a tab stop.

9. Type the next subentry.

   Airborne media include broadcast and microwave transmission.

10. Press ↵.

11. Press Shift-Tab, type **c.**, and press Tab.

12. Type the third subentry.

    New technology includes fiber optics and laser beam transmission.

13. Press ↵.

14. Press Shift-Tab twice to move the cursor to position 1, type **2.**, and press Tab.

15. Press F6 and choose Left to reset the margin.

16. Type the next entry.

    The communications protocol depends on the hardware being used, and the protocol selected by the recipient.

17. Press ↵.

18. Press F6, and choose Clear to clear the indentation.

19. Press F2, then F10 to print the outline.

If you have a long outline to type, set tab stops at each of the indentation levels so you can move the cursor quickly.

This paragraph is also a example of a hanging indentation, but it is not a numbered paragraph.

Instead of spaces separating the hanging and indented characters, the text on the first line is continuous. To create the first paragraph in this format, type until you reach the indentation position, and then press F6 and choose Left. As you complete the sentence, the remaining lines will begin at the indented position. Press ↵ when you complete the paragraph. To type additional paragraphs in the same format, first press Shift-Tab or ← to reach the regular margin position, and then type the text.

To create a hanging indentation for a paragraph that already exists, move the cursor to the indentation position in the first line, press F6, and choose Left.

HYPHENATING TEXT

At times, such as when long words are carried to the next line, justifying text results in unsightly extra spaces between words. These spaces will be most noticeable in narrow paragraphs or columns. You can avoid this problem by inserting soft hyphens.

To enter a soft hyphen, press Alt-F6, and the character to the left of the hyphen position will be highlighted or appear in a different color. The hyphen will appear on the screen and the printout only if word wrap divides the word between lines. If you later add or delete text and the word no longer has to be divided, the hyphen will disappear.

You might want to add soft hyphens to long words that are near the end or start of a line. This way, they will be hyphenated as required.

To remove a soft hyphen, delete the character to its left, and then retype the character. Even if the hyphen appears on the screen, you must delete the highlighted (or different colored) character before it, not the hyphen itself.

ADJUSTING TABS

To set and delete tab stops:

1. **Press F8, then L, then S to move the cursor to the ruler.**
2. **Enter a T to set a left tab stop or a D for a decimal tab stop. Position the cursor on the tab stop and press Del to delete it.**
3. **Press ↵ to return to the document.**

When you press the Tab key, the cursor moves directly to the closest tab stop to the right. By default, Q&A sets tab stops at positions 5, 25, 35, and 45. The following sections describe how to adjust tab stops for individual documents. To change the default tab stops for use with every new document, use the Write Global Options menu.

SETTING AND DELETING TAB STOPS

To set or delete tab stops for a specific document, press F8, select Lay Out Page, and then choose Set Tabs. The cursor will disappear from the screen and blink under the ghost cursor in the ruler.

You can set a tab stop by moving the cursor to the desired position and pressing T. Delete a tab stop by placing the cursor on it and pressing the spacebar or the Del key.

The following keystrokes can be used to move along the ruler:

Home	Moves to the first space to the right of the left margin
End	Moves to the first space to the left of the right margin
Ctrl-←	Moves five spaces to the left
Ctrl-→	Moves five spaces to the right

Tab   Moves to the next tab stop to the right

Shift-Tab   Moves to the next tab stop to the left

For example, if you want to set tabs every five characters spaces, place the cursor on the tab stop at position 5, and repeatedly press Ctrl-→, then T until you reach the right end of the ruler.

When you are finished setting and deleting tabs, press ↵ to return to the document. Press Esc if you change your mind and decide to retain the original tab positions.

When you're using real tab characters, setting or deleting tab stops affects the entire document, no matter where the cursor is placed in it (even if the cursor is below the text with real tab characters). After you press ↵ to leave the ruler after changing tab stops, you will see

formatting text…

flashing on the message line as Q&A scans the document, adjusting tab characters to align with the tab stops.

USING DECIMAL TABS

As shown in the lists below, columns of numbers are easier to read when they are aligned on their decimal points:

345.34	345.34
.09	.09
23,456.00	23,456.00
1.12	1.12

For this type of alignment, set a decimal tab. When you enter a number at a decimal tab stop, the characters shift to the left until you type a decimal point, space, tab, or ↵, and then they move to the right.

To set a decimal tab, enter a D at the tab stop position on the ruler after you choose Set Tabs from the Layout Options menu. Remember to set the tab stop where you want the decimal point to be, not where you want the number to begin or end. When planning columns, decide where you want the last decimal digit to appear, and then set the tab two spaces to the left.

CREATING TABLES

In many cases, you will set tab stops to create tables. If you're using a proportionally spaced font, or intend to merge fields into a table, you should use real tab characters and set only the tabs you will need for the columns.

Before creating the table, plan the number and positions of the columns that you will need. Next, set tabs where you want the numbers to align and delete any others. Then display the Write Global Options menu and turn on real tab characters. It's not necessary to show the tabs on the screen, but it does make it easier to set up the table.

CALCULATING IN DOCUMENTS

▐▐▐▊➤ **To perform calculations on rows and columns:**

1. **Position the cursor after the row or on the last number of the column and press Alt-F9.**
2. **Select Total, Average, Count, Multiply, or Divide.**
3. **Position the cursor where you want the result to appear and press F10.**

You can have Q&A perform arithmetic on rows and columns of numbers in a document by pressing Alt-F9. If the cursor is to the right of a number, Q&A assumes you want to perform calculations on the row of numbers to the left. If the cursor is on a number, it assumes you want to calculate the numbers in the column above.

Q&A highlights the numbers and displays this menu on the message line:

Calculations: T-Total A-Average C-Count M-Multiply D-Divide

Select the calculation you want to perform, move the cursor to where you want the result to appear, and press F10.

Results appear with a number of decimal places equal to the largest number of places in the row or column. Two additional decimal places are added when you average or divide. Numbers in parentheses or preceded by a minus sign are treated as negative values.

When calculating numbers in a row, Q&A will highlight all the text up to the first number on the line, even if there is intervening text. This means you can calculate the results in a sentence, as in

You ordered 55 items at $3.75 each, for a total of

by pressing Alt-F9, then M to multiply.

Numbers in columns, however, are only highlighted up to the first nonnumeric character or blank line. For example, if you place the cursor on the last number in this column

1
1

1
1

only the last two numbers will be highlighted, and the total would be calculated as 2.

EMBEDDING COMMANDS

To use embedded commands:

- **Use the *Linespacing *n** embedded command to space sections of text from 1 to 9 lines when printed (not on the screen).**
- **Use the *Justify Yes* embedded command before text you want to right-justify.**
- **Insert the *Justify No* embedded command to turn off justification.**

An embedded command is an instruction that tells Q&A to perform a function while the document is being printed. All embedded commands begin and end with asterisks. You can either type them in directly, or press F8, choose Print Commands, and select them from the menu shown in Figure 9.4.

The *@DATE*, *@TIME*, and *Program* commands discussed in earlier chapters are examples of embedded commands. Like all embedded commands, the codes appear in your document on the screen and are executed when the document is printed.

Unlike printer control codes—which you specify through the Print Options menu, are transmitted when printing begins, and affect the entire document—embedded control codes are transmitted to the printer as they are found in the document. This means that you can use embedded codes to turn features on and off for specific portions of text. Entering *Printer 27 73 49* before a paragraph, and *Printer 27 64* after it, for example, will print the paragraph in italics on many dot-matrix printers.

You can change line spacing using the embedded code *Linespacing *n** (or **ls *n**), where *n* is the number of the line spacing desired, from 1 to

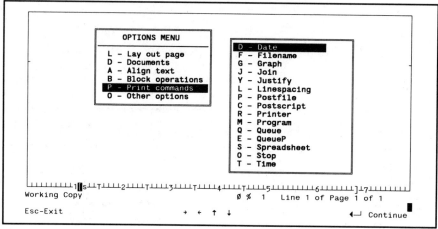

Figure 9.4: Print Commands menu

9. This has no effect on the appearance of text on the screen; it only changes the spacing on the printout.

For example, if you want one paragraph double-spaced, add the code *ls 2* before the paragraph, then *ls 1* after it to return the text to single-spacing.

You can justify selected portions of text using the *Justify* or *jy* embedded code. Enter *Justify Yes* or *jy y* at the beginning of the block you want justified; insert *Justify No* or *jy n* at the end.

PRINTING
HEADERS AND FOOTERS

▐▐▐▶ **To add headers and footers to Write documents:**

1. **Press F8, then →, and select Edit Header or Edit Footer.**
2. **Type the text of the header or footer. Use the # symbol to insert a page number and the @DATE and @TIME functions to insert the current date and time.**
3. **Press F10 to return to the document.**

Adding headers or footers to be printed at the top or bottom of each page of a Write document is similar to adding them to database reports (described in Chapter 5). However, you enter them in a separate window rather than on the Design Page menu, and they can be longer than three lines.

Headers and footers print in the top and bottom margins of the page, so their length is limited by the amount of margin space. With the default margins, you can print up to six lines of header text and six lines of footer text. If you want to add longer headers or footers, increase the margins by changing the Define Page menu settings.

CREATING A HEADER OR FOOTER

To create a header or footer or edit an existing one, follow these general steps:

1. Press F8, press →, and select Edit Header or Edit Footer. You will see a header window at the top of the screen, as shown in Figure 9.5, or a footer window at the bottom.

The header or footer window represents the actual page margins. If you type header text on the first line in the window, it will print at the very top of the page. Similarly, text on the first line of the footer window will print immediately following the last line of text on a full page. Space your header and footer text within the window just as you want it to appear on the page—with blank lines between it, the edge of the page, and the actual text of the document.

2. Type and format the text that you want to appear on every page, as well as any program instructions and functions.

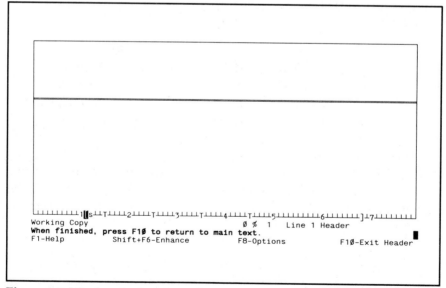

Figure 9.5: Window for header or footer text

You can use the same codes as the ones that are available for database report headers and footers. The *@DATE* and *@TIME* codes will print the current date and time (add a format number to specify the style), and the # symbol prints the page number. Remember, if you want the # sign itself to appear, such as Page #1, insert a second # sign preceded with a backslash, as in Page \##.

3. Press F10 to return to the document. You will see the header or footer on the screen within the top or bottom margin area.

Because they print within the margin areas, headers and footers do not reduce the number of text lines on the page. Some page styles call for the header and footer to appear in addition to the standard 1-inch margin. To create this style, increase the top and bottom margin settings to accommodate the desired margin space, the text of the header or footer, and the blank lines that you want to appear between it and the text of the document.

For example, suppose you want a 1-inch top margin, a one-line header, and then a $1/2$-inch line space between the header and the start of the text. Change the top margin to 10 lines, and then type the header on the seventh line of the header window.

SUPPRESSING A HEADER OR FOOTER

In some cases, you will not want your headers or footers to appear on particular pages of a document. For example, if your document includes a title page, table of contents, or other frontmatter, you will want to turn off headers and footers for those pages.

To suppress a header or footer from printing, use the Begin Header/Footer on Page # option on the Define Page menu. Enter the number of the page where you want the header and footer to first appear at the prompt

Begin page numbering with page #

This will usually be 1 unless you're printing a long document in sections as a series of files. For example, if you already printed the first 10 pages of the document in one file, set the option to 11 before printing the next file in the series.

Instead of printing a series of documents individually, however, you can use embedded commands to streamline the process, as described in the next section.

WORKING WITH LONG AND COMPLEX DOCUMENTS

If the length of your document is important, you can press Ctrl-F3 while the document is on the screen to display the Document Statistics window. As shown in the example in Figure 9.6, this window shows the total number of words, lines, and paragraphs in the document, as well as those above and below the cursor position.

Long or complex documents require some special handling. The following sections describe how to print a lengthy document divided into separate files, print spreadsheets or graphics within your text, and use PostScript files.

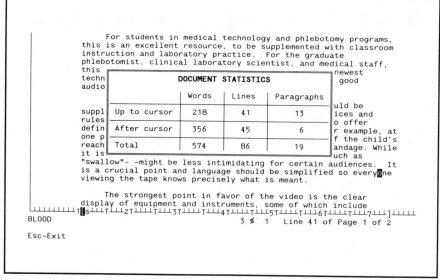

Figure 9.6: Document Statistics display

JOINING FILES

To create a master document for printing multiple files:

- Use the *Join *filename** command to insert the text of another document while printing, without a page break.
- Use the *Queue *filename** command to insert the text of another document while printing, with a page break.
- Use the *Queuep *filename** command to insert the text of another document while printing, with a page break and the pages numbered consecutively.

Long documents are often difficult to work with, especially with slower computer systems. As your document grows, you might begin to see noticeable delays in moving the cursor from one location to another or in reformatting the text after changing margins, tabs, or other settings.

One way to avoid the problem is to create a long document as a series of smaller files by typing each section or chapter as a separate document. Because each file is relatively short, you can edit and format it at maximum speed.

When you are ready to produce the final document, you can join the files together as they are being printed. This way, each file remains a separate entity because the files were never physically combined.

To join files, where you want one document to appear in another, enter the *Join *filename* command, with the complete path of the file if it is not in the QA directory. During printing, the document will be inserted at the position of the command.

If you type a long document as a series of separate files, create a master document to join the files together. The master document could contain the header, footer, and page definitions, along with the Join commands, which might look like this:

```
*Join sect1*
*Join sect2*
*Join sect3*
```

Page size, margins, pagination, headers, and footers will all be controlled by the master document. Headers and footers in the individual joined documents will be ignored.

Each file begins printing immediately after the other, not starting on a separate page. If you want a page break after each section, use the *Queue filename* or *Queuep filename* command. Each merged document will start on a new page. The page size is controlled by the master document, but the headers and footers of the queued documents will print along with them. This is one way to print different headers or footers with each section of a document.

The only difference between the Queue and Queuep commands is the way page numbering is handled. With Queue, numbering is controlled by the individual documents, based on the number you enter at the begin page numbering with prompt. Using the default settings, each document will start with page number 1. On the other hand, Queuep numbers all the pages in the merged documents consecutively, beginning with whatever number you enter at the begin page numbering with prompt.

Q&A will not check the format of joined and queued files before printing them. Files will be printed as they are found on the disk, using the page size and margins of the master document. In most cases, ASCII text files will print satisfactorily. However, documents created by other word processors may include formatting codes that Q&A cannot recognize, and those files will not be printed properly.

MERGING SPREADSHEETS AND GRAPHS INTO DOCUMENTS

To merge graphics and spreadsheets in a document:

- **Use the *Spreadsheet** *filename, range** command to insert the spreadsheet while printing.**
- **Press F8, then D, then I to use the Insert Document option to add the text of the spreadsheet before printing.**
- **Use the *Graph** *filename density** command to insert a Lotus 1-2-3 PIC or PFS:Graph file in the document.**

Embedded commands can be used to print spreadsheets and certain graphic files along with your text.

Printing Spreadsheets

Print a Lotus 1-2-3 or compatible spreadsheet with the command

*Spreadsheet *filename, range**

The *filename* is the complete path and name of the file, including the extension. If you do not designate a *range,* the whole spreadsheet will be printed. For example, this command prints an entire spreadsheet:

Spreadsheet c:\123\ENROLL.WS1

If you want to print a specific range, use either a named range or cell coordinates of the upper-right and lower-left corners of the range, separated by a hyphen, as in

Spreadsheet c:\123\ENROLL.WK1 A1-C15

Spreadsheets will not be formatted according to the placement of the Spreadsheet command on the line. If you center or right-align the command, the spreadsheet will still begin at the left margin.

If you want to format the spreadsheet or apply enhancements and fonts, you must insert it in the document as text before it is printed. Follow these general steps to bring in the spreadsheet file as text:

1. Press F8, choose Documents, and then select Insert.

2. Enter the file name or select it from the List Manager screen.

3. Choose Lotus 1-2-3 or Symphony from the Import menu. The Define Range menu will appear.

4. Press F10 to import the entire spreadsheet, or enter the coordinates or the named range and then press F10. The spreadsheet will appear at the position of the cursor.

Although this method allows you to format the spreadsheet, any changes you make to it in the spreadsheet program will not be reflected when you print the document. On the other hand, when you use the Spreadsheet command, the most recent version of the spreadsheet will be printed along with the document.

Printing Graphs

Include a Lotus 1-2-3 or compatible graphic file or a PFS:Graph file with the command

*Graph *filename density**

The file name must include the extension, as well as the path if it is not on the Q&A directory. *Density* designates the resolution of the printed image: S for single, D for double, or Q for quadruple.

With Lotus 1-2-3 graph files, you can also specify parameters in the command line, using the syntax

*Graph filename, *density, font1, font2, width, height, rotation**

where the parameters represent the following:

- *font1* is the font used for the graph's main title (BLOCK1 is the default). You must specify the full path and name of the font file, including the FNT extension.

- *font2* is the font used for all other text, such as the second title line, legends, and scale numbers. If you do not specify a second font, Q&A uses the same one as *font1*.

- *width* is the width of the graph in inches (6.5 inches is the default).

- *height* is the height in inches (4.7 inches is the default).

- *rotation* is the number of degrees counter clockwise. It can be 0 (the default), 90, 180, or 270.

If you want to specify some parameters but not others, you must use commas as placeholders for parameters to the left. For example, the command line to specify density and rotation only would appear like this

*Graph c:\123\ENROLL.PIC,Q,,,,,180"

Lotus 1-2-3 usually prints the y-axis label at a 90-degree angle to the chart, x-axis, and other titles. Q&A will always print the y-axis title in the same direction as the chart.

Figure 9.7 shows an example of a Write document that merges a spreadsheet and two graphic files. The document is shown in preview mode (without a y-axis label) in Figure 9.8.

Graphs are affected by alignment commands and the position of the Graph command on the line. If you right-align the command, the resulting graph will be right-aligned.

However, Lotus 1-2-3 graphs are contained in invisible frames—boxes that surround the graph but do not appear with it when printed. In most cases, the graph is not centered in the box, but positioned off-center toward the left. By default, the left edge of the frame is placed on the left margin of the document, so the graph will appear off-center on the page. If you centered the Graph command with the Align Center command, the frame would be centered but the graph would still appear too far toward the left. In Figure 9.7, blank spaces were added before the Graph commands to position the graph in the center of the page.

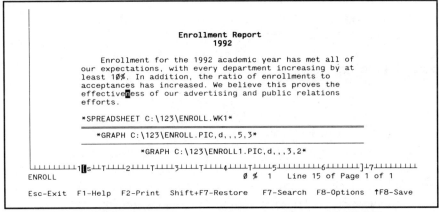

Figure 9.7: Write document with commands to merge spreadsheet and graphic files

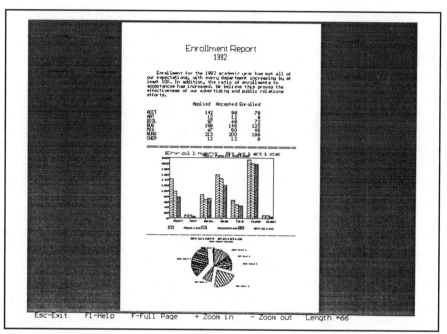

Figure 9.8: Preview of document with merged spreadsheets and graphs

USING POSTSCRIPT SUPPORT

To print PostScript files and programs:

- **Use the *Postfile *filename** command to print a PostScript file in ASCII (not Encapsulated PostScript) format.**
- **Use the *Postscript *program-line** command to transmit a Post-Script instruction.**

If you have a PostScript printer, you can print graphics that are saved as PostScript files by using the command *Postfile *filename**. The file must be in ASCII, not Encapsulated PostScript (EPS), format.

Some software programs, such as Microsoft Word, use a PostScript *preamble*, which is a separate file transmitted to the printer before it prints a document or graphic. The preamble contains definitions that must be in the printer's memory before the graphic can be generated. If you are using a PostScript file that requires a preamble, transmit the preamble first in its own Postfile command, or enter the preamble's path and name for the Printer Control Codes option on the Print Options menu.

Additional PostScript support is provided by the Postscript command. This allows you to directly transmit a PostScript command, such as

Postscript 270 360 moveto 0 72 rlineto

This command draws a 1-inch line in the middle of the page. The command must fit on one line.

IMPORTING AND EXPORTING DOCUMENTS

IIII➡ To import and export word processing files:

1. **Select Utilities from the Write menu, and then choose Import or Export.**
2. **Select the desired format.**
3. **Enter the names of the source and destination files.**

Just as you can import and export files from other database programs, you can import and export word processing documents to and from Write. Importing a file allows you to convert a document created by another word processing program into Q&A format. By exporting a Q&A document, you can edit and print it with another word processor or transmit it over a modem.

The Get option on the Write menu brings in documents that are in Q&A Write format. If you try to get a document that is in another format, and you set the Default Import Type option on the Editing Options menu to None, you will see the menu shown in Figure 9.9. Using this menu, you can import ASCII files, those created with early releases of WordStar, and Lotus 1-2-3 spreadsheets.

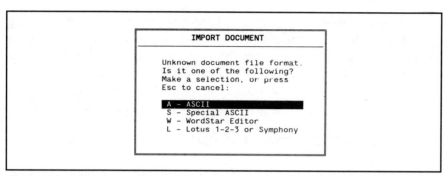

Figure 9.9: Selections when importing an unrecognized format

You can export a file in ASCII format by pressing Ctrl-F8 by selecting Print to Disk, or by choosing a basic vanilla printer assigned to the File port.

To import and export files in a wider variety of formats, select Utilities from the Write menu, then either Import a Document or Export a Document. The available formats are listed in Table 9.2.

Table 9.2: File Formats Available for Export or Import

FILE TYPE	DESCRIPTION
ASCII	ASCII text with carriage return/line feed at the end of each line.
Special ASCII	ASCII text with a carriage return/line feed only at the end of paragraphs.
Macintosh ASCII	Document created with Macintosh word processing programs. To import a Macintosh file, it must be saved as an ASCII file and on a disk readable by a PC system.
DCA	Document Content Architecture, a standard format recognized by many document conversion systems.
WordStar	Versions 3.3 and later.
WordPerfect	Versions 5.0 and 5.1.
Microsoft Word	Versions 3.0, 3.1, 4.0, and 5.0.

Table 9.2: File Formats Available for Export or Import (continued)

FILE TYPE	DESCRIPTION
Multimate	Versions 3.3 and 4, Multimate Advantage Version 3.6, and Multimate Advantage II Version 3.7.
Professional Write	Versions 1.0, 2.0, 2.1; PFS:Write version C; and PFS:First Choice versions 1 and 2.

You will be prompted to enter the path and name of the existing document, then the path and name of the document you wish to create in the new format.

IMPROVING YOUR SPELLING AND VOCABULARY

IIII➡ **To check your spelling and find synonyms:**

- **Press Ctrl-F1 to check the spelling of the word at the cursor.**
- **Press Shift-F1 to check the spelling in the entire document, starting at the position of the cursor.**
- **Place the cursor on the word for which you want to find synonyms and press Alt-F1.**

Like most full-featured word processors, Write offers both a spelling checker and a thesaurus. The following sections describe how to use these features.

CHECKING YOUR SPELLING

The Q&A Write spelling checker will report if a word in your document is not found in its dictionary. You can then tell Q&A that the word is properly spelled, correct it yourself, or select from a list of suggested spellings taken from the dictionary. The new word will be inserted into the text automatically.

Just like any dictionary, Q&A's dictionary may not contain some correctly spelled words. Many technical words and names, for instance, will be reported as possible misspellings. But if the word really is spelled correctly, you can add it to a supplemental dictionary of your own words so it will not be reported as incorrect again.

You can check the spelling of individual words or the entire document. All spelling tasks start at the position of the cursor.

To check the spelling of an individual word, place the cursor on or immediately following the word and press Ctrl-F1. To check an entire document, place the cursor at the start of the document and press Shift-F1.

If Write finds the word in its dictionary, the message

[word] is spelled correctly

appears in the message line.

When a word is not found in the dictionary, you will see the menu shown in Figure 9.10.

The first option, List Possible Spellings, displays up to nine words that are possible alternatives to the one in the text. As words start to appear in the list, you will see the message

Make a selection or wait for more.

You can select a word immediately or wait until the list is complete. When all the alternatives have been displayed, the message changes to

Select from this list or press Esc.

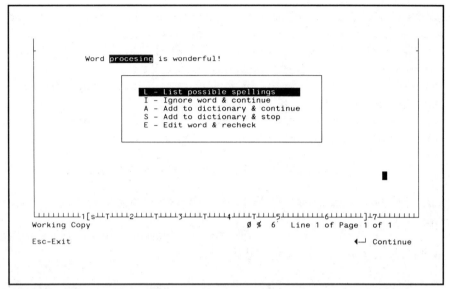

Figure 9.10: Spelling options

To select a replacement, press the number next to the word, or highlight it and press ↵.

If no alternative words are found, a box will appear with the message

No possible spellings for this word were found. Press ↵ to continue.

Press ↵ to redisplay the options. If you are checking the document, the process will continue until the end of the document.

If the word is actually spelled correctly, you may want to choose Ignore Word & Continue. This option skips over the word and continues checking the document. The same word will be ignored if it is found again during the current session.

If the word is spelled correctly, another alternative is to add it to your personal dictionary so it is not reported as incorrect during later spelling checking sessions. Choose Add to Dictionary & Continue or Add to Dictionary & Stop.

Q&A's dictionary is the QAMAIN.DCT file. When you add your own words, they go into QAPERS.DCT, an ASCII text file that you can edit or add additional words to using Q&A Write (be sure to save it as an ASCII file).

The final spelling checker option, Edit Word & Recheck, lets you edit the word without leaving the checking process. If the word contains an obvious error, it may be faster to edit the word yourself then wait until Write lists alternatives in the dictionary.

When you select this option, a box appears with the word, along with this prompt on the message line:

Enter the proper spelling for the misspelled word and press ENTER.

Edit the word and press ↵. Write will check the word again and then continue.

If the spelling checker encounters two of the same words in a row, it will highlight the second one and display

Repeated word. Press F3 to delete, ↵ to continue.

Press F3 if you want to remove the second occurrence of the word. If not, press ↵.

FINDING SYNONYMS
WITH THE THESAURUS

Sometimes the hardest part of writing is selecting just the right word. You know what you want to say, but you're not sure how to put it. Other times, you find yourself repeating a word frequently in a paragraph, and you would like to find another way to say the same thing without sounding repetitious. These times call for the Q&A Write thesaurus.

To use the thesaurus, place the cursor on or immediately following the word you would like to replace with a synonym and press Alt-F1. Six lines of text will remain on the screen above a box of suggested alternates. Figure 9.11 shows the Thesaurus screen displaying synonyms for the word *help*.

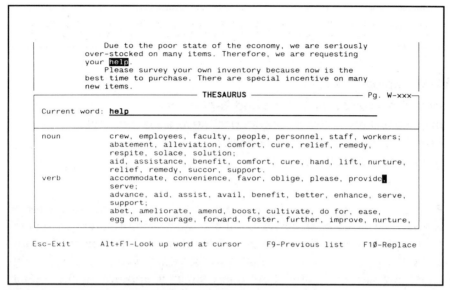

Figure 9.11: Synonyms for the word *help*

In this case, synonyms are given for the word *help* in both the noun and verb form. The words are listed in subgroups having similar connotations.

To see additional choices, highlight one of the words on the screen and press Alt-F1 again. To return to the original list, press F9.

When you find the word you want to use, select it and press F10.

If Write cannot find the word in the thesaurus, the message

> No synonyms were found for the word at the cursor. Retype the word or Escape.

will appear on the message line. Type another word with a similar meaning, and then press Alt-F1.

FINDING AND REPLACING TEXT

To find and replace text:

1. **Press F7 to display the Search and Replace menu.**
2. **Enter the text you are searching for and the replacement text (if any).**
3. **Press F7 to locate the first occurrence.**
4. **Press F7 to repeat the search.**

Have you ever misspelled the same word several times in a letter or paper, or realized that you entered the wrong information in several places? Q&A Write allows you to correct this type of error quickly and easily. You can have Write automatically locate any text and replace it with something else, no matter how many times it appears, or just search through a document to see if a certain word or phrase has been used or to locate a specific reference.

SEARCHING FOR TEXT

To search for text in a document, press F7 to display the menu shown in Figure 9.12. Type the characters that you are searching for, then press F7 again. The text can be from 1 to 45 characters, including letters, numbers, spaces, and punctuation marks. It can even include codes such as those for carriage returns, tab stops, text enhancements, and centered text.

Write scans the document, starting at the position of the cursor. When

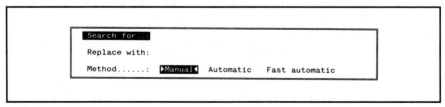

Figure 9.12: Search and replace menu

it locates a match, it places the cursor after the first occurrence of those characters and displays the message

FOUND! Press F7 to search again or ESC to cancel

To search for the next occurrence of the same characters, press F7 again. If you move the cursor between searches, press F7 twice to find the next occurrence of the same text. To search for different characters, press Esc, press F7, enter the new characters, and press F7 a second time.

At the end of the document, Write wraps around to the beginning and continues the search until it reaches the original cursor position. At the end of the search, you will see the message

Manual search COMPLETED after *n* matches

where n is the number of matches.

If no match is found, the words

Not Found

appear on the status line, and the cursor remains in its original position.

To count the number of occurrences but not locate each individual one, select Automatic or Fast Automatic from the menu. When you press F7 to begin the search, Write scans the document and displays

Automatic search COMPLETED after *n* matches

and the cursor remains at the original position.

SEARCHING FOR CODES

The text that you are searching for can include invisible codes and formats. You specify the codes by using the functions listed in Table 9.3. For example, to locate underlined text, enter @UL and press F7. The cursor will stop at the first underlined text after the cursor. To find specific formatted text, enter the format code, followed by the characters you are searching for, such as @ULPC Magazine.

Table 9.3: Write Search and Replace Codes

FUNCTION	LOCATES
@CR	Carriage returns
@TAB	Real tab characters
@NP	Newpage commands
@CT	Centered text
@RG	Regular, unenhanced text
@BD	Boldfaced text
@UL	Underlined text
@IT	Italic text
@SP	Superscript text
@SB	Subscript text
@XO	Strike-out text
@F1	Font 1
@F2	Font 2
@F3	Font 3
@F4	Font 4
@F5	Font 5
@F6	Font 6
@F7	Font 7
@F8	Font 8

CONDUCTING WILDCARD SEARCHES

Q&A Write also lets you use the wildcards ? and .. in much the same way you can specify retrieval criteria when you are working with databases. For example, searching for *r?d* will locate three-character words that begin with *r* and end with *d*, such as *rad, rid, rod,* and *red.* Searching for *r..d* will locate all words that begin with *r* and end with *d*, no matter what their length.

You can combine the wildcards in the same search, as in *?r..d* to locate words whose second letter is *r* and that end in *d*; and *W.. H??*, to locate two consecutive words—the first starting with *W*, the second a three-character word starting with *H*.

To search for the ? character, two consecutive periods, the @ symbol, or a backslash, precede them with the backslash (\), as in *WHY\?*.

REFINING YOUR SEARCH

Write locates the occurrence of the exact characters typed as a whole word, regardless of case. It will not locate words that contain the characters, such as *mission*, when you're searching for *miss*, but will locate any combination of uppercase and lowercase characters, such as *Miss* and *MISS*.

To change the search options, press PgDn when the search box is displayed. You will see the options shown in Figure 9.13.

For the Type option, select Text to find characters even if they are part of another word, such as locating *computer* when the search phrase is *compute*.

Select Pattern to locate text in much the same way you design templates in databases, where each *a* or *A* represents any alphabetic character, *9* a number, and *?* any single character. When you choose Pattern, searching for *999* will locate a three-digit number; *AA99* finds four-character words with two letters and two numbers; *(999) 999-9999* locates telephone numbers in that format; and *129* finds a three-digit number

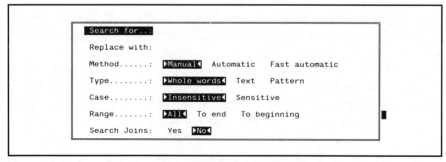

Figure 9.13: Search and replace menu advanced options

starting with *12*. Use the backslash to locate an actual *9* or *A*, such as *(20/9) 999-9999*, which would locate telephone numbers in the 209 area code.

The Case option allows you to make the search case-sensitive, matching characters only if they appear in the same case as those entered.

The Range option lets you determine the scope and direction of the search. Choose All to search through the entire document forward from the cursor position, wrapping around when it reaches the end. The To End option searches forward through the document; To Beginning searches backward toward the start, without wrapping around automatically.

The Search Joins option determines whether or not the search extends to documents that are linked to the one on the screen with the Join, Queue, or Queuep command.

You can make your new settings the defaults by pressing F8, or return to the original default settings by pressing F3. Press PgUp to remove the advanced options from display.

REPLACING TEXT

When you want to replace the text that you are searching for with other text, press F7, enter the text you are searching for, and enter the replacement text at the Replace with prompt. Then press F7.

If Method is set to Manual, Q&A will locate the first occurrence and display

> FOUND! Press F7 to search again, F10 to replace and continue, Esc to cancel.

Press F7 if you do not want to make the replacement but do want to continue searching; press F10 to make the replacement and search for the next occurrence; or press Esc to cancel the operation.

To make the replacements without stopping for confirmation, select Automatic or Fast Automatic. Both options replace the text automatically and then show the number of changes on the message line. The difference is that Automatic will display the changes as they occur. During the replacement, you can press Alt-F7 to switch between the automatic modes.

You can use all the wildcards, patterns, functions, and other options when replacing characters as well as when searching for them. For example, to change all underlined text to italics, complete the menu like this:

Search for: @UL
Replace with: @IT

Be careful when using either automatic replacement mode, especially if you change the text. For example, replacing *his* with *her* without confirmation will change *History* to *Hertory* and *this* to *ther.*

USING OTHER WRITE UTILITIES

||||➡ **To use Write file functions:**

- **Choose Recover Document from the Write Utilities menu to restore a damaged Write file.**
- **Choose DOS File Facilities from the Write Utilities menu to manipulate files without returning to the Main menu.**

If your computer's power goes off when you are editing a document, you may not be able to get the original file later. Make a backup copy of the file either from DOS or the DOS File Facilities menu, and then use the Recover Document option on the Write Utilities menu to restore the document.

The DOS File Facilities option on the Write Utilities menu works the same as the DOS File Facilities option on the Main Utilities menu. It is duplicated in Write so you can manipulate files without first saving the current document and returning to the Main menu.

This completes our discussion of Q&A Write. The following chapters introduce Q&A features that can help you find answers in your database: Query Guide and Intelligent Assistant.

10

Finding
Answers
with Query
Guide and
Intelligent
Assistant

You retrieve information from your database to answer questions. Which employees work overtime? Which clients haven't ordered lately? What's the best selling product? Where is Joe Smith? Getting complete and timely answers to your questions can help you make better business decisions.

In earlier chapters, you learned how to get information from your database by displaying and printing records and reports. These are highly structured methods because you must translate your question into the framework of retrieval, sort, and printing specifications. You have to know the criteria to use, which fields to print, the codes for calculating totals and averages, and how the data should be sorted. In this chapter, you will learn how to request information in a much more flexible, natural way.

ADVANTAGES OF INTERACTIVE REQUESTS FOR DATA

In the business world, you can ask questions without considering their structure. Rather than conform to a rigid pattern of specifications, we question intuitively, often spontaneously, with the answer from one question leading to others. Who are our best clients? Where are they located? What products do they buy? When was their last order?

If you had to create a set of specifications for every question, you would soon run out of room on your disk, and you would have little time for anything else.

For example, suppose your business needs a sudden influx of cash, so you want to know which clients owe you more than $500. Using Q&A Report, you first display the Retrieve Spec screen and decide which fields and criteria will select the records you want. You then complete the Column/Sort Spec screen, determining which fields you want to print and how to insert the calculation codes. Finally, you make selections from the Print Options menu.

Now assume that after reviewing the report, you decide to phone each client, and then visit all of them personally. You have to generate another report listing their phone numbers and addresses. Every time you need additional information, you go through the entire procedure again.

How different would it be if you had an assistant to answer your questions? You might start with the simple question, "How many clients owe over $500?" Your efficient assistant gives you the answer, so you immediately follow up with "Give me their names, address and phone numbers." Then, after thinking about it, you decide to ask, "Which ones haven't ordered since December?"

Although you might not save any time going through your assistant to get answers, you have the flexibility to adjust your line of questioning as you go along.

Q&A provides two unique and powerful features to help you interact intuitively with your database: Query Guide and Intelligent Assistant. You may or may not save time using Query Guide or Intelligent Assistant rather than Print or Report. The major advantage is that you can relate to your database in a more natural and comfortable way.

FORMING QUESTIONS WITH QUERY GUIDE

Query Guide, a new feature in Q&A version 4.0, is designed to guide you through the process of asking questions. It allows you to formulate your questions by suggesting the types of requests you may want to ask.

For example, if you want to ask, "Which clients purchased more than $1,000 worth of merchandise?" Query Guide will help you develop the request

Produce a report showing the Name and the Total Orders for records where Total Orders is greater than $1,000.

You do not have to know how Report works, fill out any specifications, or even memorize the names of your fields. Query Guide leads you step by step through developing the request, and then displays the answers on the screen.

TEACHING QUERY GUIDE ABOUT FIELD VALUES

||||➡ **To teach Query Guide about your database the first time you use it:**

1. **Select Assistant from the Main menu.**
2. **Select Query Guide, enter the database name, and press ↵.**
3. **Press ↵ at the screen asking if you want to teach Query Guide.**
4. **On the Query Guide Teach screen, enter Q in the fields you want it to learn, press F5 to mark all fields, or F3 to remove the marks.**
5. **Press F10 to continue.**

If you have text or keyword fields in your database, you can "teach" Query Guide the values in the fields so it can list the contents of those fields to help you refine your requests. For example, if you taught Query Guide about your name fields, when you are searching for a specific client, it will list the client names for you.

Let's start by teaching Query Guide something about the fields in our Clients database.

1. Start Q&A and select Assistant from the Main menu to display the Assistant menu.

On this menu, the first three options relate to the Intelligent Assistant, and the last two are Query Guide options.

2. Select Query Guide, type **Clients** at the file name prompt, and then press ↵. Because this is the first time you used Query Guide for the database, you will see the message shown in Figure 10.1, which asks if you want to teach Query Guide the values in the database fields.

Teaching Query Guide is optional and may be time-consuming. If you do not intend to access the data in text and keyword fields often, you may decide not to go through this process.

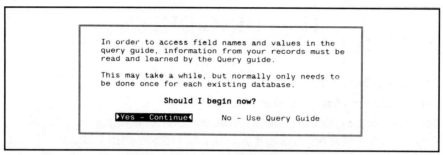

Figure 10.1: Message that appears the first time you use a database with Query Guide

3. Press ↵ to accept Yes. Q&A will display the Query Guide Teach screen, as shown in Figure 10.2.

On this screen, you can either enter Q in the fields that you want Query Guide to learn, or press F5 to teach it all the fields. If you want to clear the screen to remove the Q from fields you want Query Guide to skip, press F3.

4. Press F5 to mark every field, and then press F10 to continue.

```
                          Customer Record

Customer Code:
Name:
Address:
City:                          State:              Zip Code:

                          Primary Contact

Last Name:                     First Name:              MI:

        Type "Q" in each text or keyword field that you wish to index
        for use by the Query Guide.  For example, if you wish to have
        access to a scrollable list of cities in your database while in
        the Query Guide, type a "Q" in the "City" field.

        SUGGESTION: Start by pressing F5 to mark all fields indexable by the
        query guide with "Q"s.  Then, remove the "Q"s from those fields that
        you do not wish to index.  To unteach the database, remove all Q's.

CLIENTS.DTF                 Query Guide Teach              Page 1  of 2

Esc-Exit        F3-Clear spec        F5-Select all        F10-Continue
```

Figure 10.2: Query Guide Teach screen

You will see a prompt telling you that Query Guide is reviewing your records to collect field values. When the process is completed, you will see the main Query Guide menu, shown in Figure 10.3.

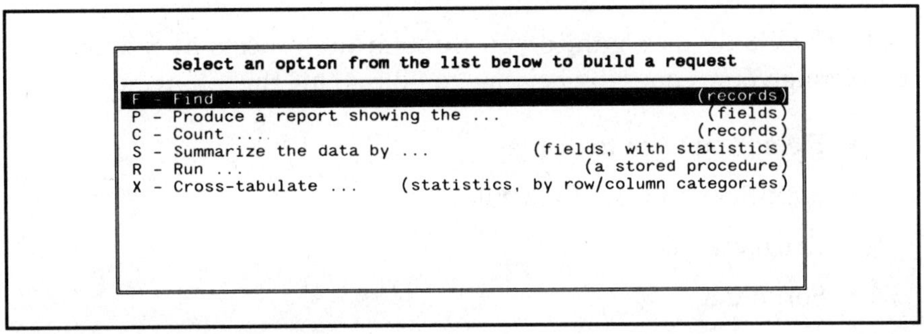

```
       Select an option from the list below to build a request

  F - Find ...                                           (records)
  P - Produce a report showing the ...                    (fields)
  C - Count ...                                           (records)
  S - Summarize the data by ...          (fields, with statistics)
  R - Run ...                                 (a stored procedure)
  X - Cross-tabulate ...    (statistics, by row/column categories)
```

Figure 10.3: Query Guide menu

From now on, whether you taught Query Guide or not, this menu will appear when you select Query Guide from the Assistant menu. If you want to teach Query Guide at a later time or change some of the marked fields, choose Teach Query Guide from the Assistant menu.

DEVELOPING REQUESTS IN FRAGMENTS

The main Query Guide menu begins the process by letting you select the first fragment, or the first words of your request to Query Guide. You select from the following options:

- Find...: Allows you to display records (similar to the Search/Update function in File).

- Produce a Report Showing the...: Generates columnar reports, including column breaks and calculations.

- Count...: Counts the number of records meeting your retrieval criteria.

- Summarize the Data by...: Generates summary reports.

- Run...: Prints data according to an existing printing specification or report format.

- Cross-tabulate...: Generates a crosstab report, allowing you to specify row, column, and summary fields.

Query Guide then guides you through the process of refining and completing your request by helping you designate the following:

- Fields you want to display

- Statistics you want to calculate

- Retrieval criteria

- Sort order

As you select options from the screen, Query Guide adds additional fragments onto the request. When your request is complete, you tell Query Guide to execute, or process, it.

The time it takes to display the results is the same as the time required to generate a report with Q&A Report. The difference is in the method of communicating your request to Q&A.

PRODUCING REPORTS WITH QUERY GUIDE

To produce reports with Query Guide:

1. **From the Query Guide menu, select Produce a Report Showing.**
2. **Select from the list of database fields displayed.**
3. **Select from the options displayed to add another field, select records, produce statistics, or execute the command.**

Let's see how the process works by seeking an answer to the question "Which clients have orders totaling $2,000 or more?" In essence, we want a columnar report showing the names of customers whose records have a value of at least $2,000 in the Total Orders field.

Remember, to select an item, highlight its name on the screen and press ↵, or click on it with the mouse. To make menu selections, type the letter shown to the left of the option.

1. Select Produce a Report Showing the…. Q&A will display a list of the fields in the database, as shown in Figure 10.4.

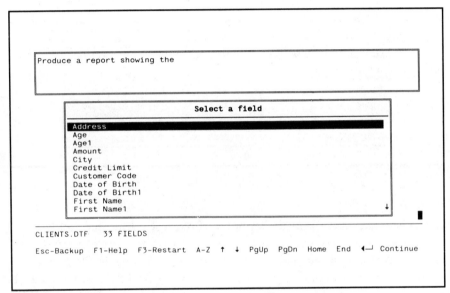

```
┌──────────────────────────────────────────────────────────────────┐
│  ┌─────────────────────────────────────────────────────────────┐ │
│  │Produce a report showing the                                  │ │
│  │                                                              │ │
│  └─────────────────────────────────────────────────────────────┘ │
│    ┌──────────────────────────────────────────────────────────┐  │
│    │                    Select a field                         │  │
│    │  ────────────────────────────────────────────────────────│  │
│    │  Address                                                  │  │
│    │  Age                                                      │  │
│    │  Age1                                                     │  │
│    │  Amount                                                   │  │
│    │  City                                                     │  │
│    │  Credit Limit                                             │  │
│    │  Customer Code                                            │  │
│    │  Date of Birth                                            │  │
│    │  Date of Birth1                                           │  │
│    │  First Name                                               │  │
│    │  First Name1                                          ↓   │  │
│    └──────────────────────────────────────────────────────────┘  │
│  CLIENTS.DTF   33 FIELDS                                          │
│                                                                    │
│  Esc-Backup  F1-Help  F3-Restart  A-Z  ↑  ↓  PgUp  PgDn  Home  End  ◄─┘ Continue │
└──────────────────────────────────────────────────────────────────┘
```

Figure 10.4: Query Guide list of database fields

The box on the top of the screen is called the *request box*. It contains the text of your request. At this point, it shows only the first fragment. As you work through Query Guide, other fragments will be added until the request is complete.

If you want to erase the entire request and start over, press F3. To erase the last fragment you added, press Esc. The fragment will be removed, and the previous menu will appear. Long requests will scroll in the request box. Press ↑, ↓, Ctrl-PgUp, and Ctrl-PgDn to scroll the text into view.

2. Press PgDn to display more field names, and then select Name. The request will now include the field Name, and the Select an Option screen will appear, as shown in Figure 10.5.

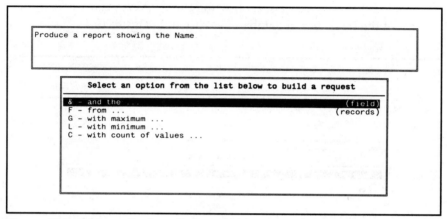

```
Produce a report showing the Name




        Select an option from the list below to build a request
    & - and the ...                                            (field)
    F - from ...                                              (records)
    G - with maximum ...
    L - with minimum ...
    C - with count of values ...



```

Figure 10.5: Options displayed after selecting a text field

This menu gives you the options to request additional fields (And The...), move on to selecting records (From...), or produce some statistics. Because Name is a text field, the statistics options are limited: find the highest name alphabetically (With Maximum...), find the lowest name alphabetically (With Minimum...), or count the number of fields (With Count of Values...).

You can select statistics for each field you add. First select the field, then designate the statistics for the field. To add other fields, select And The. To move on to specifying the retrieval criteria, select From.

3. To add the Total Orders field to the request, select And The. The field list will reappear, and the request will now read

    Produce a report showing the Name and the

4. Press PgDn three times and select Total Orders. The Select an Option screen will reappear, with the name of the Total Orders field added to the request, as in Figure 10.6.

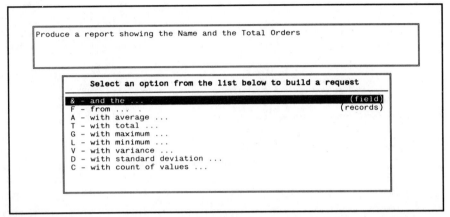

```
Produce a report showing the Name and the Total Orders


        Select an option from the list below to build a request
&  -  and the ...                                              (field)
F  -  from  ...  .                                             (records)
A  -  with average ...
T  -  with total ...
G  -  with maximum ...
L  -  with minimum ...
V  -  with variance ...
D  -  with standard deviation ...
C  -  with count of values ...
```

Figure 10.6: Options displayed after selecting a money field

Because Total Orders is a money field, all the statistics options are available. You can select as many fields and statistical operations as you want.

5. Select With Total, and the request will read

    Produce a report showing the Name and the Total Orders with total

The With Total option is removed from the menu, and the remaining options are reworded as And Average, And Count, etc.

6. Select And Average. The option will be removed from the menu, and the request will be

    Produce a report showing the Name and the Total Orders with total and average

Now that the fields and statistical operations are added to the request, the next step is to select the records you want retrieved. Instead of filling in the Retrieve Spec screen, you select the criteria from Query Guide menus.

7. Select From to add this word to the request and display the screen for selecting records, as shown in Figure 10.7.

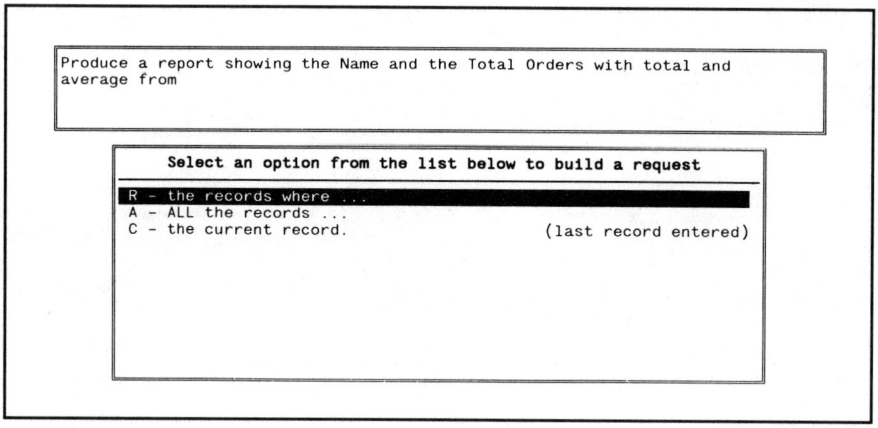

```
Produce a report showing the Name and the Total Orders with total and
average from




        Select an option from the list below to build a request
R - the records where ...
A - ALL the records ...
C - the current record.                    (last record entered)
```

Figure 10.7: Query Editor Record selection menu

From this menu, you can type R to specify retrieved criteria, A to retrieve all the records in the database, or C to use the last record you added.

We want to locate only those clients whose total orders equal $2,000 or more. This requires three criteria: the name of the field, the condition *at least*, and the amount 2000.

8. Select The Records Where. The field list will appear, and the request will be

    Produce a report showing the Name and the Total Orders with total and average from the records where

9. Press PgDn three times and select Total Orders. Q&A will display a list of constraints, or criteria, as shown in Figure 10.8.

The constraints in this menu pertain to money fields. The list is different for other types of fields.

10. Select Is At Least, and you will see the prompt

    Input an amount of money

    The request is now

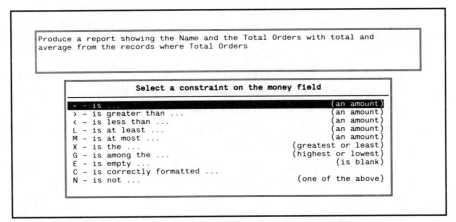

Figure 10.8: Query Editor Constraint (retrieval criteria) menu

> Produce a report showing the Name and the Total Orders with total and average from the records where Total Orders is at least

Is at least is a concise way of saying *is equal to or greater than*. If you selected Is Greater Than, Q&A would find only records with values above $2,000 in the Total Orders field.

11. Type **$2000** and press ↵. Query Guide will add the amount to the request and display additional options, as shown in Figure 10.9.

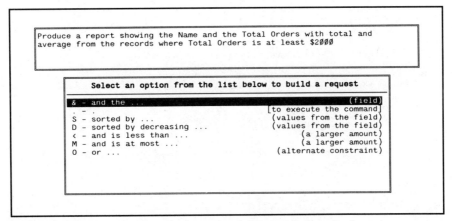

Figure 10.9: Menu displayed after completing retrieve criteria

This menu offers a wide variety of options. If your request is now complete, you can execute the command and produce the report by typing the period to end the sentence. You can also select to sort the reports by designating an order and a field, or you can add other constraints. For example, if you wanted to list records where total orders were between $2,000 and $4,000, you would select And Is At Most, and then enter $4000.

12. Select Sorted By, and the field list will appear.

13. Press PgDn three times and select Total Orders. You will see the Options menu, with the choices of executing the command or selecting an additional field for an ascending or descending sort.

14. Press . (period) to execute the command.

Query Guide constructs the report and displays it on the screen, along with the completed request, as shown in Figure 10.10. The field names are used for column headings. Since the report is too long to fit on the screen, the total and average values are out of view.

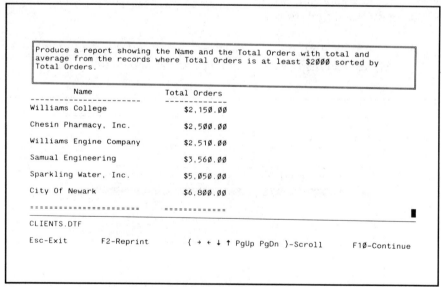

Figure 10.10: Query Guide report on screen

If your report is too large to fit on a single screen, press → and ← to scroll the report horizontally; use ↓, ↑, PgUp, and PgDn to scroll the report vertically.

15. Press ↓ until the total and average figures appear.

16. To print the report, press F2 to display the Print Options menu.

From within Query Guide, you can print reports and individual records. To print multiple records, use the Print option in Q&A File (see Chapter 5 for details).

17. Select PrtA, make sure your printer is ready, and then press F10. When the report is printed, the Query Guide menu will appear on the screen.

18. Press Esc twice, and then type **X** to leave Q&A.

The query development process may take longer than filling out the Retrieve Spec and Column/Sort Spec screens in Report, but you created the report interactively. You saw your request develop in English, just as you might write a note to a human assistant. You did not have to worry about the syntax for writing retrieval criteria or adding the proper calculation codes.

In addition, Query Guide displayed options that you might not have considered when filling out specifications. In Report, for example, you might have forgotten to display the Sort Spec screen, or to request both the total and average. By including all the possible options on menus, Query Guide helps you develop full reports.

The options on some Query Guide menus depend on the type of field you select for the report. For instance, Figure 10.11 shows the constraint options available for text or keyword fields. This menu provides for all the criteria available in Report, including SOUNDEX, for sound-alike matches.

If you select an option for a text or keyword field that you taught Query Guide, you will see a list of possible values, as in Figure 10.12. This figure shows a request being developed to report order information for a specific client. Rather than type the client's name and perhaps misspell it, you can select it from the list.

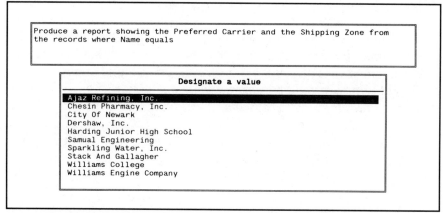

```
Produce a report showing the Amount from the records where City


          Select a constraint on the text or keyword field
  = - equals ...                        (a value in the database)
  B - begins with ...                   (a character sequence)
  E - ends with ...                     (a character sequence)
  C - contains ...                      (a character sequence)
  M - matches ...                       (a character sequence)
  S - matches the SOUNDEX pattern ...      (a letter sequence)
  A - appears alphabetically ...       (before/after/first/last)
  N - does not ...                          (one of the above)
  I - is ...                     (blank or correctly formatted)
```

Figure 10.11: Constraint options for text and keyword fields

```
Produce a report showing the Preferred Carrier and the Shipping Zone from
the records where Name equals


                         Designate a value
  Ajaz Refining, Inc.
  Chesin Pharmacy, Inc.
  City Of Newark
  Dershaw, Inc.
  Harding Junior High School
  Samual Engineering
  Sparkling Water, Inc.
  Stack And Gallagher
  Williams College
  Williams Engine Company
```

Figure 10.12: When you teach Query Guide text and keyword field values, it can display those values for selection

DISPLAYING AND EDITING
RECORDS WITH QUERY GUIDE

To display and edit records with Query Guide:

1. **Select Find from the Query Guide menu.**
2. **Select the retrieval criteria.**
3. **Select the sort criteria.**

The Find option on the first Query Guide menu lets you select records to display and edit. A typical request would be developed this way:

1. Select the initial fragment: *Find.*

2. Select the retrieval criteria: Find *the records where City is Margate and the Credit Limit is $1000.*

3. Select the sort criteria: Find the records where City is Margate and Credit Limit is $1000 *sorted by Name.*

After the first record that matches your criteria appears, you can edit and display other records using the techniques described in Chapter 3. When you press Esc or Shift-F10, the main Query Guide menu will reappear.

COUNTING RECORDS

||||➤ **To count records using Query Guide:**
1. **Select Count from the Query Guide menu.**
2. **Select the retrieval criteria.**

The Count option merely displays the total number of records meeting your retrieval criteria. You can use an OR condition in your criteria, but it must apply to only one field, as in

Count the records where City is Camden or City is Philadelphia

GENERATING SUMMARY REPORTS

||||➤ **To produce summary reports with Query Guide:**
1. **Select Summarize the Data By from the Query Guide menu.**
2. **Select the fields to include.**
3. **Select the statistics to perform and the statistics fields.**
4. **Select the retrieval criteria.**

The Summarize the Data By option generates a summary report, which includes totals, averages, and other statistics, but not individual detail lines for each record. The request begins with the initial fragment, then adds the fields, the statistics you want to calculate, the field to use for the statistics, and finally the retrieval criteria. For example, here is how you would build a request to report the average total orders by city in New Jersey:

1. Select the initial fragment: *Summarize the data by.*

2. Select the field: Summarize the data by *State.*

3. Select the next field: Summarize the data by State *and by City.*

4. Select the statistics: Summarize the data by State and by City *showing the average.*

5. Select the field for statistical operations: Summarize the data by State and by City showing the average *for Total Orders.*

6. Select retrieval criteria: Summarize the data by State and by City showing the average for Total Orders *from the records where State is NJ.*

RUNNING REPORTS AND PRINTING SPECIFICATIONS

||||➡ **To process reports with Query Guide:**

1. **Select Run from the Query Guide menu.**

2. **Enter the name of a report or printing specification and press ↵.**

If you already created a report or printing specification in File or Report, you can use it by selecting the Run option from the Query Guide menu.

When you select this option, Q&A requests the name of the file you want to run. Enter the name of an existing report or printing specification that you want to produce and press ↵. Q&A will continue as if you were generating the printout through the Report module or the Print option on the File menu.

You can make temporary changes to the report or specification before executing the command. However, you must make these changes through the Retrieve, Sort, Field, Column/Sort or other Spec screens, not through the Query Guide menus.

GENERATING CROSSTAB REPORTS

IIII➤ **To produce a crosstab report with Query Guide:**

1. **Select Cross-tabulate from the Query Guide menu.**
2. **Select the statistics.**
3. **Select the summary, row, and column fields.**
4. **Select the retrieval criteria.**

You can use Query Guide to generate crosstab and columnar reports. For a cross tabulation, you designate the summary, row, and column fields, as well as the statistics you want to generate from the summary field. The request begins with the initial fragment, then adds the statistics, and then the summary, row, and column fields. The sort order is selected with the field names. A typical crosstab report might be developed like this:

1. Select the initial fragment: *Cross-tabulate*.

2. Select the statistics: Cross-tabulate *the total*.

3. Select the summary field: Cross-tabulate the total *for Total Orders*.

4. Select the sort direction and row: Cross-tabulate the total for Total Orders *by City*.

5. Select the sort direction and column: Cross-tabulate the total for Total Orders by City *and by Total Orders*.

6. Select retrieval criteria: Cross-tabulate the total for Total Orders by City and by Total Orders *from all the records*.

Although Query Guide is certainly powerful, you have to work your way though its menus, adding fragments to the request before you can execute it. Q&A's other reporting feature, Intelligent Assistant, allows you to enter requests directly in a request box without the need to select options from menus. You can enter requests using the same syntax generated by Query Guide or by using Intelligent Assistant's own syntax.

USING INTELLIGENT ASSISTANT

Q & A's Intelligent Assistant, known as IA, offers immense potential—not only can it be used for getting information out of a database, but it also provides an insight into the learning process. By teaching IA, you can enter questions and requests, such as "What items are backordered?" and "Print a client list." You will learn how to teach IA in the next chapter.

Teaching IA new words is optional. Working with IA without teaching it requires a knowledge of Query Guide syntax, IA's own vocabulary, and the name of your database fields. By default, IA understands the words listed in Table 10.1. If you can structure your requests with only these words and your field names, you might not want to take the time to teach IA.

Table 10.1: Words That Intelligent Assistant Knows

A	AM	AT
ABOUT	AMONG	AUGUST
ABOVE	AN	AVERAGE
ACCORDING	AND	AWAY
ADD	ANNUAL	B
AFTER	ANY	BE
AGAIN	ANYONE	BEEN
AGAINST	APPEAR	BEFORE
AGO	APRIL	BEGIN
ALL	ARE	BEING
ALONG	AS	BELOW
ALPHABETICAL	ASCENDING	BEST
ALSO	ASSIGN	BETTER

Table 10.1: Words That Intelligent Assistant Knows (continued)

BETWEEN	CUT	EQUAL
BIG	DAILY	ERASE
BLANK	DATA	EVERY
BOTH	DATABASE	EVERYBODY
BOTTOM	DATE	EVERYTHING
BREAK	DAY	EXCEED
BUT	DECEMBER	EXCLUDE
BY	DECREASE	EXCLUSIVE
CALCULATE	DEFINE	EXIST
CAME	DEFINITION	F
CAN	DELETE	FALSE
CHANGE	DESCENDING	FEBRUARY
CHRISTEN	DETAIL	FETCH
CHRISTMAS	DEVIATION	FEW
COLUMN	DIFFERENCE	FIELD
COME	DISPLAY	FILE
COMMENCING	DIVIDE	FILL
CONCERN	DO	FIND
CONSTRAINT	DURING	FOLLOWING
CONTAIN	EACH	FOR
COULD	EARLY	FORM
COUNT	EITHER	FOUND
CREATE	EMPTY	FROM
CROSSTAB	END	GET
CROSSTABULATE	ENTER	GIVE
CURRENT	ENTRY	GOOD

Table 10.1: Words That Intelligent Assistant Knows (continued)

GOT	JANUARY	MINIMUM
GRAND	JULY	MINUS
GREAT	JUNE	MINUTE
HAD	JUST	MONTH
HALF	K	MORE
HALLOWEEN	KNOW	MOST
HAS	LARGE	MUCH
HAVE	LAST	MULTIPLY
HE	LATE	MUST
HELP	LEAST	MY
HER	LESS	N
HIGH	LET	NAME
HIM	LIKE	NEGATIVE
HIS	LIST	NEITHER
HOUR	LITTLE	NEW
HOW	LOOK	NEXT
I	LOW	NO
ID	M	NON
IDENTIFICATION	MADE	NOT
IF	MAKE	NOVEMBER
IN	MANY	NOW
INCLUDE	MARCH	NULL
INCLUSIVELY	MATCH	NUMBER
INCREASE	MAXIMUM	OCTOBER
INFORMATION	MAY	OF
IS	ME	OK
IT	MEAN	ON

Table 10.1: Words That Intelligent Assistant Knows (continued)

ONE	RECORD	SOUNDEX
ONLY	REDUCE	STANDARD
OR	REMOVE	START
ORDER	REPLACE	STATISTICS
OUT	REPORT	STILL
OVER	RESET	SUBAVERAGE
OVERALL	RESPECT	SUBCALCULA-TION
PAST	RESTRICTION	SUBCOUNT
PATTERN	RETRIEVE	SUBMAXIMA
PERCENT	REVERSE	SUBMAXIMUM
PLUS	RUN	SUBMINIMA
POOR	SAME	SUBMINIMUM
PORTION	SEARCH	SUBTOTAL
POSITIVE	SEE	SUBTRACT
PRECEDING	SELECT	SUBVARIANCE
PRESENT	SEPTEMBER	SUCCEEDING
PREVIOUS	SEQUENCE	SUM
PRINT	SET	SUMMARY
PRODUCE	SHALL	SYNONYM
PRODUCT	SHE	T
PROGRESSION	SHOULD	TABLE
PUT	SHOW	TAKE
QUOTIENT	SINCE	TELL
RAISE	SMALL	THAN
RANK	SOME	THANK
RATIO	SORT	THAT
RECENT	SOUND	

Table 10.1: Words That Intelligent Assistant Knows (continued)

THE	VERSUS	YES
THEIR	WANT	YESTERDAY
THEM	WAS	YOU
THEN	WE	YOU'LL
THERE	WELL	YOUR
THESE	WERE	Z
THEY	WHAT	%
THING	WHEN	(
THINK	WHERE	)
THIS	WHETHER	*
THOSE	WHICH	+
THROUGH	WHO	,
TIME	WHOM	-
TO	WHOSE	/
TODAY	WILL	/=
TOMORROW	WITH	;
TOP	WNEC	<
TOTAL	WNIC	<=
TRUE	WNRC	<>
TWICE	WON'T	=
UNDER	WORSE	>
UP	WOULD	><
US	WRITE	>=
USE	WRT	
VALUE	Y	
VARIANCE	YEAR	

USING QUERY GUIDE SYNTAX WITH INTELLIGENT ASSISTANT

||||➡ **To process requests using Query Guide syntax:**

1. **Select Assistant from the Main menu.**
2. **Choose Ask Me to Do Something, enter the database name, and press ↵.**
3. **In the request box, enter the request as it would be generated by Query Guide.**

If you are familiar with the way Query Guide formulates requests, you can save time by entering them directly into IA, without working through menus. Type the request as it would be generated by Query Guide, starting with the initial fragment, and depending on the desired processing, specifying fields, statistics, retrieval criteria, and the sort order. For example, to list the names, phone number, and total orders of clients whose orders total $1,000 or more, you would enter

> Produce a report showing Name and Phone and Total Orders where Total Orders is at least $1000 sorted by Name.

This is a quick way to reproduce a report that you already used Query Guide to generate. Make a note of the final request built by Query Guide, and then enter it directly through IA whenever you want to generate that report.

By correctly combining field names and Query Guide syntax, you can produce answers and reports quickly. The overall Query Guide command syntax, or grammar, is as follows:

- Find the records where *field-condition* sorted by *field*

- Produce a report showing the *field* with *statistic* where *field-condition* sorted by *field*

- Count the records where *field-condition*

- Summarize the data by *summary-field* showing the *statistic* for *field* where *field-condition*

- Run *report or printing-specification-name*
- Cross-tabulate the *statistic* for *summary-field* by *row-field* and *column-field* where *field-condition*

Insert the field names, type of statistics, and retrieval conditions in the order shown. You can include as many statistical operations as you want, and in all commands except cross tabulations, as many fields as you want to display. To retrieve all records, substitute

for all records

in place of

where *field condition*

As an example, to create a crosstab report for the Clients database, you could type

Cross-tabulate the average and total for Total Orders by City and Credit Limit for all records

Average and total are the *statistic*, Total Orders is the *summary-field*, City is the *row-field*, and Credit Limit is the *column-field*. The "where *field condition*" portion is replaced by "for all records."

FORMING REQUESTS WITH IA'S VOCABULARY AND STRUCTURE

To process requests using IA's vocabulary:

1. **Select Assistant from the Main menu.**
2. **Choose Ask Me to Do Something, enter the database name, and press ↵.**
3. **In the request box, enter the request using IA's built-in vocabulary words.**
4. **List the fields desired and specify the retrieval criteria in a *where* clause.**

A second way to generate a report without teaching IA is to formulate requests using IA's built-in vocabulary words in the proper structure. For example, entering

Calculate (87 + 52 + 97)/ (1.5 * .089)

will display the result 1,767.7902622.
If you typed in

What time is it?

Q&A would display the current system time and date.
You can combine IA's commands with field names to print reports, edit records, and add new records.

Reporting

To create reports, simply list the field names you want displayed, such as

Name, City, Total Orders

This will produce a report with those fields as its three columns in the order listed.
You can list fields separated by commas, spaces, or the word *and*. The entries

Name City Total Orders

and

Name and City and Total Orders

both produce the same report as the first example.
You can even start the command with the word *List*, and use complete English grammar, as in

List the name, cities, and the total orders

IA recognizes regular plurals of nouns; that is, plurals created by adding *s, es,* or *ies.* In this case, it understands that *cities* refers to the City field. However, IA cannot recognize irregular plurals, such as *mice* for *mouse.*

You can add retrieval criteria, statistical operations, and sort criteria to your requests to refine your reports.

Defining Retrieval Conditions

IA will retrieve all your records unless you specify retrieval conditions. For example, entering the request

Name and Phone where Total Orders is at least 1000

will a print a three-column report with the Name, Phone, and Total Orders fields for clients whose purchases total $1,000 or more. Any field name used in a retrieval, statistics, or sort condition will become a column. In this example, Total Orders will be a column in the report, even though it is not explicitly named in the list of fields. The fields will appear in the order they are listed in the request: Name, Phone, then Total Orders. If you want to list Total Orders, then Name and Phone, format the request as

Total Orders, Name, and Phone where Total Orders > 1000

with the fields in the proper order.

You can use the word *for* in place of *where,* as in

List names, cities, and total orders for credit limits at least $1000

When you are retrieving records based on text or keyword fields, include the search phrase in quotation marks, as in

Total Orders and Credit Limit for State = "PA"

You can retrieve records based on a yes/no field by structuring your request with one of its valid values, as in

Name and Address for Taxable = True

or by using simple Boolean expressions, such as

Name and Address where Taxable

or

Name and Address where non Taxable

Refine your retrieval criteria by using the AND or OR operators. Use AND to locate records meeting more than one criteria, such as

Name and Phone where City is "Margate" and Total Orders is at least $1000

Use the OR condition to locate records that meet one or the other criteria. Unlike Query Guide, which only allows you to use OR conditions to test the same field, IA can test different fields, as in

List the Name and Phone where Last Order Date is before 12/1/91 or Amount > Credit Limit

This request generates a list of the names and phone numbers of clients whose last order was before December 1991, or whose last order amount exceeded their credit limit—no matter what date the order was placed.

The built-in vocabulary allows you to enter requests in English-like sentences. For example, the command *is between* is a convenient way of checking for values that fall within a certain range, as in

List the names where the last order date is between November 1, 1991 and November 30, 1991

This is a shorter way to request a list of clients who made purchases in November than

Name where Last Order Date is on or after November 1, 1991 and on or before November 30, 1991

You can use retrieval criteria to locate records based on text fields, even if you are not sure of the correct spelling. For example, suppose you find a voice mail message from Mary but can't remember which company she is from. You could locate possible clients with the request

Name where first name begins with "M"

If you are not sure if she is the primary contact, secondary contact, or secretary, enter

Name where first name begins with "M" or secretary begins with "M" or first name1 begins with "M" or secretary1 begins with "M"

You can also locate records where the fields end with or include specific characters. If you are really unsure of the spelling, try a sounds-like match.

For number and money fields, the retrieval criteria can include calculations. To locate clients who are getting near their credit limit, enter

Name, Phone where Amount + 100 > Credit Limit

IA will find the records of clients whose last amount was within $100 of their credit limit.

Table 10.2 summarizes the syntax for IA retrieval conditions.

Table 10.2: IA Syntax for Retrieval Conditions

SYNTAX	CONDITION
field = value field is *value field* matches *value*	The *value* specified must match the *field* contents exactly. Enclose text and keyword values in quotation marks.
field > value field is greater than *value field* is after *value*	The *field* contents must be greater than the *value*. With text fields, the field contents must come after the value alphabetically; with date fields, the contents must be a later date.

Table 10.2: IA Syntax for Retrieval Conditions (continued)

SYNTAX	CONDITION
field < value field is less than *value field* is before *value*	The *field* contents must be less than the *value*. With text fields, the field contents must come before the value alphabetically; with date fields, the contents must be an earlier date.
field >= value field is at least *value field* is greater than or equal to *value field* is on or after *value*	The *field* contents must be equal to or greater than the *value*. With text fields, the contents must be equal to or after the value alphabetically; with date fields, the contents must be the date or later.
field <= value field is at most *value field* is less than or equal to *value field* is on or before *value*	The *field* contents must be equal to or less than the *value*. With text fields, the contents must be equal to or before the value alphabetically; with date fields, the contents must be the date or earlier.
field /= value field is not *value field* is not equal to *value*	The *field* contents must not match the *value*.
field is between *value1* and *value2*	The *field* contents must fall between *value1* and *value2*.
field begins with *value*	The *field* contents must begin with the same character or characters as *value*. Enclose the value in quotation marks.
field ends with *value*	The *field* contents must end with the same character or characters as the *value*. Enclose the value in quotation marks.

Table 10.2: IA Syntax for Retrieval Conditions (continued)

SYNTAX	CONDITION
field contains *value*	The *field* contents must include the same character or characters as the *value*. Enclose the value in quotation marks.
field is blank	The field must contain no entry. For number and money fields, Q&A distinguishes between 0 values and blanks.
field includes *value*	For keyword fields, the *field* contents must include the *value*. Enclose the value in quotation marks.
field sounds like *value*	For text fields, the *field* contents must sound like the *value*. Enclose the value in quotation marks.

GENERATING A REPORT WITH IA

As an example, we will now use IA to create a simple report. Follow these steps:

1. Start Q&A and select Assistant from the Main menu.

2. From the Assistant menu, select Ask Me to Do Something.

3. At the file name prompt, type **Clients** and press ↵. IA will scan the database to quickly review the field names and types, and then display the request box and a short Help message, as shown in Figure 10.13.

The key-assignment line includes the options Esc, to return to the Assistant menu; F1, to display Help; F6, to display a list of built-in vocabulary

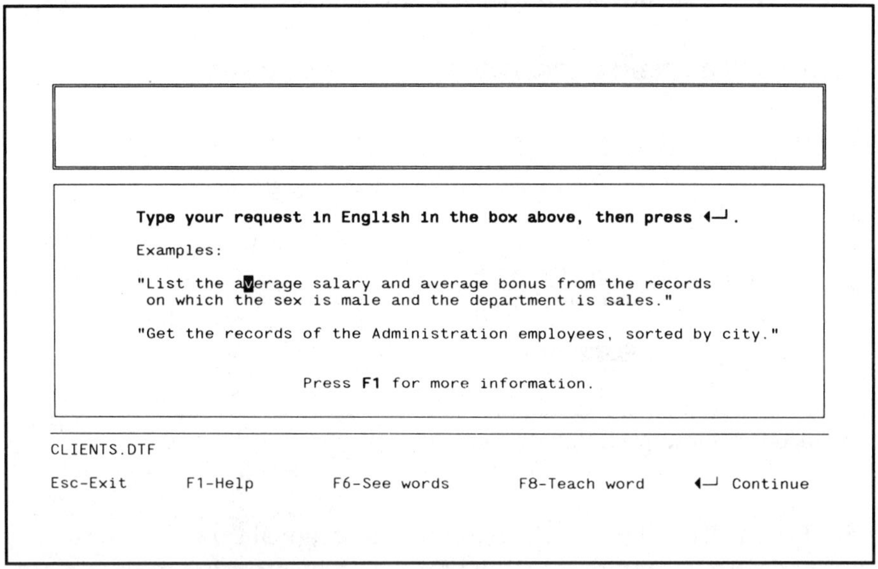

```
Type your request in English in the box above, then press ◄┘.

Examples:

"List the average salary and average bonus from the records
 on which the sex is male and the department is sales."

"Get the records of the Administration employees, sorted by city."

                  Press F1 for more information.
```

```
CLIENTS.DTF

Esc-Exit      F1-Help      F6-See words      F8-Teach word      ◄┘ Continue
```

Figure 10.13: IA screen

words and field names; F8, to teach IA new words; and ↵, to process the request.

4. Type the following request:

   list the names and cities where the total orders are at least $1000

5. Press ↵. IA will convert the entire request to uppercase, and then highlight each word as it interprets it into its own internal language.

When the entire request is highlighted, it means that IA understands and can process your instructions. You will see IA's interpretation on the screen, along with the options to continue or cancel the request, as shown in Figure 10.14. The spacing and indentation of the interpretation shows the fragments that comprise the report syntax. Select Yes if the interpretation is correct; choose No or press Esc if you want to edit the request. (You can use all of Q&A's editing features in the request box.)

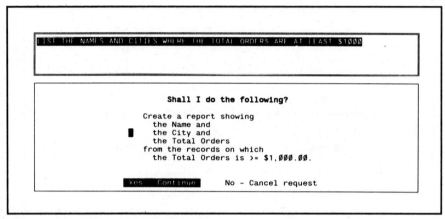

Figure 10.14: IA's interpretation of your request

6. Type **Y**. IA will return the request to its original capitalization and scan the database looking for matching records.

IA displays the report on the screen, as shown in Figure 10.15. If you

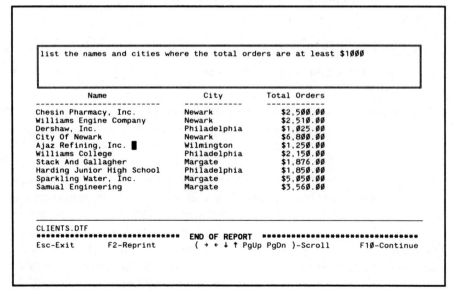

Figure 10.15: IA's response to your request

want to print the report, press F2 to display the Print Options menu.

7. Press F10 to return to the request box.

Seeing What IA Knows

While you are typing a request, you can see which words IA understands by pressing F6. This displays the menu shown in Figure 10.16, with the following options:

- Select Built-In Words to display the built-in vocabulary words.
- Choose Field Names to display field names and enter alternate names for them.
- Select Synonyms to display synonyms you have already created.

You will learn more about synonyms and alternate field names in Chapter 11.

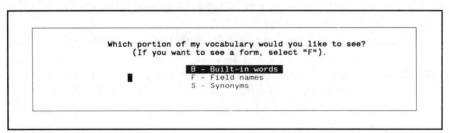

```
        Which portion of my vocabulary would you like to see?
            (If you want to see a form, select "F").

                     B - Built-in words
            ▮        F - Field names
                     S - Synonyms
```

Figure 10.16: IA vocabulary menu

Handling Unclear Requests

IA will ask for a clarification if it cannot interpret your request. Let's see how IA handles requests that it finds confusing.

1. Type the following request

   List names for not taxable

2. Press ↵. Because IA is confused by the word *not,* it will display the options shown in Figure 10.17.

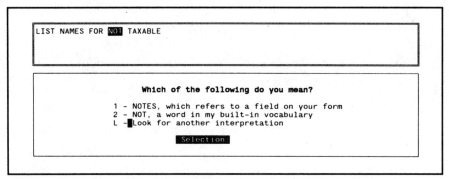

Figure 10.17: Options displayed because IA is confused by the use of *not*

IA wants to know if you are referring to the Notes field (you mistyped it) or if you want to use the word *NOT* from its built-in vocabulary. (Note that if we had used the word *non* instead, IA would have interpreted the request without a problem.)

If you select Look for Another Interpretation, IA attempts a "best guess" at your request. In this case, IA would print the names in all records, ignoring the retrieval criteria. With other requests, IA may not have enough information to continue, and it will display the message shown in Figure 10.18. Press F1 to display a Help screen, or press Esc to return to the request box.

3. Type **2** and press ↵. IA will interpret the word as NOT, and then ask you to confirm its instructions:

   Shall I do the following:
   Create a report showing
       the Name
   from the records on which
       the Taxable is NO

4. Press ↵ to display the report.

5. Press F10 to return to the request box.

```
                        ! Sorry !
    I don't understand your request well enough to do what you want.

    I am more likely to understand your request if you use words I
    already know, such as field names, synonyms, words that you have
    taught me in the Teach Lessons, data values in the database, and
    common English words in my built-in vocabulary.

      Press F1 for more help.   Press Esc to cancel this message.  █
```

Figure 10.18: This message appears when IA is unable to proceed with your request

In this example, IA identified the two most likely interpretations of your request. There may be times, however, when it is completely perplexed. This will usually occur when you use the wrong name for a field, a word not in its vocabulary, or select the Look for Another Interpretation option when there are not enough correct terms in the request for IA to interpret.

Handling Unknown Field Names

If you enter a field name that IA does not recognize, it will give you a chance to clarify your request. As an example, let's see how IA responds to the name Telephone:

1. Type the following request:

   List name and telephone numbers

2. Press ↵. Because IA cannot interpret the word *telephone*, it will display the options shown in Figure 10.19.

You can type E to return to the request box and edit the word; T to teach IA the meaning of telephone; S to see IA's vocabulary and field names (the same menu that appears when you press F6 from the request box); or G to skip the word and continue with the report if possible.

3. Type **E,** and the cursor will move to the word *telephone* in the request box.

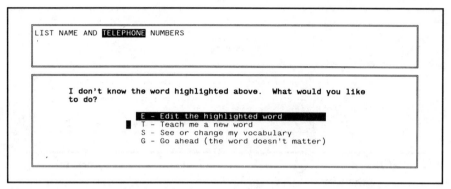

Figure 10.19: Menu displayed when IA cannot interpret your requests

4. Press Ctrl-F4 to delete the characters to the end of the line, type **phone**, and press ↵.

5. Press ↵ to display the report, then F10 to return to the request box.

6. Press Esc twice, and then type **X** to exit from Q&A.

Restricting Columns

If you do not want to include fields that are used in retrieval conditions or calculations, you can restrict the report to just those fields listed explicitly. Add WNRC (for With No Restriction Columns) or WNEC (for With No Extra Columns) to the end of the request to tell IA not to use retrieval or calculation fields as columns.

For example, to produce a report listing only the client's name and the primary contact's first and last names, for clients with total orders not above $1,000, enter

List Name, First Name and Last Name for Total Orders at most $1000 WNRC

Since Total Orders is used only for retrieval and is not in the list of fields, it will be excluded from the report.

IA REPORTING WITH STATISTICS

To use statistics in IA reports:

- **Enter the request using IA's built-in adjectives for maximum and minimum.**
- **Use the *with statistic* clause to compute the average, count, variance, or standard deviation.**

IA can calculate and display the results of statistical calculations, as well as use them as part of retrieval criteria. For example, to find the client who has ordered the most, enter the request

Name where maximum total orders

You can also take advantage of IA's built-in vocabulary by entering

Name best total orders

to display the name and total orders of the client whose record has the largest number in the Total Orders field. IA recognizes *best, greatest, most,* and *top* as synonyms for *maximum;* and *worst, smallest, least,* and *bottom* for *minimum.* With date fields, use *latest* or *most recent,* and *earliest* or *least recent,* as in

List the name with the most recent last order date

Notice that the requests above do not include the word *for* or *where* in the retrieval criteria.

The only problem with these two requests is that they will display one name, even if more than one client has the same number of maximum total orders or made a purchase on the same most recent date. For example, our database has several clients with a $1,500 credit limit. But if we request

Name best credit limit

only one client will be listed. This is because the request really asks IA to find the maximum amount in the Credit Limit field and display the name associated with it. As IA scans the database, it compares each amount in the Credit Limit field with the next value. If the value is higher, IA assigns that value to be the maximum; if the value is equal or lower, IA ignores it.

To tell IA to list the names of clients whose total order value is equal to the maximum total order value, enter

Name where total orders = maximum total orders

IA has to make two passes through the database to process this request. In the first pass, it determines the maximum value in the field. In the second pass, it locates the records that match the value.

When using *minimum, maximum,* or any of their synonyms, you can specify a range of records to display. You could list the names of the top five customers with the request

List the names with the top 5 total orders

or the five smallest most recent orders with the request

Name, Phone, and Last Name for the worst 5 amounts

Place the number after the adjective, not before it, and use numbers, not words, such as *5*, not *five*.

To include statistical operations as part of the report, use the syntax

field with *statistic*

where *statistic* can be total, average, maximum, minimum, count, variance, or standard definition, and *field* is a valid field name.

To list the total and average of our orders, for example, enter

Name and Total Orders with total and average

SORTING RECORDS WITH IA

▌▌▌➡ **To sort IA reports:**

- **For an ascending sort, use the *by field* clause to specify the field or fields to sort by.**
- **For a descending sort, use the *by descending field* clause to specify sort fields.**
- **Add statistical operations by using the *with statistic* clause.**

You sort your records in reports for two reasons: to display them in a specific order or to create column breaks. The syntax is

by *field*

for an ascending sort or

by decreasing *field*

for a descending sort.

For example, to list total orders by state and city, enter

Total Orders by State and City

The sorted field will appear in the first column, and IA will add column breaks when the sort field is not unique. In this case, the first column will contain the state, the second one will list the city, and the third will show total orders. There will be column breaks on both the State and City fields.

You can add statistical operations to the sort criteria with the syntax

field with *statistic* by

or

by *field* with *statistic*

For example, to create a three-column report breaking down total orders by state and city, enter

Total Orders by State and City with totals

The fields used for sorting will always appear; you cannot restrict the report by using the WNRC or WNEC command.

PRODUCING KEYWORD REPORTS

You can generate keyword reports with IA by sorting on a keyword field. To see the names of contacts by their hobbies, for example, enter

List Last Names and Last Name1s by Hobbies

To see which contacts are interested in specific hobbies, use the includes command, as in

list Last Names where Hobbies includes "bowling"

DISPLAYING, EDITING, AND CREATING RECORDS WITH IA

➤ **To manipulate records with IA:**
- **Display records for review or editing using the Records or List command without specifying field names in the request.**
- **Edit records automatically using the Change command.**
- **Add new records using the Create command, specifying field information in *where* clauses.**

If you do not specify any fields in a request, IA assumes you want to retrieve and display entire records, as when you use File's Search/Update option or Query Guide's Find option.

After a record appears on the screen, you can edit it, or use F10 and F9 to display additional records meeting the retrieval criteria.

To retrieve all the records in the database, just type RECORDS in the IA request box. You can retrieve selected records by adding a retrieval condition, such as

records where State = "PA"

or

List the top 5 amounts

Include sort criteria to display records in a particular order.

Changing Records

You can also edit a record by using the Change command. Specify the fields you want to change, the values you want to include, and the retrieval criteria, as in

Change Last Order Date to 12/1/91 and Amount to $651 for
Name ="Chesin Pharmacy, Inc."

Text in quotation marks will not be capitalized as IA interprets the request. IA will interpret the request, scan the database looking for matching records, and then display a message warning you that records may be altered. If you select Yes to continue, you will see the first record that meets the criteria. Press Shift-F10 to change the record and display the next, if any; press Ctrl-F10 to change all the records matching the criteria; or press F10 to see the next matching record without changing the one displayed. IA will expand a field if the inserted text is longer than can be displayed on the form.

Creating New Records

To add new records to the database with IA, use the Create command. Enter either

Create new form

or

Create new record

to insert and display a blank record into the database.

Create a new record and add data at the same time with a *where* or *for* condition. For example, entering

Create new record where Name is "Ajax Materials", Last Order Date is 12/1/91, and Amount is 673

will insert a new record with values in three fields.

This chapter has given you an introduction to Q&A's capability to understand and produce results from requests made in standard, yet very structured, English. In the next chapter, you will see how to expand this capability by teaching IA the terms you would like to use.

11

Teaching Intelligent Assistant

Perhaps the most unique and exciting aspect of IA is its capability to learn new words and grammar. Teaching IA is particularly useful when people who are not skilled with the program will have to get information from the database. Instead of training them how to follow the query structure, you can teach IA how to understand a more natural language.

You can teach IA new words as you find it necessary or through a formal series of lessons. Each lesson is designed to teach IA another set of words that you will use to communicate with it. The lessons are well worth the time they take to complete. They guide you step by step through defining a complete set of words and grammar, allowing you and others to communicate with IA in a much more natural and less structured way.

In this chapter, you will learn how to teach IA using both methods, as well as how to phrase your requests for the best results.

DEFINING SYNONYMS

To teach IA new words:

1. **Choose Ask Me to Do Something from the Assistant Menu, enter the database name, and press ⤶.**
2. **Enter a request that includes a word that is not in IA's vocabulary.**
3. **When IA reports it does not understand the word, use the Teach Me a New Word menu to define a synonym (a word IA knows) for the new word.**

When you teach IA a new word, you are telling it to interpret the word in terms of a word that is in its vocabulary, a field name, or an expression. Thus, the new word becomes a synonym for words or combinations of words that IA already knows.

For example, you can define *coolest* as a synonym for *maximum*, and then enter the request

> List the name with the coolest total order

Use synonyms for fields, such as *telephone* or *phone number* for *phone*, or the French *le nom* for *name*. You can even define synonyms for expressions or collections of fields. Defining *Contact* as a synonym for *First Name*, *MI*, and *Last Name*, allows you to request

> List contacts in "Margate"

Defining *extended* as *"Amount > Credit Limit"* allows you to enter

> List names where extended

to generate a report showing the names, amounts, and credit limits for clients who have overextended their credit.

TEACHING IA NEW WORDS

As an example, let's teach IA several new words right now.

1. Start Q&A and select Assistant from the Main menu, then Ask Me to Do Something from the Assistant menu.

2. Type **Clients** and press ↵.

3. Type **Compute 50 + 34** and press ↵. You will see a menu explaining that IA does not understand the highlighted word, *Compute*.

This menu lets you teach IA synonyms, as well as words that describe the database, alternate field names, and verbs. You'll learn how to use these other options later.

4. Type **T**, for Teach Me a New Word. IA will display the menu shown in Figure 11.1. This is the same menu IA displays when you press F8.

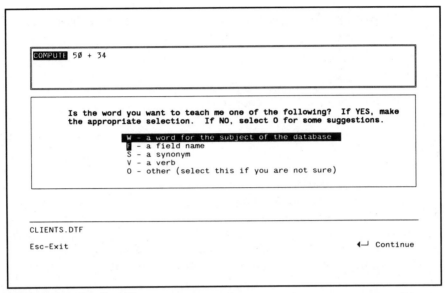

Figure 11.1: Teach options

5. Type **S** to define a synonym. IA will display the screen shown in Figure 11.2.

You type the word you want to define in the left column on the screen, and the built-in vocabulary word, field name, or expression in the right column. To delete a synonym, press F3. You can enter up to three synonyms on this screen. If you want to enter more, press F10 to save the first three synonyms and then press F8 again.

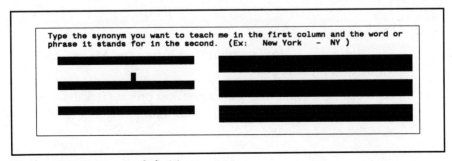

Figure 11.2: Synonym definition screen

6. Type **Compute**, press Tab, and type **Calculate**. IA will display your input in all uppercase letters.

7. Press F10 to add the synonym. On the status line, you will see the message

   I've added your new synonym

IA replaces the word *compute* with *calculate* and interprets the request, showing

   Shall I do the following:
   Evaluate the following expression:
   50 + 34?

8. Press ↵. IA will perform the calculation and display

   50 + 34

     84

9. Press F10 to return to the request box.

10. To test the new vocabulary word, type **Compute 183.45 times 6 percent** and press ↵. IA will interpret the request as

    Evaluate the expression 183.45*(6/100)

11. Press ↵ to display the results, and then press F10 to return to the request box.

Now let's define another synonym to display the primary contact's full name without requesting three fields.

12. Press F8 and type **S**.

13. Type **Fullname**, press Tab, type **First Name and MI and Last Name**, and press F10.

14. Type **List the names and fullnames** and press ↵ twice. IA will display the client names and the three fields now associated with the word *fullname*.

15. Press F10 to return to the request box.

16. Press Esc twice, and then type **X** to exit.

CLARIFYING WORDS

If you have a report or printing specification that has the same name as a built-in vocabulary word, synonym, or field, IA will ask you to clarify your request. For example, suppose you have a report named Sports that displays contact names sorted by keywords in the Hobbies field. If you also define *sports* as a synonym for *hobbies* and enter the request

List sports

IA will ask if you mean

1 - Sports, the name of a predefined report
2 - Sports, a synonym for Hobbies

ADDING AND EDITING SYNONYMS

You can also define, edit, and delete synonyms by pressing F6 from the initial IA screen to select the See Words option. Then select Synonym from the menu, and you will see a screen listing up to three existing synonyms, as shown in Figure 11.3.

To add a synonym, move the cursor to any blank line. If all the lines are full, press PgDn to display more. However, a new screen will appear

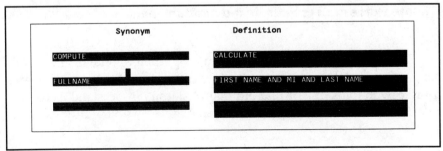

Figure 11.3: Add new synonyms or edit existing ones

only if it contains at least one synonym. If the screen does not scroll, you must add synonyms through the Teach Me a New Word menu (F8).

You can edit any of the existing synonyms in the list. To delete a synonym, select it and press F3. The words you teach IA, either spontaneously or through the formal lessons, are stored in the database's IDX file.

SYNONYMS AND OTHER FILES

Since your synonyms are stored with the database, they are not available with other files. If you want to use the word *compute* with the Vendors database, for example, you must first define it with that database.

When you copy a database using the Q&A File Copy command, you have the option of copying the design with or without IA and Query Guide definitions. If you want to copy synonyms and other words that you taught IA, select Copy Design with IA/QG.

GIVING IA LESSONS

To give IA lessons:

1. **Select Teach Me About Your Database from the Assistant Menu, enter the name of the database, and press ↵.**
2. **Choose each lesson you want to perform from the Basic Lessons menu.**
3. **Select Advanced Lessons, then choose each lesson from the Advanced Lessons menu.**
4. **Choose Exit Lessons to return to the Assistant menu.**

By teaching IA new words, you can program it to understand a wide range of natural language requests and questions. Rather than define each word as you think of it or find out that IA doesn't understand it, you can take full advantage of the program's capabilities by giving IA lessons.

As you go through each lesson in the following sections, you will learn how to phrase your requests and questions to IA. Remember, IA isn't perfect; it can be confused and misled. So it is important to understand how IA interprets your commands.

BEGINNING THE LESSONS

IA's lessons begin from the Basic Lessons menu. Follow these steps to display that menu:

1. Start Q&A and select Assistant from the Main menu.

Get Acquainted, the first option on the Assistant menu, displays three screens explaining how you can use IA. While interesting, this information has nothing to do with the actual teaching process.

2. Select Teach Me About Your Database, type **Clients**, and press ↵. IA will review some details about your database and then display the Basic Lessons menu, as shown in Figure 11.4.

You can do any of the lessons you want—you do not have to follow them all. If you decide to add words later, you can repeat the lessons or use the spontaneous method described earlier in the chapter.

Performing all the lessons provides the most comprehensive way of dealing with your database. We will go through each of the lessons to teach IA how we will request information from the Clients database.

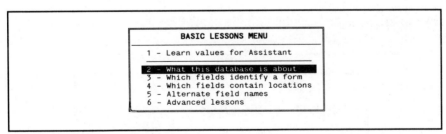

Figure 11.4: Basic Lessons menu

TEACHING IA TEXT AND KEYWORD VALUES

The Learn Values for Assistant option scans records to learn text and keyword field values. Depending on the size and nature of your database, this option can take quite some time and disk space, but when it is finished, IA will be able to process your requests with maximum speed.

You should select this option if you frequently ask IA questions regarding text or keyword fields. You only need to perform this lesson once. After that, IA will automatically update its knowledge as you edit, add, or delete records in the database.

Follow these steps for the first lesson:

1. From the Basic Lessons menu, select Learn Values for Assistant. IA will display the screen shown in Figure 11.5.

2. Select Yes-Continue. IA will report its progress as it scans your records, and then redisplay the Basic Lessons menu, with the second lesson selected.

If you select the first lesson again, you will be told that IA has already learned the values. IA will give you the options to keep the values and cancel the operation, or to delete the values and rescan the database.

Now that IA knows the values in text fields, you can give it requests without listing any field names, such as

Show me Chesin's record

IA will locate records containing the name Chesin.

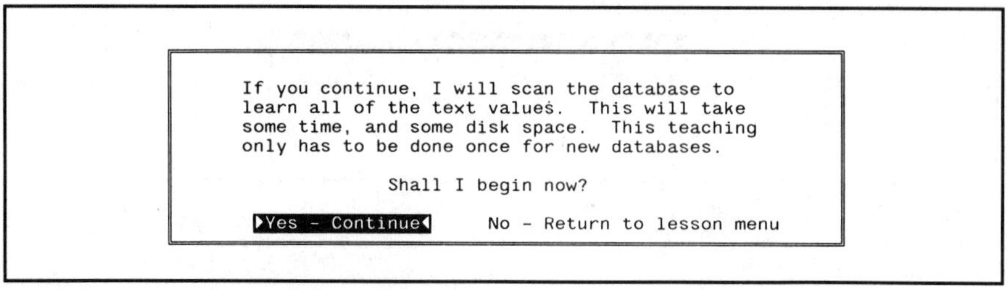

```
If you continue, I will scan the database to
learn all of the text values.  This will take
some time, and some disk space.  This teaching
only has to be done once for new databases.

            Shall I begin now?

 ▶Yes - Continue◀     No - Return to lesson menu
```

Figure 11.5: Learn values screen

TEACHING IA WHAT YOUR DATABASE IS ABOUT

In the real world, we refer to people, places, and things, not records or a list of fields. By teaching IA how you will refer to the items in your database, you can pose questions more naturally, such as

Which buyers owe over $2000?

What items are out of stock?

In addition, you gain the flexibility to refer to items in several ways. A *client* can be a *customer* or *buyer*. An *inventory item* can be an *item*, *material*, *part*, or *ingredient*. In this context, *item* refers to the overall entity represented by each database record, not by a specific field.

Follow these steps to teach IA about our Clients database:

1. Select What This Database Is About. IA will display the screen shown in Figure 11.6.

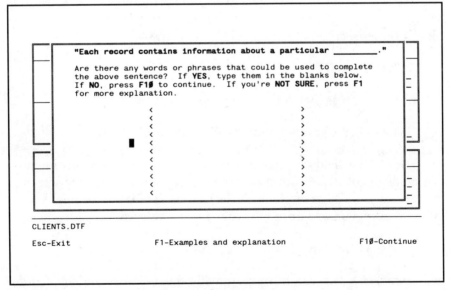

```
"Each record contains information about a particular _____."

Are there any words or phrases that could be used to complete
the above sentence?  If YES, type them in the blanks below.
If NO, press F10 to continue.  If you're NOT SURE, press F1
for more explanation.

        <                         >
        <                         >
        <                         >
        <                         >
    █   <                         >
        <                         >
        <                         >
        <                         >
        <                         >
        <                         >
```
CLIENTS.DTF

Esc-Exit   F1-Examples and explanation   F10-Continue

Figure 11.6: What this database is about screen

On this screen, you enter the words you will use to refer to database entities as if you were completing the sentence shown at the top of the screen. Enter words in their singular form unless they have irregular plurals.

2. Type **client** and press ↵.

3. Type **customer** and press ↵.

4. Type **buyer** and press ↵.

5. Type **purchaser** and press F10 to save the entries and return to the Basic Lessons menu.

The next lesson is automatically selected. If you want to add words to this list later, select this option again, or from within IA, press F8 and type W to select to teach IA a word for the subject of the database.

TEACHING IA WHICH FIELDS IDENTIFY AN ENTITY

The next option, Which Fields Identify a Form, allows you to select up to eight fields that you want to print with every report. Then you can use simple retrieval criteria, such as

Which clients?

in addition to fields that you request explicitly, as in

Which clients have amounts greater than $500?

Select as few fields as you need to identify records. Too many identifying fields might make your reports too wide to display on the screen or print on paper. For example, with the Clients database, you might select only the client name to print with each report. This way, a request such as

Which clients have total orders > 1000?

will generate a two-column report with client names and total order amounts.

You could skip this option, but then you will always have to explicitly include some identifying field in your request. Without an identifying field, the request above would result in a single-column report listing only total order amounts.

Since the client records include a customer code, you could define just the code as an identifying field. Although you would see only the code and total order amounts in response to the above request, after completing the teaching process, you will be able to follow up with questions such as

Who are they?

If you identify several fields, you can prevent them from appearing by adding the WNIC (With No Identifying Columns) code at the end of the request. With this code, only fields explicitly listed will appear.

Follow these steps to define Name as an identifying field:

1. Press ↵ to select Which Fields Identify a Form. You will see the screen shown in Figure 11.7.

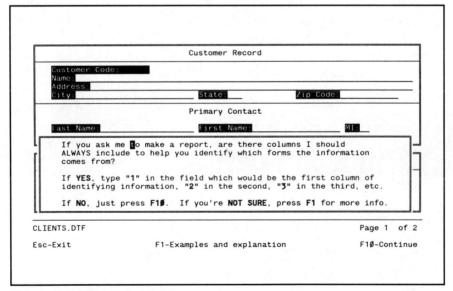

Figure 11.7: Identifying fields screen

You identify the fields and the order you want them to appear by numbering the field labels from 1 to 8.

2. Press ↵ to reach the Name field.

3. Type **1**, and then press F10 to return to the Basic Lessons menu.

TEACHING IA ABOUT LOCATIONS

If you want to be able to ask questions such as

Where are they?

you must tell IA which fields represent locations.

For our Clients database, we will define Address, City, State, and Zip Code as location fields. If your database were about employees, you might include fields such as Department, Building, Floor, or Office. With inventory databases, locate items by their shelf or bin numbers.

Your databases might include two different locations, such as home and office for employees, or campus and permanent address for students. Define the fields that you will need to see most often as the location fields. You can always create a synonym to quickly display the alternate location when needed.

Follow these steps to teach IA about the locations in our database:

1. Press ↵ to select Which Fields Contain Locations. IA will display a screen similar to the one used to define identifying fields.

As with identifying fields, you number the field labels to indicate location fields and their order.

2. Press ↵ twice to reach the Address field and type **1**.

3. Press ↵ to reach the City field and type **2**.

4. Press ↵ to reach the State field and type **3**.

5. Press ↵ to reach the Zip Code field and type **4**.

6. Press F10 to return to the Basic Lessons menu.

TEACHING IA
ALTERNATE FIELD NAMES

When you design a database, you select field labels that identify the purpose of the field. Although you do not label fields haphazardly, you may pick specific labels arbitrarily. You might use *phone* instead of *telephone*, or *customer code* instead of *customer number*.

Often, a field label that works on the form just does not seem natural when you are requesting information from IA. For example,

What are the shipping zones and preferred carriers?

is a rather wordy request. It would be easier to ask

What are the zones and shippers?

The Alternate Field Names option lets you assign alternate names to your fields. You can designate names that are shorter and easier to remember, or that will most likely be used by others who are not familiar with your database. However, if you will only refer to a field by its official name, you do not have to assign it an alternate name.

All field names, even alternate ones, must be unique. If you try to assign the same name to more than one field, IA will display the message

Sorry. This word/phrase is already used. It must be unique

Now we will assign alternate field names:

1. Press ↵ to select Alternate Field Names and display the screen shown in Figure 11.8.

The actual field name, Customer Code, is already listed as the first alternate term. You can enter up to nine alternate names for each field. Press F8 to move to the next field; press F6 to go back to the previous one.

2. Type **code** as an alternate for the field name.
3. Press ↵ and type **number**.

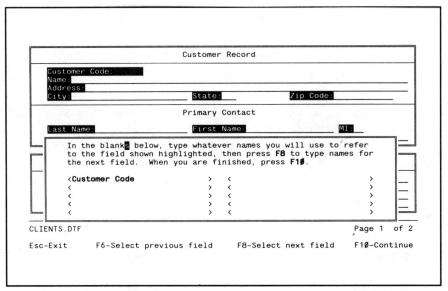

Figure 11.8: Alternate field name screen

4. Press ↵ and type **customer number**.

5. Press F8 to select the Name field.

Alternate names for this field require some thought. Common alternate field names are *company* and *firm*. It would also seem logical to use *client* and *customer,* but we already used these as words that explain what the database is about. IA would let you reuse them as alternate field names, but it would get confused when you used them in a request.

At first glance, this seems to be a problem. But remember, we already defined Name as an identifying field. Whenever we ask a question about clients or customers, IA will display the name. Since we have already associated the words *client* and *customer* with the field name, it would be redundant to reenter them as alternate field names here.

6. Type **firm**, press ↵, type **company**, and then press F8.

7. Enter the alternate field names listed in Table 11.1. Use F8 to move from field to field or F6 to move backward. You can also press ↵ or Tab to move forward from field to field, or Shift-Tab to move backward through the fields.

Table 11.1: Alternate Field Names for the Clients Database

ACTUAL FIELD NAME	ALTERNATE FIELD NAME
Customer Code	code, number, customer number
Name	firm, company
Address	street
City	town
Zip Code	zip
Primary Contact	
Last Name	surname
First Name	given name
MI	initial, middle initial
Title	position, job title
Phone	telephone, phone number, telephone number
Last Order Date	order date
Amount	last order
Total Orders	total sales
Tax	exempt
Credit Limit	credit
Products Purchased	item
Shipping Zone	zone, area
Preferred Carrier	shipper, carrier
Date of Birth	birth date
Hobbies	interests
Secretary	assistant

Table 11.1: Alternate Field Names for the Clients Database (continued)

ACTUAL FIELD NAME	ALTERNATE FIELD NAME
Secondary Contact	
Last Name	alternate's last name, alternate's surname
First Name	alternate's first name, alternate's given name
MI	alternate's initial, alternate's middle initial
Title	alternate's title, alternate's position
Phone	alternate's phone, alternate's telephone, alternate's phone number, alternate's telephone number
Date of Birth	alternate's date of birth, alternate's birth date
Age	alternate's age
Hobbies	alternate's hobbies, alternate's interest
Secretary	alternate's secretary, alternate's assistant
Notes	comments

8. Press F10 to return to the Basic Lessons menu.

To define additional alternate field names later, select this option again, or from within IA, press F8 or F6 and select to teach IA field names.

Notice that we are not assigning many alternate field names to the labels that refer to contact names. This is because IA has a special lesson for names, which you will use next.

TEACHING IA PEOPLE'S NAMES

In designing the Clients database, we divided the names of the primary and secondary contacts into three fields: one for the first name, middle initial, and last name. If we want to display a contact's full name, we must request three fields, as in

What are their first names, middle initials, and last names?

or

List first name1, MI1, last name1

It would certainly be more convenient to ask a question such as

Who are the contacts?

or

List the alternates

The What Fields Contain People's Names option on the Advanced Lessons menu allows you to designate which fields make up each person's name and specify how you will refer to that person. IA will use these names to answer "who" questions.

We refer to four people in the Clients database: the primary and secondary contacts and their secretaries. In the following steps, you will define these four names.

1. From the Basic Lessons menu, select Advanced Lessons to display the menu shown in Figure 11.9.

The options on the Advanced Lessons menu let you further enhance IA's ability to process natural language requests, including recognizing people's names.

2. Select What Fields Contain People's Names. IA will display the screen shown in Figure 11.10.

3. Press F1 to display the Help menu, shown in Figure 11.11.

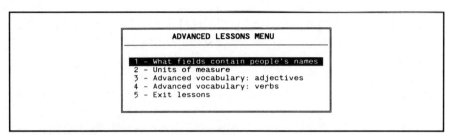

Figure 11.9: Advanced Lessons menu

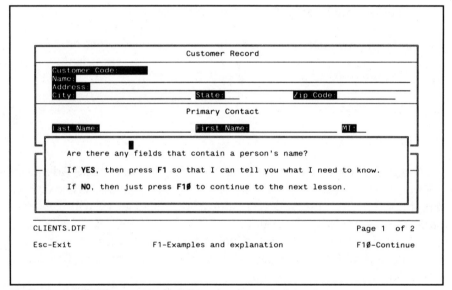

Figure 11.10: Defining which fields contain people's names

You designate a name by specifying the fields that refer to the person. Enter 1L next to the first person's last name, 1F next to the first name, and 1M next to the middle initial. Press F6 if you have to expand the field. You can also define fields that contain a title (1T) or a suffix (1S), such as Ph.D. If a field contains the whole name, use W.

4. Press Esc to return to the screen for defining names.

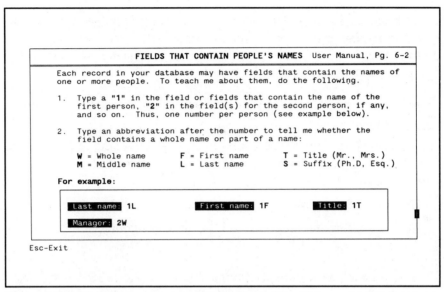

Figure 11.11: Help screen for specifying people's names

5. Press ↓ four times to reach the primary contact's Last Name field and type **1L**.

6. Press ↵ to reach the First Name field and type **1F**.

7. Press ↵ to reach the MI field, press F6, type **1M**, and press ↵.

8. Press PgDn to reach the next page of the form.

9. Press ↓ twice to reach the first Secretary field and type **2W**.

10. Press ↓ to reach the secondary contact's Last Name field and type **3L**.

11. Press ↵ to reach the First Name field and type **3F**.

12. Press ↵ to reach the MI field, press F6, type **3M**, and press ↵.

13. Press ↓ three times to reach the second Secretary field and type **4W**.

14. Press F10. IA will display a message that it is processing your information.

IA builds an index of names from the records. When the index is completed, it displays the screen shown in Figure 11.12. You use this screen to inform IA how you will refer to each of the individuals. The fields for the first person are already highlighted.

15. Type **contact**, press ↵, type **primary**, press ↵, and type **primary contact**.

16. Press F8 to highlight the next field. The field name and alternate field names that you entered through the Basic Lessons menu are already listed.

17. Press F8 to highlight the next field.

18. Type **alternate**, press ↵, and type **alternate contact**, and then press F10.

You did not have to enter additional names for the two Secretary fields because they are already identified by alternate field names.

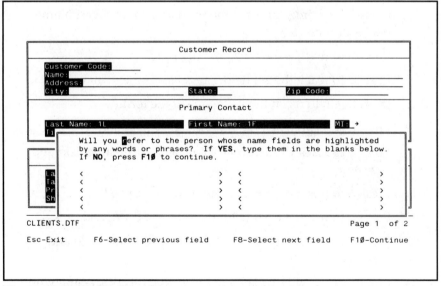

Figure 11.12: IA displays this screen so you can assign names to composite people name fields

Because the secretaries' whole names were included in a single field, the alternate field names apply to their entire names. The primary and secondary contact names were divided into three fields. Any alternate field names that you entered through the Basic Lessons menu must relate to the individual fields, not the contact's entire name. Through the Advanced Lessons menu, however, you can enter synonyms that relate to the contacts' composite name—all three fields at one time.

With these definitions, you will be able to ask questions such as

Who are the contacts' secretaries?

IA will list the names of primary contacts and their secretaries. It may appear that IA understands the possessive form contacts'. But actually, it is simply listing the fields identified with contact and secretary in the same records. We did not have to assign the alternate field name *contacts' secretary* to the Secretary field, because the request will be interpreted correctly without it.

However, we did assign terms like *alternate's secretary* to the Secretary1 field. If we had not, you would have to phrase your request as

Who are the alternates' secretary1s?

instead of the more natural

Who are the alternates' secretaries?

Without the definition, the second request would display a list of the secondary contacts' names but with the names of the *primary* contacts' secretaries, which are the names in the Secretary field. Because we assigned the alternate field names, the entire term *alternates' secretaries* is now associated with the Secretary1 field.

Using the term *alternate* by itself and as part of another alternate field name does not confuse IA. When IA sees the word *alternate's* in a request, it will look ahead to the next word. If the next word is *secretary, hobbies,* or another word used with *alternate's* in an alternate field name, IA will display the associated field. It recognizes the two words together as an alternate field name.

If the next word is some other field, as in

What are the alternates' cities?

IA interprets the request as the two separate fields Alternate and City.

These distinctions are subtle, but they are critical to your ability to get the results you intended.

There is one drawback to defining all four names: when you ask a "who" question that does not explicitly state who you are looking for, such as

Who has the highest amount?

IA may list all four names along with the client name. The exact way that IA responds, however, depends on the questions you might have asked previously. If you want only the client's name, phrase the question

What client has the highest amount?

Remember, *client* is a term describing what the database is about. Since you defined Name as identifying field, the name will appear in the report.

Another way to get the proper answer is to list the field you want explicitly, as in

What contact has the highest amount?

TEACHING IA UNITS OF MEASURE

Number and money fields contain only numbers. We can assume that amounts and total orders are in dollars, and that age is in years.

But suppose we have an inventory database with a field named Weight. Are the values pounds, ounces, grams, or kilograms? Does the field named Shelf Life refer to days, weeks, months, or years? Does the Size field refer to inches, feet, or meters?

The Units of Measure option on the Advanced Lessons menu allows you to designate the units of measure for each number field. Let's use this lesson to teach IA about the Age field.

1. Select Units of Measure from the Advanced Lessons menu. IA will display the screen shown in Figure 11.13, with the first number field, Age, already selected.

2. Type **years** and press F8. The secondary contact's Age field will be highlighted.

3. Type **years** and press F10.

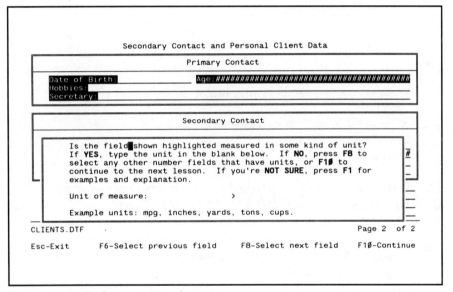

Figure 11.13: Defining units of measure

Defining Units of Currency

If your business deals internationally, you might maintain fields with several different monetary values, such as dollars, francs, yen, or lire. Money fields, however, are always treated as either dollars or pounds, depending on how you set the Global Options menu when you designed the form. When you need a field that contains some other unit of currency, define the field as number, and then assign it the unit of measure in the nation's currency.

You can program the form to convert one currency to another, or use IA to ask questions such as

Who owes more than 600 francs?

TEACHING IA ADJECTIVES

IA already knows a number of terms for the adjectives *maximum* and *minimum,* so you can ask questions such as

Who has the most total orders?

Which client has the best amount?

If you do not specify the field, as in

Who is the best client?

IA will ask you to clarify which field you are referring to, as shown in Figure 11.14. Select the field, and IA will be able to interpret the request properly.

You can use the Advanced Vocabulary: Adjectives option to teach IA other terms, such as *old* and *new,* or *expensive* and *cheap.* You link adjectives with individual number and money fields.

Now we will define adjectives for the money fields in the Clients database. We will not define adjectives for the Credit Limit field because we will assign synonyms to print reports based on this field later in the chapter.

1. Select Advanced Vocabulary: Adjectives from the Advanced Lessons menu, and you will see the screen shown in Figure 11.15.

The first money field, Amount, is selected. IA is asking you to define adjectives for high and low values. Since IA already knows words like *best,* let's just enter a new word for low values.

2. Press ↵ to reach the Low Value column and type **cheap**.

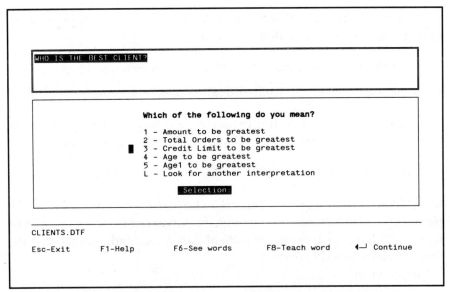

Figure 11.14: Because no field is specified, IA asks for clarification

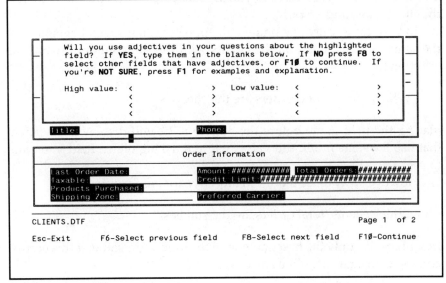

Figure 11.15: Adjective screen

You do not have to enter *cheaper* or *cheapest* because IA will automatically recognize them now that *cheap* is defined.

3. Press F8 to reach the Total Orders field, press ↵, and type **cheap**.

4. Press F10 to return to the Advanced Lessons menu.

Remember that the wording of the question will affect what names are listed and the number of records displayed. For example, if you enter

Who is the cheapest client?

IA will treat the question as a general "who" question and display all the people's names you identified through the Advanced Lessons menu. Your report will have six columns: the client name, four individuals, and the amount you selected to display.

If you enter

What client is the cheapest?

IA will prompt you for the field you are referring to, and then display just the client name and amount.

In both cases, only one name will appear, even if several clients meet the same criteria. To list all the clients with the same amount, word the question as

Which clients' total orders are the cheapest?

placing the field name before the adjective. IA will display every client that has the same minimum value, without asking which field you want to use.

However, if you use a built-in adjective for *minimum,* such as

Which clients' total orders are the smallest?

IA will display only the first name with the minimum value. If this occurs, add the field again after the adjective, as in

Which clients' total orders are the smallest total orders?

In fact, you may want to phrase all your questions explicitly to avoid possible errors.

For date fields, assign adjectives like *least recent* and *most recent*. List the fields explicitly, as in

Who is the contact with the most recent date of birth?

Who is the alternate with the least recent date of birth1?

If you do not list the fields, you will have to check IA's interpretation of your request carefully, and you may have to try different combinations of phrasing.

TEACHING IA VERBS

The Advanced Vocabulary: Verbs option on the Advanced Lessons menu teaches IA verbs that relate to your fields. By defining verbs, you can avoid using forms of the verbs *to be* and *to have*. For example, if you define the verb *bought* for a total order field, instead of entering

What client has a total order of over $1000?

you could ask

Which clients bought over $1000?

The Help screen for this lesson, shown in Figure 11.16, explains how to determine where verbs can be used. If the field name fits in the blank "has a _____ of," you can usually assign a verb to that field.

In our Clients database, we will assign verbs to the City, Phone, Last Order Date, Amount, Total Orders, and Products Purchased fields.

1. Select Advanced Vocabulary: Verbs from the Advanced Lessons menu. You will see the screen shown in Figure 11.17, with the first field in the database selected.

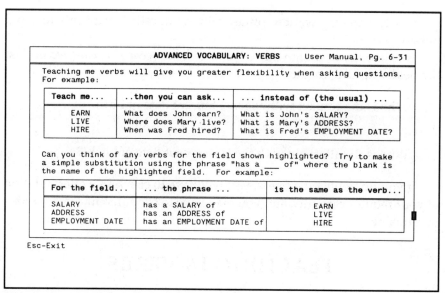

```
                    ADVANCED VOCABULARY: VERBS      User Manual, Pg. 6-31
 Teaching me verbs will give you greater flexibility when asking questions.
 For example:
 ┌─────────────────┬─────────────────────────┬──────────────────────────────┐
 │ Teach me...     │ ..then you can ask...   │ ... instead of (the usual)...│
 ├─────────────────┼─────────────────────────┼──────────────────────────────┤
 │     EARN        │ What does John earn?    │ What is John's SALARY?       │
 │     LIVE        │ Where does Mary live?   │ What is Mary's ADDRESS?      │
 │     HIRE        │ When was Fred hired?    │ What is Fred's EMPLOYMENT DATE?│
 └─────────────────┴─────────────────────────┴──────────────────────────────┘

 Can you think of any verbs for the field shown highlighted?  Try to make
 a simple substitution using the phrase "has a ___ of" where the blank is
 the name of the highlighted field.  For example:
 ┌─────────────────┬─────────────────────────┬──────────────────────────────┐
 │ For the field...│ ... the phrase ...      │ is the same as the verb...   │
 ├─────────────────┼─────────────────────────┼──────────────────────────────┤
 │ SALARY          │ has a SALARY of         │          EARN                │
 │ ADDRESS         │ has an ADDRESS of       │          LIVE                │
 │ EMPLOYMENT DATE │ has an EMPLOYMENT DATE of│          HIRE                │
 └─────────────────┴─────────────────────────┴──────────────────────────────┘

 Esc-Exit
```

Figure 11.16: Help screen for assigning verbs

```
                           Customer Record
 Customer Code:
 Name:
 Address:
 City:                          State:           Zip Code:

                           Primary Contact

 Last Name:                 First Name:                    MI:

    If you need help, press F1.  If not, type verbs you wish to use
    with the field shown highlighted, then press F8 to teach me verbs
    for the next field, if desired.  Press F10 when done.

       <                    >  <                        >
       <                    >  <                        >
       <                    >  <                        >
       <                    >  <                        >
       <                    >  <                        >

 CLIENTS.DTF                                          Page 1  of 2

 Esc-Exit     F6-Select previous field   F8-Select next field   F10-Continue
```

Figure 11.17: Defining a verb screen

2. Press F8 three times to reach the City field and type **reside**.

3. Press F8 seven times to reach the Phone field and type **reach**.

4. Press F8 to reach the Last Order Date field and type **occur**.

5. Press F8 to reach the Amount field and type **owe**.

6. Press F8 to reach the Total Orders field, type **bought**, press ↵, type **buy**, press ↵, and type **purchase**.

Since *bought* is an irregular past tense of *buy*, it must be listed separately.

7. Press F8 three times to reach the Products Purchased field and type **order**.

8. Press F10 to return to the Advanced Lessons menu.

9. Press Esc twice to return to the Assistant menu.

A request can include a verb only for one field. But since you already defined the Address, City, State, and Zip Code fields as locations, you can now ask questions such as

Where is he?

to get a complete address. Later, we will define the verb *live* as a synonym for the complete address.

With these verbs defined, you can also ask questions such as

How do I reach Chesin?

to display his phone number, or

Which clients order item 101?

to see a list of clients who have purchased that item.

To define additional verbs later, select the option again, or within IA, press F8 and choose to define a verb.

USING THE EDUCATED IA

After completing the advanced lessons, select Exit Lessons to return to the Assistant menu.

After you teach IA, you can use all the new terms in your questions and requests. You also continue using IA formal syntax or Query Guide structure. When you want to teach IA a new word, use the spontaneous method or run any of the lessons again.

Keep in mind that even after being taught, IA has its limitations. Improperly worded questions can still result in incorrect or misleading responses or display fields that you are not interested in seeing. In many cases, IA will ask you to clarify your question by indicating which field you are referring to or whether a word relates to a field, built-in vocabulary word, or a value in a field.

Now you will see just how useful the lessons you gave IA are.

DISPLAYING RECORDS

You can retrieve and display records using the commands Display, Show, and Fetch, followed by the appropriate retrieval criteria, such as

Show me the records where credit limit = 1500

You can use any of the criteria you learned in Chapter 10. However, now that you taught IA some important lessons, you can retrieve records much more efficiently. For example, now that IA knows the text and keyword values in the Clients database, it can locate records without you explicitly naming the fields.

Let's have IA show us some records:

1. From the Assistant menu, select Ask Me to Do Something, and then press ↵ to accept Clients.

2. Type **Show me Chesin's record** and press ↵. IA knows that Chesin is the name of a contact, and it will interpret the request as shown in Figure 11.18.

If you had several records containing the name Chesin, IA would ask which meaning you had in mind, as shown in Figure 11.19.

3. Press ↵, and IA will display the record for you to review or edit.

4. Press F10 to return to the request box.

5. Type **Fetch me Nancy's record** and press ↵ twice. IA will locate a record with the name Nancy in the Secretary field.

IA can retrieve records based on any word in a field identified with a person through the Basic Lessons menu. In this case, the field contains Nancy Harriet, but IA is able to locate the record on the name Nancy alone—you did not have to type the full name.

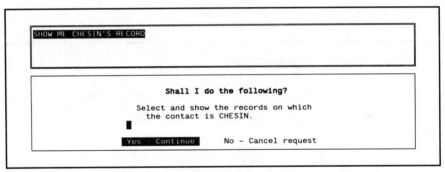

Figure 11.18: IA's interpretation shows it located the record based on text

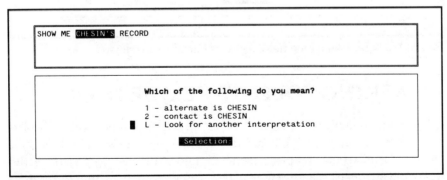

Figure 11.19: IA asks for clarification when a field value is not unique

6. Press Esc to return to the request box.

7. Type **Show me Williams' record** and press ↵. IA will display a message indicating that it doesn't know the highlighted word, even though the word Williams is part of a longer client name.

IA has the ability to identify parts of names only in fields defined as those that contain people's names through the Advanced Lessons menu. Let's try another approach.

8. Press Esc, then Shift-F4 to remove the request.

9. Type **Show me the record that contains Williams** and press ↵. IA will ask for a clarification, as shown in Figure 11.20.

10. Type **2** and press ↵ twice to display the record.

11. Press Esc to return to the request box.

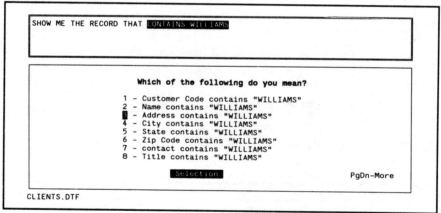

Figure 11.20: IA asks which field you want used for retrieval

ASKING FOLLOW-UP QUESTIONS

It would certainly be convenient if we always had the time to carefully plan our requests in advance. We could develop the request, or a question, so it generated a full report, complete with all the information we needed. But in the real world, we often get information in pieces, one question leading to another.

With IA, once you ask a question that retrieves a specific record or group of records, you can ask follow-up questions without repeating the retrieval criteria. Instead, you can refer to the records using the pronouns *his, hers, their, he, she,* or *they.*

Let's see how this works by developing a line of questioning relating to one record.

1. Type **How do I reach Chesin?** and press ↵ twice.

Because you defined *reach* as a verb for *phone,* IA shows you the telephone number. Now let's see if it is an out-of-town number.

2. Press F10 to return to the request box.

3. Type **Where does he reside?** and press ↵ twice.

Even without specifically including Chesin's name, IA displays the city for that client. IA understood that the *he* in the question refers to Chesin.

4. Press F10, type **Where is he?**, and press ↵ twice.

Since we indicated that the Address, City, State, and Zip Code fields are locations, they appear when you ask a "where" question. However, it would be more natural to ask "Where does he live?" In order to associate the term *live* with all four fields, we will define it as a synonym while we are using IA.

5. Press F10, then F8 to teach IA a new word.

6. Type **S** to select synonym.

7. Type **live** and press ↵.

8. Type **address and city and state and zip code**, and then press F10 to return to the request box.

9. Type **Where does he live?** and press ↵ twice to display the report.

10. To continue with our follow-up questions, press F10.

11. Type **Who is his secretary?** and press ↵ twice.

12. Press F10, type **How much does he owe?**, and press ↵ twice.

IA displays the value of the Amount field because it was associated with the verb *owe*. It also includes the count and total because we asked a "how much" question.

13. Press F10, type **What does she order?**, and press ↵.

IA does not worry about gender; even though you used the pronoun *he* in previous questions, you can change pronouns without confusing it.

However, although you defined the verb *order* for the Products Purchased field, *order* is also a built-in vocabulary word, so IA asks you to clarify your meaning, as shown in Figure 11.21. In this case, you want to use the term as it relates to a field in the database.

14. Type **1** and press ↵ twice to display the answer.

15. Press F10, type **Who buys item 101?**, and press ↵. Because the number 101 confuses IA, you will see the request for clarification shown in Figure 11.22.

IA wants to know if you are referring to a value in the Products Purchased field, a customer code, or just a number. If you had enclosed the 101 in quotation marks, IA would have been able to correctly interpret the question. But if you had just entered *Who buys "101"?* without the alternate

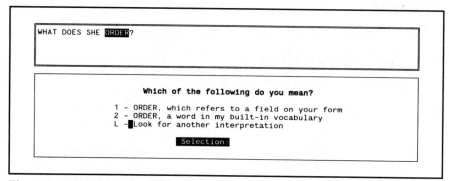

Figure 11.21: Because a verb matches a built-in vocabulary word, IA asks for clarification

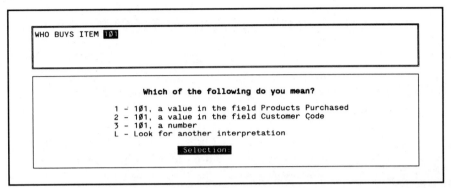

Figure 11.22: Select desired field or numeric value

field name *item*, IA would warn you that it did not have enough information to process the request. If you select to continue, IA will interpret the statement as a request for the key fields of all records. Select to cancel the request to add information or retrieve criteria.

16. Type **1** and press ⏎ twice to see a list of the clients who purchase product 101.

17. Press F10, type **Who owes over $500?**, and press ⏎.

IA interprets this "who" question in a way that would include all four people listed in the record. However, we really only want to see the client name.

18. Type **N**, and then press Shift-F4 to delete the request.

19. Type **What clients owe over $500?** and press ⏎.

20. The interpretation is now correct, so press ⏎ to display the report.

21. Press F10.

To prevent the extra fields from appearing, you had to change your command from a "who" to a "what client" question. Another way to exclude fields from a report is by using restriction codes.

RESTRICTING COLUMNS

In Chapter 10, you learned that adding WNRC and WNEC prevented fields used in retrieval criteria from printing. Now that you're using IA for more advanced purposes, you should understand the differences between these codes and WINC.

- WNRC (With No Restriction Columns) suppresses the fields used in retrieval criteria if they are not explicitly listed in the command. All identifying fields will still appear.

- WNIC (With No Identification Columns) suppresses the fields used to identify the form through the Basic Lessons menu. However, fields used in retrieval criteria will still be included.

- WNEC (With No Extra Columns) combines WNRC and WNIC. It prevents all columns not specifically listed from printing. The sort field, however, will always appear in the first column.

USING COMPARATIVE ADJECTIVES

Just as IA has many synonyms for *maximum* and *minimum*, it also has the following built-in synonyms for *more* and *less*, and *above average* and *below average*:

more	most
bigger	biggest
greater	greatest
larger	largest
higher	highest
lower	lowest
fewer	fewest
smaller	smallest
littler	littlest
less	least

above   top

below   bottom

under

In the following steps, we will use these adjectives to see which clients we should give higher credit limits.

1. Type **What clients have more credit than Dershaw?** and press ↵ twice. If your database is large, IA will display a message telling you to wait because your request is complex.

This request requires IA to make two passes through the database. In the first pass, it searches for the value in Dershaw's record. In the second pass, it looks for records with greater values in the field. Then it displays a list of clients whose credit limit is greater than the value in Dershaw's record.

2. Press F10, type **Which clients have higher credit limits?**, and press ↵ twice. IA will display a list of clients with above average credit limits.

3. Press F10, type **Which clients have smaller credit limits?**, and press ↵ twice. You will see a list of clients with below average credit limits.

4. Press F10, type **Which clients have average credit limits**?, and press ↵ twice. Instead of listing clients with an average credit rating, IA will only calculate and display the average.

To display all the clients that have the average credit limit, you must enter the request

Which clients' credit limits equal the average credit limit?

Synonyms such as *larger* and *smaller* will display all records meeting the criteria. However, synonyms for *maximum* and *minimum* (such as *highest* and *lowest*) will display only one record when used in questions such as

What clients have the highest credit limit?

To see the names of all clients with the *maximum*, you would have to enter

What clients credit limit equals the highest credit limit?

However, these requests are rather wordy. We can shorten them by defining synonyms.

5. Press F8 and type **S** to define a synonym.

6. Type **most trusted** and press ↵.

7. Type **for credit limit = maximum credit limit** and press ↵.

8. Type **least trusted** and press ↵.

9. Type **for credit limit = minimum credit limit** and press F10.

10. Press F10 to return to the request box.

You can also teach IA new words by typing commands in the request box. We will define the average credit limit as *just trusted* using this technique.

11. Type **Define "JUST TRUSTED" AS "FOR CREDIT LIMIT = AVERAGE CREDIT LIMIT"** and press ↵ twice. Be sure to use all uppercase characters.

12. Type **Which clients are most trusted** and press ↵ twice.

13. Press F10, type **Which clients are just trusted?**, and press ↵ twice. IA will not locate any records because no client has the exact average, $1,075.

14. Press ↵ to return to the request box.

TAKING SHORTCUTS

Because IA knows your fields and field values, there's a lot of information you can retrieve with simple one- or two-word requests. For example, if you type a value found in a field, IA assumes you want to display records that contain that value. Typing **Fed Ex**, for example, will show companies using Federal Express as their preferred carrier. If you type **1500** by itself, IA will ask you to select which number or money field you want displayed.

The first field is used as the retrieval criteria, so add additional fields to include more columns.

If you type **President's secretaries**, you will see a list of companies and secretaries where the contact's title is President. IA automatically interprets the request as

> Create a report showing
>> the Name and
>> the Secretary
> from the records on which
>> the Title is President

But type **Credit 1500**—a field name and then a value—to display the names of companies with a $1,500 credit limit.

With yes/no fields, enter the field name to list records that are true. For example, typing **Taxable** will display a list of client names (the identification field) with a true value in the Taxable field.

To quickly find the shipping zone for Margate, type **Margate's zone**.

These shortcuts allow you to obtain the information you need quickly.

CHANGING RECORDS

You can change a record by retrieving it with the Show or Fetch commands and then editing it on the screen. But if you know the field name and change you want to make, you can complete the task with a command to IA.

For example, if you enter

> Increase Chesin's credit limit by 500

IA asks if it should

> CHANGE THE DATABASE
> by setting Credit Limit to Credit Limit+500
> on all records on which
>> the contact is CHESIN

When you select Yes, IA scans the database looking for matching records, and then displays a message warning you that records may be altered.

Select Yes again, and you will see the first record that meets the criteria. Press Shift-F10 to change the record and display the next record (if any), press Ctrl-F10 to change all the records matching the criteria, or press F10 to see the next matching record without changing the one displayed. When the records have been updated, the request box will reappear.

You can also change field values by entering sentences such as

Chesin's secretary is "Nancy Cohen"

In this case, *Chesin* identifies the record, *secretary* is the field, and *Nancy Cohen*, in quotation marks, is the new value.

Some requests, such as

Multiply Paulson's credit limit by 2

are not interpreted automatically as a command to change a record. In this case, IA will first ask for clarification, as shown in Figure 11.23. After you select a number, IA will display the message shown in Figure 11.24. You can choose to actually change the record or to just display a report showing the new values.

You can delete a record or erase the contents of a field with the Delete command. For example, to delete the records containing Chesin, enter

Delete Chesin

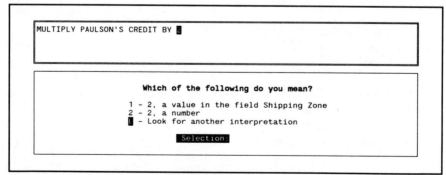

Figure 11.23: IA asks for clarification on the number 2

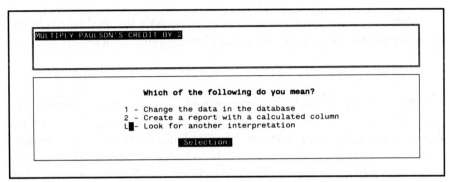

Figure 11.24: IA asks if you want to actually change the record or display
the calculations on the screen

If the name is found in more than one field, IA will ask you to select the
field you have in mind. You can, of course, be more specific to begin with,
as in

Delete the record where the contact is Chesin

If you just want to erase the contents of a field, specify the record and
field name. For instance, if Paulson's secretary quits, clear the field by
entering

Delete Paulson's secretary

USING FUNCTIONS IN IA

Most of Q&A's statistical and text functions can also be used in your
IA requests. Enter them directly starting with the @ symbol, not in Program commands as you do when creating form documents.

For example, to list the values in the Amount field rounded to whole
dollars, enter

List @ROUND(Amount,0)

With functions, field names must appear exactly as they do in the database form—IA will not recognize plural versions, such as

List @ROUND(Amounts,0)

One excellent use of text functions in IA is to change the contents of a field. If the text you are entering is wider than the space provided on the form, IA will automatically expand the field. But suppose you want to ensure that the field is not expanded so reports and print specifications you've already designed do not have to be changed. You can accomplish this by combining the @LEFT and @WIDTH functions. For example, the following command changes the Title field but inserts only as many characters as will fit on the form:

Change Title to @LEFT("Vice President for Purchasing", @WIDTH(Title)–1)

The @LEFT function tells IA to insert characters starting at the beginning of the text *Vice President for Purchasing*. The number of characters is designated by @WIDTH(Title)–1.

GIVING IA A NEW NAME

To change IA's name:

1. **Select Ask Me to Do Something from the Assistant menu, enter any database name, and press ⏎.**
2. **Type a request telling IA its new name, and select Yes when prompted.**
3. **To access the renamed IA, type the first letter of the new name from the Main menu.**

The more you teach IA, the more it understands requests in natural language. If you begin to feel like you're speaking to a real person, you can give

IA a more personal name. You can then use the name in requests, such as

Sam, what time is it?

or

Farah, who are our best clients?

To change the name, select Ask Me to Do Something from the Assistant menu, and use any database. (IA's name is one word that it learns globally, no matter which database you're using.) Then type a command such as

You are "Sam"

or

Change your name to "Raquel"

If you do not enclose the name in quotation marks, IA will change it to all uppercase.

IA will respond with

Shall I do the following?
Change my name to Raquel.

Select Yes. The new name will be listed on the IA menu and even on Q&A's Main menu, where the first letter of the name will replace A as the activating keystroke. For example, if you name IA Howard, the Main menu will include

H - Howard

and you must press H, not A, to access IA.

Be careful how you word the request, and check the interpretation carefully. For example, if you enter

You are now called Robbin

IA will interpret the request as

Change my name to NOW CALLED ROBBIN

and you would have to start IA by pressing N from the Main menu.
To change the name back to the original, enter the command

You are "Assistant"

TEACHING IA
A FOREIGN LANGUAGE

IA's ability to be taught can even extend to other languages, although it's best if the language follows the general grammatical pattern and sentence structure of English.

Teach IA a foreign-language synonym for each of its built-in vocabulary words and with all the lessons. For example, define *calculez* as a synonym for *calculate,* so you could tell IA in French to

calculez (65 + 76 + 97)/3

Create the synonyms *donde* for *where, estan* for *are,* and *ellas* for *they,* so you can display locations by asking the Spanish

Donde estan ellas?

With some experimentation and practice, you can make IA bilingual.

USING OTHER IA APPLICATIONS

By exploring the uses of IA with our Clients database, you have learned how to generate reports and answer questions that relate to customers. But we've only touched upon IA's power and flexibility.

Here are some sample questions and requests that IA could answer for other applications:

- Inventory database

    What items are backordered?

    What are the best selling items?

    Who sells us disks?

    How many printers do we have in stock?

    Increase prices by 10 percent.

    What items sell better than books?

- Personnel database

    Who has been absent more than 10 days?

    Where is Smith working?

    What is the average salary in accounting?

    How many salespersons are paid commission?

    What department has the best safety record?

    Crosstab salary by sex and department.

    Increase Barbara Wartel's salary by 5 percent.

    Decrease Salador's sick days by 1.

    Who is the highest paid manager?

- School database

    What is Jane Wyman's average?

    Where is Jane during fifth period?

List the students by GPA.

Change Chen's final grade to 90.

How many students are on honor roll?

Now it is time to move on to another powerful feature of Q&A that can make your work more efficient. The next chapter describes how to create and use Q&A macros.

12

Creating
and Using
Macros

Computers are ideal for performing repetitive tasks, such as printing multiple copies of reports or generating form letters that contain the same text. But you are probably performing many repetitive tasks yourself. Do you periodically type the same keystrokes to enter your address at the top of a letter, or work through the same series of menus to perform a function?

With Q&A, you can use a *macro* to repeat a series of keystrokes. A macro is a stored recording of a task. Every time you have to perform the task saved in the macro, you just run the macro to repeat the keystrokes. You can link macros with key combinations so that you can perform complex functions with a few keystrokes, such as pressing Alt-C to center text, or Ctrl-P to print a report. In this chapter, you will learn how to create macros by recording your keystrokes.

DEFINING A MACRO

You can select to define a macro from any Q&A menu or screen. However, you should define the macro where you plan to run it, and only run it from that location. Otherwise, the macro might delete you records or files, or even exit from Q&A without saving new records or documents. (Later in this chapter, you will learn how to construct a macro that can be run from any menu.)

Defining a macro involves actually completing the task that you want to perform. That is, as you enter the keystrokes, Q&A acts on them the same way it would if you were not creating a macro. If you press keys that select menu items, Q&A will select the items. If you press keys that print a document, Q&A will print the document. So be prepared for the function that you are recording in the macro.

CREATING A MACRO
TO RECALL A DOCUMENT

To create a macro:

1. **Press Shift-F2 and choose Define Macro.**
2. **Type the macro identifier.**
3. **Type the keystrokes you want to record.**
4. **Press Shift-F2, then F10.**
5. **Press ⏎ to save the macro to the disk, or N to create a temporary macro.**

Many times, you will start Q&A to continue working on a document that you already started. You can define a macro that will start Write and recall the document in a single keystroke. This is possible because the last document you saved or recalled is listed as the first item in the Document Options menu.

Follow these steps to define the macro:

1. Start Q&A and display the Main menu. You must begin creating the macro here because you will use it from the Main menu.

2. Press Shift-F2 to display the Macro menu, shown in Figure 12.1.

From this menu, you run, define, delete, recall, save, and clear macros. You can also create a custom menu for running macros, as explained in the next chapter.

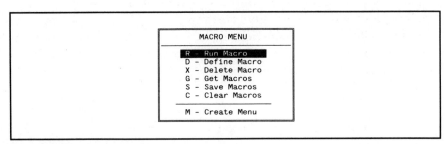

Figure 12.1: Macro menu

3. Type **D** to select Define Macro. The status line will display the message

Type the macro identifier, or ENTER for None. Example, Alt-A, Alt-B, etc.

At this prompt, you type the keystrokes you want to use to execute the macro. You can just press ↵ without entering a macro identifier, but then you will not be able to run the macro by pressing a key combination. You will learn more about macro identifiers in the next section.

4. Press Alt-L (L for last document). You will see a flashing rectangle in the bottom-right corner of the screen, indicating that Q&A is in macro record mode.

Now you press the keys that you want to be recorded as the macro.

5. Type **3** and press ↵ to start Write and display the first Write screen.

6. Press F8, type **D**, and press ↵ to recall the first document listed in the document options box. (If you did not turn on automatic menu option execution, press ↵ another time.)

When you are finished entering the keystrokes, you press Shift-F2 again. (In the next chapter, you will learn how to write a macro so that you can create it without actually performing the keystrokes until you are ready to do so.)

7. Press Shift-F2 to display the Macro Options menu, as shown in Figure 12.2. The name of your macro will appear as <altl>.

Q&A gives each macro a descriptive name. The default name is a code that represents the macro identifier. (If you did not enter a macro identifier, the name will appear as *No name #000*, numbered sequentially for all unnamed macros.) You can enter another name of up to 31 characters. Changing the name does not change its identifier.

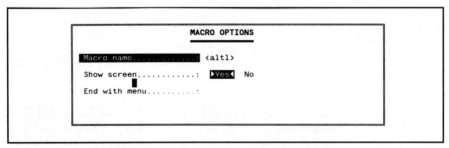

Figure 12.2: Macro Options menu

8. Type **Last Document**.

9. Press ↵ to reach the Show Screen option and type **N** to select No.

The Show Screen option determines how the macro appears as it is executing. With the default setting of Yes, you see each character or menu appear on the screen just as it did when you created the macro. If your macro runs a series of menus, the default setting can produce a distracting flashing effect as each menu appears and disappears. When Show Screen is set to No, you will not see the menus or individual keystrokes on the screen until the entire macro is run.

10. Press F10. Q&A will prompt you

    Save macros to file: C:\QA\QAMACRO.ASC

    and the message line will show

    If you want to save your macros to disk now, press ENTER. Otherwise, press ESC

11. Press ↵ to save the macro.

Because you performed the task as you created the macro, the last document you worked on now appears on the screen.

If you start to create a macro and then change your mind, press Shift-F2 to display the Macro Options menu, and then press Esc to cancel the macro definition. Do not press Esc while recording the macro because that will just add the Esc keystroke to the macro.

ASSIGNING MACRO IDENTIFIERS

Macro identifiers can be any letter, number, or function key preceded by Alt, Ctrl, or Shift. Select a key combination that will be easy to remember, such as Alt-B to boldface characters or Alt-C to center text.

Many key combinations are already used by Q&A, such as Shift-F6 to enhance text and Ctrl-F5 to copy text to a file. Also, remember that the Shift key is used in combination with letter and number keys to type uppercase letters and punctuation marks. With a few exceptions, if you enter one of the key combinations built into Q&A, you will see the message

That key is already used by Q&A. Do you want to redefine it? (Y/N):

on the message line. Redefining the key will not permanently erase Q&A's built-in function, just temporarily remove it as long as your own macro is loaded. When you delete or clear the macro, the original function will again be available.

There are a few key combinations used by Q&A that you can assign to a macro without seeing the prompt. There are some other keystrokes that Q&A does not use but cannot be assigned to a macro. If you try to use one of these as a macro identifier, nothing will happen. Press another key combination, or press Esc to cancel the macro definition.

All the key combinations used by Q&A are listed on the inside covers of this book. The following are available:

Alt-1–Alt-0	Ctrl-L
Alt-A–Alt-Z	Ctrl-O
Ctrl-↵	Ctrl-P
Ctrl-6	Ctrl-Q
Ctrl-]	Ctrl-U
Ctrl-B	Ctrl-Z
Ctrl-J	Ctrl-F10
Ctrl-K	

If you enter an identifier that you already assigned to another macro, you will see the message

That key is already defined. Do you want to redefine it? (Y/N):

Press Y to erase the existing macro from memory so you can define a new one, or press N to cancel the process. Erasing the macro from memory will not delete it from the disk file until you save the macro file.

Autostart Macros

If you want to execute a macro at the same time you start Q&A, assign it an Alt-0 through Alt-9 identifier. Then the next time you start Q&A, use the -M option from the DOS command line, followed by the number you assigned the macro. For example, entering

QA -M1

will execute the Alt-1 macro after Q&A starts. The named macro must, however, be in the default macro file. You will learn about macro files later in the chapter.

WordStar Control Keys

Included in Q&A are 16 key combinations starting with Ctrl that are designed to simulate cursor-movement and editing keys used by the WordStar word processing program. These key combinations duplicate many single keystroke or function key commands built into Q&A, such as pressing Ctrl-X instead of ↓. These combinations are good candidates for your own macros. However, there are some situations in which you might want to retain the WordStar commands instead of redefining them:

- If you are switching from WordStar to Q&A

- If you want to use your numeric keyboard for typing numbers and do not have separate cursor-movement keys

- If you have a laptop computer without a full set of cursor-movement keys (some require you to press a special function key combination to perform functions such as PgDn and PgUp)

If you do not want to retain the WordStar commands, redefine these key combinations before assigning other combinations that are used by Q&A.

Redefining Typing Keys

A macro identifier can also be any single letter, number, or punctuation mark—not preceded by another key. If you press a letter, number, or punctuation key, or one preceded by Shift, Q&A will display a prompt asking if you really want to redefine it. Since these are the keystrokes you need to input information, in most cases you will not want to redefine them. However, by redefining the keyboard, you can convert it to the Dvorak layout or a foreign-language keyboard.

Q&A can display the foreign language and special characters shown in Figure 12.3. To use the characters numbered from 128 to 244, hold down the Alt key, then use the numeric keyboard (not the numbers on the top row of the keyboard) to type the three-number code shown next to the character. When you release the Alt key, the character will appear on the screen. For example, to type the ½ symbol, hold down Alt and type 171. To type the characters numbered from 2 to 31, press Alt-F10 first, and then hold down Alt and type the number.

If you type Spanish or French documents, for example, you might find it more convenient to define the standard typing keys with macros for producing these characters. (Many computer keyboards sold overseas or designed for foreign-language applications have some of these characters programmed and displayed on the keys.)

SAVING MACROS

When you press ⏎ at the save macro prompt, you save all the macros currently in your computer's memory. If you create one new macro, it and all existing macros will be rewritten to the file. If you press Esc at the save macro prompt, none of your new macros will be recorded on disk. However, you can save macros at any time by selecting Save Macros from the Macro menu.

If you are creating a series of macros, you do not have to save each one individually. Press Esc when you see the save macro prompt, and then create the next macro. After the last macro, press ↵ at the prompt or select Save from the Macro menu to save all the macros. Just *do not forget* to save the macros before leaving Q&A.

You may want to create a macro just for the current session. In this case, you would not save the file. If you define a macro that you do want to keep during that same session, remember to delete the temporary macro from memory so it is not saved.

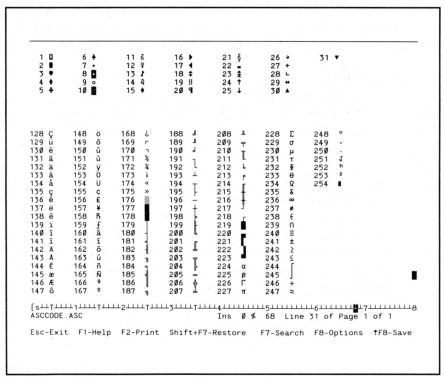

Figure 12.3: Special characters

RUNNING A MACRO

To run a macro, use one of these methods:

- **Press its identifier**
- **Press Shift-F2, then R, highlight the macro name, and press ⏎.**
- **Press Alt-F2, highlight the macro name, and press ⏎.**
- **Run an Alt-*number* macro when starting Q&A by entering the command QA -M, followed by the macro number, at the DOS prompt.**
- **Run a macro named Right Button or Center Button by clicking the mouse button.**

After you define a macro, you can run it by using any of these techniques:

- Press the macro identifier key combination. (If nothing happens, a macro with that identifier is not currently loaded in memory.)

- Press Shift-F2 to display the Macro menu, select Run, and then select the macro's name from the list that appears.

- Press Alt-F2 to display the macro list, and then select the name of the macro.

- Start Q&A with the -M option to run an autostart macro, such as Q&A -M6 to run Alt-6.

You can also execute a macro with the mouse by naming it Right Button or Center Button (if you have a three-button mouse). Run the macro by pressing its identifier keystrokes or by clicking the appropriate mouse button.

To cancel a macro as it is running, press Esc. Q&A will beep to let you know that the macro has stopped.

The macro we created earlier is ready to run—it is in your computer's memory and saved in the disk file. Let's execute it now:

1. Press Esc twice to display the Main menu.

2. Press Alt-L.

Because you set the Show Screen option on the Macro Options menu to No, the words

   macro running

flash briefly on the message line, and then the last document you used appears in the Write window. If you had left Show Screen set to Yes, you would have seen the Write and Options menus appear on the screen as the macro keystrokes were repeated.

Now let's see what happens when you do not run a macro from the same location you created it. We will run our macro again from within Write.

3. Press Alt-L.

Instead of selecting 3 from the Main menu, the macro inserted the number 3 and the carriage return on the screen, and then executed the remaining keystrokes. Since the characters were added to the current document, you are warned that your latest changes have not been saved.

4. Type **N** to cancel the operation.

If you had selected Yes, the document would have appeared on the screen.

Now let's use another method to run the macro.

5. Press Shift-F2, then type **R** to display the macro names list, as shown in Figure 12.4.

The descriptive name of each macro is on the left, and the identifier is on the right side. This list will appear when you press Alt-F2 from any location in Q&A.

6. Select Last Document.

7. Type **N** when the warning box appears.

8. Press Esc, type **C**, and then type **Y** to clear the screen.

Figure 12.4: Macro names list box

This macro recalls the last document, not a particular document. If you want to create a macro selecting a document other than the last one saved or recalled, do not do so from the document options box, because the order of files on the list changes. A document that was third on the list during one session may not be third on the list at another time. If you want to define a macro that recalls a specific document, use the Get command on the Write menu, and record the name of the document in the macro.

DELETING AND CLEARING MACROS

To delete or clear macros:

- **Delete a macro by pressing Shift-F2, then X, highlighting the macro name, and pressing ↵.**
- **Clear macros (erase all macros from memory) by pressing Shift-F2, then C.**

Deleting or clearing macros from memory does not affect the disk file until you save the file.

To delete a macro from the file, select Delete Macro from the Macro menu. Q&A will display a list of macros and menus in the loaded file. Highlight the macro you want to delete and press ↵ to display the save prompt. Press ↵ to save the file without the deleted macro. If you press Esc, the macro will only be deleted from memory, not from the file. Unless you save the file sometime before leaving Q&A, the macro will be available the next time you use the file.

When you select the Clear Macros option from the Macro menu, all the loaded macros are erased from memory. If you clear your macros and then select Save from the Macro menu before creating another, Q&A will not write a blank file over the existing one. However, after you create a macro and save it, the file will be replaced.

If you temporarily clear your macros to free memory, do not create and save a new macro. To add a new macro to the file, use the Get Macros option on the Macro menu to retrieve the file first and reload the macros into memory.

MACRO TECHNIQUES

To use macro techniques:

- **Insert a pause in a macro by pressing Alt-F2 while defining it. Press Alt-F2 again to continue creating the macro.**
- **Embed a macro within another macro by defining the embedded macro first. Then press the macro identifier while defining the main macro when you want the embedded macro to execute.**

You can create more sophisticated macros that pause for user input, execute other macros, or return to a location automatically. In the following sections, we will define macros with these features for use with Q&A Write. Later in this chapter, you will create useful macros for Q&A File and Report.

PAUSING MACROS FOR USER INPUT

Normally, pressing Alt-F2 displays a list of macros that you can run. When you are creating a macro, however, Alt-F2 inserts a pause command. This stops the macro temporarily so that you can enter any characters or keystrokes that will change each time the macro is run. The next macros you will create take advantage of the pause command to streamline character formatting in Q&A Write.

Boldfacing Macro

Enhancing characters takes several far-reaching keystrokes: Shift-F6 to begin the procedure, the cursor-movement keys to highlight the text, and then back to the function keys again to press F10. The boldfacing macro you will define in the following steps allows you to speed up the process by avoiding the function keys entirely.

1. From the Write screen, press Shift-F2 and type **D** to define the macro.

2. Press Alt-B.

3. Press Shift-F6, then ⏎ to select Bold.

4. Press Alt-F2. The cursor will change to a large blinking rectangle, and the status line will display

   Enter the variable text. Press Alt-F2 to resume saving into macro.

This means that any keystrokes that you enter at this time will not be recorded as part of the macro. For example, you could type some characters to boldface while you are creating the macro, but still use it to boldface any amount of text when you run it.

5. Press Alt-F2 again. The prompt will disappear, and the cursor will return to its normal shape.

6. Press F10, then Shift-F2 and type **Boldfacing Macro**.

7. Press ↵ to reach the Show Screen option and type **N**.

8. Press F10, then ↵ to save the macro.

The word *Bold* appears on the status line, indicating that you boldfaced the space at the cursor.

9. Press Del to erase the boldfaced space.

To use the macro, place the cursor at one end of the block you want to highlight and press Alt-B. Move the cursor to the other end of the block and press ↵. Let's see how this works.

10. Type **Macros can save a great deal of time**.

11. Press Alt-B to activate the macro.

The cursor changes to a large rectangle, indicating that the macro has paused for variable information. Write is in enhance mode, although the boldfacing message usually displayed does not appear on the message line. Instead, the message line displays

Enter text. Press ↵ to resume macro playback.

12. Press Home to highlight the entire line, and then press ↵. The sentence will be boldfaced.

The Alt-F2 keystroke paused the macro after it executed the Shift-F6 and ↵ keystrokes that selected Bold. During a pause, you can enter any characters or other keystrokes. In this case, you pressed Home to highlight the line. Pressing ↵ canceled the pause and continued the macro, which entered F10 to turn off bold enhancement.

Underlining Macro

Now let's create a similar macro to underline characters:

1. Press Shift-F2 and type **D**.

2. Press Alt-U.

3. Press Shift-F6 and type **U**.

4. Press Alt-F2 twice, then F10, then Shift-F2.

5. Type **Underlining Macro**.

6. Press F10, then ↵ to save the macro.

We left the Show Screen option set to Yes so you can see the difference this makes while the macro is running.

6. Press Alt-U to activate the macro.

The enhancement menu quickly appears then disappears as the macro reruns your keystrokes.

7. Press Esc. Q&A will beep to tell you that you've canceled the macro as it is running.

8. Press → several times.

Even though you canceled the macro, the text is still being highlighted. This is because you stopped the macro while you were in enhance mode, and the F10 keystroke was not repeated.

9. Press Esc to cancel enhancement.

10. Press Esc, type **C**, then **Y** to clear the screen.

When you cancel a macro, check the status line or look for extra characters on the screen to see if Q&A remained in a special mode.

DESIGNING MACROS
THAT RUN OTHER MACROS

A macro can include another macro as well as text and formatting keystrokes. A macro executed by another macro is said to be *embedded*. If

Macro A runs Macro B, then B is embedded in A. Q&A allows up to five levels of embedded macros:

```
Macro A
    executes Macro B
        executes Macro C
            executes Macro D
                executes Macro E
                Macro E ends
            Macro D ends
        Macro C ends
    Macro B ends
Macro A ends
```

You cannot create a macro that defines another macro, so you must define the embedded macros before you define the macros that execute them. If you were creating the five-level macro illustrated above, you would have to define Macro E before you could define Macro D, D before C, C before B, and B before A.

To embed a macro in another, while defining the main macro, press the keystrokes to run the other macro when you want it to execute.

As an example, we will define a macro that prints your standard letterhead at the top of a page. We want to center the letterhead text and insert the date. Since centering text and inserting the date are common tasks, it would be handy to have them performed by macros so you do not have to repeat the keystrokes in other documents.

Instead of including the keystrokes to center text and enter the date code in the letterhead macro, you will create separate macros and embed them in the letterhead macro. Because you are creating several macros in one session, you can save time by not saving the file after each one. Just make sure to save the file after creating the last macro.

Centering Text Macro

Follow these steps to create the macro for centering text:

1. From the Write screen, press Shift-F2 and type **D**.

2. Press Alt-C.

3. Press F8, type **A**, then **C**.

4. Press Shift-F2 and type **Center Text Macro**.

5. Press ↵ to reach the Show Screen option and type **N**.

6. Press F10, then Esc.

To use this macro, place the cursor anywhere in the line you want to center and press Alt-C.

Date Macro

Now follow these steps to create a macro to insert the date:

1. Press Shift-F2 and type **D**.

2. Press Alt-D.

3. Type ***DATE(3)*** (or use another date format code if you prefer).

4. Press Shift-F2 and type **Insert Date Macro**.

5. Press ↵ to reach the Show Screen option and type **N**.

6. Press F10, then Esc.

7. Press Esc, type **C**, then **Y** to clear the screen.

When you want to insert the date in a document, press Alt-D to run this macro.

Letterhead Macro

The final step is to create an all-purpose letterhead macro. This macro will place the letterhead at the top of the letter, even if you type the letter first and then add the letterhead.

1. Press Shift-F2 and type **D**.

2. Press Alt-H.

3. Press Home four times.

On the blank screen, the four Home keystrokes do not appear to have any effect; however, they are recorded in the macro. No matter how long the document, four Home presses will move to its beginning. Any extra Home keystrokes will have no effect.

4. Press Alt-I.

If you are inserting the letterhead at the top of an existing letter, you have to make sure that insert mode is turned on. If insert mode is turned off, the text of the letterhead will replace existing characters. You cannot use the Ins key in the macro since this toggles insert mode on and off—it would turn insert mode off if it were already on. Instead, we used Alt-I, a built-in Q&A command that always turns insert mode on. Since Alt-I is not a toggle, if insert mode is already on, the key combination will not turn it off.

5. Press ↵, then ↑.

Before typing and formatting the first line, we added a blank line at the top of the document and moved the cursor to that line. This ensures that you do not accidentally change the format of the first existing line.

6. Type your street address.

7. Press Alt-C to center the text on the screen and embed the Alt-C macro, and then press ↵.

8. Type your city, state, and zip code.

9. Press Alt-C to center the text, and then press ↵ twice to insert a blank line before the date.

10. Press Alt-D to insert the date and to embed the Alt-D macro.

11. Press Alt-C to center the date, and then press ↵.

12. Press Shift-F2 to display the Macro Options menu.

13. Type **Letterhead**.

14. Press ⏎ to reach the Show Screen option and type **N**.

15. Press F10, then ⏎ to save all three macros.

16. Press Esc, and type **C**, then **Y** to clear the screen.

Let's test the letterhead macro by using it to add the letterhead to an existing letter.

1. Type the following brief letter:

    Dear Sirs:

    Please send a copy of your new product catalog to the address above.

    Thank you.

    Sincerely,

    Alvin A. Aardvark

2. Press Alt-H. The letterhead will appear at the beginning of the letter, as shown in Figure 12.5.

3. Press Esc twice and type **Y** to return to the Main menu.

The Alt-C macro centered the text, and the Alt-D macro inserted the date. Because these are separate macros, you can use them by themselves or embed them in other macros.

DESIGNING MACROS THAT WORK FROM ANY MENU

Sometimes it is difficult to remember just where in Q&A you created a macro. Did you define it from the Main menu, Write menu, or some other location? One way to avoid problems is to define most macros from a common

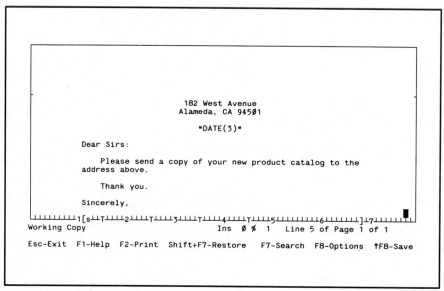

Figure 12.5: Letterhead inserted in a document using the Alt-H macro

location, such as the Main menu. But then you must always return to the Main menu to run your macros.

Another technique is to have the macros return to a common location automatically. As an example, we will create a macro that automates the process of printing our form document named Confirm, which you created in Chapter 8. This macro will be designed to run when any Q&A menu is displayed on the screen.

Merge Print Macro

Before proceeding with the following steps, be prepared to print the form letters.

1. Press Shift-F2 and type **D**.

2. Press Alt-F.

3. Press Esc five times.

Since you began from the Main menu, the Esc keystrokes do not have any effect, but they will be recorded. When you run the macro, these keystrokes will take you back to the Main menu from any Q&A menu.

4. Type **W**, then **G** to display the file name prompt.

5. Press Shift-F4, type **Confirm**, and press ↵.

When you are creating a macro that includes a file name prompt, always clear the prompt with Shift-F4 and enter the name, even if it already appears. This ensures that the correct name will be entered when you actually run the macro.

6. Press F2 to display the Print Options menu.

7. Press F10 twice.

8. Press ↵ to print the form letters.

9. Press Esc twice to return to the Main menu.

10. Press Shift-F2 to display the Macro Options menu.

11. Type **Print Form Letters**.

12. Press ↵ to reach the Show Screen option and type **N**.

13. Press F10, then ↵ to save the macros.

This macro can be run from any menu, and after the form letters are printed, it returns you to the Main menu.

HANDLING MACRO FILES

To work with macro files:

- Create a new macro file by pressing Shift-F2, pressing C to clear the current macros in memory, creating a macro, and then typing the new macro file name when saving the macro.

- Get a macro file by pressing Shift-F2, then G, typing the macro file name, and pressing ↵.

- **Change the default macro file by starting Q&A with the command QA -AD, followed by the macro file name.**

By default, Q&A saves your macros in a file named QAMACRO.ASC, but you can enter another name to save them in a different file. If you want to use the macros with most Q&A sessions, use the default name because the macros in QAMACRO.ASC are loaded automatically when you start Q&A.

You might want to create other files to store special-purpose macros. You could have a file called WP.MAC that contains macros used for creating documents and another named REPORT.MAC that contains macros that print or create reports.

You do not have to give your macro files an extension; however, adding a common extension helps you identify them on the List Manager screen. ASC stands for ASCII, and MAC stands for macro.

Creating separate macro files not only makes macros easier to manage, but saves computer memory as well. Another advantage of setting up several macro files is that it allows you to have two macros with the same identifier and name, which you cannot do in one file. For example, you could use Alt-S in one file to save a Write document, and Alt-S in another file to save a database.

CREATING A NEW MACRO FILE

To create a new macro file, clear all the current macros in memory first. Define your first macro for the file, and then enter the file's name at the save macro prompt. You will be warned if you enter the name of an existing macro file.

Creating several macros to use with Write illustrated some of the finer points of recording and running macros. You saved the macros in the default file, QAMACRO.ASC, by pressing ↵ when the file name prompt appeared.

In the later sections of this chapter, you will create macros to use with Q&A File and Report. Rather than save them with the Write macros in QAMACRO.ASC, create a new macro file:

1. Press Shift-F2.

2. Select Clear to remove all the macros from memory.

Now when you create and save your first File macro to a new file, the Write macros will not be saved along with it.

ADDING MACROS TO THE NEW FILE

To add a macro to a file other than the default, load the file first using the Get Macros option on the Macro menu. If you type the file name at the save macro prompt after you create it, you will be warned that the file will be overwritten and any existing macros already saved will be deleted.

As a shortcut to using the Get Macros option, you can name the macro file to use when you start Q&A using the syntax:

QA -AL*macro-file-name*

There must be a space before the hyphen, but not between AL and the file name. For example, to start Q&A and use the macro in WP.MAC, enter

QA -ALWP.MAC

The AL option only designates a macro file for that session of Q&A. The QAMACRO file will be used the next time you start Q&A unless you use the option again.

Combine the AL and M options to run an autostart macro in a file other than the default. For example, enter

QA -ALFILE.MAC -M1

to start Q&A, load the FILE.MAC macro file, and run the Alt-1 macro.

To change the default macro file, use the AD option, as in

QA -ADREPORT.MAC

This command makes REPORT.MAC the new default macro file. To make QAMACRO.ASC the default again, start Q&A with

QA -ADQAMACRO.ASC

To start Q&A without loading any macro file, enter

QA -AD

When you want to run a macro in a different file, press Shift-F2, select Get Macros from the Macro menu, and enter the file name. After the file is loaded, you can run the macro.

You will learn other techniques for managing your macro files in the next chapter.

MACROS FOR DATABASE TASKS

In the following sections, we will create several macros for working with your database. Now that the Write macros are cleared, be very careful when creating the next macro. When the save macro prompt appears, *do not press* ↵. If you do, the QAMACRO.ASC file will be overwritten by a file containing only one macro. Type the new file name as instructed, and then press ↵.

SORTING AND DISPLAYING RECORDS

Now you will create a macro that allows you to start Q&A and review records in the Clients database as quickly as possible. The macro includes a pause command so you can designate the sort field before displaying records.

1. Press Shift-F2 and type **D**.

2. Press Alt-1.

3. Press Esc five times.

4. Type **F**, then **S** to select File Search/Update.

5. Press Shift-F4 to delete the text at the file name prompt.

If you want to create a macro to display any database, press Shift-F2 now and after the next step as well.

6. Type **Clients** and press ↵ to display the Retrieve Spec screen.

7. Press F8 to display the Sort Spec screen.

8. Press Alt-F2 twice.

We want the macro to enter the characters 1,AS in the field that you select. Since you do not know if the field will be long enough to accept the four characters, use F6 to expand the field just in case.

9. Press F6 and type **1,AS**.

10. Press F10, and the first record will appear.

11. Press Alt-F6 to enter table view.

12. Press Shift-F2 and type **Sort and Display**.

13. Press ↵ to reach the Show Screen option and type **N**.

14. Press F10 to display the macro file name prompt, but do not press ↵.

15. Press Shift-F4, type **FILE.MAC**, and press ↵.

16. Press Esc twice to return to the File menu.

To run the macro, press Alt-1. Start Q&A and run the macro by entering QA -M1 from the DOS prompt. When the Retrieve Spec screen appears, move to the field you want to sort on, and then press ↵. The macro inserts the characters 1,AS, sorts the file, then switches to table view after the first record is displayed.

MACROS TO PROTECT YOUR DATABASE

Computers are far from perfect. Each time you access a file, the chances that something will go wrong increase. Your hard disk may crash or some other component may fail, leaving your database damaged and unusable.

There are two ways that you can help ensure the integrity of your file: making regular backups and working with the actual database file itself as little as possible. Let's create macros for just those purposes.

Backup Macro

When you are finished adding data or editing a database, you should make a backup, or duplicate, copy of the DTF and IDX files. Ideally, you should copy the files to a floppy disk. Having duplicate copies of the files on a hard disk will not help you if the disk crashes because both the original and duplicate will be destroyed.

If your files are too large to fit on a single floppy disk, you will have to back up to the hard disk, separate the DTF and IDX files, or buy some extra hardware.

Now we will define a straightforward macro that copies both the DTF and IDX files for the Clients database at the same time to files called CLBACK. There's only one small problem: after you back up the file once, Q&A will warn you that the existing CLBACK files will be overwritten, and you must press Y to confirm. This requires that the Y keystroke be recorded as part of the macro.

However, if you create the macro when the CLBACK files do not exist, you will not have a chance to include the Y when needed. To get around this, we will make a backup copy of Clients first, without recording the keystrokes, and then make another backup copy to create the macro.

1. Select File from the Main menu, Utilities, then Backup to display the file name prompt.

2. Press Shift-F4, type **Clients**, and press ↵. The backup to prompt will appear.

3. Press Shift-F4, type **Clback**, and press ↵ to make a copy of the file. If you are backing up to a floppy disk, include a disk drive letter, such as B:CLBACK, in the file name.

4. Press Esc twice to return to the Main menu.

5. Press Shift-F2 and type **D**.

6. Press Alt-2.

7. Press Esc five times.

8. Select File, then Utilities, then Backup.

9. Press Shift-F4, type **Clients**, and press ↵.

10. Press Shift-F4, type **Clback**, and press ↵. Include a disk ID if you are saving to a floppy disk.

11. Type **Y** to confirm the operation.

12. Press Esc twice to return to the Main menu.

13. Press Shift-F2 and type **Backup Clients**.

14. Press ↵ to reach the Show Screen option and type **N**.

15. Press F10, then ↵ to save the macro.

When you want to back up the Clients database, press Alt-2 from any menu. You could also automatically back up the database before adding or editing records. This way, you can retrieve the original records if you make any errors. Start Q&A and run the macro at the same time by entering QA -M2 from the DOS prompt.

POSTING DATA TO TEMPORARY FILES

If you are adding, editing, or retrieving records and your computer fails, your entire database could be wiped out. That's why many users of large databases record current transactions in special files rather than directly in the database itself. Transactions are added to the database only when they are completed and approved. In Chapters 15 and 16, you will learn how to use Q&A's posting function to add data to selected records, as well as how to create a transaction-oriented system.

In the following sections, you will create several macros to develop a system that lets you write new records to a temporary file instead of the database. This keeps the database closed as much as possible. When you are sure the new records are accurate, you can then copy them to the master database.

We will create the macros in three stages. First, you will set up the temporary file that will be used to accept the new records. Next, you will define a macro to begin the add process. Finally, you will create a macro that copies the new records to the Clients database.

Creating the Temporary File

Before you can create a macro for adding records, you must have a database file to hold the records. In order to accept client information, the database must be a copy of the Clients design, but without any records of its own.

Follow these steps to set up the temporary file:

1. Select Copy from the File menu.

2. Type **Clients** and press ↵ to display the Copy menu.

3. Select Design Only to display the copy to file name prompt.

4. Type **CTemp** and press ↵.

5. When the menu appears, press Esc twice to return to the File menu.

Add Records Macro

The macro for adding client records will begin the process by selecting Add Data from the File menu. We will include extra Esc keystrokes so records can be added from any Q&A menu.

1. Press Shift-F2 and type **D**.

2. Press Alt-3.

3. Press Esc five times.

4. Select Add Data from the File menu.

5. Press Shift-F4, type **CTemp**, and press ↵. The first blank form appears.

6. Press Shift-F2 and type **Add Clients**.

7. Press ↵ to reach the Show Screen option and type **N**.

8. Press F10, then Esc. We will save the macros later.

Now, in preparation for creating the next macro, add some data to the form.

9. Type **120**.

10. Press Shift-F10 to return to the File menu.

Posting Macro

The last step in the process is to copy the new records in the temporary file to the master database, and then delete them from the temporary database file. The posting macro will also work from any Q&A menu.

1. Press Shift-F2 and type **D**.

2. Press Alt-4.

3. Press Esc five times.

4. Select Copy from the File menu.

5. Press Shift-F4, type **CTemp**, and press ↵.

6. Type **S** to choose selected records.

7. Press Shift-F4, type **Clients**, and press ↵ to display the Retrieve Spec screen.

8. Press F10 to retrieve all the records and to display the Merge Spec screen.

9. Press F10 to merge all the fields. The File menu will reappear.

10. To delete the records from the temporary file, type **R** to select Remove.

11. Press Shift-F4, type **CTemp**, and press ↵.

12. Type **S**, press F10, and type **Y** to delete all the records.

13. Press Esc twice to return to the Main menu.

14. Press Shift-F2 and type **Post New Records**.

15. Press ↵ to reach the Show Screen option and type **N**.

16. Press F10, then ⏎ to save the macros.

Creating the macro added a fake record to the database. Let's delete it to return the database to its original state.

17. Type **F**, then **R**, then **Clients**, and press ⏎.

18. Type **S** for selected records and to display the Retrieve Spec screen.

19. Type **120** and press F10.

20. Type **Y** to confirm the deletion.

21. Press Esc twice to return to the File menu.

When you want to add records to the Clients database, run this macro by typing QA -M3 when you start Q&A, or by pressing Alt-3 from any Q&A menu. Enter the records, then return to the File menu. If a computer failure occurs as you are adding records, only the temporary file will be affected.

Review the records, and if they are correct, press Alt-4 to post them to the Clients database. Using this technique, Clients is only open as long as it takes to copy the records to it.

REPORT MACROS

One repetitive database function is generating reports. After you change a database, you might have to print copies of reports to reflect the updated records. Our next macro will print the reports that you created in Chapter 5. It includes keystrokes to return to the Main menu before and after printing a report. This way, you can execute it from any Q&A menu or run it immediately after printing one report.

1. Press Shift-F2 and type **D**.

2. Press Alt-6.

3. Press Esc five times.

4. Type **R**, then **P**.

5. Press Shift-F4, type **Clients**, and press ↵.

6. Press Alt-F2, then ↓, then Alt-F2, then ↵.

This selects one of the reports to print while you record the keystrokes.

7. Type **N** to print the report.

8. Press Esc to return to the Main menu.

9. Press Shift-F2 and type **Print Reports**.

10. Press ↵ to reach the Show Screen option and type **N**.

11. Press F10, then ↵.

When you want to print a report, press Alt-6. On the List Manager screen, highlight the report name, and press ↵. When the report is printed, you will be returned to the Main menu.

MACRO CAUTIONS

Macros are very effective time-savers, but there are some potential problems you should avoid. Two possible pitfalls are described in the following sections.

MACROS AND MEMORY

Q&A sets aside only 3000 bytes of computer memory, called the *macro buffer,* to store your macros. You can change the size of the macro buffer by starting Q&A with the -B option, followed by a number between 300 and 30000, as in

QA -B6000

But beware—if you make the buffer too large, Q&A may slow down somewhat, or you might run out of memory for performing other Q&A tasks.

If you try to define a macro when there is not enough memory, Q&A will display the message

Not enough memory. Your macro has been stopped. Press Esc.

Either delete some unneeded macros or exit Q&A and then restart it with a larger buffer.

If you try loading a macro file that's too large for memory, you will see the warning

Ran out of memory after getting macro #X. Press Esc.

Restart Q&A with a larger buffer or split the file into sections. You will learn how to edit macro files in the next chapter.

If Q&A runs out of memory as the macro is executing or as you are defining it, you will see the message

Not enough memory for this action. Try again at the main menu.

Return to the Main menu and execute the macro again. If that doesn't work, try deleting unneeded macros to free additional memory. When you have a macro that requires as much operating memory as possible, save it in its own macro file and start Q&A with a buffer size just large enough for the macro itself.

CONSIDERING ALL POSSIBILITIES

There are some macros that at first glance appear to be rather simple and straightforward, but really present some subtle obstacles. In many cases, a problem occurs because the macro doesn't take into account every possible situation that might arise.

For example, suppose that you want to create a macro that saves the current Write document and clears the screen so you can start another. You would think that the macro only has to execute Shift-F8, pause for you to enter a name, save the document, and then return to the Write menu and select Clear. But let's see what happens.

1. Select Write from the Main menu and press ↵ to display the Write screen, the starting location for this macro.

2. Press Shift-F2 and type **D**.

3. Press Alt-S.

4. Press Shift-F8, then Shift-F4.

5. Press Alt-F2, type **Temp**, and press Alt-F2 again.

Remember, the keystrokes *Temp* are not recorded as part of the macro.

6. Press ↵ to save the document, press Esc, and type **C**.

7. Press Shift-F2 and type **Save and Clear**.

8. Press ↵ to reach the Show Screen prompt and type **N**.

9. Press F10, then ↵ to save the macro.

10. Press Alt-S to run the macro.

11. Type **Newdoc** and press ↵.

As expected, the document is saved, and then the screen is cleared. If you enter a document name that has not yet been used, or resave the document by entering the same name that appears on the status line, the macro works correctly.

But now, let's see what happens when we try to save the document using a name that already is on the disk.

12. Press Alt-S, type **Temp**, and press ↵.

This time, Q&A displays the warning that you could overwrite the file. Since the macro does not include the Y or N keystroke for confirming if you want to overwrite the existing file or not, the C keystroke appears in the file name as

C:\QA\cEMP

13. Press Esc to cancel the operation.

This macro has limited use because it does not work in every situation when you are trying to save a document. Since Temp and Newdoc were created just for examples, let's delete them from the disk.

14. Press Esc twice to return to the Main menu.

15. Select Utilities, then DOS File Facilities.

16. Select Delete, type **Temp**, press ↵, and type **Y**.

17. Select Delete, type **Newdoc**, press ↵, and type **Y**.

18. Press Esc twice to return to the Main menu.

This chapter introduced macros and illustrated some practical uses for them. In the next chapter, you will learn how to make your macros more powerful.

13

Custom-
izing
Macros
and Menus

When you record macros, they include any mistakes you might have made while recording them. Also, you actually perform the procedure that you want the macro to execute, such as printing form letters or reports. By editing and writing macros, you can eliminate incorrect keystrokes, as well as have your macro perform tasks that were not recorded.

After you perfect your macros, you will probably use them frequently. You can make them easy to access by adding them to Q&A's menus or including them on your own custom menus.

In this chapter, you will learn how to edit and write macros, manage your macro files, and customize menus.

CHANGING RECORDED MACROS

|||► **To edit a macro:**

1. **Select Get from the Write menu, enter the name of the macro file, and specify the ASCII format.**
2. **Locate the macro you want to change by looking for the <begdef> code followed by the code for the macro identifier.**
3. **Edit the contents of the macro. Insert codes in angle brackets, such as <enter> for ⏎. Macros must begin with <begdef>, end with <enddef>, and be separated from each other by an asterisk (*).**
4. **Save the macro file in ASCII format by pressing Ctrl-F8, then ⏎.**

After you display the text of a macro on the screen, you can edit it just like any other text. You edit a macro using special techniques and commands that can also be used when you write a macro.

Macro files are ASCII text. They contain only letters, numbers, and punctuation marks, without any special formatting characters. To edit or write a macro, you must load and save the macro file in ASCII format.

THE STRUCTURE OF MACROS

Before you make major changes to a macro, or write one without recording keystrokes first, you should be familiar with the structure of macros and Q&A's macro codes.

The general format of macros is

<begdef><*identifier*><name><*"description"*><*video flag*> recorded keystrokes <menu> *"*menu name"<enddef>

where the codes represent the following:

<begdef>	Each macro must start with this code.
<*identifier*>	The macro identifier. If you did not assign an identifier, it appears as <nokey>.
<name>	Indicates that the descriptive name of the macro follows.
<*"description"*>	The descriptive name in quotation marks. If you did not assign a name or identifier, it appears as No<sp>name<sp>#000.
<*video flag*>	The code will be either <vidon> or <vidoff>, representing the status of the Show Screen option. Edit the flag to change the status of the option without recording the keystrokes again.
recorded keystrokes	The keystrokes, cursor, and mouse movements recorded in the macro. Cursor-movement keys are indicated with <up>, <rgt>, <dn>, and <lft>. The representation of mouse movements is quite lengthy, as shown in the more complex macro in Figure 13.1.
<menu> *"*menu-name"*	The name of a custom menu you want to appear when the macro ends. Custom menus are discussed later in the chapter.
<enddef>	Each macro must end with this code.

```
<begdef><altm><name>"Mouse<sp><sp><sp><sp><sp><sp><sp><sp><sp><sp><sp><sp>
<sp><sp><sp><sp><sp><sp><sp><sp><sp><sp><sp><sp><sp><sp>"<vidon><mouse>
1L5<mouse>ML5<mouse>MO5<mouse>MP5<mouse>MQ5<mouse>MR5<mouse>MS5<mouse>M
U5<mouse>MV5<mouse>MV5<mouse>MW5<mouse>MX5<mouse>MX5<mouse>MY6<mouse>MY
6<mouse>MY6<mouse>MY6<mouse>MZ6<mouse>MZ7<mouse>MZ7<mouse>MZ8<mouse>MZ8
<mouse>MZ8<mouse>MZ8<mouse>MZ8<mouse>M[8<mouse>M[8<mouse>M[8<mouse>M[8<mouse>
M[8<mouse>M[8<mouse>M[8<mouse>M[8<mouse>M[8<mouse>M[8<mouse>M[8<mouse>M
[8<mouse>M[8<mouse>M[8<mouse>M[9<mouse>M[9<mouse>M[9<mouse>M[9<mouse>M[
9<mouse>M[9<mouse>M[9<mouse>M[9<mouse>M[9<mouse>M\9<mouse>M\9<mouse>M\9
<mouse>L\9<mouse>1\9<mouse>L\9<mouse>1\9<mouse>M\9<mouse>M[9<mouse>MZ9<mouse>
MZ9<mouse>MY9<mouse>MY9<mouse>MY9<mouse>MY9<mouse>MX9<mouse>MV:<mouse>M
R;<mouse>MQ;<mouse>MP<caps,><mouse>MO<caps,><mouse>MN=<mouse>MM=<mouse>
MM=<mouse>MM=<mouse>MM=<mouse>MM=<mouse>MM=<mouse>MN<caps.><mouse>MN<caps.>
<mouse>MN<caps.><mouse>MN<caps.><mouse>MN?<mouse>MN?<mouse>MN?<mouse>MN
?<mouse>MN@<mouse>MN@<mouse>MO@<mouse>MO@<mouse>MO@<mouse>MO@<mouse>MO@
<mouse>LO@<del><mouse>1=:<mouse>M=:<mouse>M<caps.>:<mouse>M<caps.>:<mouse>
M?;<mouse>MA;<mouse>MD;<mouse>MF;<mouse>MG;<mouse>MH;<mouse>MH;<mouse>M
I;<mouse>MI;<mouse>MJ;<mouse>MJ;<mouse>MJ;<mouse>MJ;<mouse>MK;<mouse>ML
;<mouse>MN;<mouse>MR;<mouse>MT;<mouse>MU;<mouse>MV;<mouse>MW;<mouse>MX;
<mouse>MZ;<mouse>M[;<mouse>M\;<mouse>M\;<mouse>M^;<mouse>M_;<mouse>M';<mouse>
M';<mouse>Ma;<mouse>Ma;<mouse>Mb;<mouse>Mb;<mouse>Mc;<mouse>Mc;<mouse>M
s┴┴T┴┴┴┴1┴┴┴┴T┴┴┴┴2┴┴┴┴T┴┴┴┴3┴┴┴T┴┴┴┴4┴┴┴┴┴┴┴┴5┴┴┴┴┴┴┴┴6┴┴┴┴┴┴┴┴7┴┴┴┴┴┴┴┴8
FILE.MAC                            2 %  1    Line 41 of 48

Esc-Exit  F1-Help  F2-Print  Shift+F7-Restore   F7-Search  F8-Options  ↑F8-Save
```

Figure 13.1: Macro with complex mouse instructions

Depending on the macro, you might see other codes. For example

<wait><enter>

represents a pause inserted with Alt-F2. The <enter> code is the default keystroke used to continue after the pause. If you want to change the keystrokes used to cancel the pause, you can replace the <enter> code with something else.

When you edit a macro, be careful not to delete the <begdef>, <name>, and <enddef> codes.

CORRECTING A MACRO

To demonstrate how to edit a macro, we will first create one with some obvious mistakes. Follow these steps:

1. First, to make sure you are using the macro file FILE.MAC, press Shift-F2 to display the Macro menu, and then choose Get Macros. If the file name at the prompt is FILE.MAC, press Esc

twice. Otherwise, type **FILE.MAC** and press ⏎.

2. From the Main menu, select Write and press ⏎.

3. Press Shift-F2, choose Define Macro, and press Alt-T.

4. Type **Mason Incorporated** and press ⏎.

5. Press Backspace 13 times to erase **Incorporated**.

6. Type **Company** and press ⏎.

7. Complete the address:

    3487 Willow Way

    New York, NY 10101

8. Press Shift-F2, type **Mason's Address**, press F10, and then press ⏎ to save the macro to the file.

Now suppose that you realize that there are two things wrong with the macro you just saved. First, it contains all the actual keystrokes you pressed, so every time you run the macro it will enter then erase the word *Incorporated*. Although the error is corrected, the extra keystrokes take time. Second, the zip code recorded with the macro is incorrect; it should be 10102. Rather than redefine the entire macro, you can edit it.

Displaying the Macro Text

To begin, you must retrieve the macro file to display the macro text on the screen:

1. Press Esc to return to the Write menu.

2. Select Get, type **FILE.MAC**, and press ⏎. The warning message will appear.

3. Type **Y**. Because the file is not in standard Q&A format, Q&A will display the Import Document menu and ask you to indicate the file's format.

4. Press ⏎ to accept ASCII format. The file will appear on the screen as shown in Figure 13.2.

The macros are separated from each other with asterisks, and each starts with the code <begdef> followed by the macro identifier. Each <sp> represents a space; <enter> shows where you pressed ⏎.

5. Press PgDn until you see the macro starting with

    <begdef><altt>

    The macro will appear as shown in Figure 13.3.

Each <bks> code represents where you pressed the Backspace key to erase characters. To have the macro include just the correct keystrokes, you must delete the incorrect word *Incorporated*, the extra <enter>, and the backspace characters.

```
<begdef><alt1><name>"Sort<sp>and<sp>display<sp><sp><sp><sp><sp><sp><sp>
<sp><sp><sp><sp><sp><sp><sp><sp>"<vidoff><esc><esc><esc><esc><esc>fs<capsf4>
CLIENTS<enter><f8><wait><enter><f6>1,as<f10><altf6><enddef>
*
<begdef><alt2><name>"Backup<sp>Clients<sp><sp><sp><sp><sp><sp><sp><sp><sp>
<sp><sp><sp><sp><sp><sp><sp><sp>"<vidoff><esc><esc><esc><esc><esc>fub<capsf4>
CLIENTS<enter><capsf4>CLBACK<enter>y<esc><esc><enddef>
*
<begdef><alt3><name>"Add<sp>clients<sp><sp><sp><sp><sp><sp><sp><sp><sp>
<sp><sp><sp><sp><sp><sp><sp><sp><sp><sp><sp>"<vidoff><esc><esc><esc><esc>
<esc>fa<capsf4>CTEMP<enter><enddef>
*
<begdef><alt4><name>"Post<sp>new<sp>records<sp><sp><sp><sp><sp><sp><sp>
<sp><sp><sp><sp><sp><sp><sp><sp>"<vidoff><esc><esc><esc><esc><esc>fc<capsf4>
CTEMP<enter>s<capsf4>CLIENTS<enter><f10><f10>r<capsf4>CTEMP<enter>s<f10>
y<esc><esc><enddef>
*
<begdef><alt6><name>"Print<sp>reports<sp><sp><sp><sp><sp><sp><sp><sp><sp>
<sp><sp><sp><sp><sp><sp><sp>"<vidoff><esc><esc><esc><esc><esc>r
p<capsf4>clients<enter><wait><enter><enter>n<esc><enddef>
└s⊥⊥T⊥⊥⊥1⊥⊥⊥⊥T⊥⊥⊥2⊥⊥⊥⊥T⊥⊥⊥3⊥⊥⊥T⊥⊥⊥4⊥⊥⊥⊥⊥⊥⊥⊥5⊥⊥⊥⊥⊥⊥6⊥⊥⊥⊥⊥⊥7⊥⊥⊥⊥⊥⊥8
FILE.MAC                                Ø %   1    Line 1 of 25

Esc-Exit   F1-Help   F2-Print   Shift+F7-Restore   F7-Search  F8-Options  ↑F8-Save
```

Figure 13.2: Macro file loaded as ASCII text

```
p<capsf4>clients<enter><wait><enter><enter>n<esc><enddef>
*
<begdef><altt><name>"Mason's<sp>Address<sp><sp><sp><sp><sp><sp><sp>
<sp><sp><sp><sp><sp><sp><sp>"<vidon>Mason<sp>Incorporated<enter><bks>
<bks><bks><bks><bks><bks><bks><bks><bks><bks><bks><bks>Company<enter>
3487<sp>Willow<sp>Way<enter>New<sp>York,<sp>NY<sp>10101<enddef>
```

Figure 13.3: The Alt-T macro

Making Changes

When you are editing or writing macros, do not enter any spaces between the macro elements. Also, do not press ↵ until after the <enddef> code—let word wrap end the other lines for you.

Follow the steps below to correct the Alt-T macro. Be careful not to delete any characters except those listed in the instructions.

1. Move the cursor to the *I* in *Incorporated*.

2. Press F3, and then move the cursor just before the word *Company*. Your screen should look like Figure 13.4.

3. Press F10.

4. Change the zip code to 10102.

Saving the Edited Macro

In order to use the corrected macro, you must resave the file. However, if you save it as you would a normal document—by pressing Shift-F8—you will not be able to use any of its macros. Instead, save the file as ASCII text.

1. Press Ctrl-F8 to see the prompt

   ASCII File: C:\QA\FILE.MAC

2. Press ↵ to save the file.

3. Press Esc and select Clear to clear the screen.

Even though the edited macro is saved in the file, it is not loaded into the computer's memory. To use this macro, you get the macro file so the edited macro replaces the one in memory.

```
p<capsf4>clients<enter><wait><enter><enter>n<esc><enddef>
*
<begdef><altt><name>"Mason's<sp>Address<sp><sp><sp><sp><sp><sp><sp><sp>
<sp><sp><sp><sp><sp><sp><sp>"<vidon>Mason<sp>Incorporated<enter><bks>
<bks><bks><bks><bks><bks><bks><bks><bks><bks><bks><bks>Company<enter>
3487<sp>Willow<sp>Way<enter>New<sp>York,<sp>NY<sp>10101<enddef>
```

Figure 13.4: Select these characters to edit the macro

4. Press Shift-F2, select Get Macros, and press ↵.

5. Press Alt-T, and the corrected address will appear.

Since we created this macro just for an example, let's delete it from the file.

6. Press Shift-F2 and select Delete Macro.

7. Highlight Mason's Address and press ↵ twice.

8. Press Esc twice and type **Y** to return to the Main menu.

If you accidentally save a macro file by pressing Shift-F8, all is not lost. You will still be able to use the macros by converting the file to ASCII format.

Use the Get option on the Write menu to retrieve the macro file. When the document appears on the screen, press Ctrl-F8 and save it in ASCII format. You can then retrieve the file by using the Get Macros option on the Macro menu.

CHANGING MACRO IDENTIFIERS AND NAMES

To change the macro identifier, edit the identifier code in the macro text. For example, if you assigned Alt-1 to a macro when you defined it, you can switch it to Alt-M by changing *<alt1>* to *<altm>*.

Be careful not to change the identifier to one that already exists. Q&A will not warn you, and there will be two macros with the same identifier in the file. When you press the identifier, Q&A will execute the first macro with that identifier in the file. If you want to use an identifier that is already taken, edit the original to change the identifier keystrokes in it as well.

You can also add or edit a macro's descriptive name. In the macro text, the descriptive name is represented by the keystrokes used to enter its characters. For example, if the identifier is used for the name, the < symbol is shown as <caps,>, representing the Shift-comma keystroke. The > sign is indicated as <caps.>, for the Shift-period keystroke.

A descriptive name can be up to 31 characters. If the name has fewer characters, the extra spaces are shown as <sp> codes. For example, when an identifier is the descriptive name, the code itself takes up six positions, as in <alt1>, even though it appears as <caps,>alt1<caps.> on the screen. To reserve the unused space, 25 <sp> codes will follow. You can delete the <sp> codes and replace them with actual spaces without affecting the macro.

When you add or change a macro name, make sure it is no longer than 31 characters. To include a punctuation mark entered with the Shift key, type it in code, such as <caps,> for the < sign. Remember, the entire <caps,> code counts as just 1 of the 31 characters.

WRITING MACROS

▐▐▐▶ **To write a macro:**

1. **Select Get from the Write menu, enter the name of the macro file, and specify the ASCII format.**
2. **Type the text of the macro, using the proper macro codes.**
3. **Save the macro file in ASCII format by pressing Ctrl-F8, then ↵.**

By writing all or portions of a macro, you can create one that accomplishes tasks that cannot be recorded. For example, it would be convenient to have a macro that saves the current Write document and exits from Q&A. However, if you left Q&A while recording the keystrokes, the macro would be erased from memory before you had the opportunity to save it to a disk file. Instead, you can write the macro, following these steps:

1. To load the macro file as an ASCII document, display the Write menu, select Get, type **QAMACRO.ASC**, and press ↵ twice.

2. Press the End key four times to reach the end of the file, and then press ↵.

3. Type the following macro text. Do *not* press ↵.

   *

   **<begdef><altx><name>"Save and Exit"<vidoff>
   <capsf8><wait><enter><enter><esc><esc>x<enddef>**

   Your macro should look like the one shown in Figure 13.5.

4. Press Ctrl-F8, then ↵ to save the file.

5. Press Esc and select Clear to clear the screen.

Now let's see how the new macro works. Remember, before using the macro, you must get the file from the disk to place it in memory.

6. Press Shift-F2, select Get Macros, type **QAMACRO.ASC**, and press ↵.

7. Press Alt-X, type **Sample** at the file name prompt, and press ↵.

The document is saved and you are returned to DOS.

8. Delete Sample by typing **DEL SAMPLE** at the DOS prompt when in the QA directory.

If you enter the name of an existing document when you use this macro to save a file and exit, the operation will be canceled. The document will remain on the screen, with the X keystroke at the position of the cursor.

Rather than writing a macro entirely, it is easier to record as many of the keystrokes as possible, and then edit the macro to include those you

```
name>"Center<sp>text<sp>macro<sp><sp><sp><sp><sp><sp>
><sp><sp><sp>"<vidoff><f8>ac<enddef>

name>"Insert<sp>date<sp>macro<sp><sp><sp><sp><sp><sp><sp>
><sp><sp><sp>"<vidoff>*DATE(3)"<enddef>

name>"Letterhead<sp><sp><sp><sp><sp><sp><sp><sp><sp>
><sp><sp><sp><sp><sp><sp><sp>"<vidoff><home><home><home>
ter><up>182<sp>West<sp>Avenue<altc><enter>Alameda,<sp>CA
<enter><enter><altd><altc><enter><enddef>

name>"Print<sp>form<sp>letters<sp><sp><sp><sp><sp>█sp><sp>
><sp><sp>"<vidoff><esc><esc><esc><esc><esc>wg<capsf4>Con
<f10><f10><enter><esc><esc><enddef>

name>"Save<sp>and<sp>clear<sp><sp><sp><sp><sp><sp><sp><sp>
><sp><sp><sp><sp>"<vidoff><capsf8><capsf4><wait><enter>
nddef>

name>"Save and Exit"<vidoff><capsf8><wait><ehter><enter><esc><esc>x<enddef>

⌊⌊⌊2⌊⌊⌊⌊T⌊⌊⌊⌊3⌊⌊⌊⌊T⌊⌊⌊4⌊⌊⌊⌊⌊⌊⌊⌊⌊5⌊⌊⌊⌊⌊⌊⌊⌊6⌊⌊⌊⌊⌊⌊⌊⌊7⌊⌊⌊⌊⌊⌊⌊⌊8⌊⌊⌊⌊⌊⌊⌊⌊9█⌊⌊⌊⌊
QAMACRO.ASC                              Ø %  91  Line 29 of 29

Esc-Exit  F1-Help  F2-Print  Shift+F7-Restore  F7-Search  F8-Options  ↑F8-Save
```

Figure 13.5: Written macro added to the file

cannot record. Use the Get Macros command on the Macro menu to load the file you want to add the macro to, and then record as many of the keystrokes as possible.

For example, you could have recorded all the keystrokes in the save and exit macro except the final X. Another way to create that macro is to copy the Alt-S macro, edit the identifier and name, add the extra <esc>, and change the final C to an X.

MANAGING YOUR MACRO FILES

▰▰▰➤ To manage your macro files:

- **Divide a large file into two or more files by using Alt-F5 to move a block of macros into a new file.**
- **Combine small files by pressing F8, then D, then I to insert each macro file.**
- **Protect a macro file by selecting Design File from the File menu, then Customize Application, then Protect Macro File.**

As you build up your collection of macros, you will have to manage your macro files. You may need to split a file into two or more files or combine several files. You will also want to protect your macro files.

DIVIDING A LARGE FILE

If you add macros to a file by writing them, the file may become too large to fit in the macro buffer. Rather than increasing the buffer and using valuable computer memory, split the file into two or more separate files.

In order to create separate files, you have to divide the document into sections and save each as an ASCII file. Unfortunately, the Block Save command stores files in regular Q&A format, which means that you must save each of your sections, and then recall each one and save it again as an ASCII file.

Bring the file into Write as an ASCII document. If you want to, first organize the macros into groups (use Shift-F5 to move the blocks of macro text).

Remember that macros are separated from each other with an asterisk, but there must not be an asterisk at the beginning of the file or after the last macro. To move a macro, highlight the block from the asterisk to the end of the <enddef> code.

After the macro file is loaded and organized, follow this general procedure to divide it:

1. Place the cursor at the start of the document and press Alt-F5 to move the block of text to a new file.

2. Move the cursor to the end of the block you want to move—it should be after a macro's <enddef> code but before the asterisk for the next macro—and press F10.

3. Type a temporary file name and press ↵. The highlighted block will be deleted from the document and saved in the named file.

4. Check the document that remains on the screen. If it starts with an asterisk, delete the asterisk so the first macro starts on line 1.

5. Press Ctrl-F8, type the name you want to give this macro file, and press ↵ to save it as an ASCII file.

6. Press Esc, choose Get, type the name of the temporary file, and press ↵.

7. Check over the file to make sure it is in the correct format—no asterisk on line 1, but each macro separated by an asterisk. Don't worry if the spacing does not look correct.

8. Press Ctrl-F8, type the name for this ASCII macro file, and press ↵.

COMBINING MACRO FILES

You can combine several small macro files to form one file. For example, if you created a number of small custom macro files, you could combine them into a single file so you could use all of the macros during the same session.

Bring one of the files into Write, and follow these steps to combine macro files:

1. Place the cursor at the end of the document, type an asterisk on the line after the <enddef> code, and press ↵.

2. Press F8, choose Document, then Insert.

3. Type the name of one of the other macro files, and press ↵ twice. Make sure the first macro in this next file begins on the line immediately after the asterisk.

4. To add other macro files, repeat steps 2 and 3, after adding the asterisk to separate the macros.

5. Press Ctrl-F8 to save the file.

PROTECTING MACRO FILES

After taking the time to create your macros, you would not want them to be accidentally erased or edited. By protecting your macro file, you make it impossible for another user to add macros to it or change its macros in Write.

Be aware that the protection is not complete. The file can still be deleted from DOS and through the DOS File Facilities command in Q&A. It is also possible to load the file into Write as an ASCII file. The macros will not appear (the screen will be blank), but someone can enter text and resave the file, making it impossible for Q&A to recognize those macros.

You should also note that after you protect the macro file, you cannot unprotect it. Always have a copy of the original file so you can add to it or change it.

Follow these steps to protect a macro file:

1. From the Main menu, select File, then Design File, then Customize Application. You will see the menu shown in Figure 13.6.

2. Select Protect Macro File and enter the name of the file you want to protect. Q&A will ask you to type the name of the protected file.

3. Enter a new file name, and then press ↵.

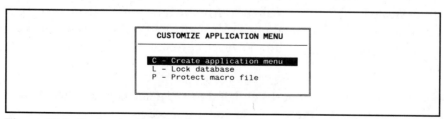

Figure 13.6: Customize Application menu

When you load a protected macro file, you will only be able to run macros. If you press Shift-F2, the list of macros will appear, not the Macro menu.

CUSTOMIZING AND CREATING MENUS

You will eventually find that you use some macros more than others. In fact, some will become so important to your everyday work that you will use them more than most of the functions listed on Q&A menus.

You might also be designing a database system for others to use. They will need to know how to execute the macros defined for the database.

Q&A allows you to organize your macros into custom menus, and even to replace Q&A's built-in menus with your own. The following sections describe how to add your own options to the Q&A Main menu, create your own menus, and replace Q&A's menus.

ADDING OPTIONS TO THE MAIN MENU

▐▐▐▶ **To add an option to the Main menu:**

1. **Select Set Alternate Programs from the Utilities menu.**
2. **For the Alternate Program option, type the macro identifier or the path and name of the external program.**
3. **For the Menu Selection option, type up to 13 characters that describe the macro or program.**
4. **Press F10 to place the new item on the menu.**

You can add to the Main menu any macro defined from that location. Then its function will be displayed and ready to select, and you do not have to memorize the keystrokes or list macros on the screen.

You can add up to six options to the Main menu by using the Set Alternate Programs option on the Utilities menu. (An alternate program can be a macro or some other software application in the QA directory.)

As an example, let's add the last document macro (Alt-L) to the Main menu so that you can start Q&A and recall the last document by pressing the letter L. Begin by starting Q&A, making sure QAMACRO.ASC is loaded as the default.

1. To start Q&A and load the macro file, enter the following command.

    QA -ADQAMACRO.ASC

2. Select Utilities from the Main menu, then Set Alternate Programs to display the menu shown in Figure 13.7.

On this screen, you enter the macro identifier as Alternate Program 1 through 6, and the text you want to appear in the menu next to Menu Selection.

3. Type **Alt-L** and press ↵.

Do not use the macro name. To add a software program, type its name as you would enter it from the DOS prompt, without an extension.

4. Type **Last Document** and press F10.

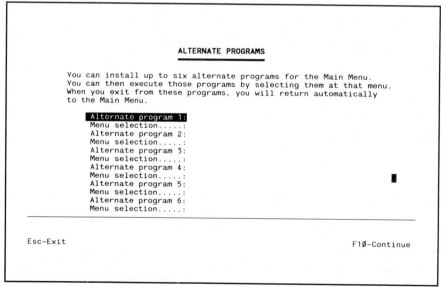

Figure 13.7: Alternate Programs screen

The menu text can be up to 13 characters long. Q&A will automatically assign the first letter of the text as the activating keystroke, so begin it with something other than a character already used by Q&A: F, R, W, A, U, and X.

5. Press Esc to return to the Main menu.

As shown in Figure 13.8, the menu now contains a second column of options. The Last Document option is listed with L as its keystroke.

6. Type **L**. The macro will be executed, and the last document will be retrieved and displayed.

7. Press Esc twice to return to the Main menu.

When you add a macro to the menu, it will appear on the Main menu whether or not the macro is actually loaded in memory. However, the macro must be loaded in order to be executed. If you add a macro to the Main menu, make sure it is in the default macro file. You might also want to copy it to all of your macro files if you plan to use the option globally.

If you add another software program to the menu, when you select it, Q&A will exit and run the application. When you exit that application, Q&A will reload itself and display the Main menu. For example, you could copy the DOS programs FORMAT, DISKCOPY, and CHKDSK to the Q&A directory, add them to the Main menu, and run them at any time with a single keystroke. However, you should be aware that leaving Q&A to run another program will erase any menus or macros that you have not yet saved to the disk file.

To remove a macro or program from the menu, display the Alternate Programs screen and delete the macro identifier or program name and its Menu Selection entry.

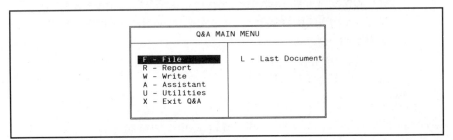

Figure 13.8: Main menu listing the macro

CREATING CUSTOM MENUS

||||➡ **To create a custom menu:**

1. **Select Create Menu from the Macro menu, then New Menu.**
2. **Complete the Macro Menu Options menu.**
3. **Press F10, then save the menu.**
4. **To use the custom menu, create a macro and enter the menu's name for the End with Menu option on the Macro Options menu.**

In addition to adding macros to the Main menu, you can create your own custom menus. Here are some uses of custom menus:

- Place macros that have a common theme all on one menu, such as a menu that prints reports or form documents.

- Replace Q&A's menus with your own to prevent users from editing or removing records.

- Develop a structure of menus to automate an entire application.

- Simulate two-keystroke macros such as Alt-KX. Press Alt-K to display a custom menu, then X to select a menu item.

When you replace a Q&A menu with one of your own, it will automatically appear in place of the original.

Menus are stored in macro files. Before you create a menu, get the macro file that contains the macros the menu will execute, and then follow this procedure:

1. Press Shift-F2 and select Create Menu from the Macro menu. (You can also select Create Application Menu from the Customize Application menu.) Q&A will display a list of menu names, as shown in Figure 13.9.

2. Select New Menu to display the Macro Menu Options menu shown in Figure 13.10.

Table 13.1 describes the options on the Macro Menu Options menu. You can easily redisplay this menu at any time to change your selections.

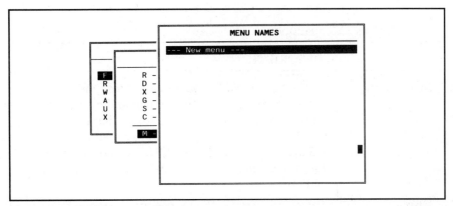

Figure 13.9: Menu names list

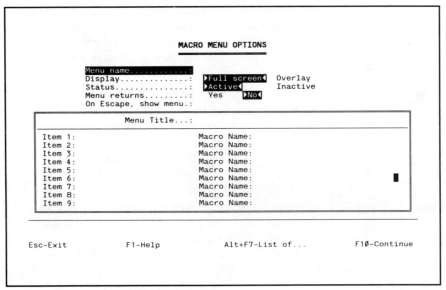

Figure 13.10: Macro Menu Options menu

Table 13.1: Macro Menu Options

OPTION	DESCRIPTION
Menu Name	Enter the name that you will use to call the menu from macros. Do not give a menu and macro the same name, because they are stored in the same file. If you use one of Q&A's built-in names for its own menus, it will replace Q&A's. To see a list of Q&A menu names, press Alt-F7 at the Menu Name option.
Display	Select Full Screen when you want the menu to appear by itself on the screen. Choose Overlay to have the menu overlap whatever is currently displayed. Overlaying menus create the same three-dimensional effect as the standard Q&A menus.
Status	When a menu is Active, it can be called from macros and macros can be run from it. Select Inactive to disable the menu. You might want to select Inactive while creating or editing the macros called from it. When all the macros are complete and tested, change Status to Active.
Menu Returns	When this option is set to Yes, after running a macro from the menu and pressing Esc to end the Q&A function, the menu will return to the screen. However, in order to return, the menu must overlap the Q&A Main menu, and all macros executed from it must be defined to start from the Main menu level. Overlapped embedded menus are considered "menu-returns" menus as long as the initial menu used to invoke them is designated as a menu-returns menu. To see a list of custom menus that can return, press Alt-F7 at the Menu Name option.
On Escape, Show Menu	Designate the menu you want to appear, if any, when you press Esc from this menu. Use this option to create a series of overlapped menus, similar to Q&A's own menu structure.

Table 13.1: Macro Menu Options (continued)

OPTION	DESCRIPTION
Menu Title	Enter the title you want to appear on the screen above the menu. This does not have to be the same as the Menu Name entry.
Item 1–9	For each item, type the text you want to appear as a menu option, such as *Insert Letterhead* or *Print Labels*. The text can be up to 21 characters. If you want to select an item with a single keystroke, enter the key as an uppercase letter, followed by a space, a hyphen, another space, and the text, as in *L - Print Letterhead*.
Macro Name	Next to each menu item, enter the name of the macro that executes it. You can press Alt-F7 to select from a list.

3. Complete the menu, and then press F10 to display the save macro file prompt.

4. Press ↵ to save the menu in the default macro file, or enter a new name and press ↵.

Defining a File and Report Menu

Now let's create a custom report for performing File and Report functions. All the macros involved include the keystrokes to return to the Main menu, so you do not have to include them in the calling macro.

The macros themselves are in the FILE.MAC macro file, so you need to get the file before creating the menu. Follow these steps:

1. Press Shift-F2, choose Get Macros, type **FILE.MAC**, and press ↵.

2. Press Shift-F2, choose Create Menu, and press ↵ to display the Macro Menu Options menu.

3. Type **File and Report** as the Macro Name.

4. Press ↵ to reach the Display option and select Overlay.

5. Press ↵ four times to reach the Menu Title option and type **My Own Menu**.

6. Press ↵ to reach the Item 1 prompt and type **B - Backup Clients**.

7. Press ↵ to reach the Macro Name prompt, press Alt-F7, select Backup Clients, and press ↵.

8. Type **C - Client Reports** and press ↵.

9. Press Alt-F7, select Print Reports, and press ↵.

10. Type **D - Display Clients** and press ↵.

11. Press Alt-F7, select Sort and Display, and press ↵.

12. Type **I - Insert Clients** and press ↵.

13. Press Alt-F7, select Add Clients, and press ↵.

14. Type **P - Post Clients** and press ↵.

15. Press Alt-F7, select Post New Records, and press ↵. Your screen should look like the one shown in Figure 13.11.

16. Press F10, then ↵ to save the menu.

In order to display a custom menu, you need to create a macro that calls the menu. You do this by entering the name of the menu for the macro's End with Menu option.

17. Press Shift-F2 and choose Define Macro.

18. Press Alt-M, then Shift-F2.

19. Press ↵ twice, type **File and Report**, press F10, and press ↵.

Using Custom Menus

You will be able to run the macro that calls the menu and displays your custom menu from any location in Q&A. But if you select a macro that was not defined from that location, it will not operate as you intended.

For example, the letterhead macro we created in Chapter 12 was designed to work from within Write. If you execute the macro from a custom

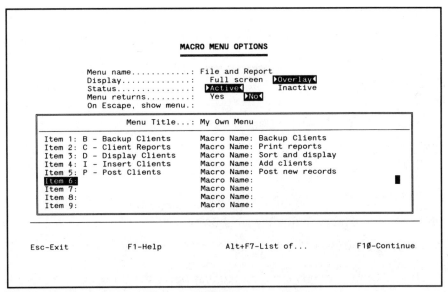

Figure 13.11: Completed menu options

menu at any other location, it will not work properly.

One way around this problem is to call the menu from a macro that returns to a set position. If the menu contains macros that are used from the Utilities menu, for example, the calling macro should include five Esc keystrokes and the letter *U*. When the macro ends, Q&A will be at the Utilities menu, the proper location for your custom menu to be displayed.

Now let's test our File and Report menu:

1. Press Alt-M. Your menu will appear on the screen as shown in Figure 13.12.

2. Type **D**. The sort and display macro will be executed, and the Sort Spec screen will appear.

3. Press ↓ three times to reach the City field, and then press ↵.

The records are sorted according to city and displayed in table view.

4. Press Alt-M again, and the menu will reappear, overlapping the table.

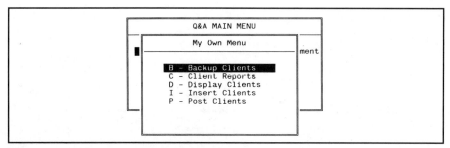

Figure 13.12: Custom menu on screen

5. Type **I** to insert new records. The macro will return to the Main menu, and then display a blank record.

6. Press Esc, type **Y**, and press Esc to return to the Main menu.

If you want your custom menu to reappear after any of its macros executes, enter its name in the macro's End with Menu option when you define it. If you already created the macro, edit it to insert the menu name just before the <enddef> code, using this syntax:

<menu>"*menu name"*

You can create a menu including macros that you have not yet defined—nothing will occur when you select an undefined macro from the menu. Similarly, you can list a nonexistent menu at the End with Menu option when creating a macro. If you think you might be using a macro in a menu, insert a menu name as a placeholder when you create it. This will make it easier to edit the macro when you have the actual menu name.

REPLACING Q&A MENUS

To replace a Q&A menu with a custom menu:

1. Select Create Menu from the Macro menu, then New Menu.
2. Give your menu the name of a Q&A menu—press Alt-F7 at the Menu Name option to display a list of Q&A menus.
3. Complete the Macro Menu Options menu and save the menu.

To replace a Q&A menu, give your menu the name that Q&A assigns to its own. For example, to replace the Main menu, name yours Q&A Main Menu.

When you replace one of Q&A's menus with your own, make sure all the macros it calls were defined from that level. Extra Esc keystrokes, like those you used in the File and Report menu macros, will create problems when the macro is called. If you want to use any of those macros, edit out the <esc> codes that precede the first character. You could then create a main menu with all your File and Report macros. This would be useful if you want a user to access those functions but not other Q&A modules.

To access the original menu functions quickly, use the function's first letter as the macro name and any letter you want as the activating keystroke. The following replacement main menu structure, for instance, will allow you to select File, Exit, Report, IA, and Write with different keystrokes:

Item 1: D - Databases   Macro Name: F

Item 2: L - Leave Q&A   Macro Name: X

Item 3: P - Printed Reports   Macro Name: R

Item 4: Q - Questions   Macro Name: A

Item 5: T - Type Documents   Macro Name: W

Pressing D will execute the F keystroke and display the File menu. You do not have to define a macro named F.

When you are replacing the Main menu, you must provide a means of exiting from Q&A. Do so by entering X as one macro name.

Now, we will create a small custom main menu. Our macro choices are limited because most begin with several <esc> codes or were designed to be activated from a location other than the Main menu. Your own menus can be more complete.

Follow these steps:

1. Press Shift-F2, select Create Menu, and press ↵ to start a new menu.

2. Press Alt-F7 to display the list of Q&A menu names shown in Figure 13.13.

3. Press PgDn to display additional names, highlight Q&A Main Menu, and press ↵ to insert it in the menu.

4. Press ↵ to reach the Display option and choose Full Screen.

5. Press ↵ four times and type **My Own Main Menu**.

6. Press ↵ to reach Item 1 and type **D - Databases**.

7. Press ↵ and type **F**.

8. Press ↵ and type **G - Get Last Document**.

9. Press ↵ and type **Last Document**.

10. Press ↵ and type **T - Type Documents**.

11. Press ↵ and type **W**.

12. Press ↵ and type **X - Exit**.

13. Press ↵ and type **X**.

14. Press F10, then Esc twice to place the menu in memory but not in the disk file. The original Main menu will appear.

15. Press Esc one more time. Your own custom menu will now be

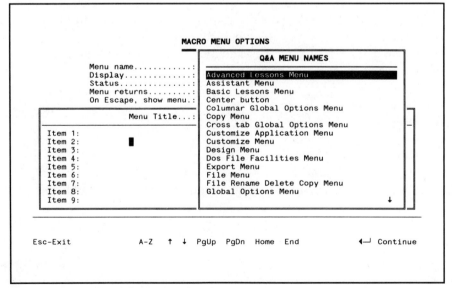

Figure 13.13: List of Q&A menu names

the main menu, as shown in Figure 13.14.

You can now run any of the macros listed on the new main menu. Notice that even though the original menu choices are not shown, their activating letters are still in effect. For example, when you run the last document macro, the first keystroke executed is W for Write. Even though Write is no longer an option on the menu, it is nevertheless selected, and the macro runs properly.

Now let's return to the original Q&A Main menu by deleting the custom menu from memory.

16. Press Shift-F2 and choose Delete Macro.

17. Highlight Q&A Main Menu and press ↵.

18. Press Esc twice to display the original menu.

19. Type **X** to leave Q&A.

Replacing Q&A menus and creating your own menu structure are typically part of the process of building complete applications. These are more advanced techniques that will be discussed in Chapters 15 and 16.

EDITING MENU FILES

The easiest way to change a menu is to select it from the list displayed when you choose Create Menu from the Macro menu. The Macro Menu Options menu for that menu will be displayed. Make your changes and press F10, then ↵ to save it.

Since menus are saved in macro files, you can also edit them in the same way that you revise macros: get the file into Write, make your changes, and

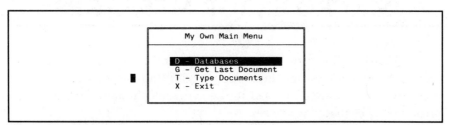

Figure 13.14: Q&A Main menu replaced with your custom menu

save the menu as an ASCII file. All entries—menus and macros—are separated by asterisks.

The general syntax of a menu entry is:

<begdef><nokey><name>*"menu-name"<menu>"menu-title,display-status-menu returns:on-escape-menu-name/ item1,macro1/item2, macro2/... itemn,macron/"<enddef>*

As with macro text, the menu entry begins with <begdef> and ends with <enddef>. All menus are assigned the <nokey> identifier. The menu's name is represented by the <name>*"menu-name"*. The <menu> code indicates that the following section includes the options listed in the menu definition.

This entire portion, enclosed in quotation marks, contains the settings and entries in the menu:

"menu-title,display-status-menu returns:on-escape-menu-name/item1, macro1/item2,macro2/...itemn,macron/"

It starts with the menu's title, a comma, then three letters representing the Display, Status, and Menu Returns settings. Enter F or O to select Full Screen or Overlay, A or I for Active or Inactive status, and Y or N for Menu Returns or not. FAN, for example, represents a full display, active status, and no menu returns.

After the colon is the name of the on-escape menu, if any, then a series of entries including the menu items and macro names. Notice the punctuation: items and macro names are separated by commas, each separated by a slash. No spaces are allowed.

The structure can be up to 255 characters, with up to nine menu items.

MACRO ERROR MESSAGES

If Q&A has difficulty loading or using a macro file, it will display a message on the message line. Along with the messages relating to memory, which were discussed in the previous chapter, there are other error messages that may appear.

When you see the message

No macros have been defined.

you are trying to run, delete, or clear a macro from an empty macro file. Get a macro file, and then try the operation again.

If Q&A displays

Macro file not found. Press Esc.

you are trying to get a macro file that is not on the disk. Check the spelling of the file name or try another path.

The error message

Macro file read error near macro #n. Press Esc.

means that Q&A cannot read the file because an error occurs near the macro mentioned. Try loading the file in Write and editing the macro. Be sure to save it as an ASCII file.

You might also see

Not able to save macro file. Not enough disk space? Press Esc.

which means that you do not have enough space on the disk to save the file. Try another disk.

A message that usually appears when you edit or write a macro that includes an error or save the macro file in standard Q&A format is

There's a bad macro definition near macro #n. Press Esc.

Try loading the file in Write and editing the macro. Be sure to save it as an ASCII file.

Creating your own macros and menus is one approach to customizing your database. The next chapter presents other ways to make your database suit your needs.

14

Custom-izing Your Database

By customizing your database, you can exercise precise control over fields. In Chapter 4, you learned how to customize a database by setting initial values for fields. In this chapter, you will explore the other ways to customize your database:

- Change field types, formats, and global options
- Restrict values that can be entered into fields
- Design templates to control field entries and their format
- Index the database to speed up record retrieval
- Design custom help messages for yourself and others
- Change screen colors and the way text, fields, and values are displayed

You will also learn how to protect your database by assigning passwords and access levels. The final sections describe how Q&A works on a network and with SQL databases.

CONTROLLING FIELD INPUT

||||➡ **To control field input:**
  - **Use the Format Values option on the Customize menu for the database (select Design File from the File menu, then Customize a File) to change field types.**
  - **Use the Restrict Values option on the Customize menu to designate acceptable input.**
  - **Use the Field Template option on the Customize menu to define the characters and format of field entries.**

Data-entry errors can have extreme results, such as when someone receives a $10 check made out as $1,000,000.00. Mistakes like this can occur in any database and with any field type. A date could be entered as 10/22/1845, or PA mistakenly typed as the state instead of CA.

You can minimize data-entry errors by controlling what will be accepted in the field. The following sections describe how to use database customization options to change field types or formats, restrict field values, and create field templates.

Begin by displaying the menu of customization options for the Clients database:

1. From the Main menu, select File, and then choose Design File.

2. Choose Customize a File, type **Clients**, and press ↵.

The Customize menu appears. In Chapter 4, we used the Set Initial Values option on this menu to have PA automatically appear in the State field of the Vendors form. Now you will see how the other customization options work.

CHANGING FIELD TYPES OR FORMATS

The Format Values option on the Customize menu lets you change the type or format of fields. It displays the Format Spec screen you completed when you designed the database. Change any of the field types or formatting instructions, and then press F10.

If the database has any money, number, date, or hours fields, the Global Options menu will appear. Make your selections from this menu, and then press F10.

Before you change a field type, you should make sure that the existing data in the field will not be affected. You can change number to money fields without any problems because the values will remain the same; only the format will change.

You can change any field type to text. Numeric values will be converted to their ASCII character equivalents, and dates will appear as text in the format 1992/12/30. You should not convert a text field to a number field unless it contains only numeric characters, such as those in the Customer Code field of the Clients database.

When you have taught IA about a database (as described in Chapter 11) and you change one of its fields to a text or keyword type, Q&A will rearrange the IA information in the IDX file. If you taught the fields to Query Guide, you will be asked if you want to teach it the new text and keyword fields.

To add, delete, or change the order of the fields, use the Redesign a File option on the Design menu (displayed when you select Design File from the File menu). The Format Values option only allows you to change the type and format.

RESTRICTING FIELD VALUES

The Restrict Values option on the Customize menu allows you to prevent data-entry errors by designating acceptable field values. If you deal with only West Coast clients, for example, you could restrict state entries to CA, WA, and OR. You could limit customer codes to three-digit numbers between 100 and 300, or you could restrict weekly salaries to $1,000 or less.

If you try to enter an unusual value or one outside the allowable range in a restricted field, Q&A will warn you

Value not in specified range. Please verify before continuing.

This is only a warning; you can still enter the value and override the restriction. Therefore, if you do have an employee who earned an unusually large commission, or an odd East Coast client, you can still add the data to the field.

Selecting this option displays the Restrict Spec screen. You enter restrictions using the same criteria you do for retrieving records, except for the MIN and MAX criteria (retrieval criteria are discussed in Chapter 3).

Requesting Versus Requiring Data

Placing a restriction on a field does not necessarily require an entry. Using PA;NJ;DE in the State field, for example, limits entries to those three states or no entry at all.

You *require* input by typing the ! symbol in the field, and *request* input by typing /=. For example, suppose you fill in the Restrict Spec screen with ! in the Customer Code field and /= in the Phone field. If you try to leave either field blank, Q&A will display the warning

This field requires a value. Please verify before continuing.

If it is a requested field, such as Phone, the message is just a warning—you can still leave it blank if you really do not have a value to enter. Just move to the next field.

A required field, however, cannot be left blank. Once you reach the field, you will not be able to leave it unless you make an entry. If you bypass the field using the arrow keys, Q&A will not let you save the record.

Before designating a field as required, make sure that you will *always* have an entry for it. Unless you do, you will not be able to enter and save any data in the record at all. You will either have to press Esc to abandon the record or type something in the field so you can continue.

To designate a field as required and restricted, place ! in front of the restriction. For example, the restriction !PA;NJ;DE requires one of the three states to be entered before the record can be saved.

Entering Restriction Criteria

Now let's enter the following restrictions for the Clients database fields:

- Limit customer codes to three-digit numbers between 100 and 300

- Require a name

- Require the state of NJ, PA, or DE

- Restrict the last order date to on or after January 1, 1991

- Set a range of order amounts between $50 and $1500

- Set credit limits to $750, $1,000, or $1,500

- Limit Product Purchased entries to numbers from 100 to 110 (these will be the numbers we will use when we create our inventory database in Chapter 16)

The Customer Code field restriction will be a slight problem. The restriction >=100..<=300, which would be fine with a number or money field, will not work. Because the field is text, the restriction does not limit entries to numbers between 100 and 300, but to character strings whose *ASCII values* are between those of 100 and 300. Thus, you could not enter numbers less than 11 or starting with a number greater than 3, but you could enter two-digit numbers above 10 and combinations of letters and numbers, such as 10A.

Instead, we will use the restriction 1??;2??;300, which limits entries to strings starting with 1 or 2 followed by any two characters, or 300. However, it does not prevent a mixture of numbers and letters, as in the obvious error 12W.

How could we ensure that the entry is between 100 and 300 without errors? One way is to change the field to a number type using the Format Values option on the Customize menu. This would allow the use of a numeric range for the restriction, but it violates the general rule of assigning the number type only to fields used in calculations. Another alternative is to list all the valid entries in one long OR restriction:

    100;101;102;103;104;...;298;299;300

But this is more than you would want to type.

Neither method is really acceptable. Instead, we will take care of the problem when we design field templates later in the chapter.

Follow these steps to restrict field values in the Clients database:

1. Select Restrict Values from the Customize menu to display the Restrict Spec screen, as shown in Figure 14.1.

2. Press F6 to expand the field.

3. Type **!1??;2??;300** and press F10.

4. Press ↓ to reach the Name field, and then type **!** to make it required.

5. Press ↵ three times to reach the State field, and then press F6 to expand it.

6. Type **!NJ;PA;DE** and press F10.

7. Press ↓ three times, press Shift-Tab to reach the Last Order date field, and type **>=1/1/91**.

8. Press ↵ to reach the Amount field and type **50..1500**.

9. Press ↓ to reach the Credit Limit field and type **750;1000;1500**.

10. Press ↵ to reach the Products Purchased field and type **100;101;102;103;104;105;106;107;108;109;110**.

11. Press F10 to save the restrictions and return to the Customize menu.

In customizing your own databases, you will have to decide how far to go to ensure proper input. Should you develop complex restrictions for every field? The decision is not an easy one.

First, consider how critical the field value is to the integrity of the database and how serious a problem the error would cause. Mistakes in

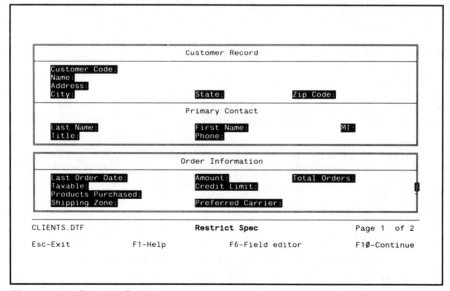

Figure 14.1: Restrict Spec screen

fields that are not used in calculations, or that are easy to spot in reports and printouts, may not require the extra effort. On the other hand, errors that involve money fields, calculations, or major decisions should be controlled as much as possible.

Second, weigh the possibility of error against the work involved in preventing errors in the first place. In some cases, range restrictions are more efficient than complex restriction criteria. For example, you would be less likely to type letters in a field that requires numbers, but more likely to enter numbers in the wrong range.

CREATING FIELD TEMPLATES

You further control how data is entered by using the Field Template option on the Customize menu to design field templates. A *field template* defines a pattern for a text field value.

Templates are useful for several purposes:

- Specify the characters that can be entered into text fields
- Disable the expansion of text fields to limit field size
- Automatically format text fields

Template Codes

The Field Template option displays the Field Template Spec screen. In the fields that will have templates, enter the characters to control which keystrokes can be entered, as follows:

- # or 9 represents a numeric character from 0 to 9
- @ represents an alphabetic character (A to Z, and a to z)
- $ represents any keyboard character

Construct a template by combining #, 9, $, or @ with any actual characters you want to include. The field entry will be limited to the number of characters used in the template.

For example, a common field template for phone numbers is (###) ###-####. After you create this template, the form will appear like this:

Phone: (   )   -

When you enter a number, the first three characters will automatically appear in the parentheses, the next three characters to the left of the hyphen, and the last four to its right. You do not have to position the cursor—Q&A does it for you.

Similarly, you could use the template 999-99-9999 to format social security numbers. Or suppose that your company assigns each inventory item a code in which the letters AN are followed by three numbers and two letters, as in AN123DK. To ensure the entry of valid codes, define the template AN999@@.

Defining the Templates

Now we will define templates for the Customer Code, City, Zip Code, and Phone fields in the Clients database:

1. Select Field Template from the Customize menu to display the Field Template Spec screen.

2. In the Customer Code field, type **999**.

This template establishes that the Customer Code field will accept only three characters from 0 to 9. Combining the template with the restriction we defined in the previous section ensures that customer codes are valid numbers between 100 and 300, even though the field is the text type.

3. Press ↵ three times to reach the City field, and then press @ until you reach the end of the field.

The template prevents the City field from being expanded.

4. Press ↵ twice to reach the Zip Code field and type **99999-9999**.

5. Press ↓ twice to reach the Phone field and type **(999) 999-9999**. Your screen should look like Figure 14.2.

6. Press F10 to return to the Customize menu.

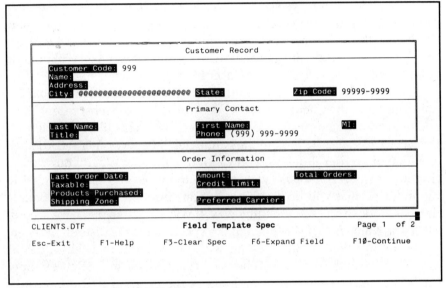

Figure 14.2: Completed Field Template Spec screen

INDEXING A
DATABASE FOR QUICK ACCESS

To index a database:

1. **Choose Speed Up Searches from the Customize menu.**
2. **On the Speed-Up Spec screen, enter S, SU (for unique values), or SE (for existing values) in each field to be indexed.**
3. **Press F10 to process the index.**

Because Q&A maintains database records in the order they were entered—new records are placed at the end of the file—adding records is quick and easy. Q&A does not have to reorder the records each time you add a new one.

However, this arrangement has the disadvantage of making it take longer for Q&A to retrieve specific records. Each time you want to recall a record that meets certain retrieval criteria, Q&A has to scan the entire database. If the records are near the beginning of the database, Q&A will find them relatively quickly. But as your database grows larger, you will notice a delay when you look for records closer to the end of your file.

For example, suppose you want to retrieve the record for Samual Engineering from the Clients database. Because this is the most recent client added to your system, its record is at the very end of the file. Before it finds the record, Q&A has to look in the Name field of every other record.

To avoid retrieval delays, you can index the file. When you want to find information in a book, you look up the topic and page number in the index so that you do not have to scan through the entire book. A database index works in the same way. If you index the database according to the Name field, Q&A maintains a special table that lists all the client names in alphabetical order, along with information that tells Q&A its exact location in the database. When you enter a name in the Retrieve Spec screen Name field, Q&A quickly looks at the index to find the record's location, then goes directly to that record.

You can index your database by as many fields as you like. However, you should limit the fields you index to those that are necessary. Indexing speeds up retrieval, but it slows down the process of entering new records because Q&A has to update the index every time you add a record.

ENTERING INDEX CODES

To index records, select Speed Up Searches from the Customize menu. On the Speed-Up Spec screen, enter S, SU, or SE in the fields you want to index. The S code simply marks the field to be included in the index.

To ensure that the values in a field are unique, enter SU. Then, if you try to enter a value that has already been used while you are adding new records, Q&A will display the message

<blockquote>This field should be unique. Please verify before continuing.</blockquote>

You may want to enter this index code in fields that contain information that should not be repeated in more than one record, such as client codes, social security numbers, or stock numbers, even if they are not important to the index. (Unfortunately, if you are indexing a file that already has records, Q&A will not report that nonunique values exist.)

The SE code works the opposite of SU. It ensures that the values in new records are not unique. If you try to enter a unique value, you will see the message

<blockquote>This value has not been entered before. Please verify before continuing</blockquote>

Use SE to ensure that a field in a new record contains a value that already exists, such as to assign new patients to physicians already on staff or place an inventory item in a location that already contains products. However, *do not* assign the SE index code to a database without records, or to a field that is blank in every record. If you do, you will not be able to add any value to the field.

Now we will index the Clients field by the Customer Code and Name fields, which are the ones usually used to locate client records.

1. Select Speed Up Searches from the Customize menu to display the Speed-Up Spec screen.

2. Type **SU** in the Customer Code field.

Combined with the field restriction and template, this index code guarantees that customer codes will be unique numbers between 100 and 300.

3. Press ↵ to reach the Name field and type **SU**.

By indexing Names as a unique field, you are ensuring that the same client will not be entered in more than one record.

4. Press F10. You will see a message telling you to wait while Q&A indexes the database. Then the Customize menu will reappear.

CREATING
CUSTOM HELP MESSAGES

▌▌▌▶ To create custom help messages:

1. **Select Define Custom Help from the Customize menu.**
2. **On the Help Spec screen, press F8 to reach each field, enter the help text, and press F10 when all the messages are entered.**
3. **To display the message and turn on help mode when using the database, press F1 in the field.**

The warning messages Q&A displays when you enter an unacceptable value in a field do not explain how to make a correct entry. You will probably remember how you constructed the restrictions, but the warning message could just frustrate another person using the database.

To make your database more user-friendly, you can add custom help messages. That way, pressing F1 in a field could display a message explaining exactly which field values are acceptable.

ENTERING HELP TEXT

To create a custom help message, select Define Custom Help from the Customize menu to display the Help Spec screen, shown in Figure 14.3. Press F8 to reach the field and type the text you want to appear in the help message. Press F6 to move backward through the fields.

Make your help messages as complete as possible. With restricted fields, tell users which values are acceptable, and whether the entry is optional, required, or just requested. Tell them how to confirm entries that seem inappropriate or outside the restricted range, as in

Hourly wages should be between $5.00 and $27.50.

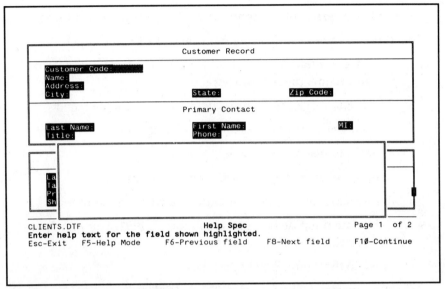

Figure 14.3: Custom Help Spec screen

Please check for an authorizing signature or contact the Personnel Department before entering a wage rate outside that range.

In fact, you could add a general help message to every field, such as

Please verify the department before continuing

↵ - next field   F10 - save record   ESC - cancel

Follow these steps to enter custom help messages for the Clients database:

1. Select Define Custom Help from the Customize menu to display the Help Spec screen.

2. Type the following message for the Customer Code field:

    You must enter a number between 100 and 300 that has not yet been assigned to a customer.

    If you do not have a customer number, press ESC twice.

Please verify the customer code entry before continuing.

3. Press F8 to reach the Name field and type the message

   A different name is required for all records. If you do not have a name, press ESC twice.

4. Press F8 to reach the Address field and type the help text

   Please verify the address before continuing.

5. Press F8 to reach the State field and type

   You must enter NJ, PA, or DE before continuing.

6. Press F8 to move to the Last Order Date field and enter

   The date must be on or after January 1, 1991. You may leave this field blank.

7. Move to the Amount field and type

   Orders should be between $50 and $1500. Please verify orders outside that range.

8. For the Credit Limit field, enter the message

   Credit limits are either $500, $1000, or $1500. Please verify any other amount.

9. Move to the Products Purchased field and enter the final message.

   Valid product code numbers are from 100 to 110. Please verify any other entry.

10. Press F10 to return to the Customize menu, and then press Esc twice to return to the File menu.

To provide the most help, you could enter a custom message for all the other fields. For fields without restrictions, use a generic message similar to the one we entered for the Address field.

DISPLAYING CUSTOM HELP

When you are using the database, pressing F1 displays the custom help message for the field. As you move from field to field, custom help screens will automatically appear. Press Esc to turn off help mode. When a custom help screen is displayed, press F1 again to display Q&A's built-in help information.

If you press F1 in a field without a custom help message, the Q&A Help screen will appear. This does not turn on help mode.

By default, help is in nonconcurrent mode, which means that your custom help message will disappear when you press a key. In concurrent mode, the message will remain on the screen as long as the cursor is in the field. You can change the mode while creating the help message. From the Help Spec screen, press F5, then type C to select Concurrent or N to choose Nonconcurrent.

CHANGING THE
HUES OF YOUR FORMS

To change the form display:

1. **Select Change Palette from the Customize menu.**
2. **Press F8 to change to the next of seven display combinations.**
3. **Press F10 to save the palette settings.**

The Change Palette option on the Customize menu lets you change the way your data-entry form appears. You can select from seven different *palettes*, which are combinations of ways that lines and headings, field labels, and the data you enter are displayed on the screen.

Press F8 to see the next palette; press F6 to see the previous one. You can enter dummy characters and move from field to field to see how the screen will look when you are actually entering data. When you find a palette that you like, press F10 to save the setting for that database. Figure 14.4 shows how the screen appears on a monochrome monitor when you select palette 1.

Depending on your hardware, not all the effects of the palette may appear. Also, you will see fewer differences between palettes on some laptop or notebook computer monitors.

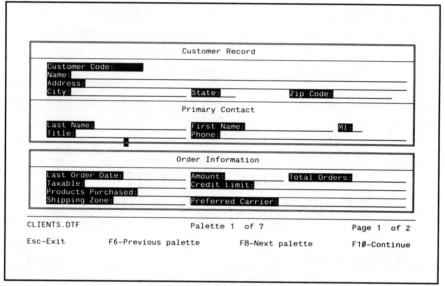

Figure 14.4: Palette screen in monochrome system

USING YOUR CUSTOMIZED DATABASE

By controlling field entries and providing help messages, you make data-entry as efficient and error-free as possible. Now that we have customized the Clients database, we can see how it is affected by the restrictions and templates.

ENTERING INVALID VALUES

We will start by trying to add a new client with an invalid customer code.

1. Select Add Records from the File menu and press ↵ to accept the Clients database.

2. Type **110** and press ↵. You will see the warning that the field must be unique.

3. Press F1 to display the custom help message.

4. Type **450** and press ↵. You will be warned that the value is outside the range.

5. Type **11p**. You will find that the letter *p* cannot be entered because the template specifies numeric characters.

6. Type **111** and press ↵. The entry will be accepted because it falls within the proper range and is unique.

7. Type **Greenwald Art Supplies, Inc.**.

8. Press ↓ four times, press Tab to reach the Phone field, and type **215**. The numbers will appear within the parentheses, and the cursor will move into position for the next number.

9. Type **5551234**. The characters will automatically appear to the left and right of the hyphen.

10. Press Esc and type **Y** to exit without saving the record.

When entering a phone number, you will have to type 000 if you do not have an area code. Because 999 is specified in the template, you cannot press the spacebar to move past the area code section. The template prevents you from moving to the right in a blank field by using the → key, although you can leave the field by pressing Tab, ↵, ↑, or ↓. This is fine if you want to strongly request an area code and will accept 000 when there is none.

If you wanted to be able to leave the area code blank—filled with spaces—you would use the template ($$$) 999-9999. However, this would allow the entry of letters for the area code. This is a case where you have to decide which route to take: would you prefer to demand 000 for a blank area code or to take the chances of an incorrect entry?

THE EFFECTS OF
TEMPLATES ON EXISTING DATA

A new template does not affect values in existing records. This means you can create a template without worrying about field values you already entered. The template will be used, however, when you add new records or fill in blank fields in an existing record.

As an example of the effects of templates, let's look at the records we have already entered into the Clients database.

1. Select Search/Update from the File menu and press ↵.

2. Press F10 to display the first form.

3. Press ↓ five times, and then press Tab to reach the Phone field.

The number in the Phone field appears as you originally entered it. Because the field is not formatted according to the template, Q&A displays the message

This field does not meet the mask specifications of (999) 999-9999

You can leave the phone numbers as you entered them or edit them to match the template. Let's change them to include the area codes.

4. Press Ins to turn on insert mode. The cursor will change from a blinking line to a blinking box.

5. Type **(609)** and press the spacebar. The remaining characters will shift to the right to conform to the template.

6. Press F10 to display the next record.

The cursor is in the record's Phone field, but pressing F10 canceled insert mode.

7. Press Ins, type **(609)**, press the spacebar, and then press F10 to reach the next record.

8. In the same manner, add area codes to all the phone numbers: **215** for clients in PA, **609** for those in NJ, and **302** for those in DE. Remember, after moving to the next record, press Ins to turn on insert mode again.

9. Press Shift-F10 after adding the area code to the final record.

You should also have noticed that a hyphen followed each five-digit zip code, as in 19116-. Since the hyphen was in the template, it appears whether or not the zip code is nine digits. If you plan to use mostly five-digit zip codes and find the hyphen unsightly, use a space in the template instead of a hyphen.

PROTECTING YOUR DATABASE

To protect a database:

- **Lock it from form and program changes by selecting Design File from the File menu, then Customize Application, then Lock Database. Enter a password and press F10. Password-protect it by selecting Design File from the File menu, then Secure a File.**
- **Enter your password by waiting until the prompt appears, or by pressing F6 from the Main menu.**

Another way to customize a database is to protect it from unauthorized access. Q&A provides several levels of protection. The protection does not prevent others from making a copy of your database, but it can block their access to data and prevent them from changing the form or associated Spec screens.

LOCKING THE DATABASE

Locking a database prevents access to selected operations. As the database designer, you might want to lock the database so that no one else can change its form, the customization, or the Program Spec screens.

To lock a database, select Design File from the File menu, and then choose Customize Application to display the Custom Application menu. Select Lock Database, and then enter the name of the database you want to protect. Q&A will display the menu shown in Figure 14.5.

Enter a password of up to 12 characters. For each menu option, select No for the functions that you want restricted; choose Yes for the functions that you want others to be able to perform. For example, if you select No for the first option, users will not be able to redesign or program the form unless they know your password.

To activate the lock, select Yes for the last option, Should the Database Lock Be Enabled. Press F10 after completing the menu.

With the lock enabled, Q&A will not let anyone, including yourself, perform any of the restricted operations. When you want to perform one of these functions or allow others to, return to the Database Lock menu

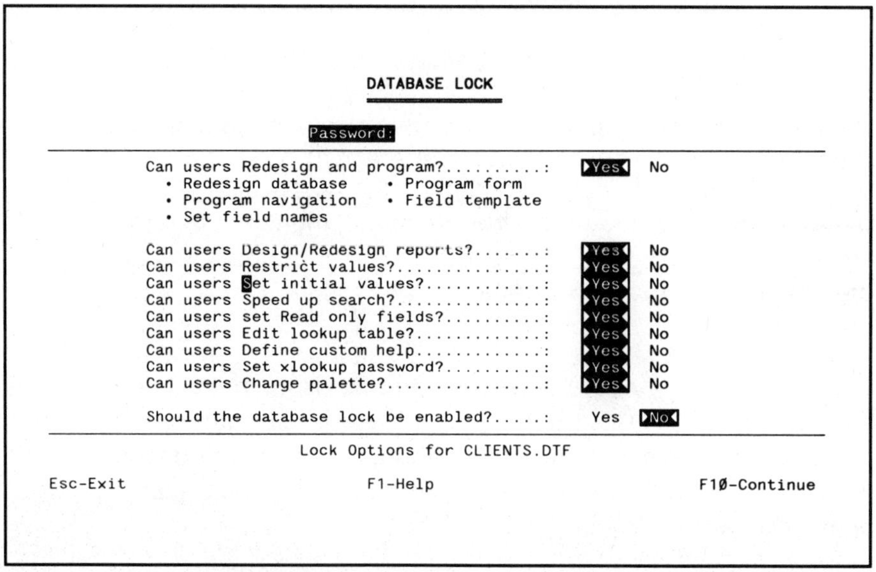

```
                        DATABASE LOCK
                        ───────────

                    Password:

        Can users Redesign and program?.........:   ▶Yes◀  No
        • Redesign database    • Program form
        • Program navigation   • Field template
        • Set field names

        Can users Design/Redesign reports?......:   ▶Yes◀  No
        Can users Restrict values?..............:   ▶Yes◀  No
        Can users Set initial values?...........:   ▶Yes◀  No
        Can users Speed up search?..............:   ▶Yes◀  No
        Can users set Read only fields?.........:   ▶Yes◀  No
        Can users Edit lookup table?............:   ▶Yes◀  No
        Can users Define custom help............:   ▶Yes◀  No
        Can users Set xlookup password?.........:   ▶Yes◀  No
        Can users Change palette?...............:   ▶Yes◀  No

        Should the database lock be enabled?....:   Yes   ▶No◀
        ──────────────────────────────────────────────────────
                    Lock Options for CLIENTS.DTF

     Esc-Exit              F1-Help              F1Ø-Continue
```

Figure 14.5: Database Lock menu

and set the final option to No. Before displaying the menu, however, Q&A will require you to enter your identification and password.

SECURING A DATABASE

Securing a database restricts access to portions of the database by assigning users their own passwords. Unlike a lock, which protects the database from every user equally, securing allows you to customize access according to work groups and individuals. You can restrict one user to adding and editing records, allow another to delete records, and let someone else redesign the Program Spec screen.

Q&A provides four levels of security:

- *Access rights* limit access to selected functions.

- *Field level security* restricts access to selected fields.

- *Sharing mode* controls access by more than one user at a time on a network.

- *XLookup password* provides access to a database through external lookup program commands.

These levels are controlled through the Security menu shown in Figure 14.6. To display this menu, select Design File from the File menu, and then choose Secure a File.

In developing security procedures, you assign each database user an identification and password. Then, a valid identification and password must be entered before Q&A will display the Security menu.

Figure 14.6: Security menu

In single-user systems, changes to the Security menu do not take effect until the next time you start Q&A.

Assigning Access Rights

You can limit an individual's ability to change and access your database by assigning specific access rights. Select Assign Access Rights from the Security menu. The List Manager screen will appear with a message asking you to enter a new user or group or select a name from the list. The user name will correspond to an identification assigned to an individual database user or to a common name assigned to a group of users who you want to have the same access. Q&A will then display the Access Control menu, shown in Figure 14.7.

For each user or group, assign a password to be entered in order to access the database. Then designate any restrictions you want to place on this access by selecting No for the options. Press F10 after making your selections. Q&A will ask if you want to assign rights to another group. Select Yes to repeat the procedure, or choose No to return to the Security menu.

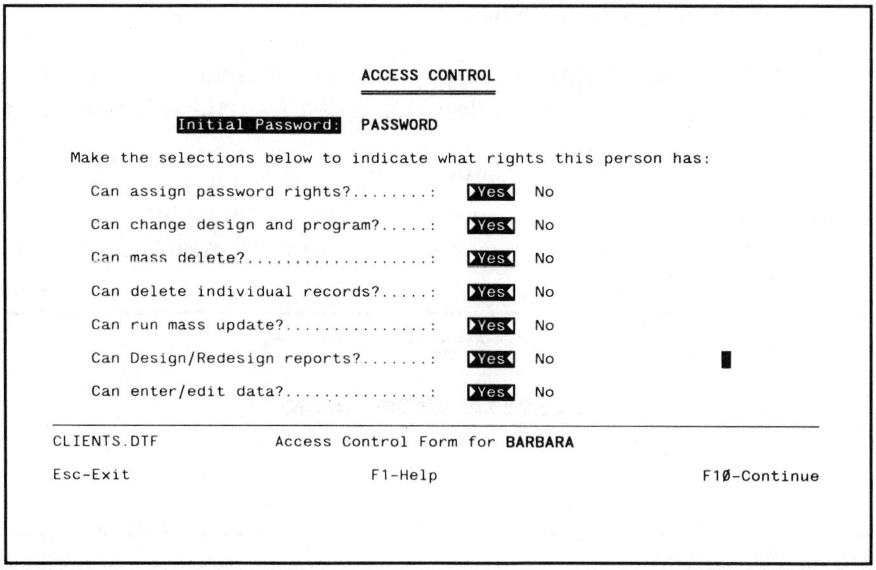

```
                           ACCESS CONTROL
                           ═══════════════

            Initial Password:  PASSWORD

        Make the selections below to indicate what rights this person has:

            Can assign password rights?........:    ▶Yes◀  No

            Can change design and program?.....:    ▶Yes◀  No

            Can mass delete?...................:    ▶Yes◀  No

            Can delete individual records?.....:    ▶Yes◀  No

            Can run mass update?...............:    ▶Yes◀  No

            Can Design/Redesign reports?.......:    ▶Yes◀  No        █

            Can enter/edit data?...............:    ▶Yes◀  No

        _____

        CLIENTS.DTF         Access Control Form for BARBARA

        Esc-Exit                    F1-Help                  F10-Continue
```

Figure 14.7: Access Control menu

After access rights are assigned, Q&A will prompt users to enter their identification and password when they attempt to use the database.

Field Level Security

You can allow access to a database but protect individual fields by assigning field level security. This lets you designate which fields a user can read, write, or even see on the screen. You can only assign field level security to users who do not have administrative rights. These are users who, according to their Access Control forms, cannot assign passwords or change the database design or program. Users who have these rights can access all the fields on the form.

To assign field level security, select the option on the Security menu. The List Manager screen will appear with a message prompting you to enter a Field Security Spec name or select one from the list. You use the Field Security Spec screen to create a view of the form. For example, if you want to prevent a user or group of users from changing the invoice fields in the Clients database, create a specification called Invoice Data Disabled. The Field Security Spec screen will appear next, as shown in Figure 14.8.

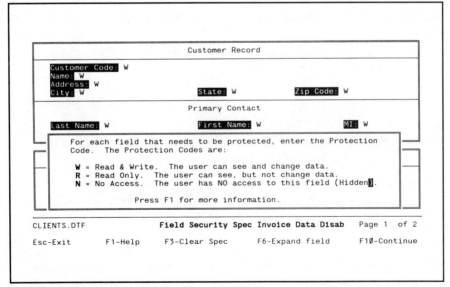

Figure 14.8: Field Security Spec screen

Mark each field with a W if you want the user to read and write its data, an R for read-only status, or an N for no access. No-access fields will not appear on screen when the form is displayed. For example, if you have a student database, you might want to prevent student helpers from seeing personal information when they enter routine data onto forms. Mark those fields as no access, and the field labels and data will not appear on the screen.

After you have marked each field, press F10 to display the User Selection screen. On this screen, enter the identification of users who should be restricted to the specified view. Press Alt-F7 to display a list of available users—those who do not have administrative rights according to their Access Control forms. If there are no such users, Q&A will display a message to that effect.

When users request a database, Q&A will ask for their identification and password. Their ability to see or display fields will depend on their access rights and the field security specification assigned to them.

Declaring Share Mode

When your database file is located on a dedicated network file server, more than one user can access the file at one time. If the file is on a local workstation, access is restricted to one user. This is called automatic sharing mode.

To change the mode, select Declare Sharing Mode from the Security menu and choose from these options:

- Automatic: The default mode, which senses whether or not the file is on a dedicated file server.

- Disallow: Permits access to only one user, even if the file is stored on a dedicated file server.

- Allow: Allows multiple access, even if the file is on a local workstation's hard disk. Select this option if you are using a distributed network such as TOPS.

XLookup Password

By assigning an XLookup password, you allow access to a database through external lookup commands, even when the user's own password is not valid for accessing the file directly. This lets you limit a user's general ability to work with a file, but allow that user to retrieve data while using another programmed form.

Select Set XLookup Password from the Security menu, enter a default identification and password, and press F10. Users can then access an external database if their own password or the default password is valid.

USING PASSWORDS

Once an Access Control form is created, Q&A will request an identification and password the first time a user requests the database. The user can also voluntarily enter his or her identification and password by pressing F6 from the Main menu.

To change your password, wait until Q&A requests it, then press F8. You will be asked for your identification, existing password, and a new password.

If you forget your password, check with the network administrator of your system. This is the person responsible for setting up and maintaining Q&A on your network. If you are the network administrator and you forget your password, you will have to mail a copy of the database files to Symantec Corporation, along with a check or money order for $50.00. Symantec will reset the password and return the disks to you.

USING Q&A ON A NETWORK

||||➡ **To use Q&A on a network, use either of these methods:**

- **Purchase and install the Network Pack to allow multiple users access to a shared database.**

- **Install single-user versions of Q&A to allow one user to access a database at a time.**

You can use Q&A on a network in either a single-user or multiuser mode. To allow more than one user to access a file simultaneously, you must purchase and install the Q&A Network Pack. If you have a single-user version of Q&A, you can still install it on a network, but only one user will be able to access a file at any one time.

To prevent problems from occurring when more than one user accesses a file, Q&A has a procedure for locking records, limiting the type of access allowed. For example, when two users request the same record, the first user is given read/write privileges; the second user can only read the record. Q&A displays a message telling the second user that the record is already in use and locked so they cannot modify it. When the first user releases the record, it becomes unlocked so another user may access it in read/write mode.

In addition, not all Q&A functions are available to every user, as summarized in Table 14.1. When multiple users are sharing a file on a network, they can access stored macros and perform the functions listed in the table, although only one user has read/write privileges to a record at a time.

Other commands are only available to one user at a time in a shared database. If another user attempts to use the same function, Q&A displays the message

This function is in use by network-ID.
Please try again later.

Finally, some functions will lock the entire database and cannot be performed if another user is accessing the file. If you attempt to perform one of these functions when someone else is using the database, Q&A displays the message

File in use by network ID.

You enter your network ID through the Set Global Options menu.

Table 14.1: Command Availability on Networks

MULTIPLE USERS SHARING A FILE	
File	Add records, print forms, search/update records, table view
Report	Print reports
IA	Search/update records, add records, print reports
Write	Mail merge
Utilities	Import and export
ONLY ONE USER AT A TIME	
File	Design a printing specification, assign passwords and access rights, access named Spec screen
Report	Design reports
LOCK THE DATABASE TO OTHER USERS	
File	Redesign database, customize database, copy forms or designs, mass update, post records, remove records, delete duplicate records
IA	Teach IA new words, mass update
Query Guide	Teach Query Guide
Utilities	DOS commands

USING Q&A WITH SQL

Using optional software drivers, Q&A can act as a *front-end* for SQL databases, such as Oracle and SQLBase. You can use Q&A to directly query the SQL database and print reports using its data.

You order SQL drivers directly from Symantec Corporation using the coupon supplied with your Q&A package. After you copy the drivers to your hard disk, select Link-to-SQL from the File Utilities menu. A special Link-to-SQL guide is supplied as part of the Q&A documentation and provided with each SQL driver you order.

In this chapter, you learned how to customize your database form to maximize its efficiency with your system. The next chapter broadens your scope of database management. It covers mass updating, posting, and other ways to work with multiple databases.

15

Advanced Database Management

The techniques you have learned so far allow you to create and manipulate databases of all types. This chapter describes the more advanced Q&A File features that can transform your databases into sophisticated business and academic applications.

You will learn how to update many records at one time and post data from one database to another. Posting introduces the concept of working with more than one database at a time, which you will explore further in Chapter 16.

Another topic covered in this chapter is how to share data between Q&A, other database programs, and spreadsheet programs. You will learn how to convert files from dBASE, Lotus 1-2-3, Paradox, and other programs into Q&A databases, as well as how to export Q&A database files to work with these programs.

MASS UPDATING

||||➡ **To update multiple records at one time:**

1. **Select Mass Update from the File menu, enter the database name, and press ↵.**
2. **Complete the Retrieve Spec screen and press F10 to display the Update Spec screen.**
3. **Enter update expressions in the appropriate fields, and then press F10.**

In Chapter 11, you learned that you could update records through IA by entering requests such as

Increase credit limit by 10 percent

Statements like this perform a *mass update*, changing all the records that meet the retrieval criteria. You can also change records through the Mass Update option on the File menu.

The first step in a mass update is to designate the records you want to change by filling out the Retrieve Spec screen (press F10 from the screen to update all the records). For example, you might want to increase the price of every item in your inventory, give every employee a 5 percent cost-of-living raise, or update payroll records to adjust for a change in tax rates.

If you want to change selected records, enter the retrieval criteria in the appropriate fields. You can change shipping charges for clients in certain zones, increase prices for your best selling products, or grant a special bonus to employees with the best attendance records.

The next step is to complete the Update Spec screen to specify how you want to change the contents of the fields. The Update Spec screen, shown in Figure 15.1, is similar to the Program Spec screen. Here, you assign a logical field number, such as #1 or #2, to each field you want to reference and enter the equation for the update, using the logical field numbers, in the field to be changed.

In an inventory database, for example, you could increase prices by 10 percent with the equation

Price: #1 = #1 * 1.10

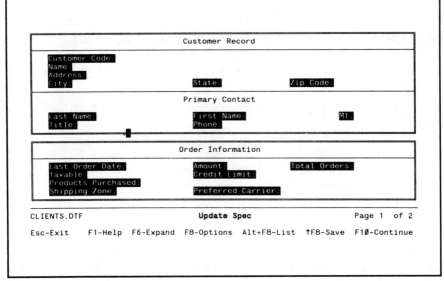

Figure 15.1: Update Spec screen

Q&A designates the field as #1 and then multiplies the value in the Price field by 1.10, which adds 10 percent to the existing value. If you want to lower prices, multiply the field times a number less than one. The expression

    Price: #1 = #1 * .90

reduces every price by 10 percent.

The expression can also be a direct replacement. Suppose that United Parcel Service changes the zone of Margate, New Jersey, to 2. On the Retrieve Spec screen, enter Margate in the City field and NJ in the State field. Then fill in the Update Spec screen with this expression:

    Shipping Zone: #10 = "2"

After you save the specifications by pressing F10, Q&A will scan the database and report the number of records that meet the criteria. You then can choose to confirm each update as it occurs, just as when you change records with IA. If you select to confirm the changes, each record will be displayed, and you can press F10 to skip the record, Shift-F10 to update it and display the next, or Ctrl-F10 to update the remaining records without confirmation.

PERFORMING COMPLEX UPDATES

Suppose that in your inventory database, you want to increase prices by 10 percent for items that are $5.00 or less, but only by 5 percent for items over $5.00.

It might appear that you can accomplish this by performing two updates:

- Retrieve items whose price is $5.00 or less, then increase their prices with the expression #1 = #1 * 1.10 (where #1 is the Price field).

- Retrieve items whose price is over $5.00, then increase their prices with the expression #1 = #1 * 1.05.

Although this procedure appears logically correct, it can lead to mathematical errors. For example, suppose you have an item that sells for $4.95. When you perform the first update, the item will be retrieved (its price is $5.00 or less) and its price raised 10 percent, from $4.95 to $5.45. When you perform the second update, the same item will be retrieved again since it now meets the criteria of being over $5.00. This time, the item's price will be increased by an additional 5 percent, from $5.45 to $5.73. The result is that you actually increased the price 15 percent.

One way to prevent such errors is to choose to confirm each of the changes in the second update. However, you would have to know which items to bypass or take the time to go through the entire database.

You could also change the records for items over $5.00 first, then those for items less than $5.00. This will work properly, but you still must make two complete passes through the database.

A much more efficient way is to update all the records in a single pass by using an If...Then programming command. This command allows you to control the updating on a record-by-record basis. The If...Then command performs an action based on a condition—whether or not the field value meets a test.

The syntax for the statement is

If *condition* Then *expression*

If the condition is met, the expression following the Then is executed. If the condition is not met, no action is performed. For example, the expression

If #1 <=5 Then #1 = #1 * 1.10

means "If the value in field #1 is less than or equal to 5, then increase the value in #1 by 10 percent. If the value is not less than or equal to $5.00, do nothing." This statement alone, however, does not solve our inventory updating problem because it would update only items selling for $5.00 or less.

To update all the records, we have to change items priced $5.00 or less by one amount, and items over $5.00 by another amount in one pass. We can accomplish this by using the If…Then…Else command. The syntax for this command is

If *condition* Then *expression* Else *expression*

When the condition is met, the expression following the Then is executed. If the condition is not met, the expression following the Else is executed. One expression or the other will always be executed.

To perform our inventory database update, we would use the expression

If #1 <=5 Then #1 = #1 * 1.10 Else #1 = #1 * 1.05

which means "If the value in field #1 is less than or equal to 5, then increase the value in #1 by 10 percent; otherwise (Else), increase it by 5 percent."

The fields tested in a condition do not have to be used in the expression.

As an example of a complex update, we will now increase the credit limit by $500 for clients whose total orders are over $2,500, but decrease credit by $500 for clients whose orders total $2,500 or less. The Total Orders field will be used for the condition, and the Credit Limit field and for the expression.

Follow these steps to update the Clients database:

1. Select Mass Update from the File menu, type Clients, and press ↵ to display the Retrieve Spec screen.

2. Press F10 to retrieve all the records. Q&A will display the Update Spec screen.

3. Press ↓ six times, press Tab twice to reach the Total Orders field, and type **#1**.

4. Press ↓ to reach the Credit Limit field, then F6 to expand it.

5. Type the following expression:

#2: If #1 > 2500 Then #2 = #2 + 500 Else #2 = #2 − 500

This means "If the value in field #1 is greater than $2,500, then increase it by $500; otherwise, decrease it by $500."

6. Press F10 to return to the Update Spec screen, and then press F10 to begin the update process. A message will appear showing that ten records will be updated and asking if you want to confirm each one.

7. Press ↵ to confirm the updates. Q&A will display the first form.

8. Press Shift-F10 to update the record.

Since the total orders were exactly $2,500, the credit limit is reduced by $500, from $1500 to $1000. Then the next record appears.

9. Press Ctrl-F10 to update all the remaining records. When Q&A has finished updating the database, the File menu will appear.

10. Press Esc and type **X** to exit.

The Then and Else expressions do not have to relate to the same field. For instance, you could update records to increase the prices of items that sell well or decrease shipping costs for items that are not selling by filling out the Update Spec screen as follows:

```
Shipping Costs: #1
Price: #2
Number Sold: #3: If #3 > 5000 Then #2 = #2 * 1.05 Else #1 = #1 * .95
```

In this case, if the condition is true, field #2 is changed and field #1 remains the same. If the condition is not true, field #2 remains the same and field #1 is changed.

Use caution in performing mass updates. Unless you are absolutely sure you want to update all retrieved records, choose to confirm each change individually. Be particularly careful when you are using conditional expressions, making sure that they mean exactly what you intend.

For example, it may seem that you could have simply reversed the signs in the If statement we used to change credit limits in the Clients database:

#2: If #1 < 2500 Then #2 = #2 − 500 Else #2 = #2 + 500

However, this subtle difference will cause a mistake when a client's total orders are exactly $2,500. The intention is to *decrease* the credit of a client with $2,500 total orders or less, but this second condition would *increase* the credit of clients who ordered exactly $2,500.

In order to accomplish the same update, the condition would have to be entered as

#2: If #1 <= 2500 Then #2 = #2 − 500 Else #2 = #2 + 500

Using AND and OR Operators

Just as a condition can test one field to update another, a condition can test several fields using the AND and OR operators, making the changes depend on two different conditions. For example, suppose you have an inventory database with the field Price assigned #1 and Number Sold assigned #2. You could increase prices of good selling products over $5.00 by 10 percent, and all other products by 5 percent with the expression:

#1: If #1 >$5 AND #2 >5000 Then #1 = #1 * 1.10 Else #1 = #1 * 1.05

For a product's price to be increased by 10 percent, the price must be over $5.00 and you must have sold at least 5000; both conditions must be met for the expression following them to be executed. If both conditions are not met, the price would be increased by 5 percent, including items over $5.00 but which sold 5000 or less, or items less than $5.00 no matter how many sold.

Use OR when you want to execute the expression when one or the other condition is met. For example, the expression

#1: If #1 >$5 OR #2 >5000 Then #1 = #1 * 1.10 Else #1 = #1 * 1.05

would increase prices by 10 percent for all items over $5.00 no matter how many have sold, and for items that sold over 5000 no matter what their price.

AVOIDING COMPLEX CONDITIONS

Any condition in the form If…Then (without the Else) can be replicated by using retrieval criteria. Just substitute each condition with the appropriate criteria on the Retrieve Spec screen.

For example, suppose you want to increase prices for items that sell for less than $1.50 and at least 10,000 have been sold. One way to accomplish this is to press F10 at the Retrieve Spec screen and enter this expression in the Price field on the Update Spec screen:

```
#1: If #1 < $1.50 AND #2 >=10000 Then #1 = #1 1.10
```

However, you could avoid writing a condition entirely by using these criteria on the Retrieve Spec screen:

```
Price: < 1.5
Number Sold: >= 10000
```

Then enter this simple expression in the Price field of the Update Spec screen:

```
#1 = #1 * 1.10
```

Because only the records that meet both retrieval criteria would be located, the intention would be fulfilled.

If you have a complex expression with more than one AND condition, you can substitute retrieval criteria for any number of them. Suppose you want to decrease prices for poorly selling items that are over $5.00 and that were received before January 1, 1991. Assuming the field Received On is assigned #3, an AND condition would appear like this:

```
#1: If #1 > 5 AND #2 < 1000 AND #3 > 1/1/91 Then #1 = #1 * .85
```

You could accomplish the same function using any of the following combinations:

Retrieve Spec	**Update Spec**
Price: > 5	Price: #1 = #1 * .85
Number Sold: < 1000	
Received On: > 1/1/91	

Price:	Price: #1: If #1 > 5 Then #1 = #1 * .85
Number Sold: < 1000	
Received On: > 1/1/91	

Price:	Price: #1: If #1 > 5 AND #2 <1000 Then #1 = #1 * .85
Number Sold:	Number Sold: #2
Received On: > 1/1/91	

CONSTRUCTING COMPOUND IF STATEMENTS

All the If statements discussed so far contain simple Then and Else expressions. This means that in each case, only one expression was executed. Although you can link several conditions together with AND, you cannot perform more than one action.

If you want two or more actions to be performed when a condition is true, you could repeat the condition in more than one field. For example, to change the shipping zone to 1 and the preferred carrier to Roadway Express for all clients in Philadelphia, complete the Update Spec screen like this:

```
City: #1
Shipping Zone: #2: If #1 = "Philadelphia" Then #2 = 1
Preferred Carrier: #3: If #1 = "Philadelphia" Then #3 = "Roadway
Express"
```

However, it would be easier to accomplish the same function by just retrieving all Philadelphia clients and completing the Update Spec screen like this:

Shipping Zone: #2 = 1
Preferred Carrier: #3 = "Roadway Express"

But what if your condition required an Else expression? You could not simply substitute retrieval criteria for the condition. In this case, you would have to construct a compound expression.

A compound expression for a simple If…Then statement has the syntax

If *condition* Then Begin *expression1*; *expression2;£expression* End

This means "If the condition is true, then begin the following series of expressions."

The compound expression starts with the word Begin and is followed by the statements you want performed, separated by semicolons. Place the word End after the last expression. Do *not* enter a semicolon between the last expression and the word End.

For example, to update the shipping zone and preferred carrier, enter a compound expression like this:

City: #1
Shipping Zone: #2
Preferred Carrier: #3: If #1 = "Philadelphia" Then Begin #2 = 1;
#3 = "Roadway Express" End

In an If…Then…Else statement, either expression or both may be compound, as in

If *condition* Then Begin *expression1; expression2;£expressionN* End
Else Begin expression1; *expression2;£expressionN* End

If *condition* Then *expression* Else Begin e*xpression1; expression2;£expressionN* End

If *condition* Then Begin *expression1; expression2;£expressionN* End
Else *expression*

THE POSTING PROCESS

III▶ To post values from one database to another:

1. Select Post from the File menu, enter the source database name, and press ↵.
2. Enter the name of the destination (or external) database and press ↵.
3. Complete the Retrieve Spec screen, and then press F10 to display the Posting Spec screen.
4. At each field you want to post, press F7 to display the posting box and fill in the information.
5. To save the posting specification, press Shift-F8, type the name, and press ↵.
6. To post records, press Alt-F8 from the Posting Spec screen, choose the specification, and press F10.

Posting is similar to updating in that it changes the contents of database fields. When you *post*, however, the new values come from another database. During the posting process, Q&A copies the fields you designate from one database to the fields you designate in the other database.

Posting requires two databases: a *source database*, which contains the existing values, and a *destination database*, which will receive the values. The databases do not have to have the same design, but the fields you post from must be the same type as the fields to which you post.

The two databases must have a common match field. A *match field* is a field that will be used to match records in one database to those in another. Having a match field means that both databases relate to the same entity; both contain records about the same clients, students, inventory items, or other information that the database contains. The destination database must be indexed on the match field (use the Speed Up Searches option on the Customize menu to index the database, as explained in Chapter 14).

As an example, suppose that you have these two databases:

Roster Database		**Student Database**		
Student Number:		ID:		
Semester:		Name:		
Locker #:		Address:		
Class 1:	Grade:	City:	State:	Zip:
Class 2:	Grade:	Telephone:		
Class 3:	Grade:	GPA:		
Class 4:	Grade:			
Class 5:	Grade:			
Average:				

Both databases relate to students in a school and include a field that contains the identifying number of the student referred to in the record. The field is called Student Number in the Roster database, ID in the Student database. When these fields contain the same value, it means that they refer to the same student. The records are said to be matched, and data from one can be posted to the other.

After a student's grades are entered into the Roster database and averaged, you can post the average to the GPA field of the Student database, using Student Number and ID as the match field.

After your source and destination databases are prepared, you define a posting specification to tell Q&A which fields should be posted and how the values should be combined.

Choose Post from the File menu and enter the name of the source database, then enter the name of the destination database. Q&A displays the Retrieve Spec screen, which you can complete to post to specific records. Next, it displays the Posting Spec screen. Select the first field to be posted, and then press F7 to display the posting box. Specify the field to be posted to and the match field, as well as the operation for combining the values. You can choose from the following operations:

- Replace: The value in the source database field will replace the value in the destination database field.

- Add: The value in the source database field will be added to the value in the destination database field.

- Subtract: The value in the source database field will be subtracted from the value in the destination database field.

- Multiply: The value in the source database field will be multiplied by the value in the destination database field.

- Divide: The value in the source database field will be divided into the value in the destination database field. If the value in the source field is zero, the destination field will remain unchanged (no error will occur).

To actually post the records, press Alt-F8 from the Posting Spec screen to get the posting specification, and then press F10 to begin the process.

SETTING UP A
TRANSACTION-ORIENTED SYSTEM

Posting is a common technique used in business applications. In Chapter 16, you will learn how to prepare client invoices and automatically post the invoice date and amount to the Clients database. In this chapter, we will use posting to solve a problem that developed back in Chapter 4.

When you created the Clients database, you programmed the Total Orders field to accumulate the values in the Amount field. But unfortunately, every time you press F8 to issue the Calculate command, the amount is calculated whether or not a new invoice had been recorded. If you press F8 to calculate the age, which was also programmed, the Total

Orders field would accumulate again. Without realizing it, you could be adding the same amount to the total orders again and again.

There is also another problem with the database. Most of the fields in the Client database will not change very often. It is a *master database* in that it contains data that you will need to refer to but not records of individual transactions. The only fields that will change frequently are Last Order Date, Amount, and Total Orders.

In order to update these fields, you must retrieve the client's entire record and move down to the fields, which are near the bottom of the form. Not only is this a waste of time, but it keeps the Client database open and susceptible to problems for longer than necessary.

You can solve both of these problems by posting. What you will create is called a *transaction-oriented* system. It will allow you to leave the master database, Clients, closed as much as possible and add the record of daily orders to a transaction file. When you want to update the master file, you will post the order date and amount from the transaction file and update the accumulated total orders at the same time.

We will create this system in five steps:

- Reprogram the Clients form to remove the total orders accumulator.

- Create a transaction database to contain the records of daily orders.

- Define the posting specification for transferring information from one database to another.

- Create an archive database to hold the transactions after they have been posted.

- Create a posting macro to perform the posting, copy the transaction records to the archive database file, and then remove all records from the transaction database file to begin a new transaction cycle.

This system ensures that transactions are not mistakenly posted twice (by removing them from the transaction database) but saves them for future reference (by copying them to the archive database).

REPROGRAMMING THE CLIENTS DATABASE

Since we are designing the posting procedure to accumulate the Total Orders field, you have to delete the programming statement that you added in Chapter 4. To remove a programming statement, delete it from the Program Spec screen.

Follow these steps to reprogram the Clients database:

1. Start Q&A and choose Design File from the File menu, then Program a File.

2. Type **Clients** and press ↵ to display the Programming menu.

3. Select Program Form to display the Program Spec screen.

4. Press ↓ six times, then Tab twice to reach the Total Orders field.

5. Press F6 to expand the field, then Shift-F4 to delete the programming instruction.

6. Press F10 twice, then Esc to return to the Design menu.

CREATING THE TRANSACTION DATABASE

The next step is to create the database that will hold the transactions before they are posted. It will be a small one with only four fields: three fields that we will be posting to Clients plus a match field for matching records.

Follow these steps to create the CPost database:

1. Select Design a New File, type **CPost**, and press ↵.

2. Type the following field labels for the form:

   Client Code:

   Order Date:

   Amount:

   Accumulate:

3. Press F10 to display the Format Spec screen.

4. Press ↵ to accept Client Code as a text field and reach the Order Date field, and then type **D** to designate it as a date field.

5. Press ↵ to reach the Amount field and type **M** to make it a money field.

6. Press ↵ to reach the Accumulate field and type **M**.

7. Press F10 twice to accept the default Global Options settings and display the File menu.

Now you need to customize the CPost database so its fields are consistent with those in Clients.

8. Select Design File, choose Customize a File, and then press ↵ to accept CPost.

9. Select Restrict Values to display the Restrict Spec screen.

10. Press F6 to expand the field, type **!1??;2??;300**, and press F10.

11. Press ↵ to reach the Order Date field and type **>=1/1/91**.

12. Press ↵ to reach the Amount field and type **50..1500**.

13. Press F10 to return to the Customize menu.

14. Select Field Template to display the Field Template Spec screen.

15. Type **999**, and then press F10 to return to the Customize menu.

We will use the Amount field in CPost to update the Amount field in Clients. Since you can only post a field to one field in the destination database, you will use the Accumulate field to update the Total Orders field. Instead of having to enter the number twice in the same record, you can program CPost to do so automatically.

16. Press Esc to return to the Design menu.

17. Select Program a File and press ↵ to accept CPost.

18. Select Program Form.

19. Press ↵ twice to reach the Amount field and type **#1**.

20. Press ↵ to reach the Accumulate field and type **#2 = #1**.

21. Press F10 to save the form, then Esc twice to return to the File menu.

Setting Automatic Calculations

By default, Q&A does not perform the program calculations in fields until you press F8. If you forget to press F8 after updating a record, programmed fields could contain the wrong data, such as a total orders value that was not accumulated by the last order. In the CPost database, manual calculation would force you to press F8 after entering each record. If you do not, the figure in the Amount field will not be carried down to the Accumulate field, and it would not be added to Total Orders field during the posting process.

When you change the default calculation mode for the database to automatic, Q&A will calculate all the fields for you.

Before you add transactions to the CPost file, follow these steps to set the calculation mode to automatic:

1. Select Add Data from the File menu and press ↵ to accept CPost.

2. Press Shift-F8 to display the calculation mode options, as shown in Figure 15.2.

3. Type **A** to choose Automatic, and then press F10 to return to the form.

Now when you make an entry or edit the Amount field, then move to the next field, the value will be moved to the Accumulate field because of

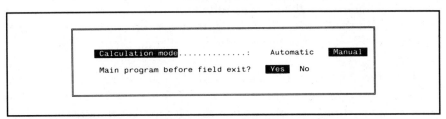

Figure 15.2: Calculation mode options

the calculation #2 = #1. If you do not change the field, no calculation will be performed.

It might appear that you could use automatic calculation to solve the accumulator problem in the Clients database. In fact, if Total Orders were the only programmed field, automatic calculation would be useful. You would not have to press F8 at all, and Total Orders would be accumulated only when you updated the Amount field.

But now the fine print: every time automatic calculation is triggered, it recalculates *every* programmed field in the form, even those which reference fields that have not been updated.

For example, suppose you have to change the primary contact for one of your clients. You retrieve the form and update the Name, Title, and Phone fields on the first page. You then press PgDn to move to the second page. Since you did not update the Amount field, the Total Orders field would not be accumulated. So far, so good.

On the second page of the form, you edit the date of birth to update it for the new contact. When you leave the field, Q&A triggers automatic calculation, and the age is inserted in the Age field. However, automatic calculation also recalculated the Total Orders field on the first page, even though the Amount field was not changed.

Automatic calculation is useful, but it does not solve the problem inherent in accumulators and counters.

Adding Current Transactions

The CPost file will contain a record of current transactions before they have been posted to the master file.

Each time a client places an order, the client number, date, and amount of the order will be inserted as another record. Since records are added as the transactions occur, the file will automatically be in date order, but not necessarily in client order. Depending on how often you post the records, you might have several transactions for a particular client, the most recent toward the end of the file.

In an invoicing system, each transaction would also include the code, quantity, and price of each item ordered. The record would be used to print an invoice and perhaps a packing order for the warehouse, as well as to update the master file. You will build this system in Chapter 16.

Now enter the first transaction in CPost:

1. For Client Code, type **101**.
2. Press ↵ to reach the Order Date field and type **3/5/92**.
3. Press ↵ to reach the Amount field, type **546**, and press ↵.

The amount is formatted and automatically copied to the Accumulate field.

4. Press F10 to display another blank form.
5. Enter the remaining transactions:

> Client Code: **105**
> Order Date: **3/7/92**
> Amount: **183**

> Client Code: **108**
> Order Date: **3/7/92**
> Amount: **297**

> Client Code: **102**
> Order Date: **3/9/92**
> Amount: **612**

> Client Code: **101**
> Order Date: **3/1/92**
> Amount: **364**

Client Code: **106**

Order Date: **3/10/92**

Amount: **611**

6. Press Shift-F10 after entering the last transaction to return to the File menu.

DEFINING THE POSTING SPECIFICATION

Although the posting macro will use the posting specification, we will not record the keystrokes while defining the specification. Instead, we will save it and then record the keystrokes for getting the posting specification from the List Manager screen. This will reduce the number of macro keystrokes.

Follow these steps to define the posting specification:

1. Select Post from the File menu. Q&A will prompt you for the name of the file you are posting from, the source database.

2. Press Shift-F4, type **CPost**, and press ↵. You will be prompted to enter the name of the file you are posting to, the destination database.

3. Press Shift-F4, type **Clients**, and press ↵ to display the Retrieve Spec screen.

When you want to post only specific records, enter the retrieval criteria here.

4. Press F10 to display the Posting Spec screen, as shown in Figure 15.3.

In this example, Client Code will be used as the match field, but it will not be posted to any field in the master file. However, match fields can be posted.

5. Press ⏎ to reach the Order Date field, and then press F7 to display the posting box, as shown in Figure 15.4.

You use this box to specify where the fields in the source database will be posted in the destination database. The current field label appears at the first prompt.

6. Type **Last Order Date** as the external field you want Order Date posted to.

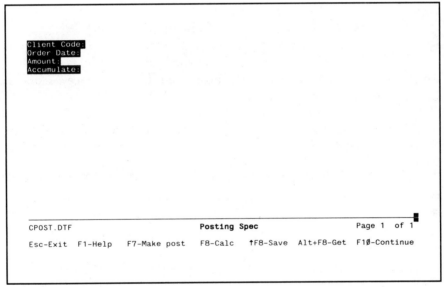

Figure 15.3: Posting Spec screen

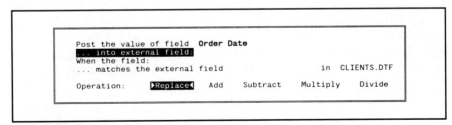

Figure 15.4: Posting box

If you are not sure of the name of the field, you can press Alt-F7 to display available fields in the destination database.

7. Press ↵ to reach the next prompt, which is where you enter the name of the match field in the source database, and type **Client Code**.

8. Press ↵ and enter the name of the match field in the destination database, **Customer Code**.

Remember, you can have only one external match field in a posting operation, and it must be an indexed field.

The operation choices at the bottom of the posting box include Replace, Add, Subtract, Multiply, and Divide, which combine values from the source database with those in the destination database as described earlier in the chapter. We want the CPost order date to replace the one in Clients, which is the default setting.

9. Press F10 to save the posting box and accept the default Replace operation.

On the Posting Spec screen, the word *post* appears after the Order Date field label, indicating that it will be posted to the destination database.

10. Press ↵ to reach the Amount field, then F7 to display the posting box.

11. Type **Amount** as the name of the field you want to post the value to.

In this case, we want to match all the records on the same two fields, Client Code and Customer Code. You can use a different match field in the source database for each posted field, but you can have only one matched field in the destination database. If you enter a new field at the matches the external field prompt, Q&A will warn you that changing the destination match field here will change it for all the fields you already entered. You can choose Yes to continue or No to cancel the entry.

12. Press F10 to accept the default match fields and operation.

13. Press ↵, then F7 to display the posting box for the Accumulate field.

14. Type **Total Orders**, and then press ↵ three times to reach the Operation options.

15. Select Add, and then press F10.

16. To save the specification, press Shift-F8, type **Post Transactions**, and press ↵.

17. Press Esc to return to the File menu.

CREATING THE ARCHIVE DATABASE FILE

When you *archive* transactions, you save them in a special file that you can place in long-term storage. Archive files are stored on tape, removable hard-disk media, or floppy disks.

Before creating the posting macro, follow these steps to create the Archive database:

1. From the File menu, select Design File, choose Design a New File, type **Archive**, and press ↵.

2. Type the following form:

   Client Code:

   Order Date:

   Amount:

Since the Accumulate field stores a duplicate value only used for posting, it is not needed in the archive file.

3. Press F10 to display the Format Spec screen.

4. Press ↵ to accept Client Code as a text field and reach the Order Date field, and then type **D**.

5. Press ↵ to reach the Amount field and type **M**.

6. Press F10 to display the Global Options menu.

7. Press F10 to accept the default settings and to display the File menu.

Creating a separate macro for archiving and purging the transaction records and embedding it in the posting macro would make the posting macro smaller and faster, but it would also provide the opportunity to run the macro by itself, archiving and purging the transaction records before they have been posted. In this case, it is better to accept a large posting macro than take the chance of such an error.

CREATING THE POSTING MACRO

Now that the posting specification and archive file have been created, you can define the macro that posts and archives the transactions, and then removes the records to prepare the transaction file for the next period.

Start defining the macro by actually posting the records in CPost to Clients.

1. Press Esc to display the Main menu.

2. Press Shift-F2 and choose Define Macro.

3. Press Alt-P.

4. Select Post from the File menu.

5. Press Shift-F4, type **CPost**, and press ↵.

6. Press Shift-F4, type **Clients**, and press ↵.

7. Press F10 to display the Posting Spec screen.

8. Press Alt-F8, type **Post Transactions**, and press ↵. Do not select the posting specification from the List Manager screen using the arrow keys, because it will not always be in the same position in the list.

9. Press F10 to begin the posting process.

Q&A scans the source database, displaying each record briefly on the screen. It then scans the destination database and displays a message showing the number of records that will be updated and asking if you want to confirm each posting.

10. Type **N** to post the records. The destination records will appear on the screen as each posting is completed, and then the File menu will reappear.

You cannot select to confirm the postings while defining the macro because then only those records would be posted every time the macro is run. If you select to confirm postings, each record will be displayed. You can press F10 to skip the record, Shift-F10 to post to it and display the next, or Ctrl-F10 to post all the remaining records without confirmation.

Now that the records in CPost have actually been posted, you can complete the macro by archiving and purging the transaction records.

11. Type **C** to select Copy and press ↵ to accept CPost.

12. Type **S** to choose selected records.

13. Press Shift-F4, type **Archive**, and press ↵.

14. Press F10 to retrieve all the records and display the Merge Spec screen.

15. Press F10 to merge all the fields. The File menu will reappear.

16. To purge the records from the transaction file, type **R** to select Remove.

17. Press Shift-F4, type **CPost**, and press ↵.

18. Type **S**, press F10, and type **Y** to delete all the records.

19. Press Esc twice to return to the Main menu.

20. Press Shift-F2 and type **Post Transactions**.

21.   Press ⏎ to reach the Show Screen option and type **N**.

22.   Press F10, then ⏎ to save the macro.

After posting, Q&A creates an ASCII text file called the posting transaction log. The file has the same name as the source file with a PST extension, CPOST.PST.

The log contains the names of the source and destination databases,
the contents of source key fields that had no matches in the destination
database, and a list of any errors that may have occurred during the posting process. If the posting was entirely successful, the log file will contain
these entries:

```
Source Filename: C:\QA\CPost.DTF
Destination Filename: C:\QA\Clients.DTF
No Errors
```

You can review the log file by bringing it into Q&A Write.

USING THE SYSTEM

The completed system allows you to record transactions as they occur
without accessing the master database. Add the transactions to the CPost
database.

At certain intervals, post the current transactions to the master file.
Posting will update the Clients database so it contains the date and
amount of the most recent order and the accumulated total orders. The
transaction file is in date order. If a client has more than one current transaction, such as two orders in the same day or between postings, the most
recent one will appear in the Last Order Date and Amount fields, but all
of them will be accumulated in the Total Orders field.

When you are ready to update the master file, display the Main menu
and press Alt-P. The transactions will be posted and archived, and then the
CPost file will be purged.

We designed the macro to run from the Main menu so you can add it
to that menu. To run the macro from any other location, edit it as explained
in Chapter 13.

CREATING NEW DATABASES

As you build your database applications, you will most likely have several databases that contain information about the same entity. With Q&A, it is easy to create a new database from two or more existing ones.

How you create the database depends on whether or not the two source databases have a match field. If they have a common field, you can build a new database by posting. If not, the existing records can be combined with the File Copy command.

CREATING A DATABASE BY POSTING

When two database forms have a matching field, you can combine fields from each to create a composite form in a new database.

Look back at the Student and Roster databases shown at the beginning of the section about posting. Suppose that after setting up these databases, you realize that you will have to notify the parents of students who have not yet cleaned out their lockers. You want to create a new database with the fields ID, Locker #, Name, and Telephone. (In Chapter 16, you will learn how to get this type of information by combining data from several databases in a printed report.)

First, you would create a database with the four fields, making sure that they have the same templates and restrictions as the corresponding fields in the Roster and Student databases. Second, copy the Student Number and Locker # fields from Roster to the corresponding fields in the new database. Finally, post the Name and Telephone fields from Students to the new database, using ID as the match field. The records of students who were not assigned a locker for the semester would not be copied to the new database.

USING FILE COPY
TO CREATE A DATABASE

▐▐▐▶ **To copy records to a database with a different form:**

    1. **Select Copy from the File menu and enter the name of the source database.**

2. **Choose Select Records and enter the name of the destination database.**
3. **Complete the Retrieve Spec screen and press F10.**
4. **Complete the Merge Spec screen by numbering the fields in the order you want them copied.**
5. **Press F10 to begin copying.**

The Copy command on the File menu can be used to copy records between databases that have different forms, as long as they contain fields with similar information. When you copy the records, Q&A merely inserts each field from one database into a field in the other database, without regard for field labels or field types.

If you do not specify fields on the Merge Spec screen, the first field in the source database will be moved to the first field in the destination database, the second to the second field, and so forth. This is fine as long as the forms are identical because entire records will be copied to matching fields. However, it can cause problems when the forms are not the same. For example, here is an example of the results of copying a record between databases that have forms with different fields:

Source Database	**Destination Database**
Name: Alvin Aardvark	Item Code: Alvin Aardvark
Address: 406 West 9th	Quantity: 406 West 9th
City: Newark	Price: Newark
State: NJ	
Zip: 08123	
Product: 101	
Cost: 5.67	
Amount: 456	

The values were copied on a field-to-field basis, even though they are totally inappropriate.

To copy just the Product, Cost, and Amount fields to the destination database, you must complete the Merge Spec screen like this:

```
Name:
Address:
City:
State:
Zip:
Product: 1
Cost: 3
Amount: 2
```

The Product field will be copied to the first destination field, Amount to the second, and Cost to the third.

Using this technique, you could create a database that contains records from several others. For example, suppose you want to create a master mailing list of clients and vendors. The database you are copying to must exist, so you would first create a database with the design shown in Figure 15.5. Make sure that the fields are the same type as in the Clients and Vendors databases and that they have the same templates and restrictions. Then copy the records from one of the databases, either Clients or Vendors, by numbering fields on the Merge Spec screen, as shown in Figure 15.6. Finally, copy records from the other database using the same merge

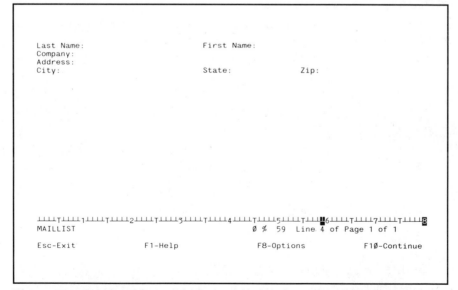

Figure 15.5: Database for combining addresses from the Clients and Vendors databases

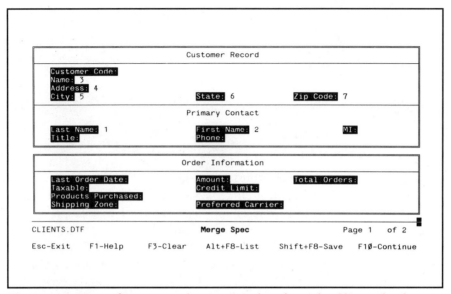

Figure 15.6: Merge Spec screen for copying data from the Clients database to a master mailing list database

specification. The resulting database will include the names and addresses of clients and vendors.

When you copy records this way, you are producing a database on a record-by-record basis. The field values from each record in the source database are used to create records in the destination database. Information from each database cannot be placed in the same record in the destination database. To combine information from each database into a composite record, you must use posting, which requires that the databases have a common match field.

IMPORTING DATABASE AND SPREADSHEET FILES

Perhaps before you purchased Q&A, you maintained your records using another database program. Now that you've seen how powerful

Q&A is, you might want to use the same data in a Q&A database. This way, you will be able to quickly generate sophisticated reports and access the information with IA—functions you cannot perform with the other program.

Or perhaps you have a disk full of records from an associate or friend who isn't lucky enough to own Q&A. He or she created the database using one of the more complex and limited database programs on the market.

Or maybe you entered a detailed spreadsheet into Lotus 1-2-3 to produce charts and graphs. Now that they are printed, you would like to use the same information in your database.

Rather than retype all the other database program or spreadsheet program data, you can convert the disk file to Q&A format through a process called *importing*, as explained in the following sections.

IMPORTING DATABASE FILES

To create a Q&A database from a dBASE, PFS:File, IBM Filing Assistant, or Paradox file:

1. Select Utilities from the File menu, then Import Data.
2. Select the format of the file you are importing.
3. Type the path and name of the file you are importing, then the name of the Q&A formatted file you are creating.
4. Complete the Format Spec screen and press F10.
5. Complete the Global Options menu (if it appears) and press F10.
6. Complete the Merge Spec screen and press F10.

When you import files created by dBASE, PFS:File, IBM Filing Assistant, or Paradox, Q&A can create the form and copy the records all in one step. The form will contain all the field labels in the original, although you can designate which fields you want copied and change their order. Fields that you do not copy to the new database are left blank.

You can also convert and copy the data to an existing database. This gives you the capability to create a database with only selected fields. When you import data to an existing database, Q&A adds the records without affecting any existing data.

To import a file created by dBASE, PFS:File, IBM Filing Assistant, or Paradox, follow these steps:

1. Select Utilities from the File menu, and then choose Import Data to display the Import menu shown in Figure 15.7.

2. Choose the format of the file you are importing, and Q&A will prompt you for its name.

3. Type the path and file name and press ↵. Q&A will prompt you for the name of the file you want to create or copy the data to.

4. Type the path and file name of the Q&A formatted file and press ↵.

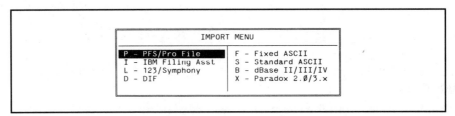

Figure 15.7: File Utilities Import menu

If the Q&A file does not exist, the Format Spec screen will appear. When you import PFS:File and IBM Filing Assistant files, all fields will be designated as text. With dBASE and Paradox files, the existing field types are displayed on this screen.

When you are importing data into an existing Q&A file, the field types are already assigned, so you can skip the next step.

5. Make any type and format changes, and then press F10. If there are any date, hours, number, or money fields, the Global Options menu will appear. Select options on the menu and press F10 to display the Merge Spec screen.

You use the Merge Spec screen to designate which fields you want to import and in what order.

6. Complete the Merge Spec screen and press F10.

If you want to copy the fields on a one-to-one basis, in the same order they occur in the original database, you do not need to fill in the Merge Spec screen. The fields will be converted and then copied, just as they would if you had used the File Copy command.

To copy selected fields, use the Merge Spec screen to number them according to the field locations in the original file. For example, place a 1 next to the field label that you want to receive the first field in the original, 2 next to the label to receive the second field, and so on. You do not have to copy all the fields. If there are more fields in the source file than in the destination file, the extra fields are ignored. If there are more fields in the destination file, they are left blank.

The critical point is to maintain the proper field types. As an example, suppose you are importing a database file with this design:

```
Employee #:
Name:
Department:        Hourly Rate:
Overtime Status:    Union:
```

The fields are ordered from top left to bottom right.

If you want Q&A to create the database but only copy the first four fields, fill in the Merge Spec screen this way:

```
Employee #: 1
Name: 2
Department: 3
Hourly Rate: 4
Overtime Status:
Union:
```

If you enter the numbers in any other order, the values will be copied to inappropriate fields.

Now suppose you already have an employee database and you want to import a few selected fields. The Merge Spec screen will display the form of the existing database, and you could number the fields like this:

```
Name: 2
Address:
City:          State:          Zip:
Telephone:
Salary: 4
Work Location: 3          Supervisor:
```

Q&A will not warn you if you fill in the Merge Spec screen incorrectly, such as when you are importing a text value into a numeric field.

If your PFS:File or IBM Filing Assistant file is more than ten pages or includes zero-length fields, you must modify the source file before importing it. If it contains attachment fields, you must add fields to the destination database.

Q&A can import only Paradox version 2 and above files. If you created your files with version 1, upgrade and convert the files before importing them.

IMPORTING SPREADSHEET FILES

IIII➤ To import a Lotus 1-2-3 or Symphony spreadsheet into an existing Q&A database:

1. Select Utilities from the File menu, then Import Data.
2. Select the 123/Symphony option.
3. Type the path and name of the file you are importing, then the name of the existing Q&A database.
4. Complete the Define Range screen.
5. To specify fields, press F8 and complete the Merge Spec screen.
6. Press F10 to import the file.

You can also import spreadsheets created by Lotus 1-2-3 (except version 3.0), Symphony, and compatible programs, but you must first create the database yourself. Each spreadsheet row becomes a record, and each cell a field. Cells that contain formulas are imported as values, so the formulas are calculated before the spreadsheet is imported into the database.

Before importing the spreadsheet, print a copy of it so you can refer to the row and column numbers. Import the values only, not column headings. The headings identify each column in the spreadsheet; your field labels will be used in the database.

Follow these steps to import a Lotus 1-2-3 or Symphony file:

1. In Q&A, create a database that contains a field for each column in the spreadsheet.

2. Select Utilities from the File menu, and then choose Import Data.

3. Select 123/Symphony from the Import menu.

4. Type the path and name of the spreadsheet file, or select it from the List Manager screen.

5. Type the path and name of the Q&A database file. Q&A will display the Define Range screen, as shown in Figure 15.8.

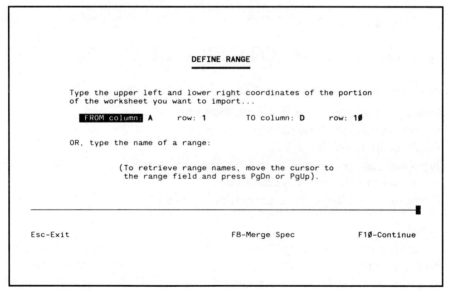

Figure 15.8: Define Range screen

If you want to import the entire spreadsheet, skip the next step.

6. Enter the range of cells you want to import.

Type the column letter and row number of the cell in the top-left corner of the range at the from column and row prompts, respectively. Type the column letter and row number of the cell in the lower-right corner of the range at the to column and row prompts, respectively. To import a named range, type its name at the range name prompt. You can press PgUp or PgDn to display a list of named ranges.

7. If you want to specify fields and their order, press F8 to display the Merge Spec screen, complete the screen, and press F10.

On the Merge Spec screen, cell or field numbers are relative to the range. If the upper-left corner of the range is A4, then cell A4 is field #1.

8. Press F10 to import the file.

The first row of the spreadsheet range will be imported into the first record, each cell becoming its own field.

IMPORTING OTHER FILE FORMATS

To import another file type into an existing Q&A database:

1. Select Utilities from the File menu, then Import Data.
2. Select the format of the file you are importing: DIF, Standard ASCII, or Fixed ASCII.
3. Type the path and name of the file you are importing, then the name of the existing Q&A database.
4. Complete the Merge Spec screen and press F10.

If your data was created by a program that is not listed on the Import menu, you may still be able to import it into Q&A. Most programs can store data in at least one of three generic formats: DIF, Standard ASCII, and

Fixed-Width ASCII. Save the file in one of these formats, then create a Q&A database to accept the data before you import it.

Importing DIF Files

DIF (Data Interchange Format) files are ASCII text with each field stored on its own line. DIF refers to each record as a *tuple*, and each field as a *vector*. Spreadsheet programs such as Visicalc and Supercalc, as well as many database programs, use this format. In addition to field values, the file contains information detailing where each vector belongs in relation to tuples.

If you created the DIF file from a spreadsheet program, the vector numbers will correspond to the cell numbers. (See the section on importing Lotus 1-2-3 files for information about cell numbers.) If the file is from a database program, the vector numbers correspond to the field numbers.

Select DIF from the File Utilities Import menu, enter the path and name of the source file, and then enter the path and name of the Q&A destination file. The Merge Spec screen will appear. Press F10 to import the entire file, or enter the vector numbers next to the field labels to import selected data.

Importing Standard ASCII Files

Standard ASCII files are also known as *delimited* or *variable-length ASCII*. The commas, called *delimiters*, indicate where one field ends and the next begins. The fields do not appear neatly aligned in columns because each takes up just the space it requires—each is of variable length.

Text in a standard ASCII file will appear something like this:

```
"101","Chesin Pharmacy, Inc.","182 Walnut Street",
"Newark","NJ","08192"
"102","Williams Engine Company","347 West Fifth Street",
"Newark","NJ","08126"
```

Each record is on one line, which ends with a carriage return/line feed character. The fields are separated by commas or some other punctuation mark, and text fields are often surrounded by quotation marks. You can usually select the delimiter and whether or not to use quotation marks when saving the file.

In most cases, the field numbers correspond to the cell in the spreadsheet or the database field in the original program. If you are not sure, bring the file into Q&A Write as an ASCII file and look at the format of each line. In the above example, you can tell that the name is the first field, the address is the second, and so on.

Select Standard ASCII from the File Utilities Import menu, enter the path and name of the source file, and then enter the path and name of the Q&A file. The Merge Spec screen will appear. Press F10 to import the entire file, or enter the field numbers next to the field labels to import selected data.

Importing Fixed ASCII Files

Fixed ASCII files do not use delimiters to separate fields. Instead, each field is assigned a specific number of character spaces, so they align neatly in columns like this:

101 Chesin Pharmacy, Inc	182 Walnut Street	Newark NJ
102 Williams Engine Comp	347 West Fifth Street	Newark NJ

The software knows where each field is by its starting position on the line and its length. For example, the customer code starts at position 1 and is 3 characters long; the name begins at position 5 and is 20 characters long. Fields that do not take up all of the positions are padded with blank spaces.

Most programs that save data in this format use the field length to determine the number of characters assigned to each field, and some add an extra space between fields. A few programs let you specify the beginning position and length manually.

To bring in this type of file, select Fixed ASCII from the File Utilities Import menu. Enter the path and name of the source file, then the path and name of the Q&A file. The Merge Spec screen will appear. When you import a file in Fixed ASCII format, you must complete the Merge Spec screen.

For each field you want to import, enter the starting position of the data and the number of characters, separated by a comma. For example, if you were importing the data illustrated above, the Merge Spec screen would include these fields:

```
Customer Code: 1,3
Name: 5, 20
Address: 26, 21
City: 48, 7
State: 57, 2
```

Q&A will insert into the Customer Code field the three characters that start at position 1. It will then insert into the Name field the 20 characters that start at position 5, and so on until all the fields specified on the Merge Spec screen have been imported.

If you are not sure about the spacing in a fixed ASCII file, bring the file into Q&A Write. Use the cursor, ruler, and position indicator on the status line to determine the starting position and length of each field.

EXPORTING DATABASE FILES

To use a Q&A database file with another program:

1. **Select Utilities from the File menu, then Export Data.**
2. **Select the format of the destination file.**
3. **Type the name of the Q&A file, then the name of the file you want to create.**

4. **Complete the Retrieve Spec screen and press F10.**
5. **Complete the Merge Spec screen and press F10.**

You might want to share data with an associate who does not have Q&A, or use your database to prepare graphics or perform more sophisticated statistical calculations with programs such as SPSS. You convert a Q&A database so it can be used by another program in a process called *exporting.*

To export a file, choose Export Data from the File Utilities menu. Q&A lets you export a database to the formats listed in Figure 15.9, which shows the File Utilities Export menu. Although there is no option for Lotus 1-2-3, that program can import files in dBASE or DIF format. If you want to use a Q&A database to prepare graphs and charts in Lotus 1-2-3, save it as a DIF or dBASE file, and then import it into 1-2-3 using that program's transfer facility.

Each export option lets you complete retrieval and merge specfications. Designate the records you want to export on the Retrieve Spec screen, and specify the fields on the Merge Spec screen. For Fixed ASCII files, you have to designate the starting position and length of each field on the Merge Spec screen.

When you select Standard ASCII, you will have the opportunity to select delimiters from the ASCII Options menu, shown in Figure 15.10. Press F10 to select the most common formats, or choose new settings. Before changing the default values, however, make sure the resulting file can be imported by the program you plan to use.

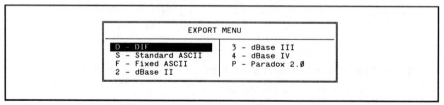

Figure 15.9: File Utilities Export menu

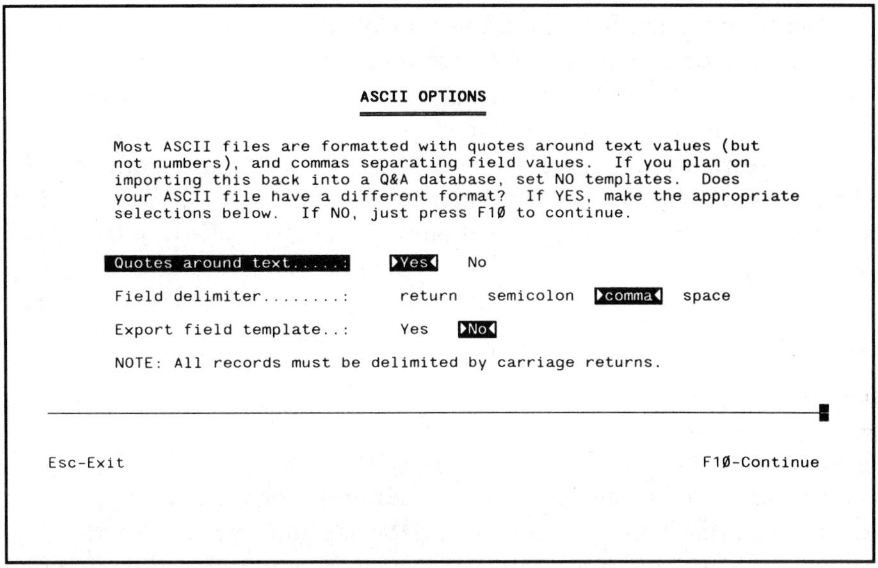

```
                         ASCII OPTIONS

        Most ASCII files are formatted with quotes around text values (but
        not numbers), and commas separating field values.  If you plan on
        importing this back into a Q&A database, set NO templates.  Does
        your ASCII file have a different format?  If YES, make the appropriate
        selections below.  If NO, just press F1Ø to continue.


    ░Quotes around text......░      ▸Yes◂   No

        Field delimiter........:    return   semicolon  ▸comma◂  space

        Export field template..:    Yes    ▸No◂

        NOTE: All records must be delimited by carriage returns.


    _____▪


    Esc-Exit                                              F1Ø-Continue

```

Figure 15.10: ASCII Options menu

RECOVERING A DAMAGED DATABASE

||||▶ To recover a damaged database:

1. Make a backup copy of the damaged database.
2. Select Utilities from the File menu, then Recover Database.

The more you access your database, the greater chance there is of it becoming damaged. However, the most common cause of damage is turning off or rebooting your computer while the file is being used.

If you have trouble accessing a file, or Q&A displays a warning that the file has been damaged, you might be able to correct the problem by using the Recover Database command.

The recovery procedure modifies the file directly, so if it fails, the file may be more damaged than it was originally. To be safe, always make a backup copy of the file before trying to recover it. This way, you will have a copy of the file and will be able to attempt another recovery if necessary.

To restore a damaged file, choose Recover Database from the File Utilities menu, and then enter the name of the database. Q&A will display a warning message. Press F10 to attempt the recovery. During the procedure, Q&A will report its progress. After the recovery attempt, Q&A will return to the Utilities menu and display a message on the status line stating whether or not the recovery was successful.

The advanced techniques you learned in this chapter can add power to your databases. By customizing a database and creating macros, you can perform an application rather than merely manipulate data in a file. In Chapter 16, you will complete the process of building an application by developing an automated invoicing system.

16

Program-
ming
Applications

In order to use traditional database languages, you must write a program—a series of instructions that you want the software to perform—that is separate from the database. Because it is separate, the program must include explicit statements for every action, including the name of the database, the fields to use, and each step you want the program to perform. It's no wonder that even some simple tasks need programs that are hundreds, if not thousands, of lines long. But do you want to be a computer programmer or a database user?

Q&A also has a programming language, but not in the traditional sense. You write a Q&A program on the database form, so each programming statement relates directly to the fields and data with which you are dealing. The statements work in conjunction with all other Q&A functions, not as a separate program that must interact with the database independently and under its own control. Often, one programming statement in Q&A is the equivalent of hundreds of lines in some other database's language.

HOW Q&A HANDLES PROGRAMMING ERRORS

Because you will be doing quite a bit of programming in this chapter, you should know how Q&A handles errors before you begin.

Q&A will check a program statement for the proper syntax when you move the cursor off the field in which it was entered. When it detects an error, Q&A will display a warning message in a box somewhere on the screen. The warning indicates that you misspelled a command, used the incorrect syntax, or have an unequal number of left and right parentheses in a complex statement. You must correct the error or delete the instruction in order to continue. (See Appendix C of the Q&A *Application Programming Tools Manual* for a complete list of error messages.)

When you press F10 to complete the specification, Q&A checks all the programming statements for correct references. It will display a message such as

You have a duplicate of field ID# 33

if it finds two fields with the same number, or

There is no field numbered 33

when a command refers to a field number that doesn't exist. Find the statements that reference the numbers and correct the error.

Q&A does not check your program statements for errors in logic—statements that are technically correct but that do not perform the task you had in mind. In some cases, this type of mistake will cause an error message to appear when the statement is executed. This usually occurs when you try to access a file or record that does not exist. Cancel the function you are performing, correct the error, and then try again.

If a statement results in dividing a number by zero or a null value, ERR will appear in the field. Rewrite the statement to avoid the possibility, as in

Rate: #40: If #10 > 0 Then #40 = #20 / #10 Else #40 = 0

Finally, there are programming errors that simply do the wrong thing. Perhaps you used the wrong mathematical formula or referenced the wrong field number. Q&A will execute the statement and display the results because it has no way of knowing that you made a mistake. These are the most difficult mistakes to correct because you might not notice them yourself. Be sure to check the results of your programming.

AN OVERVIEW OF THE INVOICING APPLICATION

In this chapter, you will learn how to program Q&A forms by developing an invoicing system. You will use Q&A's extensive array of programming statements to work with multiple databases; build lookup tables; and automate entering, posting, and printing invoices. The application will perform tasks that are typically done by a relational database.

You will be able to develop the application even if you have never written a computer program. If you have written programs in other database languages, prepare to be impressed by the power of Q&A's unique approach.

You will develop two additional databases for the invoicing application: Stock and Invoice. The Stock database will keep track of your inventory, including prices, quantities, and order details. From this database, you will be able to print backorder reports, price lists, and analyze profits.

The Invoice database will be used to record orders as they are received, as well as print actual client invoices. You will post fields in the Invoice database to update both the Clients and Stock databases.

You will also design the invoicing application to produce aging and other statistical reports to help make important business decisions.

We will develop the application in four steps:

- Modify the Clients database to store the client's last invoice number and add a lookup table to aid in filling in the Preferred Carrier field.

- Create the Stock database, which will also include a lookup table. While building this database, you will learn how to access another database during data entry.

- Develop the Invoice database. In doing so, you will learn more about working with multiple databases and automating the process of filling in forms.

- Create a posting macro to post fields from the Invoice database to the Clients and Stock databases. The macro will update the last order dates, amounts, and invoice numbers in the Clients database, and subtract the amounts ordered from the Stock database while keeping track of backorders.

After setting up the application, you will learn how to create reports that provide aging and other critical business information. The reports will include data from more than one database.

The techniques you will employ in developing this system can be applied to any Q&A database application.

PROGRAMMING WITH A LOOKUP TABLE

Some database fields should be restricted to specific values. The Preferred Carrier field in the Clients database is an example. The only possible entries are the names of shipping companies and carriers that you use, such as United Parcel and Federal Express. You control acceptable entries by restricting the field and inform users by listing the restrictions in a custom help message.

To make the system more efficient, you can allow the user to type a single letter that automatically enters the carrier's name, such as U to insert United Parcel, or F to insert Federal Express.

With Q&A, you create a built-in lookup table to handle such entries. A *lookup table* is actually a database within the database. Figure 16.1 shows the lookup table that will automate the entry of the carrier name. Each row represents a record, each column a field. The first column contains the *key*, which is the keystroke that retrieves the information in the other columns.

Let's modify the Clients database now. Then you will learn more about lookup tables. We will start by adding a field to store the most recent invoice number.

1. Start Q&A and select Design File from the File menu, then Redesign a File.

2. Type **Clients** and press ↵. Make sure you are in overtype mode. If the characters Ins appear on the status line, press Ins.

3. Place the cursor on line 19, position 35, and type **Taxable: AO**.

4. Place the cursor on line 18, position 5, and type **Last Invoice No.:**.

```
        KEY              1                 2              3            4

  U                United Parcel  7 to 1Ø days
  F                Federal Express 1 to 2 days
  P                Parcel Post    7 to 1Ø days
  T                Truck          1 to 3 weeks




CLIENTS.DTF  █                 Lookup Table                    Page 1  of 1

Esc-Exit  F6-Expand field   PgUp-Previous page   PgDn-Next page   F1Ø-Continue
```

Figure 16.1: Lookup table for shipping charges

5. Place the cursor on line 20, position 25, and press Del ten times to move the Preferred Carrier field to that position.

6. Place the cursor at position 61, press Ins to turn on insert mode, and type **ETA:**.

7. Press the spacebar six times to realign the border. Your form should look like Figure 16.2.

8. Press F10 to display the Format Spec screen.

9. Press ↓ seven times to reach the Invoice No. field and type **N**.

10. Press F10 twice. Q&A will display a message asking if you want to add the new text field to the Query Guide index.

11. Type **N** to return to the File menu.

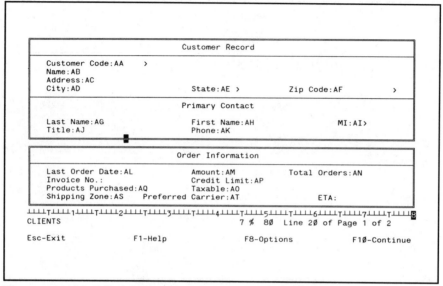

Figure 16.2: Modified Clients database form

CREATING THE LOOKUP TABLE

IIII➡ **To create a lookup table:**

1. **Select Design File from the File menu, then Program a File.**
2. **Enter the database name, press ↵, and select Edit Lookup Table.**
3. **In the Key column, enter the values that will be used to match with fields in the form.**
4. **Enter the values to be retrieved in the remaining columns.**
5. **Press F10 to save the table.**

You define a lookup table through the Edit Lookup Table option on the File Programming menu.

Now we will create the lookup table that you will use to locate carrier names and delivery times.

1. Select Design File, then Program a File, and press ↵ to accept Clients.

2. Select Edit Lookup Table. A blank lookup table will appear, as shown in Figure 16.3.

3. Type **U**, press Tab, type **United Parcel**, press Tab, type **7 to 10 days**, and press ↵.

4. Type **F**, press Tab, type **Federal Express**, press Tab, type **1 to 2 days**, and press ↵.

5. Type **P**, press Tab, type **Parcel Post**, press Tab, type **7 to 10 days**, and press ↵.

6. Type **T**, press Tab, type **Truck**, press Tab, type **1 to 3 weeks**, and press F10 to save the table and return to the Programming menu.

In this lookup table, two columns of information are used. You can enter and retrieve up to four columns based on the key value, and you can use the lookup table to store more than one class of information.

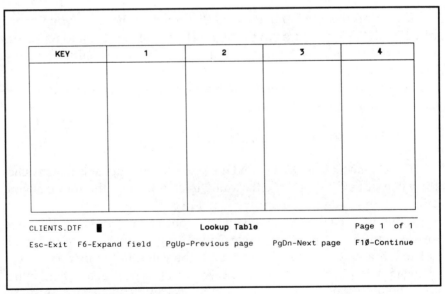

Figure 16.3: Blank lookup table

PROGRAMMING
THE FORM WITH LOOKUP

IIII➡ **To program a form with a lookup table:**

1. **Select Design File from the File menu, then Program a File.**
2. **Enter the database name, press ↵, and select Program Form.**
3. **Enter the statement in the appropriate field in the format Lookup(*key-field, column-number, destination-field-number*), or the function in the format @LOOKUP(*key-field, column-number*) as part of a formula.**

You retrieve information from a lookup table through either a statement or a function. A statement is a command telling Q&A to perform a specific task. The Lookup statement (abbreviated LU) is in the form

Lookup*(key-field, column-number, destination-field-number)*

Key-field is the number of the field that contains the value you want to match with the key column in the table. The value you want to retrieve is in *column-number* in the table, and you want to insert the value in *destination-field-number*.

For example, in the Clients database, you can program the Preferred Carrier field like this:

Preferred Carrier: #8: Lookup(#8,1,#8)

This statement tells Q&A to find the key in the lookup table that matches the value in field #8, retrieve the value in column 1 in the row that contains that key, and insert the value in field #8.

Using this statement, when you enter one of the letters shown in the key column, the full name of the carrier will appear when the record is calculated. If a matching key is not found, the value in the field is left unchanged. Because this is a statement, you could type it in any field in the form, not necessarily the field it relates to. It would still perform the same task as soon as a value is entered in field #8 and automatic or manual calculation is triggered.

The destination and key fields do not have to be the same. You can insert the value in one field based on the key in another.

A function is similar to a mathematical expression. Q&A determines the value in the function and uses it to calculate the results of a formula. The @LOOKUP function (or @LU) has the form

@LOOKUP*(key-field, column-number)*

You do not include a destination field number because you are not instructing Q&A to place the value in a specific field. Instead, the function must be used as part of an expression, such as

Preferred Carrier: #8 = @LOOKUP(#8,1)

This expression tells Q&A to assign field #8 the value found in column 1 of the lookup table in the row that matches the value entered in field #8. If a match isn't found, a null value is returned and the field is left blank.

The key field in lookup tables is always considered to be text. For example, if it contains the values 1, 2, 3, 4, and 5, Q&A will not find a match with a field entry of 1.5. Key fields must match the value exactly when used with the Lookup statement or @LOOKUP function.

For the Clients database, we have to use the statement rather than the function. This is because each time automatic or manual calculation is triggered, the lookup will be performed. If an entry has already been made in the Preferred Carrier field, no match will be found—the value in the field is no longer a single letter that matches any of the keys. The @LOOKUP function would return a null value, leaving the field blank, and you would have to reenter the letter.

Now let's program the Clients form by entering the Lookup statement.

1. Select Program Form to display the Program Spec screen.

2. Press ↓ nine times, then Tab to reach the Preferred Carrier field, and type **#8**.

3. Press ↓, then Tab to reach the ETA field.

4. Press F6 to expand the field and type the statement

#9: Lookup(#8,2#9); Lookup(#8,1,#8)

5. Press F10 twice.

Notice that this field includes two programming statements, which are separated from each other with a semicolon. This is how you include multiple statements in the same field. After you enter a single letter in the Preferred Carrier field and press ↵ or F10, automatic calculation will execute the Lookup statements. The shipping time from the second column will be inserted into field #9, then the name of the carrier from the first column in field #8, replacing the single-letter entry.

The two Lookup statements cannot be reversed. If they are, the full name of the carrier will be inserted in field #8 first. The second Lookup statement will not find a match in the key column, so the field will be left blank.

DEVISING THE FIELD RESTRICTION FOR LOOKUP

Creating a restriction for the Preferred Carrier field will ensure that the proper Lookup value is retrieved. However, we cannot use the restriction U;F;P;T, because once the lookup is performed, you will not be able to enter and leave the field a second time—the full name will not match the single letters specified in the restriction.

An alternative is to use the restriction U..;F..;P..;T.., which specifies a text string that starts with one of those letters. This would let you enter and leave the field after the lookup has inserted the proper value, but it would also allow you to enter any other word starting with those letters, such as Ups or Fed Ex. Instead, we will use a restriction that includes all the initial letters and the full names. Note that if you ever add or change an entry in the lookup table, you will have to change the restriction as well.

Follow these steps to enter the field restriction:

1. Press Esc to return to the Design menu, select Customize a File, and press ↵ to select Clients.

2. Select Restrict Values from the Customize menu.

3. Press ↓ nine times, then Tab to reach the Preferred Carrier field, and then press F6 to expand the field.

4. Type the restriction (you can enter the items in any order):

   U;United Parcel;F;Federal Express;P;Parcel Post;T;Truck

5. Press F10 twice to save the specification, then Esc twice to return to the File menu.

Next, update the current records so they conform to the new restriction and lookup table.

6. Select Search/Update, press ↵, and then press F10 to display the first record.

7. Press Shift-F8, type **A**, and press F10 to turn on automatic calculation.

8. Press ↓ nine times, then Tab to reach the Preferred Carrier field.

9. Press Shift-F4 to delete the current entry and type **U**.

The Lookup statement will not be activated until you move to another field or record.

10. Press ↵. United Parcel will appear in the Preferred Carrier field, and 7 to 10 days will be in the ETA field.

11. Press Shift-Tab, then F10 to display the next record.

12. In the same way, update all the remaining records in the file, entering **U** where you see *UPS* and **F** for *Fed Ex*.

13. Press Shift-F10 after updating the last record.

BUILDING THE
INVENTORY DATABASE

It's now time to create the inventory database, Stock. Figure 16.4 shows the database form, and Table 16.1 lists each field's width, type, restriction, and template.

Follow these general steps to create the Stock database:

1. Design the form as shown in Figure 16.4, using the field widths listed in Table 16.1.

The widths of the Stock Number, Vendor, and Location fields are critical to the application. Make sure those fields are the sizes specified in Table 16.1. Remember, if a field is three characters wide, press the spacebar four times before entering the > symbol to end the field. The other sizes represent the *minimum* width; the fields can be wider.

```
                         Inventory Data

        Stock Number:
        Item:
        Vendor:
        Location:        -   -

        Last Order Date:          Quantity:          Date Received:

        Perishable:               Shelf Life:

        Cost:                     Markup:            Price:

        On Hand:                  Reorder Point:     Minimum Order:

        Backordered:

        Weight Per Unit:          Shipper:

        ETA after shipping date:                                    ▮
        _____

        STOCK.DTF       New Record 1      of 1      Total Records: 1Ø      Page 1  of 1

        Esc-Exit   F1-Help      F3-Delete form    F7-Search     F8-Calc    F1Ø-Continue
```

Figure 16.4: Inventory database form

Table 16.1: Stock Database Fields

FIELD	WIDTH	TYPE	RESTRICTION	TEMPLATE
Stock Number	3	T	!1??;2??;300	999
Item	30	T	!	
Vendor	3	T	!1??;2??;300	999
Location	8	T		@@-99-99
Last Order Date	15	D		
Quantity	3	N	>=0	
Date Received	15	D		
Perishable	1	Y		
Shelf Life	3	N	>0	
Cost	8	M	!>0	
Markup	3	N	!0..1	
Price	8	M	>0	
On Hand	3	N		
Reorder Point	3	N	>=0	
Minimum Order	3	N	>=0	
Backordered	3	N	>=0	
Weight Per Unit	4	N	>0	
Shipper	3	T		
ETA after shipped date	15	T		

2. After laying out the form, press F10 to display the Format Spec screen.

3. Assign the field types shown in Table 16.1, and then press F10 twice to return to the File menu.

4. Apply the restrictions shown in Table 16.1.

The restrictions for the Stock Number and Vendor fields are required for compatibility with corresponding entries in the Clients and Vendors databases.

5. Apply the templates shown in Table 16.1.

The templates for the Stock Number and Vendor fields also ensure compatibility with the Vendors and Clients databases.

The template for the Location field allows it to be used to identify where the item is stored in the warehouse. The first two characters represent the building, the next two the shelf, the final two the bin. For example, the entry BN-21-34 means that the item is in building BN, shelf 21, bin 34.

6. Designate Stock Number as a unique index (speed) field (SU), and Item, Vendor, and On Hand as regular index fields (S).

7. Return to the Design menu, select Program a File, and then choose Edit Lookup Table.

8. Enter the same lookup table you added to the Clients database (Figure 16.1).

Because a lookup table is stored with the database, you have to type the same lookup table in the Stock database.

The next step in developing the inventory database is to program the form.

PROGRAMMING WITH
ON-ENTRY AND ON-EXIT COMMANDS

||||➡ **To automatically execute program commands:**

- **Create an on-field-entry or on-field-exit command by preceding the command with the < or > symbol, respectively.**

- **Create an on-record-entry or on-record-exit command by pressing F8 from the Program Spec screen and entering the number of the field that contains the command.**

The programming commands you have entered so far are called *calc* statements. They are executed when you press F8 or, if you turned on automatic calculation, when you move the cursor off a field whose value has been changed. Calc statements in a form are called the *main program*.

You can also write program commands that are executed automatically when the cursor moves to the field or out of it with a ↵, Tab, →, ↓, or F10 keystroke.

A command executed when the cursor moves into the field iscalled an *on-field-entry command*. Create it by preceding the command with the less-than symbol (<).

A command executed when the cursor moves out of the field is called an *on-field-exit command*. It is preceded by a greater-than symbol (>).

On-field-entry and on-field-exit statements are not executed when you press F8, nor are they affected by automatic calculation. They are triggered only when you move forward through the database, in or out of the field.

Calc statements are executed at different times than on-entry and on-exit statements. When you have both in the same form, the calc statements are executed first. For example, if you are in automatic calculation mode and leave a field that has an on-exit statement, all calc statements are executed before the on-exit statement.

To change the order of calculation, when you are adding a record, press Shift-F8 to display the Set Calculate options, and select No for the Main Program Before Field Exit option. Then the on-exit statement will be executed before the calc statements.

The Stock form includes on-field-entry, on-field-exit, and calc statements. The on-entry and on-exit program statements will be executed when you add or update a record. The calc statement will be used later when you post invoices.

Follow these steps to program the form:

1. Select Program Form from the Programming menu.

2. Number each of the fields consecutively, as shown in Figure 16.5.

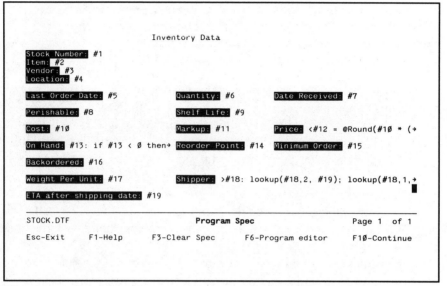

Figure 16.5: Completed Program Spec screen for the Stock form

3. Expand the Price field and enter the on-field-entry statement:

    <#12 = @ROUND(#10 * (1 + #11), 2)

This programs the form to automatically calculate the item's price when you reach the Price field. The statement multiplies the Cost field (#10) times one plus the Markup field (#11), then rounds the results to two decimal places. Because it is preceded by the < symbol, the calculation is performed immediately when you press ↵, Tab, →, or ↓ to move into the field.

4. Expand the On Hand field and enter the calc statement:

    #13: If #13 < 0 Then {#16= #16 + @ABS(#13); #13 = 0}

This statement will be used when you post order amounts from the invoices. After the posting subtracts the number ordered from the current number on hand, the calc statement will check if the result is a negative number. When it is a negative number, the If statement adds the absolute value—the number without the minus sign—to the Backordered field and sets the On Hand field to zero.

The two statements must be in the order shown; they cannot be reversed. If they were, the value in #13 would be set at zero first, then the absolute value of the field, zero, would be added to field #16. The curly brackets replace the words Begin and End to create a compound Then statement.

5. Expand the Shipper field and enter the on-field-exit command:

   >#18: Lookup(#18,2,#19); Lookup(#18,1,#18)

This command automatically retrieves values from the lookup table. It is similar to the command you entered in the Clients database, except that it is an on-field-exit statement. Again, the two lookup statements cannot be reversed.

6. Press F10 to save the programming specification.

Executing Statements on Entering and Exiting a Record

You can also designate one programming statement to execute automatically when you enter the record, and one to execute when you exit from the record. When the Program Spec screen is displayed, press F8 to display the menu shown in Figure 16.6. Enter the number of the on-record-entry and on-record-exit fields and press F10. You do not have to fill in both options.

The on-record-entry statement is executed when the record is first displayed through the Add Data or Search/Update option. The on-record-exit statement is executed when you press F10 or Shift-F10 to save the record.

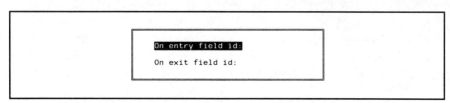

Figure 16.6: Designate on-record-entry and on-record-exit fields

WORKING WITH MULTIPLE DATABASES

||||▶ To program an external database lookup:

- **Add the statement to the appropriate field in the format XLookup(*external-file-name, field-number, external-key-field, external-field, destination-field-number*).**
- **Add the function in the format @LOOKUP(*external-file-name, field-number, external-key-field, external-field*) as part of a formula.**

The Vendor field in the Stock database corresponds to the Vendor Code field in the Vendors database. It tells you which vendor sold you the item. The restriction and template you used for the field ensure that you enter a three-digit number between 100 and 300. However, they do not prevent the entry of a number for a nonexistent vendor code—one for which there is no matching code in the Vendors database.

A solution to this problem would be to write a restriction that includes all the valid vendor numbers. But this too has a drawback: every time you added a new record to the Vendors database, you would have to modify the restriction in the Stock database. A better approach is to access the Vendors database while you are entering records in the Stock database, making sure the vendor code you enter really exists. This requires using more than one database at the same time.

Performing External Lookups

You access another database by using the XLookup statement (abbreviated XLU) or @XLOOKUP (@XLU) function. These commands perform *external lookups*—they deal with data separate from the database form itself. They are similar to the lookup table commands, except they return values from another database. The statement has the syntax

XLookup(*"x-name", field-number, x-key-field, x-field, destination*)

where the parameters are as follows:

- *"x-name"* is the name of the external database from which you want to retrieve data, enclosed in quotation marks.

- *field-number* is the number of the field on the current form that you want to use for the key.

- *x-key-field* is the name of the field in the external database that you want to match with the field on the form.

- *x-field* is the field in the external database that you want to retrieve.

- *destination-field-number* is the number of the field on the form where you want to insert the value.

For example, to include the vendor's name in the Stock database, you would need a Name field in the form programmed like this

Name: #40: XLookup("Vendors",#3,"Vendor Code","Name",#40)

The command tells Q&A to look in the database called Vendors and match the contents of field #3 of the current form with the field called Vendor Code in Vendors. When a match is found, insert the contents of the Name field in Vendors at field #40 in the current form in Stock.

If a match is not found, the field will remain unchanged and you will see this warning on the message line

The lookup file does not have the key value:

followed by the key value.

You can also use the statement to return more than one field value at the same time by specifying additional external field names and destination fields, as in

Name: #40: XLookup("Vendors",#3,"Vendor Code","Name",#40, "Address",#41,"Phone",#42)

When a match is found, the contents of three fields will be copied to the Stock database.

The corresponding function has the syntax

@XLOOKUP *(x-name, field-number, x-key-field, x-field)*

The destination field is not included because the function must be used in an expression, such as

Name: #40 = @XLookup("Vendors",#3,"Vendor Code","Name")

If a matching key is not found, the function returns a null, or empty, value.

In the Stock database, we want to make sure that only existing vendor numbers can be entered. We will do this by combining the @XLOOKUP command with field navigation.

PROGRAMMING FIELD NAVIGATION

To automatically move the cursor between fields:

1. **Select Design File from the File menu, then Program a File.**
2. **Enter the database name, press ↵, and select Field Navigation.**
3. **Enter the navigation statements in the appropriate fields of the Navigation Spec screen.**
4. **Press F10 to save the specification.**

Q&A's field navigation commands provide another way to control data entry. You can use the commands to make field entries in a different order, skip certain fields based on the information entered in other fields, and automatically enter data in a group of fields using lookup commands.

There are seven navigation commands:

Goto #*n*	Moves to field #*n*
CNext	Moves to the next field in sequence on the form, not by field number
CPrev	Moves to the previous field
CHome	Moves to the first field on the form

CEnd   Moves to the last field on the form

PgDn   Moves to the first field on the next page

PgUp   Moves to the last field on the previous page

Unlike programming statements, navigation statements do not have to begin with a field number unless the field is used in a formula or a Goto command.

Although you can enter the commands in on-field-entry and on-field-exit statements (but not calc statements), Q&A provides the Navigation Spec screen, displayed by the Field Navigation option on the Programming menu, just for this purpose. It is recommended that you use the Program Spec screen for commands that enter or change field values, and the Navigation Spec screen for commands that control movement through the form.

We will use the @XLOOKUP function and two navigation commands in the Stock database.

1. Select Field Navigation from the Programming menu.

2. Press ⏎ twice to reach the Vendor field and type the on-entry navigation command:

   >#3: If @XLU("Vendors",#3,"Vendor Code","Vendor Code")="" Then Goto #3

The restriction and template require you to enter a three-digit vendor code between 100 and 300. After you type the code and leave the field, Q&A performs the If statement by looking for a matching vendor code in the Vendors database. If no match is found, the function returns a null value. The If condition will be true, and the navigation command returns the cursor to field #3 so you can enter another vendor code.

3. Press ↓ four times, then Tab twice to reach the Price field, and type **<CNext**.

This navigation command tells Q&A to move to the next field when the cursor enters the field. On-entry programming statements are always performed before on-entry navigation commands. When you move into the Price field, the price will be calculated by the on-entry program statement, and then the cursor will automatically move to the next field.

4. Press F10 to save the navigation specification.

RECORDING INVENTORY

Now that the Stock form is programmed, we can enter records into the database. Follow these steps:

1. Press Esc twice to display the File menu, select Add Data, and press ⏎ to display the first form.

2. Type **101** and press ⏎.

3. Type **Ep-80 Ribbons** and press ⏎.

4. Type **145** and press ⏎.

Q&A will perform the lookup and find that there is no matching number in the Vendors database. The warning will appear on the message line, and the cursor will remain on the field.

5. Type **101** and press ⏎.

6. Complete the record and enter the other records using the data shown in Figure 16.7.

As you enter the records, you will notice that when you press ⏎ after entering the Markup value, the program command calculates and inserts the price, then the navigation command moves the cursor to the next field. Because of the navigation command, you cannot move the cursor into the field using the ⏎, Tab, →, or ↓ key to override the calculation manually. If you want to enter your own value, move to the field by pressing the ↑ or ← key. Note that if you do override the entry, the price will be recalculated automatically if you later move forward through the record.

When you type a letter in the Shipper field, Q&A retrieves the data from the lookup table and completes the Shipper and ETA fields.

```
Stock Number: 101
Item: Ep-80 Ribbons
Vendor: 101
Location: CD1816
Last Order Date: 3/1/92  Quantity: 15          Date Received:
3/15/92
Perishable: Y            Shelf Life: 24
Cost: 3.45               Markup: .50           Price:
On Hand: 24              Reorder Point: 10     Minimum Order: 15
Backordered: 0
Weight Per Unit: 1       Shipper: U


Stock Number: 102
Item: HPIII Cartridge
Vendor: 102
Location: CD1823
Last Order Date: 2/1/92  Quantity: 25          Date Received:
4/1/92
Perishable: Y            Shelf Life: 24
Cost: 50.75              Markup: .35           Price:
On Hand: 36              Reorder Point: 15     Minimum Order: 15
Backordered: 0
Weight Per Unit: 2       Shipper: U


Stock Number: 103
Item: DJ Cartridge
Vendor: 101
Location: CD1817
Last Order Date: 4/1/92  Quantity: 50          Date Received:
4/15/92
Perishable: N            Shelf Life:
Cost: 10.75              Markup: .33           Price:
On Hand: 102             Reorder Point: 25     Minimum Order: 25
Backordered: 0
Weight Per Unit: 1       Shipper: U


Stock Number: 104
Item: Disk 3.5" LD
Vendor: 104
Location: MW0101
Last Order Date: 6/1/92  Quantity: 3000        Date Received:
7/15/92
Perishable: N            Shelf Life:
Cost: .50                Markup: .75           Price:
On Hand: 4500            Reorder Point: 1000 Minimum Order:500
Backordered: 0
Weight Per Unit: 1       Shipper: U
```

Figure 16.7: Data for Stock records

```
Stock Number: 105
Item: Disk 3.5 HD
Vendor: 104
Location: MW0102
Last Order Date: 2/1/92  Quantity: 1500       Date Received:
3/2/92
Perishable: N             Shelf Life:
Cost: .75                 Markup: .75          Price:
On Hand:  1750            Reorder Point: 500  Minimum Order: 500
Backordered: 0
Weight Per Unit: 1        Shipper: U


Stock Number: 106
Item: AT626 Chair
Vendor: 105
Location: MW0501
Last Order Date: 1/5/92  Quantity: 2          Date Received:
3/1/91
Perishable: N             Shelf Life:
Cost: 102.35              Markup: .15          Price:
On Hand: 2                Reorder Point: 0     Minimum Order: 1
Backordered: 0
Weight Per Unit: 26       Shipper: T


Stock Number: 107
Item: Labels 5.25
Vendor: 103
Location: MW0105
Last Order Date: 3/1/92  Quantity: 1000       Date Received:
3/16/02
Perishable: N             Shelf Life:
Cost: 1.50                Markup: .10          Price:
On Hand:  1500            Reorder Point: 50   Minimum Order: 100
Backordered: 0
Weight Per Unit: 1        Shipper: P


Stock Number: 108
Item: HPII Cartridge
Vendor: 102
Location: CD1825
Last Order Date: 4/5/92  Quantity: 25         Date Received:
4/19/92
Perishable: Y             Shelf Life: 24
Cost: 55.75               Markup: .35          Price:
On Hand: 45               Reorder Point: 15   Minimum Order: 15
Backordered: 0
Weight Per Unit: 2        Shipper: U
```

Figure 16.7: Data for Stock records (continued)

```
Stock Number: 109
Item: Labels 3.5
Vendor: 103
Location: MW0106
Last Order Date: 4/15/92 Quantity: 1500      Date Received:
5/12/92
Perishable: N            Shelf Life:
Cost: 1.50               Markup: .10          Price:
On Hand: 1650            Reorder Point: 100  Minimum Order: 500
Backordered: 0
Weight Per Unit: 1       Shipper: P



Stock Number: 110
Item: Mailers 5.25
Vendor: 103
Location: MW0110
Last Order Date: 5/3/92  Quantity: 100       Date Received:
6/1/92
Perishable: N            Shelf Life:
Cost: 5.23               Markup: .25          Price:
On Hand: 150             Reorder Point: 35   Minimum Order: 100
Backordered: 0
Weight Per Unit: 1       Shipper: P
```

Figure 16.7: Data for Stock records (continued)

CREATING THE INVOICE DATABASE

The Invoice database is more than a collection of records storing information. It is a means of accepting and processing transactions as you receive orders over the phone. Since each record represents an active transaction, the form must be designed to keep the data-entry keystrokes to a minimum. We will accomplish this by making extensive use of programming and navigation statements.

The Invoice database form is shown in Figure 16.8. The form is designed to look like an actual invoice. This makes it easier for the user to enter order information, but it does impose certain limitations. In this case, to fit the invoice on one page, an order can include only five different items.

The form includes the title Invoice and the column headings Item Code, Item, Quantity, Price, and Amount. Since these are not fields, they are not followed by colons.

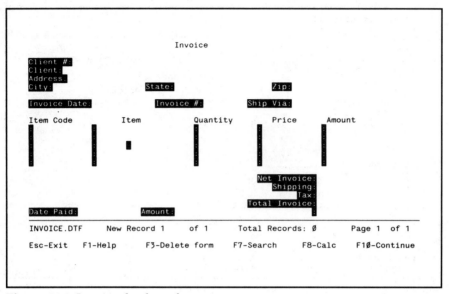

Figure 16.8: Invoice database form

Most of the form is straightforward: field labels are followed by colons. But notice the colons that do not have associated field labels. Each row of colons represents a row of the order detail: the code, item, quantity, price, and extended amount for each item ordered.

Because Q&A distinguishes field labels from field names, you do not have to have a label for each field. The colon by itself is sufficient to represent a field on the form. Q&A assigns its own internal name to each unlabeled field, starting with F0001 and numbered consecutively. If you want to change the internal names, select Set Field Names from the Programming menu and enter new, *unique* field names.

This format allows you to enter data in rows, just as you would on an actual paper invoice form. If you want the form to accommodate more than five items, enter additional rows of colons. You will learn how to use field navigation statements to quickly move from the last ordered item to the Net Invoice field.

Also notice the two fields at the bottom of the form, Date Paid and Amount. These fields will not be printed with the client's invoice, but they are included in the record to keep track of when the client makes payments. In this way, the form serves two purposes: as an invoice or order form, as well as a database record for keeping track of payments. The colon at the end of the last line represents an unlabeled field that will store a duplicate of the total invoice amount to be accumulated in the client's record.

Follow these general steps to set up the Invoice database:

1. Lay out the Invoice form using Figure 16.8 as a guide.

2. Assign the field lengths and types listed in Table 16.2.

3. Use the Customize menu to apply the restrictions and templates shown in Table 16.2.

Notice that only the first unlabeled field under the Item Code heading is required. There aren't many restrictions and templates because most of the form will be automated.

WORKING WITH RANGES

IIII➡ **To perform range lookups:**

- **Add the statement to the appropriate field in the format Lookupr(*key-field, column-number, destination-field-number*).**
- **Add the function in the format @LOOKUPR(*key-field, column-number*) as part of a formula.**

The most complex programming instruction we will include in the Invoice form will be used to calculate shipping charges. It will base the charges on the client's zone, as well as on the total amount of the invoice. The lookup is performed with the range lookup command.

The range lookup statement and function, Lookupr (LUR) and @LOOKUPR (@LUR) are similar to the Lookup commands you have already used. However, with these commands, if an exact matching key is not found, the key with the next lowest value is selected. They use the same syntax as Lookup and @LOOKUP. You can also perform an external range lookup with the statement XLookupr or the function @XLOOKUPR.

Table 16.2: Invoice Database Fields

FIELD	SIZE	TYPE	RESTRICTION	TEMPLATE
Client #	3	T	1??;2??;300	999
Client	30	T		
Address	30	T		
City	15	T		
State	2	T		
Zip	6	T		
Invoice Date	15	D		
Invoice #	4	N		
Ship Via	15	T		
Unlabeled Rows				
Item Code	3	N	(! in first row only)	999
Item	20	T		
Quantity	8	N	>=0	9999
Price	8	M		
Amount	8	M		
Net Invoice	8	M		
Shipping	8	M		
Tax	8	M		
Total Invoice	8	M		
Date Paid	8	D		
Amount	8	M		
:(Unlabeled)	8	N		

The Lookupr command we will enter can be broken down into three parts:

key-field	@RIGHT("000000"+@STR(@INT(#35)),6)
column-number	@XLU("Clients",#1,"Customer Code", "Shipping Zone")
destination-field-number	#36

Column-number is the client's shipping zone, retrieved with an external lookup command. The *destination-field-number* is #36, the Shipping field in the Invoice database.

The *key-field* definition is complex in this case because the Net Invoice amount is a calculated money field. Since keys are always text, they are compared in terms of their ASCII, not numeric, values. To use the Lookup commands with numeric ranges, the entries in the key columns and the value in the key field on the form must have the same number of digits.

The Net Invoice field will not always have the same number of digits, so it cannot be used directly in a range lookup. An order of $5.45 would locate a value in the $40-to-$69 range, not in the less-than-$10 range. In order to use the net invoice amount, it must be converted to a six-character text string that can be compared with the keys according to their ASCII values.

The @INT function returns the integer value of the net order amount. The @STR function converts the numeric value to its text equivalent. So if the invoice is $54.56, the @INT function returns the number 54, then the @STR function converts it to the text string "54."

Our goal is to pad the string to make it equivalent to a six-character text string by adding "0" characters to its left. (A six-character entry allows orders to be as large as $999,999.99.) Since we do not know in advance how many zeros an invoice will require, the command adds six zeros, then subtracts the extra ones. The zeros are added by the instruction

"000000"+@STR(@INT(#35))

With the $54.56 invoice, this results in the string 00000054. But since we can only have a total of six characters, we remove the extra characters by taking the six rightmost characters, with the command

@RIGHT("000000"+@STR(@INT(#35)),6)

The resulting six-character string can then be used in the range lookup.

PROGRAMMING THE INVOICE FORM

The Invoice form contains 38 fields that can comprise the actual invoice, but you might enter values in as few as 3 fields. The remaining fields will be filled in by programming and navigation statements. Most of the fields will use information retrieved from the Clients and Stock databases, demonstrating how Q&A can work with multiple databases even though it is classified as nonrelational.

For example, after you enter the client number, the next eight fields will automatically be filled in. Six of the fields will use information retrieved from the Clients database.

After you enter the item code number, the item name will appear. When you enter the quantity of that item ordered, the price and extended amount will appear, and the cursor will move to the next item code field. The rows of order information will be filled in by data retrieved from the Stock database.

When you enter the last item to be ordered, the net invoice, shipping, tax, and total invoice amounts will be calculated. You will even be warned if the total amount exceeds the client's credit limit.

Follow these steps to program the Invoice form:

1. From the Design menu, select Program a File, press ↵ to accept Invoice, and then select Edit Lookup Table.

2. Enter the lookup table shown in Figure 16.9, and then press F10. Make sure each of the keys has six characters.

3. Select Program a Form to display the Program Spec screen.

The completed Program Spec screen is shown in Figure 16.10, although many of the fields are extended and cannot be seen in their entirety. Since there is a great deal of programming involved here, we will go through the process step by step.

Remember, press F6 to expand the field when the programming statement is longer than the field width. Enter the statement, and then press F10 to return to the form.

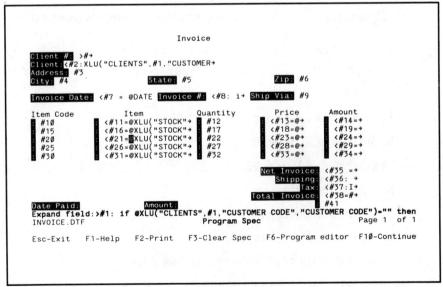

KEY	1	2	3	4
000000	1.50	2.25	3.35	
000010	2.35	3.50	4.25	
000025	3.25	4.75	5.85	
000040	4.75	6.15	7.10	
000070	6.50	7.25	10.50	

```
INVOICE.DTF                    Lookup Table                Page 1  of 1

Esc-Exit  F6-Expand field    PgUp-Previous page    PgDn-Next page    F10-Continue
```

Figure 16.9: Completed Invoice Program Spec screen

```
                               Invoice

Client #:  >#→
Client:<#2:XLU("CLIENTS",#1,"CUSTOMER→
Address: #3
City: #4                State: #5                Zip: #6

Invoice Date: <#7 = @DATE Invoice #: <#8: i→ Ship Via: #9

Item Code          Item           Quantity        Price       Amount
 #10        <#11=@XLU("STOCK"→   #12         <#13=@→    <#14=→
 #15        <#16=@XLU("STOCK"→   #17         <#18=@→    <#19=→
 #20        <#21=@XLU("STOCK"→   #22         <#23=@→    <#24=→
 #25        <#26=@XLU("STOCK"→   #27         <#28=@→    <#29=→
 #30        <#31=@XLU("STOCK"→   #32         <#33=@→    <#34=→

                                         Net Invoice: <#35 =→
                                           Shipping: <#36: →
                                               Tax: <#37:I→
                                      Total Invoice: <#38=#→
                                                     #41
Date Paid:           Amount:
Expand field:>#1: if @XLU("CLIENTS",#1,"CUSTOMER CODE","CUSTOMER CODE")="" then
INVOICE.DTF                   Program Spec                Page 1  of 1

Esc-Exit   F1-Help   F2-Print   F3-Clear Spec   F6-Program editor   F10-Continue
```

Figure 16.10: Lookup table for Invoice database

4. In the Client # field, type

   >#1: If @XLU("Clients",#1,"Customer Code","Customer Code")="" Then Goto #1

This statement ensures that you enter a code number that has already been assigned to a customer. Although it is actually a navigation statement, it is included on the Program Spec screen for two reasons. First, a valid entry in this field is critical to the remainder of the invoice. Second, you will be entering an on-entry navigation statement for this field later.

5. In the Client field, type

   <#2:XU("Clients",#1,"Customer Code","Name",#2,

   "Address",#3,

   "City",#4,

   "State",#5,

   "Zip Code",#6,

   "Preferred Car -

   rier",#9)

This statement retrieves six fields from the customer's record in the Clients database in one external lookup. It is an on-field-entry statement, so the values will be retrieved and inserted when the cursor enters the field. You will add an on-exit command on the Navigation Spec screen to automatically move the cursor out of the field.

6. In the Address field, type **#3**.

7. In the City field, type **#4**.

8. In the State field, type **#5**.

9. In the Zip field, type **#6**.

10. In the Invoice Date field, type **<#7 = @DATE**.

11. In the Invoice # field, type

   <#8: If @ADD AND #8 = "" Then #8 = 100 + @NUMBER

This statement automatically numbers your invoices, starting with a number one higher than the last invoice you entered, even if the last invoice was recorded during an earlier session or you already removed existing records.

The @ADD function returns a true value if you are using the Add Data function, not when you are updating an existing record. If you are adding a record and the field is currently blank, the field is assigned the next consecutive number plus 100. Since the @NUMBER function starts at 1, this creates invoice numbers beginning with 101. The @ADD function ensures that the invoice number is not recalculated when you update the record with date paid and amount paid values.

If you ever need to reset the invoice numbers (or any other @NUMBER counter), when adding or updating records, press Ctrl-F8 and type the number you want to start with.

12. In the Ship Via field, type **#9**.

13. In the first unlabeled field under the heading Item Code, type **#10**. (Refer to Figure 16.10 for the position of the unlabeled field entries.)

14. In the field to its right, the first unlabeled field under the Item heading, type

   <#11 = @XLU("Stock",#10,"Stock Number","Item")

15. In the next field, under the heading Quantity, type **#12**.

16. In the next field, under the heading Price, type

   <#13 = @XLU("Stock",#10,"Stock Number","Price")

17. In the next field, under the heading Amount, type

   <#14 = #13 * #12

18. Enter the remaining programming statements for the next four rows of order information, which are shown in Figure 16.11. Type the programming statements only, not the field label and colon.

19. In the Net Invoice field, type

   <#35 = #14 + #19 + #24 + #29 + #34

This calculates the sum of the values in the Amount column.

20. In the Shipping field, type

<#36: LUR(@RIGHT("000000"+@STR(@INT(#35)),6),

@XLU("Clients",#1,"Customer Code","Shipping Zone"),#36)

This command uses a range and external lookup to calculate shipping charges, as explained in the previous section.

21. In the Tax field, type

<#37: If @XLU("Clients",#1,"Customer Code","Taxable")
Then #37 = #35 * 0.06

This statement checks the taxable status of the client. If the client is taxable, Q&A adds a 6 percent sales tax, based on the net order excluding

```
Row 2

Item Code:      #15
Name:           <#16 = @XLU("Stock",#15,"Stock Number","Item")
Quantity:       #17
Price:          <#18 = @XLU("Stock",#15,"Stock Number","Price")
Amount:         <#19 = #18 * #17


Row 3

Item Code:      #20
Name:           <#21 = @XLU("Stock",#20,"Stock Number","Item")
Quantity:       #22
Price:          <#23 = @XLU("Stock",#22, "Stock Number","Price")
Amount:         <#24 = #23 * #22


Row 4

Item Code:      #25
Name:           <#26 = @XLU("Stock", #25,"Stock Number","Item")
Quantity:       #27
Price:          <#28 = @XLU("Stock",#25,"Stock Number","Price")
Amount:         <#29 = #28 * #27


Row 5

Item Code:      #30
Name:           <#31 = @XLU("Stock",#30,"Stock Number","Item")
Quantity:       #32
Price:          <#33 = @XLU("Stock",#30,"Stock Number","Price")
Amount:         <#34 = #33 * #32
```

Figure 16.11: Program statements for item detail lines

shipping charges (your state sales tax and how it is calculated may be different).

22. In the Total Invoice field, type

> **<#38 = #35 + #36 + #37; #41 = #38;**
>
> **If @XLU("Clients",#1,"Customer Code","Credit Limit")<#38**
>
> **Then @MSG("Client has insufficient credit for this order")**

This statement totals the order amount, shipping charges, and sales tax, and copies the amount to the field we will use to accumulate total orders. The If statement compares the total invoice amount with the client's credit limit. If the order exceeds the credit limit, the @MSG function displays the message in parentheses on the message line.

23. In the unlabeled field under Total Invoice, type **#41**.

24. Press F10 to return to the Programming menu.

We programmed the Total Invoice field in the form so the user can override the credit limit warning and still process the invoice. However, you can include some additional programming here depending on your company's policy. For instance, if you do not want to allow an invoice to be processed when the client does not have enough credit, program the field this way:

```
<#38 = #35 + #36 + #37; #41 = #38
If @XLU("Clients",#1,"Customer Code","Credit Limit")<#38
Then {@MSG("Client has insufficient credit for this order");
Goto #10}
```

When the credit limit is exceeded, the cursor returns to the first order row. Notice that the Goto #10 command is part of a compound Then condition; it is included in the brackets that substitute for the Begin and End commands. If the Goto command were outside the If statement, like this:

```
Then @MSG("Client has insufficient credit for this order");
Goto #10
```

the cursor would always return to field #10 regardless of the credit limit.

NAVIGATING THROUGH INVOICES

The final step in creating the Invoice form is to add the navigation statements to the Navigation Spec screen. You will use these commands to bypass the fields filled in automatically by external lookup statements, so the only fields you have to fill in yourself are Client #, Item Code, and Quantity.

Follow these steps to complete the Navigation Spec screen, as shown in Figure 16.12:

1. Select Field Navigation from the Programming menu to display the Navigation Spec screen.

2. In the Client # field, type

    <If @UPDATE Then Goto #8

This statement will move the cursor directly to the Date Paid field when you enter the record through the Search/Update function so you

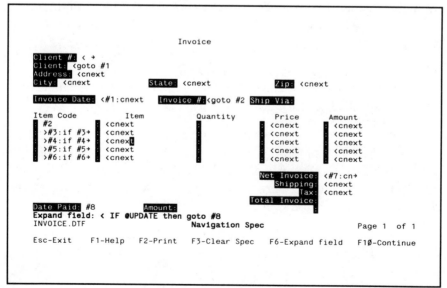

Figure 16.12: Invoice Navigation Spec screen

can quickly add the date the invoice was paid and then the amount received. However, it does not prevent you from manually moving the cursor backward through the form if you need to change other information on the invoice.

An on-field-entry navigation statement will be executed before an on-field-exit programming statement. When you are adding records, the If condition is false, so the cursor remains in the Client # field. When you press ⏎, the on-exit programming statement is executed, and its If condition is executed.

3. In the Client field, type **<Goto #1**.

This bypasses the Address, City, State, and Zip fields, which are filled in by the external lookup statement in the Client field.

4. In the Invoice Date field, type **<#1: CNext**.

5. In the Invoice # field, type **<Goto #2**.

This bypasses the Ship Via field, which will be filled in by the external lookup statement in the Client field.

6. In the first row under the Item Code heading (the first column in the first row), type **#2**.

7. In the second row under the heading Item Code (the first column in the second row), type

    >#3: If #3 = "" Then Goto #7

The restriction you entered in the first row under Item Code requires you to enter at least one item in each invoice. However, if you do not enter a value in the second row, it means that you are finished entering items, and the cursor will move directly to field #7, Net Invoice.

8. Enter a similar command in each of the other fields in that column:

    >#4: If #4 = "" Then Goto #7

    >#5: If #5 = "" Then Goto #7

    >#6: If #6 = "" Then Goto #7

9. Enter **<CNext** in each of the fields under the Item, Price, and Amount headings.

You do not have to enter the command in the Quantity column because you must manually enter a value there.

10. In the Net Invoice field, type **<#7: CNext**.

11. Enter **<CNext** in the Shipping and Tax fields.

12. In the Date Paid field, type **#8**.

13. Press F10 to save the navigation specification.

The programming and navigation commands you entered will automate filling in the Invoice form. If you have a slower computer system and a large Clients database, however, you might notice a slight delay each time Q&A performs an external lookup.

Later in the chapter, we will explore some advanced programming techniques that you can use in your own applications.

ADDING INVOICES

Now let's see how the programming works by adding several invoices to the system. Assume that two orders were just phoned in, and you want to process the invoices.

Follow these steps:

1. Press Esc twice to reach the File menu, select Add Data, and then press ⏎ to display the first form.

2. Type **101** and press ⏎.

The XLookup command inserts the client's data in the appropriate fields, the date is filled in, and the invoice is numbered.

3. Type **104** and press ⏎.

The item's name appears, and the cursor moves to the Quantity column.

4. Type **10** and press CR.

The price is inserted, the extended amount is calculated, and the cursor moves to the next row. Now let's see what happens if we enter an invalid item number.

5. Type **145** and press ↵.

The cursor moves to the Quantity column, but an item name does not appear. The message line displays

The lookup file does not have the key value: 145

6. Press Shift-Tab twice to return to the Item column.

7. Type **102** and press ↵. The name of the item is inserted.

8. Type **1** and press ↵ to retrieve the price and calculate the extended amount. The cursor moves to the next row.

9. Press ↵ without making an entry. The net invoice, shipping charges, tax, and total invoice amounts are calculated and displayed.

10. Press F10 to save the invoice and display the next record.

11. Type **106** and press ↵.

12. Type **101**, press ↵, type **10**, and press ↵.

13. Type **107**, press ↵, type **20**, and press ↵.

14. Type **103**, press ↵, type **2**, and press ↵.

15. Press ↵ to complete the invoice, then Shift-F10 to return to the File menu.

DEFINING THE POSTING MACRO

The next step in building the invoicing application is to create a macro to post the transactions. The macro will perform the following tasks:

- Post the invoice date, amount, and number to the Clients database and accumulate the total orders. This portion of the macro will replace the posting macro you created in Chapter 15.

- Post the amounts ordered to the Stock database, subtracting them from the values in the On Hand fields and calculating any backorders.

- Copy the posted records to an archive transaction database file. You will use this file to update records when invoices are paid and for printing reports.

Most of the steps for creating the posting specifications and macro are similar to those you followed in Chapter 15.

CREATING THE ARCHIVE FILE

First we need to set up the archive file where invoices will be stored after they have been posted. To save disk space, the file will not include the unlabeled field that we use to accumulate total orders.

Rather than retype the entire form, you will make a copy of the Invoice database design, and then delete the extra field. We also have to delete any programming or navigation statements that refer to the deleted field.

1. Select Copy from the File menu and press ↵ to accept Invoice.

2. Type **D** to select Design Only.

3. Press Shift-F4, type **Archive**, press ↵, and type **Y**.

4. When the menu appears, press Esc to return to the File menu.

5. Select Design File, choose Redesign a File, type **Archive**, and then press ↵.

6. Delete the entire unlabeled field at the bottom of the form, *:Ao >.*

7. Press F10 twice to save the form and return to the Design menu.

8. Select Program a File, press ↵ to accept Archive, and then select Program a Form.

9. Expand the Total Invoice field, delete *#41 = #38;,* and press F10.

10. Press F10 to save the edited specification, then Esc twice to return to the File menu.

POSTING
TRANSACTIONS TO CLIENT RECORDS

Next, we will create a specification to post fields from the Invoice database to the Clients database.

1. Select Post from the File menu, type **Invoice**, and press ↵.

2. Type **Clients** and press ↵ to display the Retrieve Spec screen.

3. Press F10 to display the Posting Spec screen.

4. Press ↓ four times to reach the Invoice Date field.

5. Press F7 to display the posting box.

6. Type **Last Order Date** as the field you want Order Date posted to.

7. Press ↵ to reach the when the field prompt and type **Client #**.

8. Press ↵ to reach the matches the external field prompt and type **Customer Code**.

9. Press F10 to return to the Posting Spec screen, accepting Replace as the operation.

10. Press ↵ to reach the Invoice # field, then F7 to display the posting box.

11. Type **Last Invoice No.** and press F10.

12. Press ↓ nine times to reach the Total Invoice field, and then press F7.

13. Type **Amount** as the name of the field you want to post the value to, and then press F10.

14. Press ↓ to reach the unlabeled field under Total Orders, and then press F7.

15. Type **Total Orders**, and then press ↵ three times to reach the Operation options.

16. Select Add and press F10.

17. Press Shift-F8, type **Post Transactions**, and press ↵ to save the specification.

18. Press Esc to return to the File menu.

POSTING ON-HAND
AMOUNTS AND BACKORDERS

Now create the posting specification for updating the on-hand amounts in the Stock database.

1. Select Post from the File menu and press ↵ to accept the Invoice database.

2. Type **Stock** and press ↵, then F10 to display the Posting Spec screen.

3. Press ↓ five times, then Tab to reach the Quantity field in the first detail row, then F7 to display the posting box.

4. Type **On Hand** as the field you want the quantity posted to.

5. Press ↵ to reach the when the field prompt, type **F0001**, press ↵, and type **Stock Number**.

6. Press ↵, type **S** to select Subtract, and then press F10.

7. Press ↓ to reach the Quantity field in the next row, then F7.

On Hand already appears as the external posting field, and Stock Number as the external key field. You have to change the field you want to use for the match.

8. Press ↵ to reach the when the field prompt and type **F0006**.

9. Press ↵ twice, type **S** to select Subtract, and then press F10.

10. Press ↓ to reach the Quantity field in the next row, then F7.

11. Press ↵ and type **F0011**.

12. Press ↵ twice, type **S**, and press F10.

13. Press ↓ to reach the Quantity field in the next row, then F7.

14. Press ↵ and type **F0016**.

15. Press ↵ twice, type **S**, and press F10.

16. Press ↓ to reach the Quantity field in the next row, then F7.

17. Press ↵ and type **F0021**.

18. Press ↵ twice, type **S**, and press F10.

19. Press F8 to display the recalculation options, as shown in Figure 16.13.

By default, calculation, on-entry, and on-exit programming statements are not executed when you post to a record. When you post the invoice to update the on-hand amounts, however, you want the calculation statement to update the backordered field, if necessary.

The Batch Post Calculation Options menu allows you to change the default setting. Select Yes for the statements you want to execute during posting. As stated in the note at the bottom of the menu, on-field-entry and on-field-exit statements are never executed during posting. This menu controls

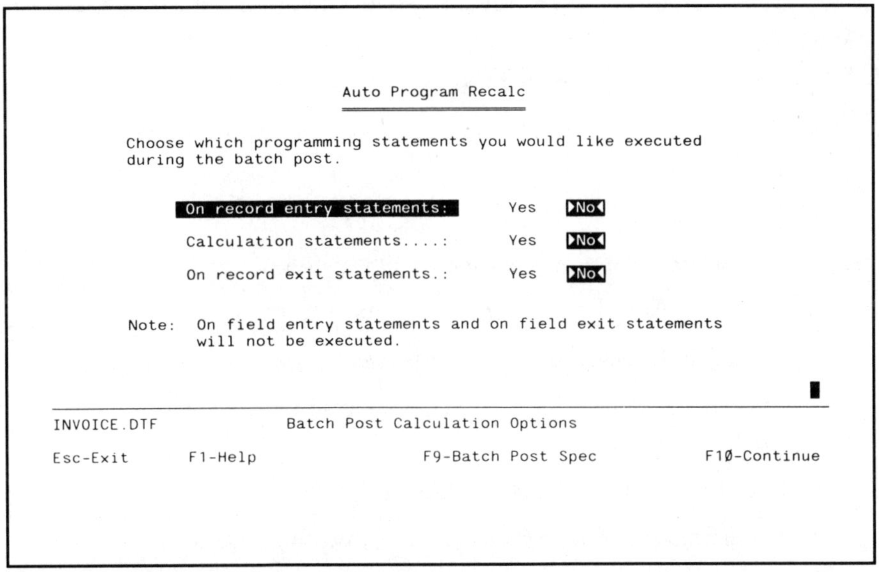

```
                         Auto Program Recalc

        Choose which programming statements you would like executed
        during the batch post.


           On record entry statements:      Yes    ▶No◀

           Calculation statements....:       Yes    ▶No◀

           On record exit statements.:       Yes    ▶No◀


        Note:  On field entry statements and on field exit statements
               will not be executed.


                                                                    ▮

        ───────────────────────────────────────────────────────────
        INVOICE.DTF           Batch Post Calculation Options

        Esc-Exit      F1-Help             F9-Batch Post Spec        F10-Continue
```

Figure 16.13: Batch Post Calculation Options screen

regular calculation, on-record-entry, and on-record-exit statements.

Note that when you are filling in the Update Spec screen, you can press F8 to display this menu and select the statements you want executed during a mass update.

20. Press ↵ to reach the Calculation Statements option, type **Y**, and press F9 to return to the Posting Spec screen.

21. Press Shift-F8, type **Post Stock**, and press ↵.

22. Press Esc to return to the File menu.

RECORDING THE POSTING MACRO

The final step is to create the macro that posts and archives the transactions, then removes the records to prepare the transaction file for the next period. This is similar to the posting macro you created in Chapter 9, but it will perform two postings: from Invoice to Clients, then from Invoice to Stock.

Start the macro by posting the records to Clients.

1. Press Esc to display the Main menu, then press Shift-F2 and type **D**.

2. Press Alt-P and type **Y** to replace the existing posting macro.

3. Select Post from the File menu, press Shift-F4, type **Invoice**, and press ↵.

4. Press Shift-F4, type **Clients**, and press ↵.

5. Press F10 to display the Posting Spec screen.

6. Press Alt-F8, type **Post Transactions**, and press ↵.

7. Press F10 to begin the posting process.

8. Type **N** to post the records. The File menu will appear when the posting is complete.

9. Select Post and press ↵ to accept Invoice.

10. Press Shift-F4, type **Stock**, press ↵, and then press F10.

11. Press Alt-F8, type **Post Stock**, and press ↵.

12. Press F10 and type **N** to post the records.

Now that the data is posted, you can archive and purge the invoices.

13. Type **C** to select Copy, press ↵ to accept Invoice, and type **S** to select records.

14. Press Shift-F4, type **Archive**, and press ↵.

15. Press F10 twice to display the Merge Spec screen and merge all the fields. The File menu will reappear.

16. Type **R** to select Remove and press ↵ to accept Invoice.

17. Type **S**, press F10, and type **Y** to delete all the records.

18. Press Esc twice to return to the Main menu.

19. Press Shift-F2 and type **Post Transactions**.

20. Press ↵ to reach the Show Screen option and type **N**.

21. Press F10, then ↵ to save the macro.

22. Type **X** to exit.

RUNNING THE APPLICATION

With the application complete, you can record transactions in the Invoice database as they occur. When you want to update the Clients and Stock databases, display the Main menu and press Alt-P. The transactions will be posted and archived, and then the Invoice file will be purged.

When a client pays an invoice, locate the invoice in the Archive database. The @UPDATE function in line 1 will move the cursor directly to the Date Paid field. Enter the date and amount, and then save the record.

How often should you post invoices? Until you post, the transaction fields in Clients and the on-hand amounts in Stock will not be accurate. If you access these databases regularly, post after each invoicing session. Make sure you post before printing client or inventory reports that include transaction and on-hand fields.

If you develop an application for another user, create a system of menus and macros to automate the entire process. Begin by deciding which functions you want the user to perform, and then plan a series of custom menus. Figure 16.14 shows an example of a menu system that includes a main menu and several submenus for an invoicing application. It could also include additional menus listing specific reports. Define macros that run each process in the submenus, and macros that call the submenus from the main menu.

Next, develop the menus themselves. On the Macro Menu Options menu for submenus, select Overlay and enter the main menu name for the On Escape option. This way, the menus will be linked together as in Q&A's

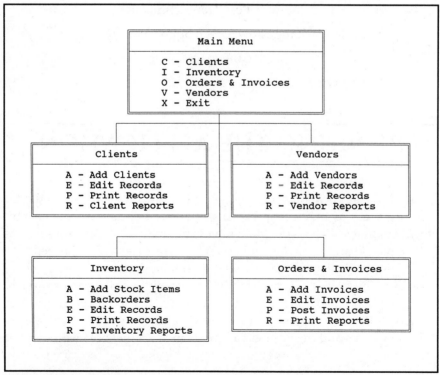

Figure 16.14: Menu structure for client-invoicing system

own menu structure. By replacing Q&A's main menu with your own, you can create a totally automated, turnkey system.

CUSTOMIZING AND PROGRAMMING FORMS ON THE FLY

If you find you need to modify a customization or programming option while you are adding or updating records, press Shift-F9 to display the menu shown in Figure 16.15.

You must fill in all required fields before Q&A will display the menu, because selecting an option saves the record and displays the designated Spec screen. If there are unfilled required fields when you press Shift-F9, the cursor will move to the nearest one and display a warning message. When all required fields have been completed, press the letter corresponding to the specification you want to change:

F - Frmt   Format Fields

R - Rstrct   Restrict

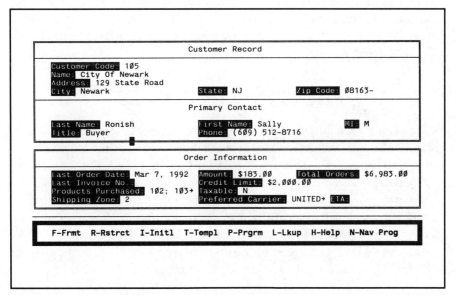

Figure 16.15: Custom Spec menu

I - Initl	Initial Values
T-Templ	Template
P - Prgrm	Program
L - Lkup	Lookup tables
H - Help	Custom help messages
N - Nav Prog	Navigation

When you leave the Spec screen, the Customize or Programming menu will appear.

PRODUCING INVOICES AND REPORTS

With the Stock and Invoice databases created, you can print any number of useful reports. In addition to the techniques you learned previously, you can include information from several databases in a report by using external lookup commands in derived columns and in form documents.

As an example, let's examine how you could print invoices and back-order and aging reports.

PRINTING INVOICES

You can print a quick copy of your invoice for review by pressing Shift-PrtSc after the total invoice amount is calculated. A copy of the on-screen form will be sent to your printer. However, the output will include the status, message, and key-assignment lines, but will not show any data in extended fields.

To print an invoice more suitable for mailing, design a printing specification using the coordinate method. Figure 16.16 shows a completed printing specification, and Figure 16.17 is a sample printout. The word INVOICE was entered as a header. Be sure to use a top-margin setting that is large enough to accommodate your preprinted letterhead.

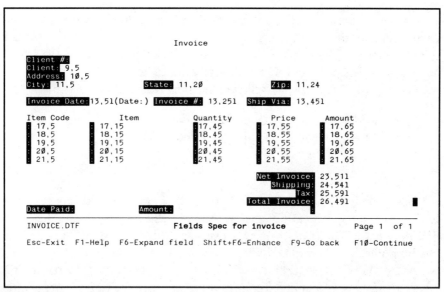

Figure 16.16: Fields Spec screen for printing invoices

```
                         INVOICE


        Chesin Pharmacy, Inc.
        182 Walnut Street
        Newark          NJ   08192


        Date: Jan 11, 1992  Invoice #: 106      Ship Via: UNITED PARCEL


        104      Disk 3.5" LD                  10        0.88      $8.80
        102      HPIII Cartridge               1        68.77     $68.77




                                          Net Invoice:  $77.57
                                             Shipping:   $6.50
                                                  Tax:   $5.43
                                        Total Invoice:  $89.50
```

Figure 16.17: Sample invoice

Notice that the invoice does not include headings above the Item Code, Item, Quantity, Price, and Amount columns. If you feel they are necessary, you can print headings by designing the form with a blank field just above the screen headings. On the Set Initial Values Spec screen, add a text string that includes the headings as a field value. That section of the form would appear like this:

```
:Item Code    Item     Quantity   Price    Amount
Item Code     Item     Quantity   Price    Amount
:             :        :          :        :

:             :        :          :        :
```

Use a navigation statement to bypass the field when adding records. In the printing specification, assign the field the number just before the first item code. The text string will print as a field value but appear as a heading over the columns.

As an alternative to using a printing specification, press F2 or Ctrl-F2 when the invoice is displayed to print it. Make sure the options are set for one form per page, and then press F10. This way, you could enhance the form with lines and boxes and print them by selecting to print field labels.

But for the greatest control and flexibility, print invoices as a merge document in Q&A Write. Figure 16.18 shows a merge document that was used to print the invoice in Figure 16.19. It illustrates how to use external lookup commands in merge documents to access more than one database. Most of the information comes from the Invoice database, but the contact's name, shipping zone, and estimated delivery time are retrieved from the Clients database. Note that the series of program commands to print the contact's name should be entered as one long line (Q&A divides it with word wrap).

The spacing in the merge document may not seem right, but it is necessary to align the net invoice, tax, shipping, and total invoice amounts with the last column in the detail lines. To create the columns and other aligned numbers, you have to carefully set and use decimal tab stops.

Set a left margin at 10 and a right margin at 75. Using the position indicator on the status line, set a left tab at position 10 and decimal tabs at 34, 45, and 55. Use the Editing Options menu to turn on real tab characters. This will ensure proper alignment when the data is merged from the lookup files.

GENERATING BACKORDER REPORTS

A backorder report lists the item number, name, amount backordered, and the vendor name of items in the Stock database that contain a value greater than zero in the Backorder field.

Since the vendor name is not stored with the Stock record, you have to create a report that accesses two separate databases, Stock and Vendors. Use Stock as the primary database and access Vendors with an external lookup command in a derived column.

Figure 16.20 shows one format a backorder report can take. It lists the vendor's name, then the stock number, item name, and amount backordered.

```
                          Invoice

*Client*
*Address*
*City*, *State*  *Zip*


Attention: *program {@XLOOKUP("CLIENTS",#1,"Customer Code","First
Name")}* *program {@XLOOKUP("CLIENTS",#1,"CUSTOMER CODE","MI")}*
*program {@XLOOKUP("CLIENTS",#1,"Customer Code","Last Name")}*,
*program {@XLOOKUP("CLIENTS",#1,"Customer Code","Title")}*

Date:  *Invoice Date*          Invoice #: *Invoice #*

Item       Description        Quantity       Price      Amount

*F0001*    *F0002*            *F0003*     *F0004*     *F0005*
*F0006*    *F0007*            *F0008*     *F0009*     *F0010*
*F0011*    *F0012*            *F0013*     *F0014*     *F0015*
*F0016*    *F0017*            *F0018*     *F0019*     *F0020*
*F0021*    *F0022*            *F0023*     *F0024*     *F0025*



                       Net Invoice:            *NET INVOICE*
                              Tax:           *TAX*
                         Shipping:        *SHIPPING*
                    Total Invoice:           *TOTAL INVOICE*


                  Shipping Information

Ship Via: *Ship Via*     to Zone: *program
{@XLOOKUP("CLIENTS",#1,"Customer Code","Shipping Zone")}*

Expected Delivery: *program {@XLOOKUP("CLIENTS",#1,"Customer
Code","ETA")}*
```

Figure 16.18: Merge document for printing invoices

```
                              INVOICE

          Dershaw, Inc.
          17th And Locust Streets
          Philadelphia, PA  19101

          Attention: Terry  Dershaw, President


          Date: Jan 11, 1992              Invoice #:132



           Item      Description     Quantity    Price    Amount

           101 Ep-80 Ribbons             1        5.18      5.18
           103 DJ Cartridge             12       14.30    171.60
           105 Disk 3.5" HD              1        1.31      1.31




                              Net Invoice:        178.09
                                     Tax:          10.69
                                Shipping:          10.00
                           Total Invoice:         198.78



                         Shipping Information

          Ship Via: FEDERAL EXPRESS      to Zone: 1

          Expected Delivery: 1 to 2 days after shipment
```

Figure 16.19: Sample merged invoice using information from two databases

Vendor	Stock Number	Item	Backordered
Marvin Supply, Inc.	103	DJ Cartridge	40
Siravo, Inc.	102	HPIII Cartridge	2
	108	HPII Cartridge	1
Capital Manufacturing	107	Labels 5.25	150
	110	Mailers 5.25	50

Figure 16.20: Backorder report using data from two files

The report was created with the retrieval criteria

    Backordered: > 0

and the entries on the Column/Sort Spec

    Stock Number: 3
    Item: 4
    Vendor: 1,AS,I
    Backordered: 5

and a derived column

    Heading: Vendor
    Formula: @XLU("Vendors",#1,"Vendor Code","Name")
    Column Spec: 2,AS

The Vendor Code field is used as an invisible first column to serve as the key to match records in the external lookup. The @XLU command serves the same function and uses the same syntax in reports as it does in programming statements. You can create derived columns using fields from any database as long as they contain a key that matches a field in the form.

PRINTING AGING REPORTS

Since cash flow is often the most critical problem facing a small business, an aging report is essential to good management. An aging report is a record of unpaid invoices based on the number of days they have been outstanding.

Use the Archive database for the aging report because it is the database you update with the date and amount paid.

Figure 16.21 shows a sample aging report. It was created with these

Client #	Invoice #	Invoice Date	0-30 Days	31-60 Days	Over 60 Days
101	110	Jan 7, 1992	$88.72	$0.00	$88.72
103	114	Mar 3, 1992	$0.00	$0.00	$172.00
106	121	May 9, 1992	$0.00	$130.25	$0.00
108	131	Jun 5, 1992	$219.42	$0.00	$0.00
Total:			$219.42	$130.25	$260.72

Figure 16.21: Sample aging report

entries on the Column/Sort Spec screen:

    Client #: 1,AS
    Invoice Date: 3
    Invoice #: 2,AS
    Total Invoice: 4,I

And it uses these derived columns:

    Heading: 0-30 Days
    Formula: (@DATE − #3 < 31) * #4
    Column Spec: 5,T

    Heading: 31-60 Days
    Formula: (@DATE − #3 > 31 AND @DATE − #3 < 61) * #4
    Column Spec: 6,T

    Heading: Over 60 Days
    Formula: (@DATE − #3 > 60) * #4
    Column Spec: 7,T

The amount of the total invoice is an invisible column used to calculate the derived columns. The derived columns use the formula @DATE − #3 to calculate the number of days since the invoice was created, and Boolean operations that return a 1 if true, 0 if false.

For example, let's consider the first derived column. If the invoice is less than 31 days old, the formula (@DATE − #3 < 31) will return a value of 1. When the row's entry for that column is printed, the total invoice amount will be multiplied by one. Since any number times one is the number itself, the total invoice amount will appear unchanged. If the invoice were not less than 31 days old, the formula would return a 0. Since any number times zero is zero, a 0 will print in that column.

The second derived column prints the total invoice amount if the invoice is between 30 and 60 days old; the last derived column prints the invoice amount if it is over 60 days old.

Notice that the heading in the second derived column starts with a colon. Q&A will normally ignore numbers, except 0, that start a heading, so without the colon, the heading would appear as -60 Days. The colon tells Q&A to treat the numbers following as text.

ADVANCED PROGRAMMING CONCEPTS

||||➤ **To use advanced programming techniques:**

- **Use the @SELECT function to insert text or numeric values in fields.**
- **Protect a field from being changed by selecting Read Only Fields from the Programming menu and entering an R in the field.**
- **Construct lookup tables with groups of values (but do not duplicate keys).**

Q&A's programming language is easy to use and powerful because it is totally integrated with the database form. In fact, there is still quite a bit of programming you can add to fine-tune the invoicing application. In the following sections, you will learn additional details on controlling data input and working with ranges in lookup tables.

USING THE SELECT FUNCTION

Another way to quickly insert data into a field is through the @SELECT function, which has the syntax

@SELECT*(field-number, value1, value2, value3,...valuen)*

If the field value is 1, the first value in the list is returned; if it is 2, the second value is returned; and so forth. The values can be separated by commas or semicolons. Values in the function can either be text or numeric.

For example, in our Clients database, we could have used this statement:

#8 = @SELECT(#8,"United Parcel","Federal Express","Parcel Post","Truck")

If you enter 1 in the field, United Parcel will appear when the function is calculated. If you enter 3 in the field, Parcel Post will appear. When you enter a number smaller than 1 or larger than the number of items in the function, the last value will appear.

Q&A will take the integer of a decimal number in returning the elements; 2.66 will return the second item in the list.

DESIGNATING READ-ONLY FIELDS

In our Stock database, the programming statement in the Price field will calculate the price automatically from the Cost and Markup fields when the field is entered as you move forward through the record. However, if you press ↑ or → to enter the field, you could override the calculation and change the price manually.

To prevent a calculation from being overridden, designate the field as read-only. A *read-only* field is one that can only be altered by programming statements or during a post, update, or copy operation. You cannot move the cursor manually into a read-only field.

To create a read-only field, select Read Only Fields from the Programming menu, and then enter an R next to the field labels on the Spec screen that appears. If you want to insert a fixed value into a field, enter it as an initial value (through the Set Initial Values option on the Customize menu), and then designate the field as read-only.

USING GROUPS IN LOOKUP TABLES

The method we used for computing shipping charges in our Invoice database does not consider the carrier. If the charges vary with the carrier as well, you would have to construct a table something like the one shown in Figure 16.22.

Notice that the keys, now seven characters long, are grouped according to the first letter of a shipper. The first group contains charges for United Parcel, the second for Federal Express, and so on. The number of rows and ranges vary with each group.

To access the keys, the key field in the range lookup command would appear like this

```
@LEFT(@XLU("Clients",#1,"Customer Code","Preferred Carrier"),1)+
@RIGHT("000000"+@STR(@INT(#35)),6)
```

KEY	1	2	3	4
U000000	1.50	2.25	3.35	
U000010	2.35	3.50	4.25	
U000025	3.25	4.75	5.85	
U000040	4.15	6.15	7.10	
U000070	6.50	7.25	10.50	
F000000	6.50	6.50	6.50	
F000005	12.50	12.50	12.50	
F000025	17.50	17.50	17.50	
P000001	1.25	1.25	1.25	
P000005	2.50	2.50	2.50	
P000015	3.75	3.75	3.75	
P000025	4.75	4.75	4.75	
T000050	18.26	21.50	26.75	
T000100	35.00	38.95	42.50	

```
INVOICE.DTF                        Lookup Table                      Page 1  of 1

Esc-Exit  F6-Expand field   PgUp-Previous page    PgDn-Next page    F10-Continue
```

Figure 16.22: A lookup table may contain different groups of data

This adds the first letter of the carrier to the beginning of the string. The shipping charges will now vary with the amount of the invoice, zone, and carrier.

Lookup tables can contain groups of several types as long as no keys are duplicated. The table in Figure 16.23, for example, contains six rows of shipping charges and three rows of state sales tax rates. If you wanted the tax amount on the invoice to depend on the state, use this statement in the program specification:

Tax: <#37: If @XLU("Clients",#1,"Customer Code","Taxable") Then
#37 = #35 * @LU(#5,1)

The @XLOOKUP function retrieves the state's tax rate from the table.

RETRIEVING DBASE
RECORDS WITH LOOKUP

You can use external lookup commands to retrieve field values directly from a dBASE file without performing any special conversion or importing

```
┌──────────────────────────────────────────────────────────────────────────┐
│                                                                            │
│   ┌──────────┬──────────┬──────────┬──────────┬──────────┐                 │
│   │   KEY    │    1     │    2     │    3     │    4     │                 │
│   ├──────────┼──────────┼──────────┼──────────┼──────────┤                 │
│   │ 000000   │ 1.50     │ 2.25     │ 3.35     │          │                 │
│   │ 000010   │ 2.35     │ 3.50     │ 4.25     │          │                 │
│   │ 000025   │ 3.25     │ 4.75     │ 5.85     │          │                 │
│   │ 000040   │ 4.75     │ 6.15     │ 7.10     │          │                 │
│   │ 000070   │ 6.50     │ 7.25     │ 10.50    │          │                 │
│   │ 000100   │ 9.25     │ 10.15    │ 11.25    │          │                 │
│   │          │          │          │          │          │                 │
│   │ DE       │ .03      │          │          │          │                 │
│   │ NJ       │ .07      │          │          │          │                 │
│   │ PA       │ .06      │          │          │          │                 │
│   │          │          │          │          │          │                 │
│   │          │          │          │          │          │                 │
│   │          │          │          │          │          │                 │
│   └──────────┴──────────┴──────────┴──────────┴──────────┘                 │
│                                                                            │
│   CLIENTS.DTF              Lookup Table              Page 1  of 1          │
│                                                                         ▋  │
│   Esc-Exit  F6-Expand field   PgUp-Previous page   PgDn-Next page  F10-Continue │
│                                                                            │
└──────────────────────────────────────────────────────────────────────────┘
```

Figure 16.23: Lookup table to charge by amount, zone, and carrier

the file. The dBASE file must not be encrypted and must be indexed on the field you want to use as the external key. For the external file name, enter the full path and name of the dBASE file, including the .DBF extension.

If you are retrieving data from a dBASE IV file, enter the name of the dBASE field as the external key. Q&A assumes the index is in a file having the same name as the database but with the .MDX extension. For earlier versions of dBASE, which use separate files for each indexed field, enter the path and name of the index file, including the .NDX extension, in place of the external key field.

Appendix B summarizes all of Q&A's programming commands and functions. By combining them with the techniques you learned in this and previous chapters, you can program entire business applications.

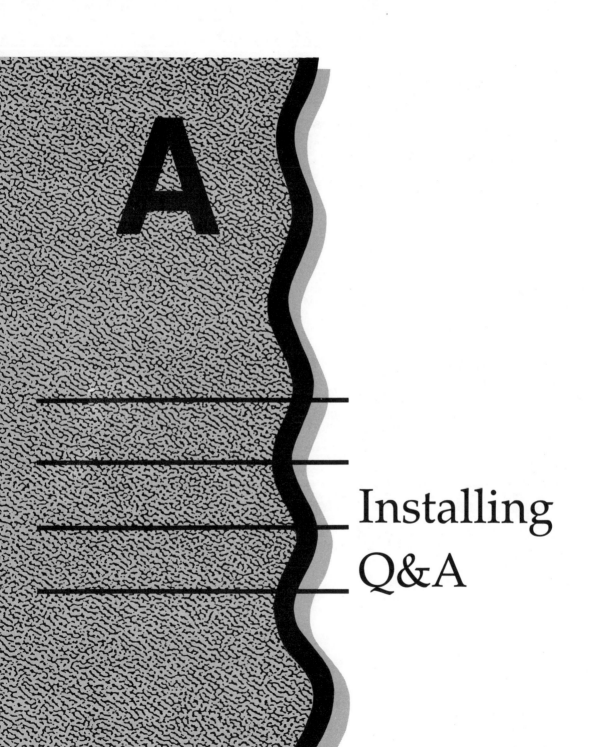

A

Installing
Q&A

Before using Q&A, you must install it on your hard disk drive. The Q&A floppy disks contain compressed files that cannot be used directly, even if you copy them to the hard disk. (A *compressed* file contains any number of individual files that are squeezed together to save room.)

The Install program provided with Q&A decompresses the files and copies them to the hard disk. It also lets you select font files that you will need to print documents and gives you the opportunity to install tutorial and sample database files.

BACKING UP YOUR Q&A DISKS

Before you install Q&A, make a backup copy of your Q&A disks. Then use the backup as your working copy and store the original in a safe place. Because disks can wear out or become damaged, having an extra set of disks is a precaution against losing this valuable program.

You will need a DOS disk, all your Q&A disks, and a number of blank disks, either 5¼-inch or 3½-inch, depending on your computer system. Make sure you have a blank disk for each disk supplied with Q&A.

First, *write-protect* your Q&A disks to ensure that you do not accidentally erase your Q&A program. With 5¼- inch disks, place a write-protect tab over the small notch on the edge of each disk. The write-protect tabs are the small rectangular stickers that are packaged with blank diskettes. If you have 3½- inch disks, protect the disk by pushing the small tab toward the end of the disk. If the small square is blocked, the disk is unlocked and the files can be erased. Lock the disk by pushing the tab so the hole is uncovered.

Do not lock or write-protect the blank disks that you will be copying onto. You want these disks free so that you can transfer Q&A to them.

BACKING UP WITH TWO
IDENTICAL FLOPPY DISK DRIVES

Follow the steps below to back up your Q&A if your system has two disk drives that are the same size. If you have two different size disk drives, follow the procedure in the next section for a single disk system. In this procedure, *never* place one of your original Q&A disks in drive B. If you do, the Q&A program could be destroyed.

1. Turn on the computer and respond to the date and time prompts if they appear. Wait until the drive prompt appears. It will usually be C>.

2. To make sure the DOS program DISKCOPY.COM is on the current directory, type **DIR** and press ↵ to display the programs on the main, or *root*, directory. If the directory listing scrolls off the screen too quickly, use the command DIR/P. The listing will pause when the screen becomes full—press any key to display the next screen. If DISKCOPY.COM is not there, make a note of the subdirectory names (marked with <DIR>). Move to each subdirectory by entering **CD** followed by the subdirectory's name, and then use the DIR command again to check for the copying program, DISKCOPY.COM. If you cannot find it, insert a DOS disk into your floppy drive, log onto the drive, and continue.

3. Type **DISKCOPY A: B:** and press ↵. (DOS commands can be entered in either uppercase or lowercase.)

The screen will display a message similar to the following, depending on your version of DOS:

    Insert the source diskette in drive A: and the destination diskette in
    drive B:
    Press Return when ready

The *source* diskette is the original Q&A disk that you will be copying from. The *destination* disk is the blank diskette that you are copying onto.

4. Place one of your Q&A disks in drive A and a blank disk in drive B.

5. Press ↵ to begin copying.

When the copy is completed, you will see the message

Copy Another (Y/N)?

6. Remove the disks and immediately label the copy accordingly.

Write the name of the disk on the label before sticking it on the disk. If you write on the disk itself, the impression of a pen or pencil could damage the recording surface. If you must write on a disk, use a felt-tipped pen and write very lightly.

7. Press Y and repeat this process for all your disks.

Place the original Q&A disks in a safe location and use the copies for everyday work.

BACKING UP WITH ONE FLOPPY DISK DRIVE

Follow the steps below to back up your Q&A disks with a one floppy disk drive system or a system with two different sized drives. During this procedure, you must be very careful to follow the instructions displayed on the screen. Remember to install write-protect tabs on your Q&A disks as a precaution against accidentally erasing them.

1. Start your computer and log onto the directory that contains the DOS program DISKCOPY.COM. (Refer to step 2 in the previous section for details.)

2. Type **DISKCOPY A: A:** and press ↵. The screen will display

Insert source diskette in drive A:
Strike any key when ready

You will be making a copy using only one disk drive. During the process, you will be instructed to insert either the source diskette or the destination diskette into drive A. The *source* diskette is the original Q&A disk that you will be copying from. The *destination* diskette is the blank disk that you are copying onto. *Never* insert the original Q&A disk when you are asked to insert the destination disk. If the write-protect notch is not covered, the Q&A program will be erased.

3.   Place one of your Q&A disks in drive A.

This will be one of the original disks supplied with Q&A. You should have a write-protect notch on it; or with 3-1/2 inch disks, the tab should be moved to the locked position.

4.   Press any key. Soon you will see the message

   Insert destination diskette in drive A:
   Strike any key when ready

5.   Remove the Q&A disk and insert a blank disk in drive A.

6.   Press any key to begin copying.

You may be told several times to switch disks until all the information on the Q&A disk has been copied onto the blank disk. Be certain that the original Q&A disk is in the drive only when the screen requests the source diskette.

When the copy is completed, you will see the message

   Copy Another (Y/N)?

7.   Remove the disk and immediately label the copy accordingly.

Write the name of the disk on the label before sticking it on the disk. If you write on the disk itself, the impression of a pen or pencil could damage the recording surface. If you must write on a disk, use a felt-tipped pen and write very lightly.

8.   Press Y and repeat this process for all your disks.

Place the original Q&A disks in a safe location and use the copies for your everyday work.

INSTALLING Q&A

After you have made a set of backup disks, follow these steps to install Q&A:

1. Insert the Q&A disk labeled #1 - Install Disk in drive A.

2. Type **A:** and press ↵ to log onto drive A.

3. Type **Install** and press ↵. You will see the initial screen shown in Figure A.1.

4. Press ↵. You will see a screen listing the disk drives available in your system and asking you to designate the source drive.

5. Press ↵ to accept drive A. Q&A will display the message

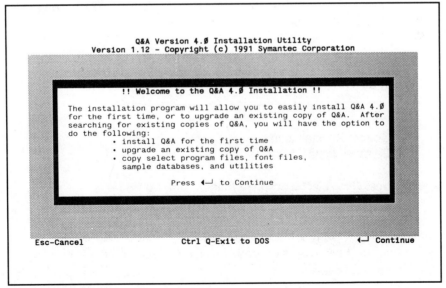

Figure A.1: Initial installation screen

Preparing for Installation

and then ask you to select the destination drive.

6. Press ↓ until the letter of your hard disk is highlighted, and then press ↵.

As Install searches your hard disk for an already installed version of Q&A, you will see the message

Scanning for Other Copies of Q&A

If this is the first time you are installing Q&A, you will see the message

Enter Pathname: C:\QA\

If you have a version of Q&A already installed, you will see a screen showing the directory and the option Create Directory. Select the existing directory if you want to replace the installed version, or select Create Directory and enter a directory name to install the new version separately.

7. Press ↵ to accept the default directory name, or press the Backspace key to erase the directory, enter another one, and then press ↵.

If your are updating a previous version of Q&A, you will be warned that it will be deleted during installation. Press ↵ to continue or Esc to cancel.

Next, Q&A will display a menu with two options:

C - Complete Installation
S - Selective Installation

8. Press ↵ to select Complete Installation.

If you are updating a previous version of Q&A, you can choose to upgrade custom mailing labels and to make a backup copy of the existing Q&A program files. Based on your selections, Install will either copy or delete your old program files.

Install will decompress and copy the files from the disk in drive A to your hard disk. Follow the messages on the screen to replace the disk in drive A with other Q&A disks. When all the files have been decompressed and copied, you will see the message

Installation of Program Files Successfully Completed

9. Press ↵ to see the message

Hit ↵ to install fonts, or Esc to cancel

10. Press ↵. The Install program will display a list of printers supported by Q&A, as shown in Figure A.2.

In order to use your printer's fonts and special features, you must copy the appropriate font files to the Q&A directory. The name of the Q&A font file is shown on the left side of the list; the printer, model name, and type of fonts are on the right side. There may be several different font files available for your printer.

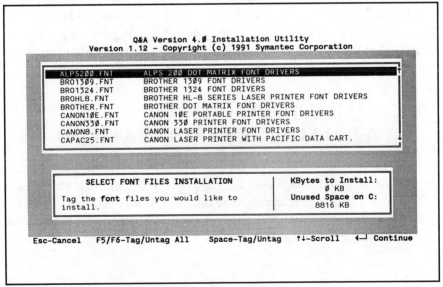

Figure A.2: Select the printers and fonts you want to install

11. Press ↓ or PgDn to find the printer and fonts you want to use. Highlight the name and press the spacebar to tag the name, indicating that you want it copied.

12. Repeat step 11 to tag all the font files you might be needing, and then press ↵ to copy the files to your hard disk. (You will be able to add additional font files at any time after you install Q&A.)

13. Follow the instructions that appear on the screen to install optional Q&A files and to complete the installation process.

You will be given the opportunity to install tutorial files, utilities, and ready-to-use files. The tutorial files include a sample merge document and the database that is used to illustrate functions in the Q&A manual. Utility files include QABACKUP, a program for backing up database and document files from the DOS prompt; QAFONT, for adding softfonts to font files; HIMEM.SYS, for managing extended memory; and several sample files for testing your printer. The ready-to-use files are sample database files for a customer invoicing system. Since you will be creating your own customer invoicing system in this book, you might not want to copy the ready-to-use files at this time.

You may also be asked if you want to modify the CONFIG.SYS file read by the operating system when you start your computer. Select Yes if that option appears. Q&A will modify the file or display a message indicating that no changes were necessary. When the installation process is completed, you are ready to use Q&A.

PERFORMING
A SELECTIVE INSTALLATION

Any time after you have performed a complete installation, you can copy additional font or optional files to your hard disk by performing a selective installation. You can also use this procedure to recopy Q&A program files—perhaps after accidentally erasing a necessary file or receiving an update disk from Symantec.

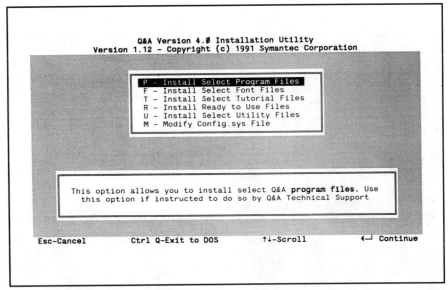

Figure A.3: Selective Installation options

Follow the procedure outlined in the previous section, but choose Selective Installation rather than Complete Installation. The Install program will display the options shown in Figure A.3. Choose the files you want to install, and then follow the instructions that appear on the screen.

B

Q&A
Cursor-
Movement
Keys and
Programming
Functions

Use this appendix as a quick reference guide to the Q&A cursor-movement keys and programming functions. The function-key commands are shown on the inside covers of the book.

CURSOR-MOVEMENT KEYS

The following keys and key combinations move the cursor through a document, form, or Spec screen.

Key	Movement
↑	Up a line
↓	Down a line
→	One character to the right
←	One character to the left
Ctrl-→	One word to the right
Ctrl-←	One word to the left
Home	
First press	Beginning of the line or field
Second press	Top of the screen
Third press	Top of the page or form
Fourth press	Beginning of the document
Ctrl-Home	To the beginning of the document or form
End	
First press	End of the line or field
Second press	Bottom of the screen

Key	Movement
Third press	Bottom of the page or form
Fourth press	End of the document
Ctrl-End	End of the document or form
PgUp	Top of the previous screen (Write)
	Previous page (File)
Ctrl-PgUp	Top of the previous page (Write)
PgDn	Top of the next screen (Write)
	Next page (File)
Ctrl-PgDn	Top of the next page
Tab	Next tab stop or field
Shift-Tab	Previous tab stop or field

WORDSTAR COMMANDS

The following key combinations simulate the cursor-movement and some editing keystrokes of WordStar. You can use these keystrokes to move the cursor in documents, records, and Spec screens (or redefine them in macros).

Key	Function
Ctrl-E	Moves up a line
Ctrl-X	Moves down a line
Ctrl-D	Moves one character to the right
Ctrl-S	Moves one character to the left
Ctrl-F	Moves one word to the right
Ctrl-A	Moves one word to the left
Ctrl-R	Moves to the top of the previous screen
Ctrl-G	Moves to the top of the next screen

Key	Function
Ctrl-G	Deletes the character at the cursor
Ctrl-T	Deletes the current word
Ctrl-Y	Deletes the current line
Ctrl-N	Inserts a blank line

Q&A FUNCTIONS

Q&A provides a complete set of functions and commands for use in programming statements. Many of the functions can also be used in *Program* commands for preparing form documents.

FINANCIAL FUNCTIONS

The parameters in the following functions represent numeric values, the numbers of fields containing a numeric value, or expressions that results in a numeric value.

@CGR(p,f,l)   Calculates the compound growth rate (rate of return), where p is principle, f is the future value, and l is the length of the loan.

@FV(p,i,n)   Calculates the future value of a series of payments, where p is the amount of each payment, i is the interest rate per period, and n is the number of payments.

@PMT(p,i,n)   Calculates the payments due on a loan, where p is the principle, i is the interest rate, and n is the number of payments.

@PV(p,i,n)   Calculates the present value of *an* annuity, where p is the amount of each payment, i is the interest rate per period, and n is the number of payments.

@IR(*p*,*pa*,*n*)   Calculates the interest rate of a loan, where *p* is the principle, *pa* is the payment amount, and *n* is the number of payments.

MATHEMATICAL FUNCTIONS

In the following functions, *n* and *m* represent numeric values, the number of a field containing a numeric value, or an expression that results in a numeric value. *List* represents a series of numeric values.

@ABS(*n*)
@AB(*n*)   Returns the absolute value of *n*.

@AVG(*list*)
@AV(*list*)   Produces the average of the values of all items in *list*.

@EXP(*n*,*m*)
@EX(*n*,*m*)   Raises *n* to the *m*th power.

@INT(*n*)
@IT(*n*)   Returns the integer portion of *n*.

@MAX(*list*)
@MX(*list*)   Returns the maximum value in *list*.

@MIN(*list*)
@MN(*list*)   Returns the minimum value in *list*.

@MOD(*n*,*m*)
@MD(*n*,*m*)   Returns *n* modulo *m*.

@ROUND(*n*,*m*) Rounds off *n* to *m* decimal digits.
@RND(*n*,*m*)

@SGN(*n*)   Returns the sign of *n*.

@SQRT(*n*)
@SQ(*n*)   Returns the square root of *n*.

@STD(*list*)   Calculates the standard deviation of *list*.

@SUM(*list*)	Returns the sum of the values in *list*.
@VAR(*list*)	Returns the variance of all nonblank items in *list*.

TEXT MANIPULATION FUNCTIONS

In the following functions, *x, y,* and *z* represent a string in quotation marks, the number of a field containing a string value, or an expression that results in a string. The parameters *n* and *m* represent numeric values, the number of fields containing numeric values, or an expression that results in a numeric value. *List* represents a series of fields.

@ASC(*x*) @AS(*x*)	Returns the ASCII decimal value of the first character of *x*.
@CHR(*n*) #CH(*n*)	Returns the ASCII character equivalent of *n*.
CLEAR(*list*)	Clears, or empties, a series of fields.
@DEL(*x,n,m*) @DE(*x,n,m*)	Returns *x* with *m* characters deleted, starting at position *n*. For example, @DEL("BARBARA",5,3) returns BARB.
@DITTO(*list*) @DI(*list*)	Copies the values from a list of fields from the previous record, in Add Data function only.
@FILENAME @FN	Returns the name of the current file.
@HELP(*n*) @HP(*n*)	Displays user-defined help for field *n*.
@INSTR(*x,y*) @IN(*x,y*)	Returns the position of the first occurrence of *y* in *x*. For example, if field #10 contains Philadelphia, the function @INSTR(#10,"d") returns the value 6.
@LEFT(*x,n*) @LT(*x,n*)	Returns the leftmost *n* characters of *x*.

@LEN(x) @LN(n)	Returns the length of the value in field x.
@MID(x,n,m) @MD(x,n,m)	Returns m characters from x starting at position n. For example, the function @MID("BARBARA",4,2) returns the string BA.
@MSG(x)	Displays the message x on the message line.
@REPLACE(z,x,y)	Replaces every occurrence of the character x with character y in the expression in field z. The resulting string is inserted in field z. For example, if field #10 contains 19116, the statement #20 = @REPLACE(#10,"1","2") modifies #10 to contain 29226.
@REPLFIR(z,x,y)	Replaces just the first occurrence of the character x with character y in the expression z.
@REPLLAS(z,x,y)	Replaces just the last occurrence of the character x with character y in the expression z.
@RIGHT(x,n) @RT(x,n)	Returns the rightmost n characters of x.
@TEXT(n,x) @TXT(n,x)	Produces a text value consisting of n characters of x.
@WIDTH(n) @WTH(n)	Returns the width of field n.

DATE AND TIME FUNCTIONS

In the following functions, d represents a field containing a Q&A date or time, n represents a date format, and x represents a text string containing date or time information.

@DATE(n) @DA(n)	Inserts the current data in format n (the format parameter is optional).
@D(x)	Converts the text string into a Q&A date.

@DOM(*d*) @DM(*d*)	Returns the day of the month (1, 2, 3...) in date *d*.
@DOW$(*d*) @DW$(*d*)	Returns the name of the day (Monday, Tuesday,...) in date *d*.
@MONTH(*d*) @MT$(*d*)	Returns the month (1, 2, 3,...) in date *d*.
@MONTH$(*d*) @MT$(*d*)	Returns the name of the month (January, February,...) in date *d*.
@TIME(*n*) @TME(*n*)	Inserts the current time in format *n* (the format parameter is optional).
@T(*x*)	Converts the text string into a Q&A time.
@YEAR(*d*) @YR(*d*)	Returns the year (1991, 1992,...) in date *d*.

FIELD CONVERSION FUNCTIONS

The following functions convert field values from one format to another. The parameter *x* represents a field number.

@NUM(*x*)	Removes all nonnumeric characters from a text string. For example, if field #10 contains 128 West 45th Street, the function @NUM(#10) returns 12845.
@STR	Returns *x* as a string expression.
@TONUMBER(*x*) @TN(*x*)	Returns *x* as a numeric value.
@TOMONEY(*x*) @TM(*x*)	Returns *x* as a monetary value.
@TODATE(*x*) @TT(*x*)	Returns *x* as a date value.
@TOTIME(*x*) @TT(*x*)	Returns *x* as a time value.

@TOYESNO(*x*)   Returns *x* as a Boolean (yes/no) value.
@TY(*x*)

LOOKUP COMMANDS

The following commands retrieve data from lookup tables or external database files.

Lookup Table Statements and Functions

In the following commands, *key* is the field number, value, or expression in the current record that you are attempting to match; *column* is the column in the lookup table that you want to return; and *d-field* is the name or number of the destination field in which to place the returned data.

LOOKUP(*key,column, d-field*)
LU (*key, column, d-field*)

Returns the corresponding value from *column* only when an exact match for *key* is found and puts the result in the *d-field*. For example, LOOKUP(#10,1,#20) inserts in field #20 the value in column 1 where the key matches the value in field #10. If no match is found, the destination field is unchanged.

@LOOKUP(*key, column*)
@LU(*key,column*)

Returns the corresponding value from *column* when an exact match for *key* is found. For example, #10 = @LOOKUP (#5,2) inserts in field #10 the value in column 2 where the key matches the value in field #5. If no match is found, the destination field is changed to blank.

LOOKUPR(*key, column,d-field*)
LUR(*key,column, d-field*)

Returns the corresponding value from *column* when an exact match for *key* is found, or the next lowest value for *key* if an exact match is not found, and puts the result in the *d-field*.

| @LOOKUPR(*key,* *column*) @LUR(*key,column*) | Returns the corresponding value from *column* when an exact match for *key* is found, or the next lowest value for *key* if an exact match is not found. |

External Lookup Commands

The following commands retrieve data from external databases. The functions can be used in preparing form documents in Write and in calculating derived columns in Report. They use the additional parameters *fn* for the name of the external file from which you want to retrieve data, surrounded by quotation marks; *x-key* for the name of the key field in the external database that you want to match with the key value from the current record, surrounded by quotation marks; and *x-field* for the name of the field in the external database that you want to retrieve, surrounded in quotation marks.

| XLOOKUP(*fn,key,* *x-key,x-field,d-field*) XLU(*fn,key,x-key,* *x-field,d-field*) | Searches the database *fn*, looking for a match between key in the current record and *x-key* in the external database. When a match is found, the value in *x-field* in the external database is inserted into *d-field* of the current record. For example, XLOOKUP ("Vendors",#3,"Vendor Code","Name",#40) places in field #40 the value in the Name field of Vendors, when the Vendor Code field in Vendors matches the contents of field #3 of the current record. |

@XLOOKUP(*fn,key, x-key,x-field*) @XLU(*fn,key, x-key,x-field*)	Returns the value in *x-field* of the database *fn*, when a match is found between the key field of the current record and field *x-field* of the database *fn*. For example, #50 = @LOOKUP("Clients",#20,"Client Code", "Total Orders") inserts in field #50 the value in the Total Orders fields of Clients, when the Client Code field in Clients matches the contents of field #20 of the current record.
XLOOKUPR(*fn,key, x-key,x-field,d-field*) XLR(*fn,key,x-key, x-field,d-field*)	Like XLOOKUP, except if an exact match is not found, it returns the field value from the record having the next lowest value in the external key field.
@XLOOKUPR(*fn,key, x-key,x-field*) @XLR(*fn,key,x-key, x-field*)	Like @XLOOKUP, except if an exact match is not found, it returns the field value from the record having the next lowest value in the external key field.

MISCELLANEOUS FUNCTIONS

The following functions can also be used in programming statements.

@ADD @AD	Returns a true when the program is adding forms.
@ERROR	Returns true if the most recent XLOOKUP failed; false if it was successful.
@FIELD(*x*) @(*x*)	Returns the value from field *x*, where *x* is a reference to a field.
@GROUP	Returns the name of the user's field security group.

@NUMBER @NMB	Returns a unique number, incremented by 1.
@NUMBER(n) @NMB(x)	Returns a unique number, incremented by n.
@REST(x,m)	Returns true if the field referred to by x has a value that matches m.
@SELECT($n,m,n,...$)	Returns the nth value of the list that follows.
@UPDATE @UD	Returns a true when the program is updating forms.
@USERID	Returns the user ID number of the current user of the database.

PROGRAM CONTROL COMMANDS

You can control the flow of program logic using the following commands in program statements. In addition, use the If statement, discussed in detail in Chapter 15, for conditional logic commands.

GOSUB	Transfers control of programming to the field given by the command. Each GOSUB command must have a matching RETURN.
RETURN	Returns control to where the GOSUB command was issued. Each RETURN command must have a matching GOSUB.
STOP	Cancels all pending returns and halts the program execution.

FIELD NAVIGATION COMMANDS

In programming statements, precede the field # with < or > to use the following commands. The less-than sign (<) causes the statements to be executed when the cursor enters the field; the greater-than sign (>) when the cursor exits the field.

GOTO *n*   Moves directly to field *n*, where *n* is a field identifier.

CNEXT   Moves to the next field.

CPREV   Moves to the previous field.

CHOME   Moves to the first field in the form.

CEND   Moves to the last field in the form.

PgDn   Moves to the first field on the next page.

PgUp   Moves to the first field on the previous page.

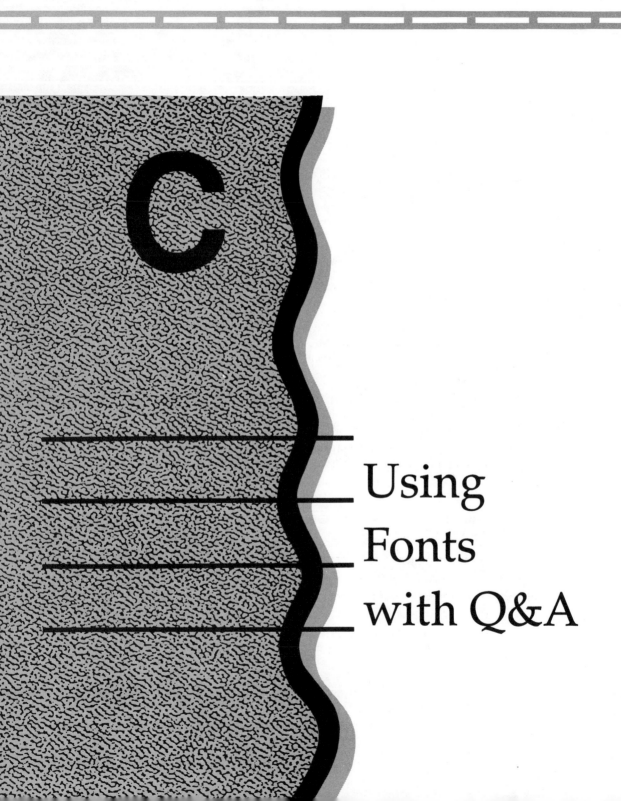

C

Using Fonts with Q&A

A *font* is a collection of characters, numbers, and symbols in one size and style. Printers gets their fonts from three possible sources:

- *Internal fonts* are built into the computer's hardware. You can select from the various internal fonts but you cannot change them.

- *Cartridge fonts* are plugged into the printer. They add greater variety to your printing and, like internal fonts, are available immediately when you turn on your printer.

- *Softfonts* (or downloadable fonts) are typefaces stored on a disk and transferred to your computer's memory when needed. Since they can consume a great deal of disk space, you should have a hard disk drive to use softfonts. Q&A will not download softfonts for you; they must be downloaded in the printer before you start Q&A.

Q&A allows you to enhance documents and reports with character formats such as boldface and underlining, and to print up to nine different fonts in one document. However, unless you configure Q&A to work with your fonts, you will be able to access only your printer's default font—the font that is immediately available when you turn on your printer. In this appendix, you will learn how to set up Q&A to print in any of the fonts and type sizes you have available.

SETTING UP Q&A TO USE FONTS

In order to use fonts with a Q&A document, you must install the printer with a font definition file, and then specify the fonts you want to use in a font assignment menu.

INSTALLING FONT DEFINITION FILES

When you install Q&A, you are given the opportunity to copy font description files to the hard disk. The files contain information telling Q&A how to access and use the fonts; they do not contain the fonts themselves. Font description files have the extension FNT. For example, data on PostScript fonts is stored in a file called POST.FNT, and information on LaserJet internal and cartridge fonts is in HPLASERJ.FNT. (The file named BLOCK1.FNT is a Lotus 1-2-3 font file, which is used in the tutorial for merging sample Lotus 1-2-3 PIC files; it is not a Q&A font description file.)

But placing the correct font definition file on the hard disk may be just the first step. You might have to link the font file with the printer as you install it. In most cases, the appropriate font file will be linked with the file by default, especially with dot-matrix printers and laser printers using only internal or cartridge fonts.

If you are using softfonts with a laser printer, or have trouble assigning fonts, you have to select Special Options when you install the printer, as discussed in Chapter 1. This will display the menu shown in Figure C.1.

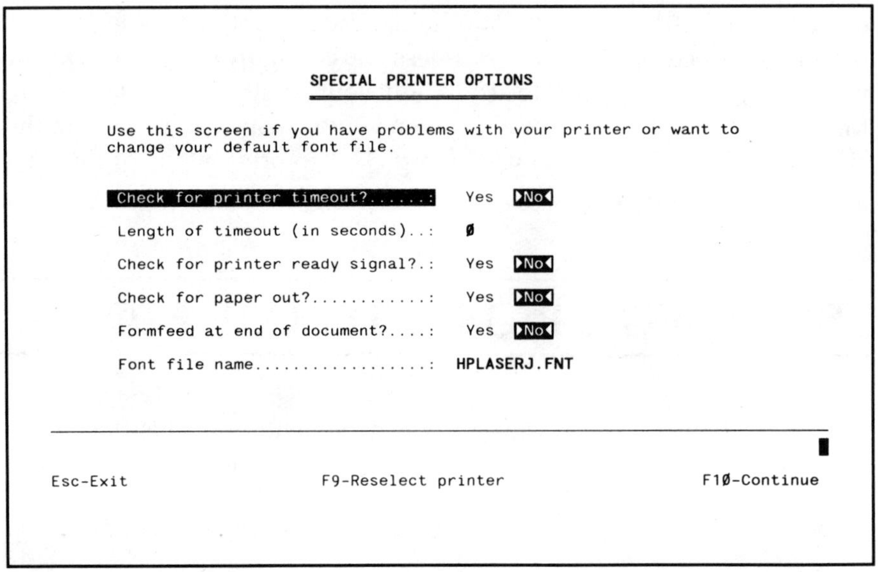

```
                        SPECIAL PRINTER OPTIONS

        Use this screen if you have problems with your printer or want to
        change your default font file.


        ┌─────────────────────────────────┐
        │Check for printer timeout?......:│   Yes  ▶No◀
        └─────────────────────────────────┘
         Length of timeout (in seconds)..:   Ø

         Check for printer ready signal?.:   Yes  ▶No◀

         Check for paper out?............:   Yes  ▶No◀

         Formfeed at end of document?....:   Yes  ▶No◀

         Font file name..................:   HPLASERJ.FNT


    ──────────────────────────────────────────────────────────────────  ■


        Esc-Exit              F9-Reselect printer            F1Ø-Continue
```

Figure C.1: Special Printer Options menu

The font definition file that you want to use must be listed at the font file name prompt. To use softfonts with a LaserJet printer, for example, you must change the font file to HPLJSOFT.FNT. To access the Pro cartridge, use the HPPRO.FNT file.

Follow the steps given in Chapter 1 to install the printer and display the Special Options menu. Enter the font file name at the prompt, and then press F10 to complete the installation process.

ADDING SUPPORT FOR ADDITIONAL SOFTFONTS

The font definition files for Hewlett-Packard LaserJet printers support the softfonts supplied by Hewlett-Packard at the time your copy of Q&A was created. The PostScript font definition file supports the standard fonts supplied with PostScript devices.

You must add support for other softfonts to the font definition file using the utility QAFONT.EXE, which you can copy to the hard disk during the installation process. This program will insert the necessary information into the appropriate font definition file from LaserJet softfonts or PostScript AFM font files. QAFONT will also let you convert font files from earlier versions of Q&A into version 4 format.

To use the program, copy it to the hard disk by selecting to install it during a full or selective installation. Make a note of the directory storing your softfonts, AFM files, or font files from an earlier version of Q&A. Log onto the QA directory, run QAFONT, and then follow the instructions that appear on the screen.

MAKING FONT ASSIGNMENTS

After the font file is on disk and your printer is installed, you make font assignments. You assign fonts to tell Q&A which one to use for the default and the eight fonts to be included on the enhancement menu.

Follow these steps to make font assignments:

1. Select Write from the Main menu, and then choose Type/Edit to display the Write screen.

610   MASTERING Q&A

APPENDIX C

You can assign fonts with a document already in memory, but the process is faster if you do so before creating or retrieving a document.

2. Press F2 to display the Print Options menu, select the printer that contains the fonts you want to use, and press F9 to return to the document.

3. Press Ctrl-F9 to see the Font Assignments screen, shown in Figure C.2.

You can also display the Font Assignments screen by pressing Shift-F6 from the document to display the enhancement menu, and then typing A.

4. Type the name of the font definition file you want to use, or press ↵ and select the file name from the List Manager screen.

5. Press ↵ to reach the Regular option.

Your entry for the Regular option establishes the default font that will be used for all nonenhanced characters. If you are pleased with the current default font, skip to step 8.

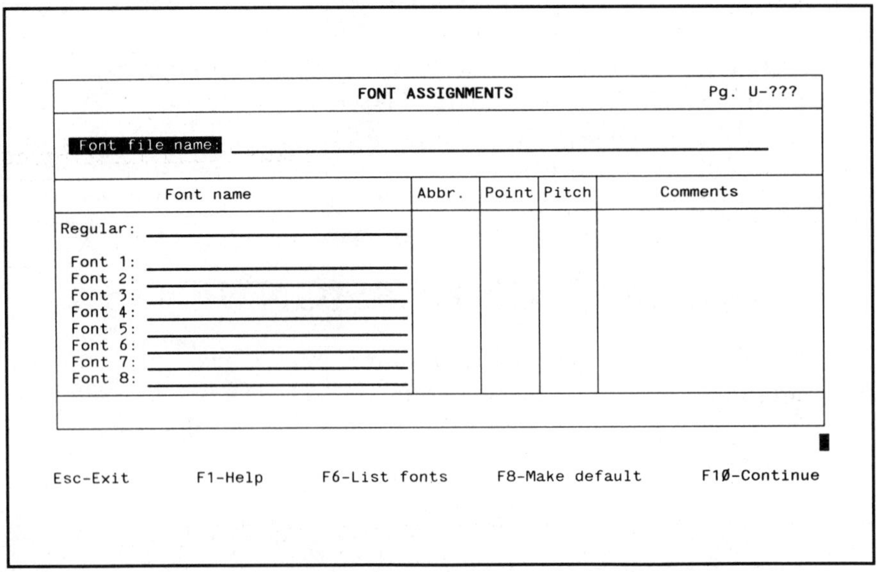

Figure C.2: Font Assignments screen

6. Press F6 to list the available fonts in the file.

As shown in the example in Figure C.3, the list shows each font's name, style, and point size. Those that do not have a point size are scalable fonts, such as those used with PostScript and some LaserJet printers.

7. Select the font you want to use as the default for the document, and then press ↵.

The name of the font, its abbreviation, point size, pitch, and some optional commands appear on the screen.

8. Press ↓ to reach the Font 1 option.

9. Repeat steps 5 through 8 to select up to eight fonts to be listed on the enhancement menu.

The selections you make will be saved along with the document. If you want to make them the default for every new document, press F8. Q&A

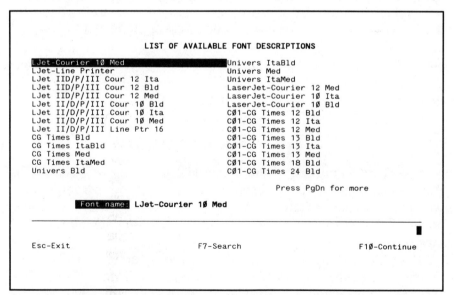

```
                    LIST OF AVAILABLE FONT DESCRIPTIONS
LJet-Courier 10 Med               Univers ItaBld
LJet-Line Printer                 Univers Med
LJet IID/P/III Cour 12 Ita        Univers ItaMed
LJet IID/P/III Cour 12 Bld        LaserJet-Courier 12 Med
LJet IID/P/III Cour 12 Med        LaserJet-Courier 10 Ita
LJet II/D/P/III Cour 10 Bld       LaserJet-Courier 10 Bld
LJet II/D/P/III Cour 10 Ita       C01-CG Times 12 Bld
LJet II/D/P/III Cour 10 Med       C01-CG Times 12 Ita
LJet II/D/P/III Line Ptr 16       C01-CG Times 12 Med
CG Times Bld                      C01-CG Times 13 Bld
CG Times ItaBld                   C01-CG Times 13 Ita
CG Times Med                      C01-CG Times 13 Med
CG Times ItaMed                   C01-CG Times 18 Bld
Univers Bld                       C01-CG Times 24 Bld

                                     Press PgDn for more

          Font name: LJet-Courier 10 Med



Esc-Exit                 F7-Search                 F10-Continue
```

Figure C.3: Select from a list of fonts supported by the font definition file

will save the settings and display the message

These settings are now the default

To return to the standard default fonts, delete all the entries on the Font Assignment screen, and then press F8 again.

10.   Press F10 to return to the document. The fonts will now be available for use with Q&A.

If you selected a font description file that is not linked with the installed printer, Q&A will display a message similar to

Font file HPLJSOFT.FNT not valid for the selected printer

Reinstall the printer selecting the proper file, or reassign the fonts with the correct file.

It may take some time for the Write screen to reappear if the current document already has text. Font selections in a document are saved as markers (invisible codes that tell Q&A which font to use for sections of text). When you press F10 after assigning fonts, Q&A reformats the entire document according to the new font selections, applying the new regular font and searching for font markers to apply other enhancements. For example, text enhanced as Font 1 will automatically be changed to your new Font 1 selection. This is why it is generally more efficient to assign the fonts first, and then type the text or load an existing document.

Scalable Font Support

Most LaserJet printers require softfonts that are presized. This means that you must have a separate font for each typeface and size you want to use in your document. To print in 6-, 10-, 12-, 14-, 18-, and 24-point fonts, you must have each of them on your disk and already downloaded into the printer.

PostScript and some LaserJet printers use scalable fonts. These are generic outlines that describe the shape and characteristics of a typeface. When you want to print in a particular size, the printer creates the characters "on the fly," forming the properly sized characters at the time of printing. You only need one outline for each typeface, not separate fonts in every size. (PostScript printers are also capable of slanting, rotating, and shading characters as they are made, as explained later in the appendix.)

When you assign a scalable font, you will not see the point sizes next to the font on the screen, just the font name. After selecting the font, you will see a dialog box with the message

Enter Point Size:

Enter a point size between 1 and 999 and press ↵.

Fonts for Daisy-Wheel Printers

Font description files are not provided for daisy-wheel printers. With a daisy-wheel printer, just insert the wheel you want to use and set the character pitch on the Define Page menu before printing.

If you want to change wheels during printing, such as to substitute an italic or another font, insert the *Stop* code where you want the font change to occur. Q&A will stop printing when it reaches the code. Change the print wheel, and then press ↵ to continue printing. Make sure to include another *Stop* code where you want to reinsert the original wheel. For example, a line of text that includes a wheel change to print characters in italic might appear like this:

Use *Stop*italic*Stop* type to add emphasis to text.

USING FONTS

The font you designated as regular will be used for all characters that you do not enhance. When you want to use another font in the document for existing text, press Shift-F6 and select the font from the enhancement menu. Move the cursor over the text you want to format, and then press

F10. The text will be displayed in a different color, and the font's abbreviated name will appear on the status line.

If you insert text in a paragraph that has already been enhanced with a font, the new characters will take on the same format. You do not have to apply the enhancement again.

When you press F2 to print a document that has been enhanced with fonts, you will see

Reminder: Make sure fonts are installed in the printer before printing

on the message line of the Print Options menu. Insert the cartridge you plan to use; or save the document, exit from Q&A, and download the softfonts before continuing.

FORMATTING AS YOU TYPE

The standard procedure for assigning fonts is to format text that already exists as a block. To apply fonts as you type, press Shift-F6, select the font, and then press F10 without highlighting a block. The space where the cursor is located contains the font marker, and the font abbreviation appears on the status line. Characters you type from that position will be formatted according to the designated font. When you want to return to the regular font, press → or ↓ to move off the marked text.

As a shortcut, create macros that apply each font to a single space, such as recording the keystrokes Shift-F6 1 F10 as macro Alt-1, Shift-F6 2 F10 as macro Alt-2, and so on. When you want to type in a particular font, press the corresponding Alt-key combination, type the text, and press ↓ to return to the regular font.

CHANGING FONT ENHANCEMENTS

Storing fonts as markers makes it easy to quickly change the fonts used in your document. For example, if you formatted all headlines as 24-point Times Roman assigned as Font 1, you can change them all to 18-point Helvetica in one step by reassigning Font 1.

Blocks that you move or copy retain their font markers. When you insert an enhanced block into another document, the markers format the block according to the document's font assignments. You can take advantage of this to quickly change fonts between draft and final printouts, or for printing the same document on different printers.

For example, suppose you use a dot-matrix printer for draft copies and a laser printer for the final output. Start with a clear document, select the dot-matrix printer, and make the font assignments that you plan to use. Save the document without any text, using a name such as EPFX.TMP. Clear the screen, then repeat the process for the laser printer, saving the file with a name such as HP.TMP.

When you want to print a draft copy of a document, get the file EPFX.TMP, and then insert the document into it. The font assignments will be applied to each of the font markers. To print a final copy, get the file HP.TMP and insert the document into it.

FONTS AND THE POSITION INDICATORS

In Chapter 1, you learned that the position indicator on the status line shows the character position of the cursor. Using the default printer font, ten characters print in each inch of space. There are ten spaces between each inch position along the ruler, and the position of the ghost cursor represents the character distance from the left edge of the paper.

When you assign a regular font that is not 10 characters per inch (cpi), the ruler adjusts to indicate the number of characters that will fit in each inch of space.

With fixed-width fonts, no matter what their size, word wrap will always occur when you reach the right-margin indicator. The spacing of characters in a proportionally spaced font, however, varies with the width. Because the screen can only display characters in a fixed width, word wrap will still occur, but it may appear as though it is in the wrong location, with characters extending beyond the margin or far short of it. Q&A measures the size of each character on the line and wraps when the combined width reaches the margin.

Figure C.4 shows two lines of type in a 24-point typeface. Notice that more lowercase *i* characters will fit between the margins than uppercase *W* characters. When you are using proportionally spaced fonts, the location of the ghost cursor on the ruler represents character positions, not actual inches. Use Print Preview to see how the document will appear when it is printed.

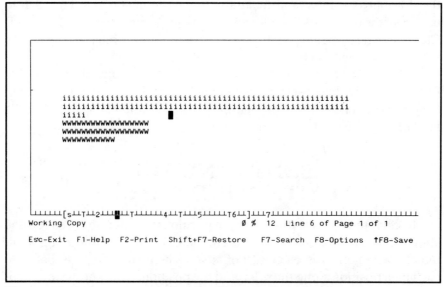

Figure C.4: With proportionally spaced fonts, Q&A displays as many characters as will fit on the actual printed line

INDEX

Selections from
The SYBEX Library

DATABASES

The ABC's of dBASE III PLUS
Robert Cowart
264pp. Ref. 379-1
The most efficient way to get beginners up and running with dBASE. Every 'how' and 'why' of database management is demonstrated through tutorials and practical dBASE III PLUS applications.

The ABC's of dBASE IV 1.1
Robert Cowart
350pp, Ref. 632-4
The latest version of dBASE IV is featured in this hands-on introduction. It assumes no previous experience with computers or database management, and uses easy-to-follow lessons to introduce the concepts, build basic skills, and set up some practical applications. Includes report writing and Query by Example.

The ABC's of Paradox 3.5
(Second Edition)
Charles Siegel
334pp, Ref. 785-1
This easy-to-follow, hands-on tutorial is a must for beginning users of Paradox 3.0 and 3.5. Even if you've never used a computer before, you'll be doing useful work in just a few short lessons. A clear introduction to database management and valuable business examples make this a "right-to-work" guide for the practical-minded.

Advanced Techniques
in dBASE III PLUS
Alan Simpson
454pp. Ref. 369-4
A full course in database design and structured programming, with routines for inventory control, accounts receivable, system management, and integrated databases.

dBASE Instant Reference
SYBEX Prompter Series
Alan Simpson
471pp. Ref. 484-4; 4 ¾" × 8"
Comprehensive information at a glance: a brief explanation of syntax and usage for every dBASE command, with step-by-step instructions and exact keystroke sequences. Commands are grouped by function in twenty precise categories.

dBASE III PLUS Programmer's
Reference Guide
SYBEX Ready Reference Series
Alan Simpson
1056pp. Ref. 508-5
Programmers will save untold hours and effort using this comprehensive, well-organized dBASE encyclopedia. Complete technical details on commands and functions, plus scores of often-needed algorithms.

dBASE IV 1.1 Programmer's
Instant Reference
(Second Edition)
Alan Simpson
555pp, Ref. 764-9
Enjoy fast, easy access to information often hidden in cumbersome documentation. This handy pocket-sized reference presents information on each command and function in the dBASE IV programming language. Commands are grouped according to their purpose, so readers can locate the correct command for any task—quickly and easily.

dBASE IV User's Instant Reference (Second Edition)
Alan Simpson
356pp, Ref. 786-X

Completely revised to cover the new 1.1 version of dBASE IV, this handy reference guide presents information on every dBASE operation a user can perform. Exact keystroke sequences are presented, and complex tasks are explained step-by-step. It's a great way for newer users to look up the basics, while more experienced users will find it a fast way to locate information on specialized tasks.

Mastering dBASE III PLUS: A Structured Approach
Carl Townsend
342pp. Ref. 372-4

In-depth treatment of structured programming for custom dBASE solutions. An ideal study and reference guide for applications developers, new and experienced users with an interest in efficient programming.

Mastering dBASE IV Programming
Carl Townsend
496pp. Ref. 540-9

This task-oriented book introduces structured dBASE IV programming and commands by setting up a general ledger system, an invoice system, and a quotation management system. The author carefully explores the unique character of dBASE IV based on his in-depth understanding of the program.

Mastering FoxPro
Charles Seigel
639pp. Ref. 671-5

This guide to the powerful FoxPro DBMS offers a tutorial on database basics, then enables the reader to master new skills and features as needed—with many examples from business. An in-depth tutorial guides users through the development of a complete mailing list system.

Mastering Paradox 3.5
Alan Simpson
650pp, Ref. 677-4

This indispensable, in-depth guide has again been updated for the latest Paradox release, offering the same comprehensive, hands-on treatment featured in highly praised previous editions. It covers everything from database basics to PAL programming—including complex queries and reports, and multi-table applications.

Mastering Q & A (Second Edition)
Greg Harvey
540pp. Ref. 452-6

This hands-on tutorial explores the Q & A Write, File, and Report modules, and the Intelligent Assistant. English-language command processor, macro creation, interfacing with other software, and more, using practical business examples.

Power User's Guide to R:BASE
Alan Simpson
Cheryl Currid
Craig Gillett
446pp. Ref. 354-6

Supercharge your R:BASE applications with this straightforward tutorial that covers system design, structured programming, managing multiple data tables, and more. Sample applications include ready-to-run mailing, inventory and accounts receivable systems. Through Version 2.11.

Understanding dBASE III
Alan Simpson
300pp. Ref. 267-1

dBASE commands and concepts are illustrated throughout with practical, business oriented examples—for mailing list handling, accounts receivable, and inventory design. Contains scores of tips and techniques for maximizing efficiency and meeting special needs.

Understanding dBASE III PLUS
Alan Simpson
415pp. Ref. 349-X

A solid sourcebook of training and ongoing support. Everything from creating a first database to command file programming is presented in working examples, with tips and techniques you won't find anywhere else.

Understanding dBASE IV 1.1
Alan Simpson
900pp, Ref. 633-2

Simpson's outstanding introduction to dBASE—brought up to date for version 1.1—uses tutorials and practical examples to build effective, and increasingly sophisticated, database management skills. Advanced topics include custom reporting, managing multiple databases, and designing custom applications.

Understanding Oracle
James T. Perry
Joseph G. Lateer
634pp. Ref. 534-4

A comprehensive guide to the Oracle database management system for administrators, users, and applications developers. Covers everything in Version 5 from database basics to multi-user systems, performance, and development tools including SQL*Forms, SQL*Report, and SQL*Calc. Includes Fast Track speed notes.

Understanding Professional File
Gerry Litton
463pp. Re. 669-3

Build practical data management skills in an orderly fashion with this complete step-by-step tutorial—from creating a simple database, to building customized business applications.

Understanding R:BASE
Alan Simpson
Karen Watterson
609pp. Ref. 503-4

This is the definitive R:BASE tutorial, for use with either OS/2 or DOS. Hands-on lessons cover every aspect of the software, from creating and using a database, to custom systems. Includes Fast Track speed notes.

Understanding SQL
Martin Gruber
400pp. Ref. 644-8

This comprehensive tutorial in Structured Query Language (SQL) is suitable for beginners, and for SQL users wishing to increase their skills. From basic principles to complex SQL applications, the text builds fluency and confidence using concise hands-on lessons and easy-to-follow examples.

Up & Running with Q&A
Ranier Bartel
140pp. Ref. 645-6

Obtain practical results with Q&A in the shortest possible time. Learn to design and program forms, use macros, format text, use utilities, and more. Or use the book to help you decide whether to purchase the program.

WORD PROCESSING

The ABC's of Microsoft Word (Third Edition)
Alan R. Neibauer
461pp. Ref. 604-9

This is for the novice WORD user who wants to begin producing documents in the shortest time possible. Each chapter has short, easy-to-follow lessons for both keyboard and mouse, including all the basic editing, formatting and printing functions. Version 5.0.

The ABC's of WordPerfect
Alan R. Neibauer
239pp. Ref. 425-9

This basic introduction to WordPefect consists of short, step-by-step lessons—for new users who want to get going fast. Topics range from simple editing and formatting, to merging, sorting, macros, and more. Includes version 4.2

The ABC's of WordPerfect 5
Alan R. Neibauer
283pp. Ref. 504-2

This introduction explains the basics of desktop publishing with WordPerfect 5: editing, layout, formatting, printing, sorting, merging, and more. Readers are shown how to use WordPerfect 5's new features to produce great-looking reports.

The ABC's of WordPerfect 5.1
Alan R. Neibauer
352pp. Ref. 672-3

Neibauer's delightful writing style makes this clear tutorial an especially effective learning tool. Learn all about 5.1's new drop-down menus and mouse capabilities that reduce the tedious memorization of function keys.

The Complete Guide to MultiMate
Carol Holcomb Dreger
208pp. Ref. 229-9

This step-by-step tutorial is also an excellent reference guide to MultiMate features and uses. Topics include search/replace, library and merge functions, repagination, document defaults and more.

Encyclopedia WordPerfect 5.1
Greg Harvey
Kay Yarborough Nelson
1100pp. Ref. 676-6

This comprehensive, up-to-date Word-Perfect reference is a must for beginning and experienced users alike. With complete, easy-to-find information on every WordPerfect feature and command—and it's organized by practical functions, with business users in mind.

Introduction to WordStar
Arthur Naiman
208pp. Ref. 134-9

This all time bestseller is an engaging first-time introduction to word processing as well as a complete guide to using WordStar—from basic editing to blocks, global searches, formatting, dot commands, SpellStar and MailMerge. Through Version 3.3.

Mastering Microsoft Word on the IBM PC (Fourth Edition)
Matthew Holtz
680pp. Ref. 597-2

This comprehensive, step-by-step guide details all the new desktop publishing developments in this versatile word processor, including details on editing, formatting, printing, and laser printing. Holtz uses sample business documents to demonstrate the use of different fonts, graphics, and complex documents. Includes Fast Track speed notes. For Versions 4 and 5.

Mastering MultiMate Advantage II
Charles Ackerman
407pp. Ref. 482-8

This comprehensive tutorial covers all the capabilities of MultiMate, and highlights the differences between MultiMate Advantage II and previous versions—in pathway support, sorting, math, DOS access, using dBASE III, and more. With many practical examples, and a chapter on the On-File database.

Mastering WordPerfect
Susan Baake Kelly
435pp. Ref. 332-5

Step-by-step training from startup to mastery, featuring practical uses (form letters, newsletters and more), plus advanced topics such as document security and macro creation, sorting and columnar math. Through Version 4.2.

Mastering WordPerfect 5
Susan Baake Kelly
709pp. Ref. 500-X

The revised and expanded version of this definitive guide is now on WordPerfect 5 and covers wordprocessing and basic desktop publishing. As more than 200,000 readers of the original edition can attest, no tutorial approaches it for clarity and depth of treatment. Sorting, line drawing, and laser printing included.

Mastering WordPerfect 5.1
Alan Simpson
1050pp. Ref. 670-7

The ultimate guide for the WordPerfect user. Alan Simpson, the "master communicator," puts you in charge of the latest features of 5.1: new dropdown menus and mouse capabilities, along with the desktop publishing, macro programming, and file conversion functions that have made WordPerfect the most popular word processing program on the market.

Mastering WordStar Release 5.5
Greg Harvey
David J. Clark
450pp. Ref. 491-7
This book is the ultimate reference book for the newest version of WordStar. Readers may use Mastering to look up any word processing function, including the new Version 5 and 5.5 features and enhancements, and find detailed instructions for fundamental to advanced operations.

Microsoft Word Instant Reference for the IBM PC
Matthew Holtz
266pp. Ref. 692-8
Turn here for fast, easy access to concise information on every command and feature of Microsoft Word version 5.0—for editing, formatting, merging, style sheets, macros, and more. With exact keystroke sequences, discussion of command options, and commonly-performed tasks.

Practical WordStar Uses
Julie Anne Arca
303pp. Ref. 107-1
A hands-on guide to WordStar and MailMerge applications, with solutions to comon problems and "recipes" for day-to-day tasks. Formatting, merge-printing and much more; plus a quick-reference command chart and notes on CP/M and PC-DOS. For Version 3.3.

WordPerfect 5.1 On-Line Advisor Version 1.1
SYBAR, Software Division of SYBEX, Inc.
Ref. 934-X
Now there's no more need to thumb through lengthy manuals. The On-Line Advisor brings you answers to your Word-Perfect questions on-screen, right where you need them. For easy reference, this comprehensive on-line help system divides up each topic by key sequence, syntax, usage and examples. Covers versions 5.0 and 5.1. Software package comes with 3½" and 5¼" disks. **System Requirements:** IBM compatible with DOS 2.0 or higher, runs with Windows 3.0, uses 90K of RAM.

Understanding Professional Write
Gerry Litton
400pp. Ref. 656-1
A complete guide to Professional Write that takes you from creating your first simple document, into a detailed description of all major aspects of the software. Special features place an emphasis on the use of different typestyles to create attractive documents as well as potential problems and suggestions on how to get around them.

Understanding WordStar 2000
David Kolodney
Thomas Blackadar
275pp. Ref. 554-9
This engaging, fast-paced series of tutorials covers everything from moving the cursor to print enhancements, format files, key glossaries, windows and MailMerge. With practical examples, and notes for former WordStar users.

Visual Guide to WordPerfect
Jeff Woodward
457pp. Ref. 591-3
This is a visual hands-on guide which is ideal for brand new users as the book shows each activity keystroke-by-keystroke. Clear illustrations of computer screen menus are included at every stage. Covers basic editing, formatting lines, paragraphs, and pages, using the block feature, footnotes, search and replace, and more. Through Version 5.

SYBEX ®

FREE CATALOG!

Mail us this form today, and we'll send you a full-color catalog of Sybex books.

Name _____

Street _____

City/State/Zip _____

Phone _____

Please supply the name of the Sybex book purchased.

_____

How would you rate it?

_____ Excellent   _____ Very Good   _____ Average   _____ Poor

Why did you select this particular book?

_____ Recommended to me by a friend

_____ Recommended to me by store personnel

_____ Saw an advertisement in _____

_____ Author's reputation

_____ Saw in Sybex catalog

_____ Required textbook

_____ Sybex reputation

_____ Read book review in _____

_____ In-store display

_____ Other _____

Where did you buy it?

_____ Bookstore

_____ Computer Store or Software Store

_____ Catalog (name: _____)

_____ Direct from Sybex

_____ Other: _____

Did you buy this book with your personal funds?

_____ Yes   _____ No

About how many computer books do you buy each year?

_____ 1-3   _____ 3-5   _____ 5-7   _____ 7-9   _____ 10+

About how many Sybex books do you own?

_____ 1-3   _____ 3-5   _____ 5-7   _____ 7-9   _____ 10+

Please indicate your level of experience with the software covered in this book:

_____ Beginner   _____ Intermediate   _____ Advanced

Which types of software packages do you use regularly?

_____ Accounting	_____ Databases	_____ Networks
_____ Amiga	_____ Desktop Publishing	_____ Operating Systems
_____ Apple/Mac	_____ File Utilities	_____ Spreadsheets
_____ CAD	_____ Money Management	_____ Word Processing
_____ Communications	_____ Languages	_____ Other _____

(please specify)

Which of the following best describes your job title?

_____ Administrative/Secretarial	_____ President/CEO
_____ Director	_____ Manager/Supervisor
_____ Engineer/Technician	_____ Other _____

(please specify)

Comments on the weaknesses/strengths of this book: _____

_____

_____

_____

_____

PLEASE FOLD, SEAL, AND MAIL TO SYBEX

SYBEX, INC.
Department M
2021 CHALLENGER DR.
ALAMEDA, CALIFORNIA USA
94501

SYBEX ®

SEAL

Q&A FUNCTION KEYS

F1	Get help information
Alt-F1	Thesaurus (Write)
Ctrl-F1	Spell check the current word
Shift-F1	Spell check the entire document
F2	Print the current document or record
Alt-F2	List macros and menus
Ctrl-F2	Print multiple records (File)
	Print a block of text (Write)
Shift-F2	Access macros and menus
F3	Delete a block of text (Write)
	Delete the current record (File)
	Clear the spec screen
	Restart Query (Query Guide)
Ctrl-F3	Display document statistics (Write)
	Display system information (Main menu)
F4	Delete the word
Ctrl-F4	Delete characters to the end of line
Shift-F4	Delete the line
F5	Copy the field from the previous record (when adding records)
	Copy selected item (List Manager)
	Copy a block of text (Write)
Alt-F5	Insert the current time (File)
	Move a block of text to a new file (Write)
Ctrl-F5	Insert the current date (File)
	Copy a block of text to a new file (Write)
Shift-F5	Copy the previous record (when adding records)
	Move a block of text (Write)
F6	Expand the field (File)
	Set and clear temporary margins (Write)
	Display vocabulary (Intelligent Assistant)
	Add a description to a database or document (List Manager)
Alt-F6	Enter table view (when updating records)
	Insert a soft hyphen (Write)
Ctrl-F6	Add records (when updating records)
	Define page settings (Write)